W9-BSZ-545

Faulkner in Cultural Context
FAULKNER AND YOKNAPATAWPHA
1995

Faulkner in Cultural Context

FAULKNER AND YOKNAPATAWPHA, 1995

EDITED BY
DONALD M. KARTIGANER
AND
ANN J. ABADIE

UNIVERSITY PRESS OF MISSISSIPPI
JACKSON

00   99   98   97   4   3   2   1

The paper in this book meets the guidelines for permanence and durability of the
Committee on Production Guidelines for Book Longevity of the
Council on Library Resources.

Library of Congress Cataloging-in-Publication Data

Faulkner in cultural context : Faulkner and Yoknapatawpha, 1995 :
edited by Donald M. Kartiganer and Ann J. Abadie.
p.   cm. — (Faulkner and Yoknapatawpha series)
Papers from the 22nd Faulkner and Yoknapatawpha Conference sponsored
by the University of Mississippi between July 30 and August 4, 1995.
Includes index.
ISBN 1-57806-001-X (cloth : alk. paper). — ISBN 1-57806-002-8
(paper : alk. paper)
1. Faulkner, William, 1897–1962—Criticism and interpretation—
Congresses.   2. Literature and society—United States—
History—20th century—Congresses.   3. Southern States—In
literature—Congresses.   I. Kartiganer, Donald M.   II. Abadie, Ann
J.   III. Faulkner and Yoknapatawpha Conference (22nd : 1995 :
University of Mississippi)   IV. Series.
PS3511.A86Z783211852   1997 5
823'.912—dc21   97-6956
CIP

British Cataloging-in-Publication data available

Contents

Introduction   vii
DONALD M. KARTIGANER

A Note on the Conference   xv

Faulkner's History: Sources and Interpretation   3
DON H. DOYLE

"Like a Virgin": Faulkner, Sexual Cultures, and the
Romance of Resistance   39
ANNE GOODWYN JONES

The Social Psychology of Paternalism: *Sanctuary*'s
Cultural Context   75
KEVIN RAILEY

X Marks the Spot: Faulkner's Garden   99
DAWN TROUARD

The Guns of *Light in August*: War and Peace in the
Second Thirty Years War   125
WARWICK WADLINGTON

Light in August: A Novel of Passing?   148
GENA MCKINLEY

Faulkner and Proletarian Literature   166
JOHN T. MATTHEWS

If I Forget Thee, Jerusalem and the Great Migration:
History in Black and White   191
CHERYL LESTER

Faulkner and the Frontier Grotesque: *The Hamlet* as
    Southwestern Humor 218
    PETER ALAN FROEHLICH

Faulkner and the Post-Confederate 241
    NEIL SCHMITZ

Race Fantasies: The Filming of *Intruder in the Dust* 263
    CHARLES HANNON

Culture in a Faulknerian Context 284
    SACVAN BERCOVITCH

Contributors 311

Index 315

Introduction

I'm inclined to think that my material, the South, is not very
important to me. I just happen to know it, and dont have time
in one life to learn another one and write at the same time.
                                        WILLIAM FAULKNER

1

The topic of the 22nd annual Faulkner and Yoknapatawpha conference—"Faulkner in Cultural Context"—encapsulates the changes
of the last decade in the way we read Faulkner. Clearly there has
been a major shift in focus, one that has led us to incorporate into
our interpretations of Faulkner's texts the various contexts that
surround them—the historical, political, economical, social, ideological, and aesthetic conditions that were contemporary with
Faulkner's creation of those texts—as well as those contexts that
are contemporary with our reading of them: this latter concern a
natural consequence of the conviction that no one, neither author
nor critic, is free from the contextual impact. From a mode of
criticism in which the text was regarded as autonomous, a
uniquely transcendent form of utterance somehow remote from
contextual implication—a mode of criticism which received its
most significant American impetus in the South during Faulkner's
lifetime—we have moved to an acknowledgment of context: the
situation of any created text as both a product of, and a contributor
to, the circumstances of its time and place.

What Faulkner once referred to as his "material, the South,"
can possess the most substantive kind of reality—the materiality
of war and peace, wealth and poverty, race and sexual identity—
and yet it is ultimately cultural in the sense that that reality must
be understood in terms of an entire way of life: a complex of beliefs, fears, values, prejudices, aesthetic tastes: a cluster of meanings which make up the cultural language of a society. That

language is finally the arena within which, and of which, the literary text is formed. The task of cultural criticism, as Anne Goodwyn Jones asserts in one of the essays in this volume, is to trace the connections between the literary text and the surrounding cultural life, to "look for the ways in which works of art—as cultural productions—produce meanings together with other elements of culture." If the literary text does not transcend its context, neither is it entirely of a piece with it. Its distinction is its power of critique as well as reflection, its capacity to avail itself of the current cultural language while aspiring to move that language toward meanings seemingly outside, or contrary to, the meanings it has been accustomed to stand for.

The "cultures" of the texts of William Faulkner, as the scope of the twelve essays in this volume testifies, are many and varied, for every human act and thought predicates itself within a cultural stance, one which the cultural critic tries to identify as an enabling armature of act and thought. Each of the following essays constitutes the staging of a specific encounter, as a reader isolates a set of cultural conditions within and against which to situate Faulkner's text. The cultures touching Faulkner's work range from prevailing sexual attitudes to the social revolutionary thought of the thirties; from familiar rubrics such as the frontier to newly identified modes such as the post-Confederate. In every case the critical effort is to trace a continuing dynamic of textualized cultural interaction, as Faulkner's fiction fleshes out its particular cultural moment, giving it a powerful narrative existence, even as, within the very language of cultural constraint, it resists that moment, projecting new possibilities.

2

Don H. Doyle's "Faulkner's History: Sources and Interpretation" is a fitting opening for the volume, for, as befits Doyle's historical discipline, it seeks to distinguish between the factual history of north Mississippi, which supplies much of the underpinning for Faulkner's fiction, and what Faulkner makes of it. Doyle summarizes a good deal of what, for Faulkner, were the most relevant parts of that history, and tries to determine both the historical reliability of Faulkner's retellings and their significance. Tracing the development of Lafayette County from its antebellum origins through the Civil War, Reconstruction, and the emergence of the New South, Doyle explores the history behind key incidents and characters in *Absalom, Absalom!*, *Light in August*, *The Unvanquished*, *The Hamlet*, and *Requiem for a Nun*. Not surprisingly, Doyle discovers both accuracy, as in Faulkner's ability to capture "wonderfully the sudden genesis of government and economy on the cotton frontier" in *Requiem for a Nun*, and inaccuracy, his tendency, for example, in *The Unvanquished* to distort the facts of Reconstruction along the lines subscribed to by white segregationists.

With Anne Goodwyn Jones's " 'Like a Virgin': Faulkner, Sexual Cultures, and the Romance of Resistance" the volume turns from historical fact to cultural practice. Her concern is specifically with the sexual contexts of Faulkner's work, the way in which his texts negotiate the emerging conflict between a traditional Southern paternalistic culture and a modern American and international popular culture. The former culture emphasizes the sexual innocence and essential helplessness of white women and their dependency on white males; the latter at least ostensibly acknowledges sexual desire in all women as well as their independence. The complexity of Faulkner's texts is that they resist *both* cultures to a certain degree, using the values of one to undermine the other, although finally, according to Jones, Faulkner's loyalty is with the Southern commitment to male responsibility and power. Interestingly enough, the partial "feminization" of the male—which is one of the consequences of the modern revision of male/female relationships—is more comfortable for Faulkner than its corollary, the masculinization of the female. The male gender crossing, a clear violation of Southern convention, can occasionally be compatible in Faulkner with male control and autonomy; whereas in the opposite case, when the female dares to resist her traditionally subservient role, the outcome is disastrous.

The dominant cultural context of *Sanctuary*, according to Kevin Railey, is the "aristocratic, paternalist, noblesse oblige world associated with the Old South." Despite the significant socioeconomic transitions taking place during the 1920s, Railey argues that the paternalist ideology continues to control the world of *Sanctuary*, particularly the mind of Horace Benbow, and continues as well to project a social vision that effectively determines the subjectivity and perception of women and the lower classes. Borrowing from Klaus Theweleit's studies in male fantasy, Railey establishes connections between aristocratic background and the repression of sexual desire as low and base, leading to a subsequent social rejection of the lower classes as similarly base. Although Horace fails in his attempt to reassert paternalism by defending successfully the innocent Lee Goodwin, the ideology he represents survives as a controlling force: dividing women into "ladies" and "whores," projecting an ethic of severe emotional control, and punishing those like Temple who most threaten to disturb those divisions and that control.

As evidence for a revisionary reading of the closing paragraphs of *Sanctuary*—the scene of Temple Drake and her father sitting in the Luxembourg Gardens, not far from where "the dead tranquil queens in stained marble mused"—Dawn Trouard unearths the largely implicit cultural presence of Flaubert as well as the identities of the queens themselves as an important context for the novel. Working closely with both versions of *Sanctuary* and the remains of the still undiscovered "2000 words about the Luxembourg Gardens and death" that Faulkner wrote and waxed euphoric about in 1925, Trouard explores the affinities Faulkner may have felt with Flaubert. Finally she contrasts Temple's ending with that of Emma Bovary, finding more of a sense of survival than despair, as Temple sits among the statues, "queens and powerful women . . . excluded and diminished by official history."

For Warwick Wadlington, a dominant cultural context for virtually all of Faulkner's work, from *Soldiers' Pay* to *A Fable*, is war and peace, understood as the regional, national, and international cultural attitudes that interact with each other between 1915 and

1945. In "The Guns of *Light in August*: War and Peace in the Second Thirty Years War," the cultures of war and peace, complicated by the occasional claims of "just wars and unjust peaces," appear in Faulkner's texts as a rhythm of violence and tranquility, outrage and calm, enthusiasm for expansionism and regret for dispossession—and with such ambivalence that "neither war nor peace are quite believed or quite awakened from."

In "*Light in August*: A Novel of Passing?" Gena McKinley considers Faulkner's characterization of Joe Christmas in the literary and cultural context of the highly varied depictions of mulattoes in nineteenth- and twentieth-century fiction by abolitionists, white racists, and black writers of the Harlem Renaissance, particularly James Weldon Johnson. The unique quality of Faulkner's Christmas is his own firm commitment to the prevailing social constructions regarding racial difference. Despite the flimsy evidence that he is part black, he remains forever a prisoner of those constructions—giving emphasis both to their weight and their arbitrariness: "fictions" he cannot escape and that ultimately destroy him.

In John T. Matthews's "Faulkner and Proletarian Literature" the relevant cultural context is the attempt of numerous artists and intellectuals during the 1930s "to imagine and instigate a class revolution in the United States." Challenging the common reading of Faulkner's fiction—and modernism generally—as inherently conservative, if not reactionary, Matthews finds in Faulkner's radical experimentalism a "textual politics" that can constitute a profound critique of capitalism. In *Absalom, Absalom!*, for example, he claims that Thomas Sutpen is the representation of a form of logic and abstract thought that epitomizes the principles of capitalist domination; yet the modernist aesthetics of the novel as a whole "formalize . . . ways of thinking and experiencing that shake or deconstruct this economic logic."

In "*If I Forget Thee, Jerusalem* and the Great Migration: History in Black and White," Cheryl Lester expands the concept of cultural context by pointing to a largely suppressed one—one that exerts a genuine power within Faulkner's novel (published as *The Wild Palms*), although surfacing only indirectly, "symptomatically." Referring to a wide array of historical facts and interpretations, Lester argues that the African American migration from the South between 1915 and 1940 is a significant yet buried component of the Southern white mind, producing a complex and contradictory stance blending denial and guilt, regret and resentment. Both in "Wild Palms" and "Old Man," Lester contends, Faulkner is alluding to that migration and the kinds of cultural blindness, hysteria, and fear that characterized Southern response to it. Within what is in some respects an unconscious strategy of displacement, Faulkner enacts a characteristic Southern (and American) ambivalence as he relegates race to a minor place, yet brings to the fore materials inextricable from African American experience: the "migration" northward of Harry and Charlotte, the alienated tall convict, the powerful imagery of the 1927 flood, and the novel's enormously suggestive original title.

The cultural context Peter Alan Froehlich invokes in his "Faulkner and Frontier Grotesque: *The Hamlet* and Southwestern Humor" is that of the frontier, which he defines not as a line between settlement and wilderness, between an area characterized by "high" culture and one characterized as a state of nature or "barbaric" culture, but as a space in which the two interact and engage each other. The frontier is the tension-filled space of "settlement located *within* wilderness": the site of the meeting that takes place when people Europeanized in the settlement strike out into the wilderness and encounter "low European and native cultures," creating a new fluidity, a grotesque confusion of categories. *The Hamlet*, like the stories of the Southwest humor tradition, is situated within "a late-stage frontier" context, which accounts for the novel's apparently dual loyalties to traditional high culture and convention as well as to the radical individualism that threatens them. In several major episodes in the novel we see how *The Hamlet* invokes "familiar cultural matrices and call(s) them into question," compelling readers to experience precisely the kind of category confusion and opposing loyalties that constitute frontier experience.

Neil Schmitz proposes the term "post-Confederate" as a way of describing the fiction of such Southern writers of the 1870s and 1880s as Twain, Harris, Page, and Cable, each of whom sought, in different ways, to gain access to the national literary market. Such access mandated that Southern writers put aside certain aspects of "Confederate" language and attitude and become part of the "postwar Unionist national narrative," even while maintaining the particular regional identity that was in some ways the basis of their appeal. The emergence of this complex discourse, another version of what Allen Tate once referred to as the "double focus" of the Southern writer, becomes for Schmitz a significant cultural frame for Faulkner's fiction, in particular his late novel *Intruder in the Dust*. Schmitz reads the novel in terms of its reference to and occasional revision of the post-Confederate, its loyalties and its innovations, what it tentatively suggests and what it refuses to give up.

In "Race Fantasies: The Filming of *Intruder in the Dust*" Charles Hannon argues that both Faulkner's novel and its film version—in its content and in the process of its production in Oxford—participate in a cultural dynamic of dependency and disavowal in their portrayal of black-white relations. The communities of Jefferson and Oxford "project a segregationist fantasy that excluded blacks from a protected white center, but maintained their availability as binary references in both the social and psychological construction of white racial identity." A comparable act of simultaneous dependency and disavowal takes place in the novel's and film's emphasis on the middle-class character of Jefferson and Oxford. Lower-class whites are sacrificed, and yet remain essential as a means of identifying that middle class as the members of a unified, progressive, and enlightened—within the system of segregation—New South.

Unique among this group of essays that generally demonstrate the power of various cultural contexts to situate and shape Faulkner's fictional texts, Sacvan Bercovitch's "Culture in a Faulknerian Context" suggests an opposing perspective, one that demonstrates how the literary text performs its own act of contextualization. Through its imagery of specific people in a specific time and place, the fiction questions, tests, at times undermines the larger abstractions. It counters the totalizing impulse of "disciplinarity" with the concrete characters and events that subvert absolutes, force us into new interpretations, remind us of the limits of all disciplines and, as corollary, the *un*limitedness of the real world: the fact that "we are always more . . . than our culture tells us we are." In the example of *Light in August*, Bercovitch argues that the novel revises some of its most powerful contextualizing frameworks, such as Fate and Christ, by embodying them in the figures of Percy Grimm and Joe Christmas, at once confirming the truth of tradition and opening, once again, its possibilities.

Donald M. Kartiganer
The University of Mississippi
Oxford, Mississippi

A Note on the Conference

The Twenty-second Annual Faulkner and Yoknapatawpha Conference sponsored by the University of Mississippi in Oxford took place July 30–August 4, 1995, with nearly three hundred of the author's admirers from around the world in attendance. The twelve lectures presented at the conference are collected in this volume. Brief mention is made here of other activities that took place during the week.

The conference opened with a reception hosted by the University Museums and an exhibition entitled *Square Art: Images of a Town*. At the opening session Chancellor Robert C. Khayat welcomed participants, and William Ferris, director of the Center for the Study of Southern Culture, presented the 1995 Eudora Welty Awards in Creative Writing to Natalie Tropp of Oxford and Casey Crosthwait of Jackson. The awards are selected annually through a competition held in high schools throughout Mississippi. Following the presentation was *Voices from Yoknapatawpha*, readings of passages from Faulkner's fiction selected and arranged by former conference director Evans Harrington.

Conference participants then gathered at Faulkner's home, Rowan Oak, for the announcement of the winner of the sixth annual Faux Faulkner write-alike contest, sponsored by *American Way* magazine, the University of Mississippi, and Yoknapatawpha Press and its *Faulkner Newsletter*. Authors Barry Hannah, George Plimpton, and Willie Morris selected Peter Stoicheff, a professor of English at the University of Saskatchewan, for his winning parody "A Rose for Hemingway." After a buffet supper, held on the lawn of Dr. and Mrs. M. B. Howorth Jr., and sponsored by *American Way*, Sacvan Bercovitch delivered the opening lecture and Square Books hosted a party.

Monday's program consisted of four lectures and the presentation "Knowing William Faulkner," during which J. M. Faulkner presented slides and stories of his famous uncle. Other highlights of the conference included a panel discussion by local residents—Howard Duvall, Mildred Murray Hopkins, Chester McLarty, and Patricia Young—moderated by M. C. Falkner, another of the writer's nephews; "Teaching Faulkner" sessions conducted by visiting scholars James B. Carothers, Robert W. Hamblin, Arlie E. Herron, and Charles A. Peek; a lecture on American literature and history by writer Marilynne Robinson; and bus tours of North Mississippi and the Delta. Social highlights were a party at Tyler Place hosted by Charles Noyes, Sarah and Allie Smith, and Colby Kullman; a walk through Bailey's Woods and a picnic at Rowan Oak. The closing party, originally scheduled to take place at the Gary home, was shifted to Off Square Books because of rain.

The conference planners are grateful to all the individuals and organizations who support the Faulkner and Yoknapatawpha Conference annually. In addition to those mentioned above, we wish to thank Mrs. Jack Cofield, Dr. William Strickland, Mr. Richard Howorth of Square Books, Mr. James Rice of Holiday Inn/Oxford, the City of Oxford, and the Oxford Tourism Council.

Faulkner in Cultural Context

FAULKNER AND YOKNAPATAWPHA

1995

Faulkner's History:
Sources and Interpretation

DON H. DOYLE

This conference offers me a special opportunity to cross boundaries that exist between history and literature, disciplines that use different currency and speak different languages, but share, nonetheless, a common interest in the past. While my aim is to traverse those boundaries, it is not my purpose to deny or obliterate them. On the contrary, I hope to shore them up a little, to define some important distinctions between the worlds of history and literature, but, at the same time, illustrate how they can enrich one another. I can think of no author and no place more inviting to the collaboration between history and literature than William Faulkner's Yoknapatawpha County.

Many historians before me have seen in Faulkner a credible authority on the South, a writer of fiction who had something important to offer about the region and the meaning of its past. The renowned Southern historian C. Vann Woodward credits Faulkner, Robert Penn Warren, and other writers of the Southern Renaissance with leading the attack on the stubborn myths that enshrouded the region's past and, thereby, helped clear the way for historians to take up the task of revising the traditional narratives that had dominated Southern history since Reconstruction. But more than that, Woodward tells us, it was Faulkner's fiction that framed his reading of that past. After reading Faulkner, Woodward asked, how could one write about the New South without thinking about Flem Snopes or Jason Compson? How could one discuss the planters without recalling such vivid characters as

Thomas Sutpen or Old Carothers, and how could a historian ex-
ploring the world of black people or the issue of race not have in
mind Joe Christmas, Lucas Beauchamp, or Dilsey Gibson? When
Woodward refers to the New South as the "age of the Snopeses,"
it becomes clear that Woodward's plot of Southern history, as well
as the ironic and tragic tone of his interpretation, owes much to
Faulkner's fictional rendering. Confessing himself to be a historian
"dedicated to fact" but "inspired by fiction," Woodward speaks for
many historians of the South who cite Faulkner or his characters
alongside documented evidence as though Faulkner's people, his
South are—if not real—historically true.[1] This exchange between
fiction and history began with Faulkner's absorption of local and
regional history into his works of fiction, but at some point this
fiction began seeping back into the narratives and plots historians
impose upon the South's past.

Historians and Faulkner critics rarely pause to ask: by what authority does Faulkner inform our understanding of the South and
its history? He was quite free to interpret the past uninhibited by
the rules of evidence that discipline the historian's craft. Indeed,
he often expressed contempt for factual accuracy, or even consis-
tency, and claimed that he never did an hour of research for any
of his books. "Poets," he wrote, "are almost always wrong about
facts. That's because they are not really interested in facts: only in
truth." "I believe that 'fact' has almost no connection with 'truth,'"
he wrote impatiently to one editor who was nit picking over some
"factual" inconsistencies.[2]

Faulkner took full advantage of his poetic license not only to
invent colorful characters and dramatic events, but also to go inside the minds of his actors, to explain their psychology and motivations. Historians both suspect and envy this creative freedom.[3]
No amount of archival research by the most earnest historian is
ever going to reveal the kind of interior world Faulkner opens to
us in his description of Thomas Sutpen and the trauma of his
youth, how that shaped his destiny, what he thought and how he
came to be what he was. Even relatively minor characters, like
Mink Snopes and Jack Houston, are brought on stage dragging

along with them a full biography, richly nuanced and emotionally penetrating. Throughout Faulkner's writing we get observations about people and places that appear to be carefully set within a particular historical, social, and geographical context, as though what he describes could not have happened except in that particular place and time. "The land, the people, and their history," Robert Penn Warren wrote, "—they come to us at a realistic level, at the level of recognition."[4]

But can we rely on him, not for facts of course, but for a more general historical realism that is, if not true *to* life, true *of* life? He once explained that he wrote about things his subjects "could have done," or "would have done" when no one was "there to record the action."[5] As he once put it, he was "sublimating the actual into the apocryphal." This would all be reassuring to the historian were it not so well known that Faulkner also had a habit of taking liberties with the truth, that through much of his adult life, for example, he deliberately and repeatedly distorted the facts about his personal history, often in self-serving ways. Why should we trust him or grant him authority just because he was a good writer, or a native Southerner, or because he allegedly had "universal truths" well beyond mere factual accuracy to communicate? Even if we grant an *intention* to get at the truth about his region's past, he was looking at it from his own peculiar angle: the descendant of a prominent Mississippi family of conservative Democratic loyalties, a white male with particular views of blacks and women, a young Southerner coming of age in the twilight of the old order and the disturbing emergence of a new one.[6]

It seems obvious that one way to test Faulkner's reliability as an authority on the South is to examine closely the historical world that was the primary source for much of his fiction. This is what I set out to do, determined from the outset to put the history center stage and give Faulkner's fiction a supplementary role in helping interpret the action and its meaning, in other words to use the historical fiction to inform the history—to sublimate the apocryphal into the actual. Where else in America is there a place whose history is so richly complemented with such a large body of fine fiction?

As I immersed myself in the history of this place, and simultaneously in Faulkner's fictional world, I found myself confusing the two. Names of people, events, places, and countless little details that emerged from the historical record began to blur with what I was absorbing from Faulkner. It must have been the same for him. In the attic of the courthouse I come across the deed with the "X" of Hoka, the Indian woman who in 1836 sold her allotted land to the three men who then donated a portion of this land to the county so that it would be chosen as the county seat. In church records I come across a slave named Dilsey who ran away with the Yankees and was excommunicated. Dozens of other names that made their way into Faulkner's fiction emerge in the historical record. I read countless stories from the Civil War era of buried silver and one about an old plantation whose front yard was pocked with holes from treasure hunters. Another local story gives account of a Chickasaw Indian who asked that his black slave and treasure be buried with him.

There is already a rich and valuable stock of linkages between the actual and the apocryphal in the voluminous scholarship on Faulkner. The origin of this work can be traced back to the local sport among readers and friends who guessed at the sources of his characters and stories. Scholarly critics built upon this local lore, beginning with Ward Miner and then Joseph Blotner's monumental biography, which seemed to trace every fictional detail to some experience or historical incident. Evans Harrington put much of this into the film script of *Land Into Legend*. Arthur Kinney has juxtaposed historical documents and fictional accounts of Faulkner's families. Charles Aiken has examined the geographical correspondence between fact and fiction, a theme that takes on expanded meaning in a new book by Gabriele Gutting.[7] The annual Faulkner and Yoknapatawpha Conference, with its bus tours and panels featuring local people, lends credence to the realism of Faulkner's imaginative world by immersing its participants in the historical world from which it was created.

The voluminous coincidences between fact and fiction revealed through all the scholarship, films, and guided tours confirm that the actual was often the source for the apocryphal. It is precisely because Faulkner's fiction is so accurate in so many of its historical details that we must be careful about accepting the larger historical picture of the South we see—or *think* we see—in Yoknapatawpha. It is this larger plot of history that I want to turn to now.

*   *   *

Southern history is most often told within the framework of a three-act morality play that portrays, first, the Old South dominated by the honorable but flawed slave master aristocracy, then the crisis of Civil War and Reconstruction, which destroys the foundations of the old ruling class, followed by the New South, which witnesses the rise of a new calculating class of urban entrepreneurs.

One of the pillars in the mythology of the Old South is the belief that it was a society ruled by aristocratic planters, a class whose values were not only fundamentally opposed to the Northern bourgeoisie but also at odds with the New South, whose leaders emerged from inferior social origins after the Civil War. This is essentially what many Faulkner critics see as a contest between the Sartoris and Snopes families, which are thought to embody the larger historical drama.[8]

The Old South's planter class, those with large acreage and at least twenty slaves, were a small and wealthy elite, but they were far from being an aristocracy of unbought ease whose wealth and status were insured by inherited privilege. To be sure, the old planter families of tidewater Virginia and the low country of South Carolina did all they could to garner the trappings of aristocracy, and, arguably, they came closer than any American elite to imitating the European model. But even these "long-tailed families" were deeply troubled by economic insecurity during the antebellum period as their land became exhausted due to repeated plantings of tobacco and cotton and a heedless disregard for soil conservation. It was the voracious hunger of the cotton plantation economy for new land that put so much pressure on President Jackson—himself a western planter—to open up the Old Southwest to white settlement by removing the Indian tribes there.

Lafayette County was born in 1836 amid an enormous land grab, a carnival of land speculation that brought a swarm of white land agents, surveyors, land lookers, lawyers, and settlers into negotiation with the Chickasaw chiefs and family heads. After 1830 when the Indian Removal Act was passed and when the state of Mississippi abolished tribal government, the Chickasaw nation was doomed. Perhaps it had been doomed three centuries earlier when DeSoto first entered their lands in 1540 and when, in the years that followed, alien European germs wiped out some 80 percent of the native people. Or maybe they were doomed only a century before removal when they began trading with the English: first deerskins for guns, knives, and metal pots, then Indian slaves for African slaves, and then tribal land for money with which they bought jewelry, clothing, and whiskey from white traders. Their leaders (by this time a group of mixed-blood—white and Indian— families led by Levi Colbert) made the best deal they could with Jackson and his agents; they agreed to allot land to each family head, according to the size of his or her family (including their African slaves) and throw the land on the open market. At the land office in Pontotoc in January 1836 speculators and planters brought bags of gold as the land—six million acres—all neatly divided by invisible lines into square mile sections, went under the gavel at one of the largest land auctions in American history.[9]

Hoka's "X" was one of hundreds of transactions by which the Chickasaws transferred land title to whites. (During the county centennial in 1936 Hoka's deed was celebrated as the origin of Oxford, a legitimate, voluntary, legal transfer—a symbol that obscured a more troubling history of forcible removal.)[10] The state-appointed county commissioners quickly set up an election for the first county government, setting in motion a self-perpetuating machine of local self-government, a replica of the American republic. The new officials immediately selected a site for the seat of the new government, to which Hoka's land was quickly converted. Faulkner's maternal great-grandfather, Sheriff Charles Butler, laid out the new town lots using a hickory tree as the base point with the courthouse square at the center and a grid of rectangular streets superimposed on the hitherto untouched forest land. Among their first acts, the county officials called for bids on a courthouse, which they specified was to be made of brick, with thick stone foundations, rising two stories and topped by a cupola. At the same time they authorized construction of a dungeon, of thick oak logs, with iron strapping, secured with "strong prison locks . . . a double bolt pad lock."[11] The law, government, courts, and a jail were at the center of a new economy that required clear legal title to ownership of land, cotton, and slaves. The new government quickly laid out roads, authorized bridges and ferries, all to facilitate the rapid emergence of a cotton economy that linked this remote frontier to the markets of the world and the textile factories of the industrial revolution.

Many important dates and events in Faulkner's account do not agree with the history of the early formation of the county, but he captured wonderfully the sudden genesis of government and economy on the cotton frontier, a process driven by land greed and accompanied by no small amount of swindling. The Mississippi frontier was no place for fastidious, honor-bound gentlemen. Much of the so-called Old South was barely a generation from its crude beginnings when the Civil War destroyed it.

Faulkner's Mohataha, the Indian queen in her silk dress and slave-borne parasol, inscribes her "X" on the land deed and turns her wagon westward, removed "like a float or a piece of stage property dragged rapidly into the wings across the very backdrop and amid the very bustle of the property-men setting up for the next scene and act before the curtain had even had time to fall."[12] The last act for the Chickasaws in Mississippi was the opening one for white settlers. The stage for the next act was indeed set up with amazing rapidity. A whole new plantation economy was laid out within a year or two. Lafayette County filled rapidly with people, over 6,500—far more than the entire Chickasaw nation in this one county—and it would grow to over 16,000 by 1860. More than half were white people who came voluntarily; about 40 percent were slaves who migrated with their masters or were sold to the West, part of a massive and barely studied movement that might be called the "first Great Migration."

The large planters took up land in the northern portion of the county around College Hill and on Woodson's Ridge, exactly where Faulkner puts the Sutpen, McCaslin, and Sartoris families. These lands were flat, covered with a deep brown loam soil and located near the Tallahatchie River, site of the nascent cotton port of Wyatt, which promised briefly to rival Memphis. The large planters sent ahead an advance party, a younger son or overseer along with a work force of male slaves to clear the land and set up housing. They built crude dogtrot cabins made of logs, chinked with mud, and furnished rather primitively. The master's house was not markedly different from the slave quarters, according to many astonished travellers. On the Jones plantation on Woodson Ridge the slaves ate outside, eating their hoecakes and "potliker" with their hands from a crude trough made from a hollowed out log. Alexander Pegues and his father, Malachi, one of the richest families in Lafayette, lived in a "rude bachelor affair of logs." Alexander Pegues could be seen riding about the county, a rifle over his shoulder and a pack of hounds following him. After he married a cousin from Alabama, he built a more refined country home surrounding which was an abundance of flowers she had carefully planted. But her rough-shod husband retreated to a separate masculine den, a cabin fenced off and flowerless, where he entertained his hunting friends.

It was in the late 1840s and 1850s, when a more steady prosperity took hold in Lafayette that many wealthy planters built grand looking mansions in Oxford or on their country estates. The locally renowned Pegues mansion, now called Ammadelle on North Lamar Street, was built by Alexander's brother-in-law, Thomas E. B. Pegues. He began construction on 100 acres of land, lined the drive with magnolias and planted trees all the way down North Street to the square. Built of bricks his slaves made from local clay and said to be designed by Calvert Vaux, whom townspeople referred to as the New York architect with the French name, the mansion he called Edgecomb was known locally as "Pegues' Folly" for it remained unfinished when the war began.[13]

Whether the Pegues family helped inspire the Thomas Sutpen story or not, several other pioneer planter families could have served as models. A Sutpen on the Mississippi frontier would hardly have stood out as an alien pretender among a refined gentry; they were all a striving, calculating breed whose stock in trade was land, slaves, and the cotton they produced. They came west to reclaim wealth and land that had eroded in the East, and to a degree they were all reinventing themselves on the cotton frontier. I will "change to Yankee shrewdness and perseverance," one planter's son wrote home. "Here I see a field to operate in and here I can make *money money*." He hoped to make a fortune in Mississippi and then return home, "but I fear I shall be like the rest of mankind, not satisfied with a sufficiency but wish to grasp after *more more more*."[14]

But the dream of wealth proved elusive for most. The bubble of land speculation burst suddenly in the Panic of 1837, which hit Mississippi full force two years later, dashed the hopes of land speculators, sent cotton prices plummeting, and ruined the schemes of town boosters in Wyatt and other places. "[T]he splendid lie of a false credit burst into fragments," Joseph Baldwin wrote. "Men worth a million were insolvent for two millions: promising young cities marched back again into the wilderness. The ambitious town plat was re-annexed to the plantation, like a country girl taken home from the city. The frolic was ended, and what headaches, and feverish limbs the next morning!"[15]

Masses of the newly settled population moved on, farther West to the next Mississippi, anywhere to escape creditors and begin over. "GTT" became a common shorthand in church records, land sales, and credit reports for those who had gone to Texas to try again. The churning of the county's population continued long after the economy began to recover in 1840. One in three of the 1840 population could be found ten years later, and the same was true of the next two decades. Except for a stable core of the population, Lafayette County was just a temporary stop in a restless search for opportunity.[16]

As cotton prices recovered, the soil in Lafayette County was ruined by the expansion and repetitive planting of cotton, which between 1840 and 1860 rose rapidly from a little over 2,600 to nearly twenty thousand bales each year. Following a short-term strategy aimed at quick profits, farmers paid no heed to the rapid erosion of the soil. Made of the windblown refuse from ancient glaciers to the North, the loosely packed loam soil made the land remarkably easy to clear and "break." But once exposed to the elements, the soil melted like sugar in the rain and washed away or, when the winds came, it blew away in huge clouds of dust—a recurrent image in Faulkner's landscape.[17] It would be a century after the land was first tilled that the federal Civilian Conservation Corps set up camp near Abbeville and planted thousands of kudzu vines over the scarified land of Lafayette County. Soon the kudzu formed a thick green gauze that covered—but would never heal—the wounds left from a century of reckless land use. The John McCready painting *Oxford on the Hill*, which is featured on this year's Faulkner and Yoknapatawpha Conference poster, gives an ominous view of the ravaged land just before the kudzu took over in 1939.[18]

The Old South that took form in northern Mississippi was far from a stable, hierarchical, traditional community in harmony with nature, as the latter-day Agrarians imagined, and the planter elite was all too much a part of the larger market revolution that extended itself rapidly westward across antebellum America. Lincoln's election in 1860—among other things—threatened further expansion of slavery, and therefore the well-being of slavery where it already existed. This election led radical proslavery leaders to secede from the Union rather than remain a beleaguered minority at the mercy of free-soilers hostile to slavery.

*   *   *

Act 2, the Civil War, was an event Faulkner kept coming back to, partly to cash in on the popular taste for Civil War stories but also because the war was the central crisis in the history of the South from which all else followed. "In the broadest sense," one critic wrote, "most of Faulkner's fiction is concerned with the defeat of the South or the effects of that defeat."[19]

Faulkner anticipated historiographical trends that are only now reshaping scholarship on the Civil War by viewing the war through the eyes of the women, children, and slaves at the Southern home front.[20] In this first "total war" the civilian population at home was active supplying men, uniforms, arms, and moral support. The Confederate home front was exposed to invasion and massive destruction of property and the liberation of slave property. It was at the home front, not the battle field, that the South was defeated, something Faulkner (and before him General Sherman) fully realized. It was here that the deepest tensions within Southern society, between rich and poor, masters and slaves, men and women all came to the surface under the pressure of war, massive death tolls, conscription, invasion, and slave rebellion.

Lafayette County went into the war divided over the issue of secession, but it was the fire-eaters, led by L. Q. C. Lamar, who prevailed. Lamar cast the election of Lincoln as a perilous threat to slavery and the whole Southern economy on which it rested. The South, he insisted, was left with no choice but to declare its independence. Mississippi's secession from the Union was heralded by the leading slaveholders in the county who lent their full support to the war by private donations of money for arms and uniforms and by sponsoring military companies: Thompson's Cavalry, Avant Southrons, Pegues Defenders, and the Lamar Rifles were among the seventeen companies that formed in the county that winter and spring.[21]

The wealthy women of Lafayette county played a vital role in the war effort: sewing uniforms and battle flags, preparing food, and lending their moral support to the recruitment campaign. The most poignant expression of this came at the numerous flag presentation ceremonies. There, the young daughters of the slave-holding elite, dressed in white dresses with sashes indicating the Confederate states they represented, would present a company battle flag to the men about to go off to defend them. Through these rituals the war became something other than a defense of slavery or states rights; it became a defense of feminine virtue at the home front. "Our safety is endangered, and our honor is at stake," young Miss Wiley told a large crowd of soldiers at one such ceremony. "Our State has nobly resolved that she will submit to no denial of her rights; and you, by volunteering to bear her flag, have shown your determination to uphold her in that resolution. . . . Receive it and bear it with you in your marches and upon the field of danger, remembering when you gaze upon it, that our eyes are also upon you. . . . Woman, bereft of honor, is not less unworthy of the love of man, than is man, devoid of courage, incapable of inspiring her with reverence."[22]

If the young men were asked to fight in exchange for the respect and love of these women, those who refused to fight would suffer emasculating humiliation. J. E. Robuck was twenty-four years old, the son of a small farmer near the Yoknapatawpha River. He opposed secession on principle and sat out the first year of the war, resisting tremendous pressure from the recruiters or "out pushers" as they were known. Then a slave girl arrived with a present from some young women: a hoop skirt, sun bonnet, and Mother Hubbard frock intended as an insult to his masculinity. (Robuck defiantly put on the outfit, posed for a photographer, and gave copies of his outlandish portrait to his tormentors.) But after conscription was in force he finally joined the Lafayette Rifles. Not one of his comrades owned a single slave, he recalled pointedly. When they gathered at the train station to go off to war the wealthy planters' wives showed up, giving out ten dollar gold pieces to the soldiers and promising to look after their families while they were away.[23]

Dissident voices were mostly silenced in the initial euphoria of secession and military pomp. "[T]he first seconds of fall always seem like soar," Faulkner wrote of Yoknapatawpha's—and the South's—plunge from its precipice of wealth, power, and pride into the war that would almost destroy all three. For a time in that exhilarating winter and spring of 1861 it seemed like they were soaring, with that "upward rush of earth . . . a soar, an apex, the South's own apotheosis of its destiny and its pride" before—a year or more later—they were to hit the ground and even then with that "preliminary anesthetic of shock so that the agony of bone and flesh will not even be felt."[24]

It was about a year after Fort Sumter that Lafayette County hit the hard ground. The war came home that spring not in the form of dashing men in uniform with flags and brass bands but in train loads of mutilated bodies from the battlefield of Shiloh. The university buildings were transformed into a hospital for hundreds of wounded men, while others were nursed in private homes. (About half of them died and are buried in the Confederate cemetery on the edge of campus, a reminder of the carnage that remains overgrown and neglected, far less visible than the unvanquished soldiers who stand proudly on the two Confederate monuments in town.) The women who served at home or at the university hospital nursing the men, bringing them food, and preparing bandages and clothing, now saw before them the horrifying face of a war to which they had sent their own sons, husbands, and brothers. Like Judith Sutpen, who joined the women of Jefferson "in the improvised hospital where (the nurtured virgin, the supremely and traditionally idle) they cleaned and dressed the self-fouled bodies of strange injured and dead and made lint of the window curtains and sheets and linen of the houses in which they had been born."[25]

After Shiloh the Confederacy introduced America's first conscription policy, with a provision that would exempt one white man for every plantation with twenty slaves—bitterly referred to as "the twenty nigger law" by poor white families who were sending their own sons to what they contemptuously referred to as a "rich man's war and poor man's fight." Many joined grudgingly rather than be shamed by being drafted, but they formed a resentful and despised band among the Southern armies. Others resisted the draft outright, "laying out" in the woods to evade conscription officers. These "moss backs" were supported by family and neighbors who brought them food and warned them when to hide. One

man in Abbeville hid out in his attic, a story that must have inspired Faulkner's tale of Goodhue Coldfield in *Absalom, Absalom!*[26]

Others escaped north seeking protection behind Union lines;
many joined the Union army and took up arms against their own
people. As the war dragged on, as supplies grew scarce, growing
numbers in northern Mississippi began engaging in "blockade
running," trading with the enemy across the lines in and around
Memphis (a practice Faulkner's own great-grandfather, the "Old
Colonel," had engaged in). Wagons full of cotton moved north by
back roads at night, returning with food, salt, and other supplies.
Others, known as "bushwhackers," were often deserters and those
willing to take advantage of a war-torn society that left women and
old men unprotected. One band of horse thieves in the Cambridge
community, in the hill country east of Oxford, was led by Ross
Boyd and Bill Winn, who stole horses and mules from destitute
old women and once threatened to burn a baby unless the mother
gave them food. Like Faulkner's Grumby, Boyd was victim of his
own violent justice and was eventually caught and hanged.[27]

The pressure on the home front intensified at the end of 1862
when a force of 40,000 men under the command of General Grant
invaded the county and set up headquarters in Oxford. Hundreds
of men, thinking the Union army was here to stay, flocked to the
courthouse in Oxford to take the amnesty oath and declare their
loyalty to the Union. But when Van Dorn's raid at Holly Springs
cut off supplies, their new protectors quickly withdrew, leaving
them at the mercy of their pro-Confederate neighbors. Before
evacuating, Grant ordered his troops to scour the countryside.
They confiscated every mule and horse they could find, pillaged
every pantry, cellar, and corn crib and left behind hundreds of
depleted farms and desperate families. Lafayette County, Grant
wrote later in his memoirs, offered a rehearsal for a strategy that
would emerge full blown in Sherman's ruthless march to the sea.[28]

A war originally defined as a defense of the women at home had
exposed them instead to the hardship and humiliation of invasion.
Many of Mississippi's soldiers had been sent to Virginia; others

were about to be sent east when Grant's army drove south into Mississippi. Desertions rose alarmingly as men came home to protect their families and restore their homes. Those who remained on the front lines received demoralizing letters from parents and wives. When Grant's army withdrew north of the Tallahatchie just before Christmas on a cold wet December day "the country [was] literally devastated for ten miles in all directions around Oxford. The horrors of the situation at the university were unspeakable."[29] "A melancholy gloom overhangs our beloved community," the Presbyterians of College Hill recorded, wondering what they had done to so displease God.[30]

While the loyalty of whites was being undermined by the draft and Union invasion, many within the slave population suddenly abandoned their masters in a massive flight north to freedom following Grant's retreat. Lincoln's Emancipation Proclamation had been issued in September 1862, effective on the first day of the new year. Union soldiers made certain the slaves of Lafayette County knew the Day of Jubilee was at hand.

Not long after Grant's retreat one woman wrote her sister describing the depredations of the soldiers who had occupied her house and taken her food. What shocked her the most was the disloyalty of her slaves: "they (the negroes) were so deceitful . . . they talked against the Yankees and I never suspected any of them going away so soon. . . . Old Harry assured me that they were none of them going to the yankees and they all deceived me very well for I was shocked as I had rang the bell several times and no answer or noise[.] I hurried on my clothes and all were gone. Hester and Bet slept in the house and as usual went to the kitchen after getting up to wash their faces and I kept thinking they would come indirectly [sic]."[31]

Long after Grant's army left, the slaves of Lafayette were continually running off to Memphis or somewhere behind Union lines. During 1863 and 1864 the Oxford Baptist Church excommunicated several of its runaway slave members.[32] It was this exodus from slavery that Faulkner described so vividly (if not quite accurately) in *The Unvanquished* where droves of runaways raise huge

clouds of dust along the roads going north, drawn like lemmings
by faith— "reasonless, . . . blind to everything but a hope and a
doom"—to a river they call Jordan, and to something called "freedom" to which Jesus and the Yankees, led by the angel Sherman,
were going to deliver them. Faulkner's Yankees are reluctant
emancipators who beat the runaway slaves back with their scab-
bards, blow up the bridge they hope to cross, and urge them to
return home, an ironic and not misleading depiction of Yankee
ambivalence.[33]

John Eaton, the Army chaplain in charge of the slave refugee
camps in Holly Springs and Grand Junction, Tennessee (the origin
of the Freedmen's Bureau), described in remarkably similar language the flight to freedom that winter: "Imagine, if you will, a
slave population, springing from antecedent barbarism, rising up
and leaving its ancient bondage, forsaking its local traditions and
all the associations and attractions of the old plantation life, coming
garbed in rags or in silks, with feet shod or bleeding, individually
or in families and larger groups,—an army of slaves and fugitives,
pushing its way irresistibly toward an army of fighting men. . . .
The arrival among us of these hordes was like the oncoming of
cities. There was no plan in this exodus, no Moses to lead it. Unlet-
tered reason or the mere inarticulate decision of instinct brought
them to us."[34]

The slaves who stayed behind were in some measure no longer
fully slaves. Various sources indicate a general breakdown of discipline and deference. Confederate officials in Jackson were alarmed
by reports of insurrection: "the Negroes have driven overseers
from plantations in Lafayette county and taken possession of everything," one Confederate officer reported. Another related that
they were "dividing the mules and other property of their masters
among themselves." The details of this slave uprising have proved
difficult to unearth—as are many details in the hidden history of
the period—but this slave uprising was sufficient to warrant a
mounted regiment dispatched to Lafayette County.[35]

Local records reveal a multitude of small rebellions among the
slaves who remained, and the brutal means whites employed to

regain control. One member of the College Hill Presbyterian Church defended himself before the session in September 1864 for shooting and killing a young female slave of his mother; the servants, he explained, had become "unmanageable, rude and insolent, setting at defiance all authority." He apologized for having offended "God and the church," and the church session let him continue as a member "in view of the peculiar state of things in the country, and the demoralized condition of the servants."[36]

As the war exposed northern Mississippi to recurring raids from the Yankees, in Lafayette County the stress of war put more pressure on the fault lines that crossed local society, setting slaves against masters, poor against rich, and Unionists against Confederates. Women's support for the war effort, so essential at the outset, was tested by the demoralizing experience of losing their men at the battle front while on the home front the Confederacy left them exposed to invasion, depredation, and slave rebellion. Faulkner echoed a familiar jest when he said that had it been up to the women the South would never have surrendered, but the evidence from the home front reveals more about women who were despondent over the absence or loss of their sons and husbands, fearful of invading armies and rebellious slaves, and simply exhausted by the hardships and deprivation war had brought.[37]

The final act of devastation and humiliation came in August 1864 when Union forces burned the courthouse and nearly all the buildings on the square, then ransacked and burned several homes of Confederate leaders and sympathizers. Among the soldiers in Oxford for this carnival of destruction were former slaves from Mississippi who had joined the army and now returned to the land of their enslavement wearing Yankee uniforms and bearing arms. They entered the homes of wealthy slave masters and Confederate supporters to loot and destroy (imagine Faulkner's Loosh torching the Sartoris home). It was after that day, Faulkner wrote, that the county passed through its own Appomattox well before the end of the war, reconciled to defeat—and to rebuilding. What he does not say is that many were scarred by the humiliation and wanton destruction of this day, by the disloyalty of slaves and fellow white

Southerners, by the insults and threats the Union soldiers had inflicted on their women. If, according to the code of chivalry, a man's honor was defined by his ability to protect his women, to guarantee their safety and reputation, especially against assaults from other men, the war for most of those who left northern Mississippi to go to battle had been an emasculating, ignominious ordeal. The Confederate soldiers may have returned defeated, but they were not conquered, and when the opportunity arose, they would settle some scores with those who had shamed them.[38]

* * *

Act 2, scene 2, brings us to the "dark and bloody ground" of Reconstruction. The military defeat of the Confederacy was accepted with little resistance, just as Faulkner wrote of Jefferson's stoic resignation. The soldiers came home, and the South prepared to rejoin the Union. But another struggle over white supremacy was still at issue, and in this contest white Southerners would not surrender, would not comprise, and would not accept defeat.

Faulkner captured the onset of this second civil war in a comic but perceptive exchange in *The Unvanquished*: "This war ain't over, Hit just started good," Ringo says to Bayard, his friend and former master's son. Bayard's father, Colonel John Sartoris, and the other leading white landowners of the county were preparing to do battle with the Republican carpetbaggers and scalawags who were organizing the blacks and preparing to consolidate their control over Yoknapatawpha's local government. Ringo had slipped away from the plantation to visit Jefferson, the county seat, and came back with astonishing news about the revolution that had been going on since the Yankee victory: "You know what I ain't?" he asked Bayard. "I ain't a nigger any more. I done been abolished." Just what *was* he then, Bayard wanted to know. Ringo answered by showing a scrip dollar signed by Cassius Q. Benbow, former slave and carriage driver for the Benbow family (before he ran off with the Yankees during the war), and now acting marshal of Yoknapatawpha, preparing for permanent election as marshal.

That, Ringo explained, was what John Sartoris and "the other white folks is so busy about." "A nigger?" Bayard asks incredulously, "A nigger?" " 'No,' Ringo said. 'They aint no more niggers, in Jefferson nor nowhere else.' " The carpetbaggers, led by the Burdens, a zealous family of abolitionists from Missouri, were here to "organise the niggers into Republicans." *That* is what they were, or were becoming; they were being "organized into" Republicans—citizens, voters, office holders, equals in the eyes of the law—by these outsiders.[39]

But not if John Sartoris and the whites of Yoknapatawpha County had anything to say about it. Faulkner employed the familiar plot of heroic former Confederate leaders challenging the sinister Northern carpetbaggers and their ignorant black dupes who threaten to take over the county and menace the white population. It was part of the same Black Legend immortalized by Thomas Dixon and D. W. Griffith, and ensconced in scholarship by the Dunning School.[40]

Reconstruction was part of a prolonged struggle over the future of former slaves, a struggle that began in 1863 when slaves took flight or otherwise defied their masters, and was resolved in 1875 when the Conservative Democrats "redeemed" the state. The issue of white supremacy was settled more conclusively in 1890 when a new constitution stripped the freedmen of political power and set Mississippi on what historian Neil McMillen calls the "dark journey" of racial subjugation, violence, and segregation that lasted three quarters of a century.

During Reconstruction Lafayette County witnessed a violent political and racial war. Republicans built a biracial coalition between the newly enfranchised freedmen and pro-Union, anti-Confederate whites; together they formed about half the electorate. Opposing them were most of the white voters and a small but important segment of "loyal" former slaves allied in the Conservative Democratic coalition. The electorate was evenly divided, and Lafayette County became violently contested ground. The conflict was not simply over local and state government, nor was it solely

over control of black labor. Both these political and economic issues were part of a larger struggle over white supremacy.

The fear with which whites regarded the former slaves was
grounded in terrifying interracial violence. Sometime early in
1866 in the southeast corner of the county, the area Faulkner
called "Frenchman's Bend," Sam Ragland, a sixty-five-year-old
overseer for the Price plantation near Delay, was asleep in bed
with his wife, Elizabeth. A group of black men, apparently looking
for money, entered the house and, according to one of several
different accounts, struck each of the Raglands in the head with
axes while they lay sleeping. Mrs. Ragland escaped to the yard,
where the intruders found her and slit her throat, nearly decapitat-
ing her. Sam Ragland was left for dead but survived. The white
men in the neighborhood, many of them Confederate veterans,
rounded up the Negroes and questioned them. They also watched
carefully as the Freedmen's Bureau agent conducted more questioning. Meanwhile, some local "private detectives" found derrin-
ger pistols stolen from Ragland's house in the possession of a
seventy-five-year-old black man, "Old Jess," who confessed under
pressure. Whoever actually committed the crime, the person they
blamed was a Northern woman who came South to teach in a
freedman's school set up on the Price plantation. Whites in the
neighborhood had already run her out of the county with threats
of tar and feathering and had shut down the school. Now a quiet
program of revenge began against those thought to be Elizabeth
Ragland's killers. An unidentified group of white vigilantes executed some twenty blacks, men and women, one by one. The accounts of the reign of terror that winter are inconsistent, vague,
and cloaked in secrecy. Some refer to lynchings, and one reports
that a group of suspects, bound by chains and vines, were pushed
into the Yoknapatawpha River to drown. Most of the victims simply disappeared while away from their homes. Skeletons were
later reported rising to the surface of the Yoknapatawpha.[41] This
was the violent corner of the county which Faulkner described as
remote from law "straddling into two counties and owning alle-

giance to neither" through which no "strange Negroes" would
dare pass after dark.[42]

The struggle over white supremacy was most visible in politics.
Once granted voting rights in 1867 the freedmen became the base
of the Republican party in Mississippi. Republicans organized a
county Loyal League to enlist black support and organized party
rallies and barbecues. The League also staged magnificent torchlight parades, where the freedmen marched wearing red oilcloth
caps festooned with bright red feathers, wrapped in large blue and
red sashes, with badges and flowing ribbons on their breasts, and
the ubiquitous Republican drums beating proudly and torches and
transparencies held aloft. In such moments every freedman must
have felt himself a citizen, belonging to something larger than his
family or church, something that defined itself in opposition to his
former master but also in alliance with whites eager for his support
in an unprecedented spirit of shared interest.[43]

The Loyal League also provided security and party discipline,
particularly on election days, when black voters travelled to and
from the polls in large groups, drums beating, marching through
gauntlets of armed and angry whites, some of whom conspicuously
wrote down the names of black voters in order to intimidate them.
Republican domination has been greatly exaggerated in the Black
Legend, but the party did manage against great odds to win state
and local contests. Most of the Republican office holders in county
government were not elected but appointed by Governor Adelbert
Ames (as Faulkner's Cassius Q. Benbow apparently had been) and,
contrary to the Black Legend, most Republican officeholders were
white. Republicans did manage to win local offices by election,
and in at least two cases with black candidates: Jerry Fox and Mack
Avent.[44]

Republicans were not the only ones to cater to the new black
voters. Democrats appealed to what they called the "loyal" former
slaves, who were given a tin badge as an emblem of their allegiance to the whites. To those who refused the Democrats or were
reported in the newspaper as having voted Republican, landlords
threatened to refuse contracts the coming year. On some planta-

tions the owners had fresh graves dug and markers without names put up as an ominous threat to the fearful new voters.[45]

Once Republicans rose to power at the state level, Democrats organized what amounted to a terrorist wing of the party, the Ku Klux Klan, whose purpose was to intimidate Republican leaders and voters. The Klan was most active where Democrat and Republican constituencies were evenly balanced. Lafayette County's first Klan was organized by General Nathan Bedford Forrest (in the law office later occupied by James and Phil Stone) in 1867.[46] The Lafayette County Klan included five dens, one in each beat of the county, led by Grand Cyclops Colonel R. W. Phipps, an Oxford lawyer and Democratic party leader, and Sam Thompson, editor of the *Falcon*.

Prior to the election of 1868 the Klan targeted Republican leaders black and white: they burned cabins, shot one man with shotguns, and flogged others. Violence and election fraud were so rampant that the results for Lafayette County had to be thrown out. The next year, when another election was held, a near riot broke out in Oxford after a white man shot black Republican leader Alexander Phillips. U.S. troops were brought in to occupy Oxford during the election and stayed on in an attempt to quell further violence. In fear for their lives, Republicans had to stage their rallies in the shadow of the army garrison. But with the polls secured by the Republican-appointed governor, the party managed to win amid a staggering statewide victory in 1869. Once Republicans gained power, the levels of violence only escalated, for it was the opposition's purpose to deny the very legitimacy of Republican rule and, with it, black citizenship and equality.[47]

This is exactly what Faulkner portrays through John Sartoris, who in broad daylight enters the polls, shoots two opposition leaders, takes the ballot box back home and stages a whites-only election at the plantation. The most absurd moment in this story comes when John Sartoris insists on turning himself in to the sheriff while his followers abscond with the ballot box: "Dont you see," he tells them, "we are working for peace through law and order?"[48]

The freed people of Lafayette County sought much more than

political power; they wanted education, economic independence, religious autonomy, and control over their lives. Northern agents and the Freedmen's Bureau were often blamed for stirring up the former slaves, but what is striking in the historical records is that it was the freedmen who were pushing their white benefactors for a fuller conception of freedom and not the other way around. Freedmen's Bureau agent Charles Austin wrote in August 1865: "The colored people of this town have done nobly towards raising a school fund to support schools for the instruction of the colored children here[;] [A]lready seven hundred thirteen and a half dollars have been subscribed. . . . They are continually plying one with questions as to when the school will commence[.] What can I answer them[?]" They were moving forward on their own, Austin later reported: "On the Jacob Thompson place stands the walls of a brick building[.] The Freedmen think they can cover this and use it for a school house." "The harvest is abundant here," Austin implored his supervisors; "what we want are teachers. I feel for this people. I would like to see them raised from their degradation."[49]

Most whites seemed intent on doing all they could to continue that degradation. They burned down school houses, harassed, beat, and shot teachers, and threatened worse if they did not leave.[50] The most tenacious teacher was Alexander Phillips, a black Methodist preacher and Republican organizer from Holly Springs.[51] Phillips was a fearless advocate of black rights who endured relentless harassment, threats, and violent assaults, including a bullet in his face. Students at the university led the assault on his school. After he was forced out of his rented school room and no one else would rent him space, "he retired to the woods and constructed a temporary house of brush in which he has since been teaching."[52]

The Black Legend of Reconstruction warned that if blacks were ever again allowed the power to vote they would dominate government, they would aspire to power beyond their capability, they would refuse honest work, and they would insist on full social equality, including access to white women. This belief was the

historical foundation for the policy of racial subjugation that followed Reconstruction, and to challenge it was to go up against the
wall of white solidarity that defended it. What is disappointing
about Faulkner's light treatment of Reconstruction is not just that
it parrots the prevailing party line that supported segregation. He
may well have believed that version of history, as most white Mississippians in the 1930s did, and also may have believed, at that
time anyway, in the social system that followed logically from it.
Yet his treatment of other venerated elements in Southern historical narratives had often demonstrated the subversive disposition
of a young Southerner, one impatient with the "plug hats and hoop
skirts" mythology that enshrouded his region's past. Earlier, in
Light in August, he had explored the psyche of the Burdens in an
interesting way, even if it pointed out the peculiar racism of the
Northern missionary in the South.

Faulkner's story "Skirmish at Sartoris," which dealt directly
with the events of Reconstruction, was originally written in 1934
during one of the author's desperate scrambles for quick cash from
popular magazines. The *Saturday Evening Post* had agreed to publish the series that later made up the major part of *The Unvanquished*, published in 1938. Perhaps this popular venue demanded
more superficial treatment of what was still a sensitive historical
subject, or maybe it was just that he was, as he admitted at the
time, simply writing "trash" for income. Yet within the earlier stories in the series he had already introduced strong characters, with
great iconoclastic potential, notably the outspoken slaves, Ringo
and Loosh, but also young Bayard Sartoris and the venerable ma-
triarch, Granny Millard, whose attitude toward the war and the
Yankee invaders played against type. They, along with such figures
as the bushwhacker Ab Snopes, were all characters who might
easily have been employed to explore some of the historical complexities and ironies of the Reconstruction era. But following
Ringo's pithy account of what Reconstruction meant to blacks, he
and these others disappear in favor of the cardboard characters
and stilted dialogue that carries the thin story line of "Skirmish
at Sartoris." Faulkner confessed to having trouble writing about

Reconstruction. After "stewing" over the subject for three weeks, he then changed course and put off confronting Reconstruction in favor of going back to the Civil War era. In the end, the story dealt only superficially with the historical events of Reconstruction; it was more about Drusilla Hawk and John Sartoris's wedding than about the conflict with the carpetbaggers that disrupted it. Later, when Faulkner put the magazine stories together for the book, he took the opportunity to rewrite and add depth to many passages, but he did little to alter the Reconstruction story. It remained the one period in Southern history he avoided and seemed unable or unwilling to attack. I suspect it was more than just the creative problems of plot or character; it was the subject, the history, and all that it meant for what the South was that made Reconstruction so difficult—especially for the probing and sometimes heretical mind of William Faulkner—to reassess.[53]

*   *   *

Act 3 in the conventional drama of Southern history brings on the New South (the first of many "New" Souths as it turned out). It was thought to be a time of reconciliation and of great economic rejuvenation and social change following Reconstruction. But the New South was also a slogan, a creed that captured the optimistic spirit of a post-war generation, especially the rising urban bourgeoisie whose eloquent spokesman, Henry Grady of Atlanta, claimed had put the past behind them and placed "business above politics." It was a period of urban growth, railway expansion, industrial development, and new fortunes for the winners, chief among whom were the industrialists, bankers, merchants, and lawyers in the towns. For the losers, most notably the white and black sharecroppers, it was a period of grinding poverty, declining cotton prices, and increasing dependence on landlords, furnishing merchants, railroads, and distant cotton markets.[54]

Class antagonisms were intensified by the new arrangements surrounding farm tenancy. The hill country yeomen who in antebellum times had managed a hardscrabble existence out of semi-subsistence farming on small plots of hilly land, raising corn for themselves and neighboring planters or running hogs and cattle on unclaimed land. The postwar devastation and the lure of quick profits in cotton pulled many of the Southern yeomen more fully into the market economy. Most had no capital or land and bank loans were difficult to qualify for, so small farmers of both races used next year's cotton crop as collateral to guarantee advances in rent charged for land and equipment, farm supplies, food, clothing, and all their needs during the year. Some land owners moved into mercantile activities, as Thomas Sutpen did with his plantation commissary, but more often it was country merchants, like Will Varner, who were becoming landlords. They extended credit to farmers for supplies, then (under the terms of Mississippi's lien law) they could foreclose on land, which was, in turn, rented out to more tenants. Contracts usually required the tenant to purchase all supplies from the merchants and at high mark-ups. At the end of the year the farmers and their creditors settled up by dividing shares of the crop and charging all expenses against the farmer's share. When merchants like Varner controlled the gins and bought the cotton, their dominance over the local economy was nearly complete. As cotton prices declined, foreclosures passed more and more land into the hands of the rising merchant-landlord class.[55]

The South's white small farmers were *falling* from a condition of modest competence and autonomy into a state of dependence as sharecroppers, a status they now shared with former slaves. The resentment that boiled within them could be directed *above* at landlords, merchants, or railroads, but also *below* at their new black rivals who competed for land and credit. Adding to this antagonism was the tendency for black tenant farmers to be preferred by landlords who considered them willing to work harder, pay more, and protest less than whites.[56]

Faulkner captured this mingled resentment of class and race perfectly in his story "Barn Burning." Ab Snopes goes to his landlord, the man who will own him "body and soul for the next eight months," approaching his large white house with a "ravening and jealous rage," brushing past the Negro servant at the front door and smearing horse manure on the carpet. Returning toward his own rented cabin, which "ain't fitten for hawgs," he looks back at the large white plantation house built with the sweat of black labor and remarks: "Maybe it ain't white enough yet to suit him. Maybe he wants to mix some white sweat with it."[57]

Barn burning was a prepolitical form of individual retribution, motivated by class enmity and desire for revenge, to be sure, but with no political aim of redistributing power. In the late 1870s this class resentment also took collective form with gangs known as "bull dozers," protective clubs that carried out campaigns of terror against the merchants and the farmers who cooperated with them. The bull dozers took to whipping, mutilation, robbery, rape, and murder.[58] These acts of violence were prelude to the politicalization of the grievances farmers began to voice through the Grange, Farmer's Alliances, and Populist Party. In Mississippi the farmers' revolt more often took the form of insurgency within the Democratic party through which they worked effectively to gain control of government, to shift political power from the Delta to the hill counties, and then to use the power of the state to help the farmer, the "forgotten man."

The "Revolt of the Rednecks," as it was known, brought genuine efforts toward democratic, progressive reform of government and society; it also became identified with extreme racism and a harsh regime of black disfranchisement, lynchings, and segregation. This was the movement that James K. Vardaman and Theodore Bilbo rode to power in the early twentieth century. When the Delta planter Leroy Percy ridiculed Vardaman's followers as "voting cattle" and "rednecks," they embraced the insult as an emblem of pride and took to wearing red neck ties at rallies while their champion, the "Great White Chief," rode in an ox cart.[59]

The successor to Vardaman and Bilbo was Lee Russell, who grew up near Dallas in the southeast corner of Lafayette County—not far from Faulkner's Frenchman's Bend. Lee Russell's family was not of the poor white class, as it is sometimes asserted. They owned a large farm along Mucaloon Creek and rented land to tenant farmers. But prospects were not good for even large farmers at

the end of the nineteenth century. Lee Russell's mother was credited with a burning ambition for her son that drove him to walk
miles along the dusty roads to a rural schoolhouse and later to
nearby Toccapola Normal College. He came to the University of
Mississippi to study law in 1903, according to legend walking the
twenty-three miles from Dallas. Students then were predominantly the wealthy sons of planters and townspeople. They scorned
the rise of the rednecks whose hero, Vardaman, had just won the
governorship. Russell was blackballed by a fraternity and then humiliated one day when he passed one of the fraternities and was
doused with water. He transformed his rage into a political attack
against what he considered aristocratic, secret societies. They encouraged "dissipation," gambling, harassment of women, undermined scholarship, and ostracized nonfraternity men from the
social life of Oxford. He went to Jackson and succeeded in per-
suading the University's Board of Trust to regulate fraternities.
Lee Russell became a law partner with J. W. T. Falkner, who may
have looked down on the likes of Russell but could not afford to
ignore the rising power of white farmers. Russell began to gather
a following, especially among the poor white farmers in Lafayette
County, and from that base launched a successful career in state
politics. As a state legislator in 1912, his resentment of the fraternities still smoldering, he led a campaign to have them banned from
the University. By 1920 Russell had followed his allies, Vardaman
and Bilbo, to the governorship of Mississippi.[60]

While poor white farmers were challenging the power of the
planters and townspeople, many were also quietly rising economically and socially, abandoning the washed-out land and endless
drudgery of rural life for opportunities in the town. It is this striving that Faulkner chronicled with a combination of amazement
and contempt in the Snopes novels.

It is his father's threat of barn burning that opens the door for
Flem Snopes to pass from the squalor of poor white sharecropping
into the lower rungs of the commercial class in Frenchman's Bend
as a clerk in Varner's store. Ab Snopes gets mad; Flem gets even.
He beats his social superiors at their own game, a game whose

customs and rules Varner, Ratliff, and others, including Ab Snopes and Pat Stamper, have been practicing long before Flem Snopes arrives. He is no alien invader bringing corruption and greed to the agrarian garden, just a quick learner and skillful player.[61]

We will better understand the character of Flem Snopes if we grasp the historical and social meaning of "redneck" class resentment and if we move beyond the Agrarian shibboleths against the evils of modernity which often rest on a romantic image of the "honorable aristocracy" of the Old South. Flem Snopes has much in common with his antebellum predecessors in fiction and history who swindle Indians, ruthlessly exploit the land and slaves, and are consumed by ambition for wealth and power. Like Sutpen before him, he is a poor white man scorned by his social superiors and driven by an unarticulated but intense desire to rise in wealth and status. Among his contemporaries Flem Snopes merely imitates and excels in practicing the shrewd skills of the country trader. He gets the better of his rivals in the game of trade primarily by taking advantage of *their* greed and lust—his own greed is under carefully calculated control, and his lust is altogether repressed or lacking.

Faulkner and his friend Phil Stone looked down on the Snopeses and the redneck class they supposedly represented, Stone from the vantage point of a descendant of the declining planter class, Faulkner from his position as offspring of the established Mississippi bourgeoisie. His brother, John Faulkner, gave a more charitable assessment of the country people who moved into town; he wrote, "for a better living for themselves and better education for their children, and by their initiative they secured both." They lived in shacks on the edge of town, worked diligently at menial labor, then opened small cafes and groceries, finally arriving on the square, in charge of the banks, stores, and local government. Their children "studied harder than we did" John Faulkner admitted, and had "the same driving urge their parents had." "Before you actually knew they were coming, to your surprise they were already there."[62] An ambitious, industrious people were coming in from the country, escaping rural poverty to make their way

in town. These country folk simulated rather than corrupted values
which townspeople had already acquired. The more successful
among them acquired wealth and position, and before anyone noticed they had passed the descendants of established town families, some of whom, like the Stones and Falkners, were sliding into
genteel poverty.

The Avent family is thought by many to have served as a model
for Flem Snopes and his clan, but the differences are as revealing
as the similarities. The Avents of Faulkner's time descended from
a pioneer family who had settled in the eastern part of Lafayette
County in 1839. Benjamin Avent, the family patriarch, fathered
fourteen children with his first wife and four more with his second
wife, the last when he was seventy-six years of age (no problem
with impotence in that line!). They were not rootless poor whites.
Benjamin owned eleven slaves in 1860 and $19,000 in property;
he was a man of wealth compared to his neighbors. His grandson,
Thomas Wesley Avent, began the migration from the hill country
into town. In the area around Liberty Hill, he owned some 2,000
acres of land and operated a cotton gin; he was more Varner than
Snopes. He married Sidney Parks, daughter of another large and
ambitious family in this part of the county. Following the tragic
death of their small daughter in an accident at the gin, they sold
the gin and all their land and moved to Oxford. There he discovered he had been duped; the business he bought was heavily en-
cumbered. Despite this shaky beginning, T. W. Avent eventually
became a founder and director of the First National Bank. His
partner was J. W. T. Falkner, the author's grandfather.

T. W. Avent and his wife had fifteen children, but only five sons
survived. All five rose to positions of considerable prominence in
banking, farming, medicine, and business of all kinds. Thomas Ed-
ison (known as "T. E.") Avent, whose prominent nose and other
facial features may have inspired Faulkner's Flem Snopes, became
well known as a shrewd business man. He began as a pharmacist
in Avent's Drug store, opened Avent Dairy in 1920, and after
World War II developed Avent Acres, a historical model for Flem
Snopes's Eula Acres and a Mississippi version of Levittown, which

produced small, affordable tract houses to the veterans returning home. Adjacent to this neighborhood is Avent Park, which he donated to the city. The Avent clan was involved in a remarkable array of businesses from banks, cotton gins, and dairies to boarding houses, groceries, and real estate. They were also well represented in local government and church affairs and were notable for their philanthropy.[63]

Joe Parks, another ambitious new man from the country, probably served as another prototype for Flem Snopes. He wore a black bow tie and was known as a shrewd trader and aggressive entrepreneur. It was Joe Parks who, with one of the Avents, promoted a spectacular oil drilling venture in Lafayette County in 1919 with bombastic claims that in the end yielded more gas than oil. Parks became a partner in J. W. T. Falkner's First National Bank and then managed to oust the "Young Colonel" and take over as president in 1920.[64]

The Parks, Avents, and others among the new men in Oxford were coming in from the hill country, and all its grinding poverty, worn-out land, and depressed cotton prices, to seek every opportunity they could find to secure wealth and win respect. The old established families, like the Falkners and Stones, may have looked down their noses at these country people who were taking over the town's economy and positions of influence. They no doubt ridiculed their rustic manners, dress, and ways of living. The old families in town may also have despised the new political demagogues who appealed to white farmers through racism and class resentment, though it is worth noting that J. W. T. Falkner, as well as making business partnerships with these men, joined political forces with Vardaman and his movement. In the end, these new people from the country were not so different from the old elite. I suspect Faulkner knew this at some level and created in Flem Snopes not so much a demon with alien values but a pure distillation of traits pervasive in his community, a mirror ungilded by any class pretensions of gentility.

In his own day he was confronting the changes that history had brought to his land and people, and in much of his best writing

Faulkner was working toward an understanding of the past and the ways it impinged upon the present. "The past is never dead"; he has one of his characters tell us, "It's not even past." It is a phrase often thought to evoke Southern traditionalism, but it may better reveal Faulkner's knowledge of the tragic burden history had inflicted on the South, a burden that weighed on the minds of thoughtful young Southerners who struggled through his writing to understand and help others understand how the past haunted the present.

NOTES

1. C. Vann Woodward, *The Burden of Southern History*, rev. ed. (Baton Rouge: Louisiana State University Press, 1968), 38; Woodward, *Thinking Back: The Perils of Writing History* (Baton Rouge: Louisiana State University Press, 1986), 109, 145.

2. Faulkner, *Snopes: The Hamlet, The Town, The Mansion* (New York: Modern Library, 1994), 426; Joseph Blotner, *Faulkner: A Biography*, 2 vols. (New York: Random House, 1974), 2:1730.

3. Richard King, "The Discipline of Fact/The Freedom of Fiction?" *Journal of American Studies* 25 (1991): 171–88, offers some thoughtful views on the relationship between history and literature with reference to Faulkner.

4. Robert Penn Warren, "William Faulkner" in *William Faulkner: Four Decades of Criticism* (East Lansing: Michigan State University Press, 1973), 96.

5. David Minter, *William Faulkner: His Life and Work* (Baltimore: Johns Hopkins University Press, 1980), 78, paraphrasing Frederick L. Gwynn and Joseph L. Blotner, *Faulkner in the University* (1959; Charlottesville: University of Virginia Press, 1995), 59–60.

6. Daniel Joseph Singal, *The War Within: From Victorian to Modernist Thought in the South, 1919–1945* (Chapel Hill: University of North Carolina Press, 1982), 153–97.

7. Ward L. Miner, *The World of William Faulkner* (New York: Grove Press, 1952); Blotner, *Faulkner*; *Faulkner's Mississippi: Land Into Legend*, film, directed by Robert Oesterling, script by Evans Harrington, 1965; Arthur F. Kinney, ed., *Critical Essays on William Faulkner: The Compson Family* (Boston: G.K. Hall, 1982); Kinney, ed. *Critical Essays on William Faulkner: The Sartoris Family* (Boston: G.K. Hall, 1985); Kinney, ed. *Critical Essays on William Faulkner: The McCaslin Family* (Boston: G.K. Hall, 1990); Charles S. Aiken, "Faulkner's Yoknapatawpha County: Geographical Fact into Fiction," *Geographical Review* 67 (January 1977): 1–21; Aiken, "Faulkner's Yoknapatawpha County: A Place in the American South," *Geographical Review* 69 (July 1979): 331–48; Gabriele Gutting, *Yoknapatawpha: The Function of Geographical and Historical Facts in William Faulkner's Fictional Picture of the Deep South* (Frankfurt am Main: Peter Lang, 1992).

8. Malcolm Cowley's editorial introductions to *The Portable Faulkner* lay out this historical narrative, building upon George Marion O'Donnell's influential 1939 essay, reprinted as "Faulkner's Mythology," in *William Faulkner: Four Decades of Criticism* (East Lansing: Michigan State University Press, 1973), 83–93.

9. For an overview of Chickasaw history see Arrell M. Gibson, *The Chickasaws*, The Civilization of the American Indian Series, v. 109 (Norman: University of Oklahoma Press, 1971).

10. See *Oxford Eagle*, 10 December 1936. Hoka's name, like many Chickasaw words, is spelled inconsistently. The deed she marked appears to have her name as Haka, and other

versions include Ho-Kah. I have retained th[e] [c]urrent usage adopted by the theater and
restaurant in Oxford named in her hon[or]

11. "Minutes, Board of Po[lice,"] [Cler]k's Office, Lafayette County Courthouse,
1836–18[4]6 ...

linquish)," in *Portable*, 672.

[R]ebecca Ann Evans Pegues, 1840–1882]
sketch of family history apparently ex-
[o]f *My Father's Family* (n.p., n.d.). For
see James Durwood Cole, "Origin of
[t]hesis, University of Mississippi, 1935),
[hist]ory of Lafayette County Mississippi,"
of Mississippi, Mississippi Collection
H. Pegues; *Oxford Eagle*, Centennial
[fi]le "Lafayette Springs" MDAH (Mis-
Mississippi); Mrs. Calvin S. Brown,
[M]rs. Calvin S. Brown Papers, Box 2,
Pegues, his daughter.
[...]th [Lowndes County, Miss.] 3 Au-
Duke University Library, mf "Re-
[...]eth M. Stampp (Frederick, Md.,

[...]d *Mississippi: A Series of Sketches*
[...]87), 90.
[...]t emphasizes their striving, inse-
[...]akes, *The Ruling Race: A History*
[...]s, 1982). For a contrasting view, see the
[...], which stress the paternalism and antibourgeois character

[...]o[...] [Geno]te: *The World the Slaveholders Made: Two Essays in Interpretation* (New
[Y]ork: Pantheon Books, 1969); *The Political Economy of Slavery: Studies in the Economy
and Society of the Slave South* (New York: Vintage Books, 1967).

17. For observations on the land and its early ruination, see Herbert Anthony Kellar, ed., *Solon Robinson Pioneer and Agriculturalist: Selected Writings*, 2 vols. (Indianapolis: Indiana Historical Bureau, 1936), 1:460.

18. On the kudzu planting: WPA, Source Material for Mississippi History, Lafayette County, Box 2, file on "History of Lafayette County," MDAH. The manuscript originals of this collection are more complete than the microfilm edition, which is also cited below.

19. Douglas T. Miller, "Faulkner and the Civil War: Myth and Reality," *American Quarterly* 15 (1963): 200; see also Matthew C. O'Brien, "William Faulkner and the Civil War in Oxford, Mississippi," *Journal of Mississippi History* 35 (May 1973): 167–74.

20. Drew Gilpin Faust, "Altars of Sacrifice: Confederate Women and the Narratives of War," *Journal of American History* 76 (March 1990): 1200–28; and George Rable, *Civil Wars: Women and the Crisis of Southern Nationalism* (Urbana, 1989); Catherine Clinton and Nina Silber, eds., *Divided Houses: Gender and the Civil War* (New York: Oxford University Press, 1992); Leon F. Litwack, *Been in the Storm So Long: The Aftermath of Slavery* (New York: Knopf, 1978); Clarence L. Mohr, *On the Threshold of Freedom: Masters and Slaves in Civil War Georgia* (Athens: University of Georgia Press, 1986); Wayne K. Durrill, *War of Another Kind: A Southern Community in the Great Rebellion* (New York, 1990).

21. Accounts of military mobilization are found in the *Oxford Intelligencer*, throughout 1861.

22. *Intelligencer*, 20 March 1861.

23. J. E. Robuck, *My Own Personal Experience and Observation as a Soldier in the Confederate Army During the Civil War, 1861–1865 also during the Period of Reconstruction* (Birmingham, Alabama: Leslie Printing and Publishing Co., 1911), 15, 17.

24. *Portable Faulkner*, 678, 679.

25. Faulkner, *Absalom, Absalom! The Corrected Text* (1936; New York: Vintage Books, 1987), 155–56, quoted in Matthew C. O'Brien, "William Faulkner and the Civil War in

Oxford, Mississippi," *Journal of Mississippi History* 35 (May 1973): 167–74. *The Oxford Eagle*, Centennial Edition, 27 March 1969; Miss Ella F. Pegues, "Recollections of the Civil War in Lafayette County," Maude Morrow Brown Papers, Box 1, f. 5, MDAH; Maude Morrow Brown, "At Home in Lafayette County, Mississippi, 1860–1865," pp. 54–57, in Maude Morrow Brown Manuscript, MDAH. See also Johnson, "The University War Hospital," *Publications of the Mississippi Historical Society*, IX.

26. *Absalom*, 100. There is a hint of antislavery sentiment in Coldfield's protest. He refused to own slaves and had immediately freed two slaves he had received as compensation for a debt, keeping careful account of the labor each owed him as they paid him back at their fair market value. Among the few white critics of slavery in Yoknapatawpha are the elderly McCaslin brothers, who are nonetheless such ardent supporters of the Confederacy they have to settle which one of them could go off to war with a game of poker—the loser to stay home and look after the slaves. The account of the draft dodger in Abbeville is found in WPA Source Material, Lafayette County, "Civil War: Deserters," microfilm of MDAH collection.

27. WPA Source Material, Lafayette County, "Outlaw Days," [c1935] mf. Little more is known of Boyd and his exploits.

28. "I was amazed at the quantity of supplies the country afforded," Grant recorded in his memoirs. "It showed that we could have subsisted off the country for two months instead of two weeks. . . . This taught me a lesson which was taken advantage of later in the campaign. . . ." Ulysses S. Grant, *Personal Memoirs of U.S. Grant*, 2 vols. (New York, 1885–86), 1:435–36, quoted in James W. Silver, ed, *Mississippi in the Confederacy as Seen in Retrospect* (Baton Rouge, Louisiana State University Press, 1961), 267.

29. Brown, "Lafayette County at Home," 100.

30. Quoted in Brown, "Lafayette County at Home," 105–8.

31. Unsigned to sister Dona, Oxford, 27 January 1863, H. W. Walter Papers, UM; photocopy, original in Holly Springs Historical Society.

32. "Minutes of Oxford Baptist Church," vol. 1, mf., entries for March 1863, November 1864, Skipwith Historical and Genealogical Society Collection, Oxford-Lafayette County Public Library.

33. Faulkner, *The Unvanquished* (New York: Vintage Books, [1938] 1966), 92.

34. John Eaton, *Grant, Lincoln and the Freedmen: Reminiscences of the Civil War* (1907; New York: Negro Universities Press, 1969), 2.

35. W. W. Loring to Colonel J. R. Waddy, Grenada, 17 January 1863, National Archives and Records Administration, Washington, D.C., hereafter NARA, Pemberton Papers. See also, John K. Bettersworth, *Confederate Mississippi*, 163–64, who cites T. C. Tupper to J. R. Waddy, 14 February 1863, and W. W. Loring to Waddy, 17 January 1863, both in the John C. Pemberton Correspondence, Confederate Archives, NARA.

36. Minutes, College Hill Presbyterian Church, mf; Brown, "At Home," 220–22.

37. My evidence on white social divisions during (and after) the war draws on the Lafayette County files of the Southern Claims Commission, NARA. For a fuller study of internal divisions during the war, see Wayne K. Durrill, *War of Another Kind: A Southern Community in the Great Rebellion* (New York, 1990), and Orville Vernon Burton, "On the Confederate Homefront: The Transformation of Values from Community to Nation in Edgefield, South Carolina," unpublished paper. My thanks to Professor Burton for making available of his work in progress. On the morale of women, local evidence of demoralization is found in Maude Morrow Brown, "Lafayette County, 1860–1865: A Narrative," typescript, Brown Papers, MDAH. Brown's unpublished manuscript was researched and written at the same time Faulkner was writing the stories that went into *The Unvanquished*. Her knowledge of the home front and her decidedly feminine perspective on the war may well have informed his interpretation. We know Faulkner was a friend of Maude and Calvin Brown (an expert on Mississippi Indians, incidentally), that he visited their home, but there is no evidence of any direct influence by them on his interpretation of the war or of Indian life. Recent scholarship has stressed the opposition of Southern women to the war; see Drew Gilpin Faust, "Altars of Sacrifice: Confederate Women and the Narratives of War," *Journal of American History* 76 (March 1990): 1200–28; and George Rable, *Civil Wars: Women and*

the Crisis of Southern Nationalism (Urbana: University of Illinois Press, 1989), Catherine Clinton and Nina Silber, eds., *Divided Houses: Gender and the Civil War* (New York: Oxford University Press, 1992).

38. Faulkner, "The Jail (Nor Even quite Yet Relinquish)," in *Portable*, 681.

39. Faulkner, *Unvanquished*, 228–29.

40. The Dunning School consisted of a series of dissertations and books emanating from graduate training at Columbia University under the direction of Professor Dunning. See James Wilford Garner, *Reconstruction in Mississippi* (1901; Gloucester, Mass.: Peter Smith, 1964).

41. Robuck, *My Own Personal Experience*, 72–73; Julia Kendel, "Reconstruction in Lafayette County," *Publications of the Mississippi Historical Society*, 1913, 241–42. Kendel was confused about the time and motivation for the assault on the Raglands, which she thought was in response to Ku Klux Klan violence against blacks; that would place it sometime between 1867 and 1871. Later, Sam Ragland would become a leader in the Ku Klux Klan, but it was not organized until 1867. Both accounts say blacks were after money. It is Kendel's account that reports Mrs. Ragland's escape and death by knife; Robuck thought she died immediately. See also *Oxford Eagle*, 20 March 1941, an account by Ragland's grandson, which says his father and a friend were upstairs when the attack took place and intervened, saved Sam, and recognized some of the attackers. He reports nineteen "hangings" in revenge, and he also has the date in 1869 or 1870. Elizabeth Ragland's grave stone reports her death in 1866. I am grateful to C. T. Hill, Sam Ragland's great-grandson, for assisting me in this research. John B. Cullen, *Old Times in the Faulkner Country* (Chapel Hill: University of North Carolina Press, 1961), 100, identifies the Price place (renamed "Prince" for anonymity) as the model for the Old Frenchman's place.

42. Faulkner, *The Hamlet*, in *Snopes: The Hamlet, The Town, The Mansion* (New York: The Modern Library, 1994), 7, 9.

43. Wharton, *Negro in Mississippi*, 166; Kendel, "Reconstruction," 247–54.

44. Kendel, "Reconstruction," 228–35, 265–66.

45. Kendel, "Reconstruction," details the local strategies of intimidating voters, and her informants were veterans of the Klan and other opponents of Republican rule in Lafayette County.

46. Susan Snell, *Phil Stone of Oxford: A Vicarious Life* (Athens: University of Georgia Press, 1991), 30.

47. For testimony on the violence in Lafayette County see the correspondence of Alexander Phillips to the Freedmen's Bureau: Alex Phillips to Freedmen's Bureau Headquarters, Oxford, 2 May 1868; Alexander Phillips to Gen Gillem, Oxford, 21 May 1868; NARA, RG 105, Records of the Assistant Commissioner for the State of Mississippi, Freedmen's Bureau, mf. M 826, roll 25, Letters Received, January 1868–May 1869.

48. Faulkner, *Unvanquished*, 239.

49. Austin to Donelson, Oxford, Miss., 1 September 1865, NARA, RG 105, entry 2188, "Registered Letters Received, July 1865–March 1866, Jackson, Miss., Acting Assistant Commissioner of the Northern District of Mississippi. For more on the hostility of whites to the plans for a "colored school" see letters from Reverend A. J. Yeater, Oxford, Miss., 28 November 1865; Lt. Jno. W. Pancoast, Oxford, Miss., 28 September 1865; Yeater, Oxford, Miss., 4 January 1866, all in RG 105, Records of the Assistant Commissioner for the State of Mississippi, Freedmen's Bureau, mf M 826, roll 6, Register of Letters Received, June 1865–February 1866.

50. Rev A. J. Yeater to [Bureau Headquarters], Oxford, Miss., 28 November 1865; 4 January 1866, NARA, RG 105, Records of the Assistant Commissioner for the State of Mississippi, Freedmen's Bureau, M 826, roll 6, Register of Letters Received, June 1865–February 1866; A. J. Yeater to Col Saml Thomas, Concordia, Bolivar Co., Miss., 18 January 1866, NARA, Ibid., roll 17, Letters Received, January 1866-February 1867. See also Charles Arthur Williamson, "Reconstruction in Lafayette County," typescript in Franklin Riley, ed., Reconstruction essays, UM, 14–15.

51. Williamson, "Reconstruction," 3.

52. Preuss to Sunderland, 30 September 1867; Rossiter to Preston, 12, 31 May 1867,

NARA, RG 105, entry 2307, Vol 239, Mississippi, "Oxford Miss., Letters Sent from 29 April 1867 to 31 October 1867"; ibid. On Alexander Phillips, see Kendel, "Reconstruction," 234; *Falcon*, 16 March 1867.

53. Blotner, *Faulkner*, 1:849, 860; 2:958–59.

54. For overviews of the New South era, see C. Vann Woodward, *Origins of the New South, 1877–1913* (Baton Rouge: Louisiana State University Press, 1951), and Edward L. Ayers, *The Promise of the New South: Life After Reconstruction* (New York: Oxford University Press, 1992); Howard N. Rabinowitz, *The First New South: 1865–1920*, The American History Series (Arlington Heights, Illinois: Harlan Davidson, 1992).

55. Faulkner summarized the terms of one of these contracts in the verbal exchange between Ab Snopes and Jody Varner at the opening of *The Hamlet*. Faulkner, *Snopes*, 12. By this agreement the Varners would allow Snopes to work the land with his family of six hands and Snopes would pay him one third of the corn and one fourth of the cotton crop and purchase all supplies out of the store paying a dollar for every seventy five cents worth of goods. No cash would exchange hands, only crops and store goods. Albert D. Kirwan, *Revolt of the Rednecks: Mississippi Politics 1876–1925* (New York: Harper, 1951), 43–45. For an overview of the plight of the Southern yeoman, see Stephen Hahn, *The Roots of Southern Populism: The Transformation of the Georgia Upcountry, 1850–1890* (New York: Oxford University Press, 1982). On Populism see Robert C. McMath, *American Populism: A Social History, 1877–1898* (New York: Hill and Wang, 1993).

56. Kirwan, *Revolt*, 45n.

57. Faulkner, "Barn Burning," in *Collected Stories of William Faulkner* (New York: Vintage Books, 1977), 9–12.

58. Kirwan, *Revolt*, 45–46.

59. Ibid., 212.

60. Blotner, *Faulkner*, 1:81–82; Kirwan, *Revolt*, 292–97.

61. Joseph R. Urgo, *Faulkner's Apocrypha: A Fable, Snopes, and the Spirit of Human Rebellion* (Jackson: University Press of Mississippi, 1989), 149f, offers an intelligent reading of *Snopes*.

62. John Faulkner, *My Brother Bill: An Affectionate Reminiscence* (1963; Oxford, Miss.: Yoknapatawpha Press, 1975), 269–70. I have used the surname spelling John Faulkner used as author, but he normally spelled his name Falkner.

63. On Avent family see *The Heritage of Lafayette County* (Oxford, Miss.: Skipwith Historical and Genealogical Society, 1986), 215–18; Blotner, *Faulkner*, 1:143, 173, 234. Avent Acres is an obvious model for Flem Snopes's Eula Acres, but it is worth noting that it was Faulkner's friend, Phil Stone, descendant of the planter class, who first sold off land in his family's estate and chopped it up into small lots for federally subsidized housing in the Stone Subdivision north of the University. Snell, *Phil Stone*, 246–47.

64. Blotner, *Faulkner*, 1:258–60.

"Like a Virgin": Faulkner, Sexual Cultures, and the Romance of Resistance

ANNE GOODWYN JONES

"Culture," wrote Raymond Williams, "is one of the two or three most complicated words in the English language."[1] Indeed, when he wrote this, "culture" 's complications had already led Williams himself to write one of his best known works, *Culture and Society*.[2]

One of the most familiar complications within cultural studies is the distinction between "culture" as anthropologists use it, to describe a way of life, with all its practices and meanings, and "culture" in a narrower and perhaps now outdated sense, to describe a socially privileged relation to knowledge and especially to the arts. Consider the difference between these two claims: "She was a woman of culture" and "She was a woman of the Chinese/Maori/Southern culture." (I ignore entirely the biologist's "culture," by whose meaning our woman might now have a sore throat.) The first claim is evaluative; it presumes that one. "has" or "lacks" culture, and that to "have" culture (knowledge of and sensitivity to the arts, for example) is better. The second is descriptive; it presumes that everyone "has" culture, that no one can "lack" it; to "have" one culture is no better than to "have" another.

In a sense, the second claim disempowers the first by offering a way to analyze it, to "break it down" into its components. Our woman may indeed think she is "a woman of [intellectual or aesthetic] culture"; she may *be* a "woman of culture" as that is defined within her "[anthropologist's] culture." Cultural anthropology, though, is concerned not with acknowledging or appreciating her high degree of "culture," but rather with understanding the *mean-*

ings of naming her as "cultured" within the codes, signs, and practices of her entire "culture," her community, her way of life. The
interest is analytical rather than evaluative. One might say it seeks
to know her way of life from "outside," "objectively," rather than
to judge her level of accomplishment from within it.

There is a connection, perhaps obvious, perhaps obscure, between "culture" in its more traditional meanings—as cultivation,
civilization, "high" culture—and a more traditional theory of art.
By this theory, art has a unique way of touching and teaching its
audience. This process has something to do with its form and with
its way of referring to its objects; because of it, art differs from, for
example, scientific writing, whose form and referentiality depend
on different values, epistemologies, and perhaps ontologies. A
work of (written) art "refers" to a world it invents in writers' and
readers' imaginations; however "realistic" that world may be, it is
not conventionally presumed to be identical with the "real" world
"outside" it. The organization of its language—its form—is designed to create an experience rather than to provide a transparent
window onto "objective reality," as science—and, silently, much
literary criticism—claims. Thus works of art, in this view, can
stand alone, outside of time, universal in their meanings and accessible to readers without a knowledge of cultural context. All one
needs is the work of art and the ability to read. One reads, then,
or looks at or listens to a work of art without a need to understand
its times and cultures, the conditions of its production, the limitations of the "author." One reads—and thus acquires "culture" in
this traditional sense of the word—in a process that, like certain
forms of religious experience, itself takes one "outside of time."

One version of such a theory evolved out of the South during
Faulkner's lifetime, calling itself the New Criticism. Indeed, key
Faulkner scholar Cleanth Brooks, with Robert Penn Warren, was
a leader of the New Criticism, especially in the widely influential
textbook *Understanding Poetry*.[3] But such convictions were by no
means limited to the South, though that was their primary American origin. Russian formalism, British close reading, and even the
German Frankfurt school, articulated and struggled with similar

ideas. Theodor Adorno's critique of mass culture rested in part on the distinction he found between the corrupting influence of commodified "art" and the salutary effects of reading autonomous "high" art. In Faulkner critic John T. Matthews's words, "For [Max] Horkheimer and Adorno, what the culture industry produces violates art's essential purposelessness, its expression of individuality through style, its insistence on beauty and pleasure in their pure uselessness, and hence its fundamentally negative function in society. Art ought to *resist* [my italics]—impassively, through its willful beauty—the social and economic practices in which it is embedded."[4] Walter Benjamin's notion of the power of high art's "aura" is similar.[5]

The anthropologically minded literary critic, however, sees all texts as located well within time and space, and thus fully open to historical and cultural analysis.[6] Just as there is a connection between traditional meanings of "culture" and theories of art, so there is for "culture"'s newer meanings, a newer set of theories of art. These approaches—one of which is "cultural studies"—no longer privilege the work of art or knowledge of it, no longer find it "unspotted by the world." On the contrary, such analyses look for connections between art and history, between aesthetics and daily life, between the writings of "high modernism" and stories of true detectives and popular romance. In short, such criticism looks for the ways in which works of art—as cultural productions—produce meanings together with other elements of culture. The interest lies not in deciding the "quality" or celebrating the "autonomy" of a work of art, but in understanding and describing how it connects to the culture(s) that gave it birth and that it now shapes. Its focus is on art's immanence, not its transcendence. Following this theory, even the New Critical belief that the experience of art allows transcendent "timeless" knowledge, then, is itself subject to historical and cultural analysis. What purposes did such a belief accomplish (critics have asked), what effects did it produce, in the time and place of its cultural sway?[7]

It is my sense that the writers for this volume are using this second sense of "culture," the anthropologists' sense—and the critical practice that accompanies it—without exception. No one has discussed Faulkner's "level" of "culture" ("was Faulkner a real man of culture or only a Count No 'Count?") or even his texts in isolation; indeed, no one, as the volume title promises, has analyzed any text *without* regard for its cultural context. Kevin Railey, for example, quite explicitly treats "culture" as a way of life (paternalism), from its psychology to its social ideology. John T. Matthews, though he treats "art"—proletarian novels, modernism, contemporary literary criticism—treats it not in isolation or as a sign of superior refinement but as a symptom of shared values, a trace of a way of life.

I intend to follow suit in this essay, looking at Faulkner's writing as deeply embedded within the cultures of sexuality that marked his time and place. But there are risks and limitations to this second theory and method, just as there were to the first (the New Criticism, the Frankfurt school, and, even earlier, Matthew Arnold's idea of ["high"] culture as the counterweight to anarchy). It is my hope in this essay to think about some of the risks of cultural studies while at the same time carrying out a cultural study of some of Faulkner's fictions.

One such risk, it seems to me, is too easy a polarization of these two general meanings of "culture" and therefore of the two general literary theories and critical methods, as in fact I have just done, by dividing them between aesthetics and science, participation and observation, ahistoricity and historicism, even mystification and truth. Whereas anthropologists can turn to a disciplinary history of thought and practice concerning the ambiguities of "participant observation" and the art of science, cultural studies literary critics—lacking a coherent theorized practice of "textual" participant observation, for example—may find it all too easy to believe our own rhetoric of implicit detachment and objectivity. Yet of course literary "descriptions" carry unconsciously or deliberately evaluative freight, like any other "objective description." As a result the traditionalists' belief in art's timelessness may be disturbingly similar—instead of opposite—to the innovative cultural critic's implicit faith in his own writing's transcendence of culture, in its "objectivity," or in its descriptive credibility, its truth.

In this essay, I focus on one example of such a phenomenon. A key concept in contemporary cultural criticism is represented by the term "resistance." It is this concept whose use and limitations, whose descriptive and implicitly evaluative freight, I hope to point out through this analysis (and, no doubt, implicit evaluation) of the sexual cultures that formed a context for Faulkner's writing.

Romancing "Resistance"

By now "resistance" has become a common term in American cultural studies lingo. Virtually every speaker at the Faulkner and Yoknapatawpha Conference, "Faulkner in Cultural Context," used it. But what does it mean? And how is it relevant to Faulkner studies?

Resistance can be overt or covert, conscious or unconscious, organized or personal; it has to do in each case with the refusal to accept the advances of the dominant or hegemonic culture. And since those advances take place in the most personal as well as the most public arenas, resistance to them can appear—can be read—virtually anywhere. Resistance thus seems to offer multiple threads to pull in the effort to unravel the net of dominant discourse. It sits on the cultural plane in the place of revolution or rebellion on the political plane, as a means for change.

Matthews's reading of Faulkner's popular market fictions as an example of Adorno's theory of "resisting" the culture industry, cited above, is a case in point. "For a writer like Faulkner," Matthews writes, "even works aimed at the mass market possess reflective and *resistant* [my emphasis] features that make their *relation* [Matthews's emphasis] to the culture industry and the social order it endorses the very heart of the problem."[8] The term appears with frequency in American literary criticism as well as Southern and Faulkner criticism. See, for example, Lora Romero's "Bio-Political Resistance in Domestic Ideology and *Uncle Tom's*

Cabin," or Diane Roberts's "Ravished Belles: Stories of Rape and Resistance in *Flags in the Dust* and *Sanctuary.*"⁹

As these titles suggest, feminists have found the concept espe-cially useful, particularly because it allows for such a range of be-haviors to be read as "resistance," opening the way for private and subtle behaviors as well as the public and obvious. A similar usefulness appeared in slavery studies: barred from overt rebel-lion, most slaves had access to strategies like slowing down work in the field, or, in the kitchen, spitting in the master's food.¹⁰ In her early book *The Resisting Reader*, Judith Fetterley claimed, for example, that most American fiction assumes a male reader. Thus in order to retain a sense of female identity, female readers have to read such narratives as *Moby Dick* and *Huckleberry Finn* resist-ingly, read against the grain of the text, refuse fundamental as-sumptions about the contract between text and reader. To read resistingly, then, is in this case to monitor one's reactions, to ob-serve where the reader's identity is being assumed or constructed, and to choose deliberately whether or not to consent. Fetterley shows how this can be done in a series of exemplary readings, one of them a reading of "A Rose for Emily."

Let's see how resistingly we can read Faulkner ourselves. How about "Dry September"? Did Minnie Cooper spread the story about Will Mayes? Of course, we say dutifully, we don't know for sure. But there's circumstantial evidence to suggest . . . dot dot dot. . . . What circumstantial evidence? I submit that before we see any of that evidence we as readers have already been uncon-sciously persuaded by Hawkshaw's own sexism, a sexism that ap-pears on the first page of the text and that is easy to consent to since we are so involved at the moment in supporting his resis-tance to racism. Listen to how he argues for Will Mayes by slan-dering Minnie Cooper: "She's about forty, I reckon. She aint married. That's why I dont believe. . . . I leave it to you fellows if them ladies that get old without getting married dont have notions that a man cant—" "Then you are a hell of a white man," the client jumps in.¹¹ Here Faulkner has staged a contest for consent to conflicting culturally hegemonic assumptions. One assumption emerges from the culture of Southern racism, which defines a white man by his ability to protect sexless white women from lascivious black men; since Hawkshaw won't, he isn't a real "white man." The other is less clear, because Hawkshaw's words are so vague. If he is implying that Miss Minnie's "notions" emerge from sexual frustration, his assumption may emerge from the national sexual culture as defensive exaggeration of that culture's claim that women are as sexually interested as men: women—including aging spinsters—desire, fantasize about, and even demand sex and sexual attention at any price. If he is implying that her lack of sexual experience leads her to sexual paranoia, it may emerge from more traditional Southern assumptions. But in either case, Hawkshaw is appealing to dehumanizing clichés about women's sexuality in order to distract these men from their clichés about black men's sexuality and white men's manhood.

If we read resistingly, we can avoid being seduced by the text at such moments. And if we read against the grain of the story, "as a woman," then McLendon's physical abuse of his wife at the end of the story—a compelling but puzzling detail—becomes more critical to the story. It can be read as the logical outcome of the same assumptions about women that Hawkshaw appeals to here, assumptions that may even have shaped Faulkner's telling of Minnie's history so that it is focussed on romantic failure. Thus we may better understand how Minnie's world, offering no alternatives, encouraged Minnie to "consent" to, even create, her own victimization in the interests of consolidating white male control. Even if Hawkshaw had succeeded in stopping the lynching; even if his view had prevailed in the barber shop, this resisting analysis points out that women would still as a category in the story remain fixed in mental, verbal, and physical abuse.

Minrose Gwin and, inspired by Gwin, Diane Roberts offer two of the most persuasive and passionate feminist resisting readings of Faulkner in their essays and books.[12] Roberts, for example, reads *Sanctuary* through Temple's eyes as a sustained act of resistance against a series of rapes. Rather than blame Temple Drake, as so many critics have thoughtlessly done, Roberts uses contemporary knowledge about patterns of response to rape to understand Temple's fantasies, her drinking, her refusal to escape, even her attachment to Red, as varieties of resistance, efforts to hold onto a scrap of self in the face of numerous efforts—beginning with Ruby's words—to dismantle and remake her. Thus Roberts uses the text to resist the text, locating within Faulkner's words the possibility of an alternative, less obvious narrative that nevertheless, when "read" from Temple's point of view, is coherent and plausible. Roberts resists the call not only of the text but of the generations of Faulkner scholars whose distaste for Temple has been so palpable through the years.

I would like to try out this reading practice on *Sanctuary* from a somewhat different point of view. Is Temple Drake a virgin when she is ravished by Popeye's cob? What have you always assumed? The text certainly seems to want us to think so. Ruby thinks so, and the text seems to want us to like Ruby and to believe her words and her sexual experience. Not only does she believe Temple is a virgin; she has lectured Temple on the evils of teasing men, leading them on and then not coming across with the goods. Miss Reba too thinks Temple was a virgin before Popeye's "sexual" experience with her; she calls the blood that even in Memphis is still seeping from Temple's body "thousand dollar" blood, the proof of virginity.[13] But unless we as readers buy into their cultural assumptions—Ruby's that college girls are afraid of "real men" and "real sex," Miss Reba's that Popeye has (at last) become a "real man"—we will have to remain less certain.

Although nothing in the text that I can find gives us a definitive answer, I think the evidence, both textual and contextual, goes against Ruby and Miss Reba. Temple's bleeding must have been caused by the cob. The multiple sorts of wounds a cob could cause to her body can account for the excess of blood far more readily than can a torn hymen. So the bleeding is no proof of virginity. Moreover, her name is not only in the mouths of town and college boys; it is written on the wall of the bathroom at the train station. American teenagers' sexual behavior in the twenties and thirties included not only necking and petting but premarital and even nonmonogamous sexual intercourse, for girls as well as, if less openly than, for boys. Temple's name on the wall suggests her availability as well as her desirability. Or it may—with its promise— have set her up for earlier rapes. It is certainly plausible that Temple is no virgin.

But if Temple is no virgin, why is she perceived as one by Ruby and Miss Reba? Both characters have personal and cultural stakes in seeing her as virginal. Ruby needs to preserve her sense of her own identity and worth, which are based in turn on her acceptance of a patriarchal cultural myth that divides men and women into clear (and classed) categories. Those categories, for Ruby, name women as either rich, "good" (virginal) man teasers, afraid of actual sex, or whores with hearts of gold, "jazzing" to get their man out of jail. Apparently she—and perhaps we—cannot hear Temple's whisper: " 'I have been called that [whore].' " Ruby clearly needs to split women in this way, to believe that "good" girls will " 'take all you can get, and give nothing' "; perhaps the belief justifies the suffering she experiences for giving all.[14] On the other hand, Miss Reba needs to preserve her sense of identity and worth as a good mother figure to Popeye and a good professional. Hence her pride in his choosiness among women and her conviction that he has been a "real man" to Temple, has penetrated her with his body. In both cases, personal stakes in cultural myths determine their perceptions of Temple's sexuality. Whether Temple is or is not a "real" virgin, then, she is "like a virgin"[15] for their cultural and personal purposes.

To be "like a virgin," however, is to breach a fundamental dichotomy within Faulkner's world, a dichotomy that troubles Quentin Compson in *The Sound and the Fury*. That dichotomy is the clear distinction between virgin and nonvirgin; it is associated with the equally clear split between women (or not-men) and men. "In the South you are ashamed of being a virgin. Boys. Men. They lie about it. Because it means less to women, Father said. He said it was men invented virginity not women. Father said it's like death: only a state in which the others are left and I said, But to believe it doesn't matter and he said, That's what's so sad about anything: not only virginity and I said, Why couldn't it have been me and not her who is unvirgin and he said, That's why that's sad too; nothing is even worth the changing of it, and Shreve said if he's got better sense than to chase after the little dirty sluts and I said Did you ever have a sister? Did you? Did you?" Conjoining the present (where Harvard students call Shreve Quentin's "husband") and the past (the conversation with his father), Quentin shows the agonizing effects that the gender differences in meanings of virginity have on him. As a virgin, he is not a man; as a nonvirgin, his sister is in the place he should occupy. Their father's insensitive response shows only his self-preoccupation: his insistence that men invented virginity is less feminist or postmodern than a habit of generalizing his personal cynicism.

Later, his father asks of Quentin: ". . . did you try to make her do it and i i was afraid to i was afraid she might and then it wouldn't have done any good but if i could tell you we did it would have been so and then the others wouldnt be so and then the world would roar away." Here Quentin's view of virginity seems to have changed from the commonsense literal meaning of the first passage, the meaning that so agonizes him as the virgin brother, to a remarkably postmodern conviction, or at least hope, that words will be more potent in constructing reality—the past as well as the present and the future—than can any other acts of the body, such as sex. But it seems unlikely Quentin's real feelings have changed; this is a desperation move to identify with his father's views.[16]

Nevertheless, if anyone can perform "like a virgin" as Quentin hopes and as Florence King so wittily points out in her description of the Southern self-rejuvenating virgin,[17] then does authentic virginity matter any more? Does it even exist? Temple—not a virgin (and by the same token not *un*virgin: we never know for sure) but *like* a virgin, a simulacrum of a construct— becomes a postmodern protagonist far more certainly than Quentin or Mr. Compson. Even her name is close kin to Madonna's: one is the Virgin Mary and the other the Temple of the Holy Ghost.

To read *Sanctuary* without assuming Temple's virginity—to resist the apparent desire of the text—inevitably has consequences for one's sense of the entire novel. Although this is not the place to explore them in any detail, one of those consequences surely would be to foreground both the violence of Temple's rape(s) and the loneliness of her silence about her own body's history.

Resisting Resistance

Reading resistingly, reading against the grain, is a critical strategy that works in the sense that it produces new, provocative, and sometimes persuasive readings of even the most fully read texts. "Resistance" seems in academic cultural contexts to signify something that opposes dominance or hegemony (here, the dominant designs of the text) and hence is generally good, on the grounds that dominance is generally not so good. The excitement and generativity of such readings continue to be major strengths.

Yet the use of the term in a vague and merely evocative sense must obscure its intellectual history and the history of its use, as well as any internal contradictions and complications. Without careful definition, its appeal may rest—ironically—on its ability to mystify, on silent evaluation disguised as description. But resistance as a concept—despite or because of its increasingly frequent use—seems to be increasingly *in*frequently defined, at least within contemporary academic culture, as though it can go without saying.

To look even briefly at the intellectual history of the concept must cause us to wonder about its usefulness as an unequivocally positive marker; to look at its use, especially in the South, increases that doubt, and a look at the logic of the concept erodes its romance still further.

In her excellent inquiry into the status and history of another key word for cultural studies, "ideology," Michele Barrett glances upon the history of "resistance" as well. "Resistance" becomes more difficult to achieve and to define as the course of cultural studies theory is followed. Antonio Gramsci, who first circulated the term "hegemony," introduced more complexity into a model of resistance that can be attributed to Marx. That model, in its most familiar form, had been based on the "truth" of an economic base and the "illusory" quality of ideological superstructure. "Resistance" within the earlier Marxist model had been easier to conceptualize. Since "ideology" was untrue, its purpose being largely to mystify reality and in that way protect the interests of the ruling class, in order to *resist* ideology one had simply to locate, and stand by, the truth. When the term remains undefined even today, it may unintentionally suggest just such a simple, dichotomous meaning.

Gramsci complicated this dichotomy by arguing that the dominant group within a society maintained its dominance through hegemonic strategies. By hegemony Gramsci meant power that depended not simply on coercion—the army, the police—but on consent. Consent means consent of the nondominant to the values endorsed by and serving the interests of the dominant class. Consent means that people agree to and even participate in their own oppression. It takes place quietly, subtly, and constantly, through the agencies of culture, especially in a capitalist market economy where consumption is so closely tied to identity. In such a model, it is not so easy to locate and to stand by the "truth." Resistance to hegemony in Gramsci's formulation is difficult not only because of the psychological power of "consent." It is also difficult as a concept because Gramsci's solution to capitalist hegemony required its successful displacement by another (Communist) hegemony. At that point, resistance for Gramsci is no longer an absolute good.

With Gramsci's complications, then, consent became internalized, the "truth" harder to locate, and resistance to hegemony a contextual but not an absolute good. And with Michel Foucault, truth itself would become an effect. How does one "resist" the false when the division between the true and the illusory is itself a political effect? For Marx, even for Gramsci, the capacity to resist comes from learning the "truth"; for Foucault, "truth" itself has its own politics, such that to learn the "truth" is not the same as being "within the true" of a given cultural moment, that is, within that culture's understanding of what is true.[18] Moreover, if we are all "subject" to the cultural discourses that construct our "subject"ivities, from what position could we resist the "true" of our time? Barrett notes the charge made against Michel Foucault that his "earlier position left little room for 'resistance.' "[19] But as Barrett sees it, Foucault, with his still more complex understanding of power as the (sometimes anonymous) exclusionary workings of discourse, offers the most useful post-Marxian theory of the relation between power and knowledge. However, Foucault's more subtle arguments also damage the coherence of "resistance"—perhaps the very coherence that makes it so evocative a word in so much current literary criticism on Faulkner in particular.

I would like to suggest too that such a notion of resistance, as a coherent, "good," opponent to dominance, depends logically on the very ideology it hopes to critique—an ideology of binary oppositions, of unified subjectivity, and—not so very far below the surface—of competitive masculinity. To use deconstructive terms, one might say that dominance is only one half of a binary opposition whose "other half" is resistance. Flipping that opposition over does not deconstruct it. Perhaps, even, buried within the concept of resistance is the desire for dominance. Certainly Gramsci had no difficulty with the concept of shifting rather than eliminating hegemonic control. Michèle Barrett notices, in another context, that "the discourse of a critique of ideology is simply a means of expanding the sway of rationalism within a position that is as much bounded by the 'philosophical' as the one being criticized."[20] To challenge the master using the tools of the master might, perversely, keep the very problem and structure of mastery alive.

Perhaps as a result of imprecision and the lingering power of American cultural values such as competitive individualism as well as its embeddedness in a logic of dichotomy, which is the logic of the illusorily unified subject, the use of the term "resistance" in some hands suggests a unified and rather traditionally masculine subject position. In this use, the subject position for resistance reverts to an older notion of organized, focused political resistance as a model. Organized, focused, goal-directed behavior, because it depends on a logic of exclusion and opposition, runs the risk of constructing and demonizing its own opposition, as we saw with the Marxian model of truth and illusion. What does it mean when scholars habitually use words from a military vocabulary—strategy, tactic—to describe textual events? Is battle a foregone conclusion? Yet the more sophisticated understandings of resistance as diffused or unconscious can be accused of ineffectiveness. This is not a new irony, of course, but it does re-emerge in the discourse of resistance.

A related difficulty with "resistance" becomes apparent when the dominant or hegemonic culture is the admirable one, and resistance therefore is retrogressive. We do not need Gramsci's Communist hegemony to make this point; Southern history provides a wealth of examples.

In the American South the question of resistance takes this more complicated turn. Here, resistance has a history that is not always so desirable to emulate. Resisting the Reconstruction not only meant episodes like Faulkner's story of Drusilla and John's stealing the voting box, in *The Unvanquished,* but meant the origins of the Ku Klux Klan, as the world knows from *Birth of a Nation* and *Gone with the Wind.* Resisting federal desegregation orders a century later meant torching black churches, burning crosses, blowing up children.

Nor, to be blunt, has resistance been very *successful* in the white South—at least until Jesse Helms and Newt Gingrich resisted their way to the top, and even that promises to be a short stay. Resisting the Yankee invaders failed; resisting Reconstruction failed; resisting civil rights legislation failed. Even today in the South, resisting the cultural hegemony of New York and Los Angeles is at best difficult, as anyone with a Southern accent, including Bill Clinton, knows.

In the South, then, resistance to a dominant culture and ideology must be understood with some complexity. Those who resist may well have in mind a future in which they are the dominant class. If they are white men (or women for that matter), they may well have in mind the bitterness of a past in which their resistance failed. And if they are white men they may well feel some anxiety about joining forces in the present with other nonhegemonic

American groups such as blacks, women, and the working class. Take the scene from "Skirmish at Sartoris" in which Drusilla and John have brought the voting box back to Sartoris after killing the carpetbaggers who were filling it with black men's votes. At Sartoris, one of their friends simply writes "No" on all the votes, and fills the box with them. There is no question about the resistance to Yankee Reconstruction here; but notice also that it is the white men—Drusilla is shedding her ascribed gender for the last time here—who resist in order to reinstate their own hegemony. Notice also how the white women collaborate in what we might now call their own oppression, by rigorously protesting both Drusilla's putative heterosexual outrages and Drusilla's evident gender-crossing clothes and behavior. They stuff her back into a dress and a marriage, containing her transgressions. In Gramsci's terms, the women's consent to traditional Southern sexual ideology reinforces the men's resistance to the Yankee's removal of Southern male hegemony, just as, in "Dry September," Hawkshaw's consent to traditional Southern sexual ideology is a tool in his effort to sway Southern men.

In scenarios where dominance is represented as institutionally powerful and resistance as isolated and brave, it is hard to see the limitations of resistance. At least in segments of our culture, it can go without saying that resisting male or white dominance or the dominance of institutional power is courageous and needful. But to privilege "resistance" categorically is to assume that all "dominance" is by definition in need of resistance. Clearly this is not the case. I think, as a last example, of the federal enforcement of the 1964 Civil Rights Act. Was institutional state power to be resisted then? White Citizens' Councils certainly thought so.

If resistance is not always so admirable, then by the same logic can dominance, or hegemony, be admirable, not only as a tactic but as a policy? Antonio Gramsci thought so; as we saw, his goal was to supplant the hegemony of the right with the hegemony of the left, of the Communist Party, using similar tactics of coercion and consent. For myself, I prefer not to try to make the case for dominance, for the reasons suggested above: dominance and resistance, like criminals and the police, sanity and insanity, the pure and the polluted, as I see it, depend on one another for their meanings. Hidden within the meaning of each term is both the fear of and the desire for its opposite; each term is its other's secret sharer. Moreover, dominance is historically the object and goal of many forms of cultural masculinity, as I suggested earlier. Arguably, a "masculine" subject position by cultural definition is dominant. By the same token, as we saw, certain forms of resistance may require a "masculine" subject position—a sense of one's "individuality," perhaps, or a strong "ego," or a belief that one "possesses the phallus." My goal in this analysis is simply to suggest and to illustrate that because "resistance" may bear such ideological freight, freight that is not always simply brave or otherwise laudable, it needs to be analysed (and politically exercised) with considerable sensitivity to context.[21]

We will see Faulkner setting out these and other questions relating to resistance in the context of two opposing sexual cultures, one of which (the national) achieved popular dominance in part through representing itself, ironically, as a form of rebellion and resistance against a putatively repressive Victorianism, and the other of which (the regional) achieved a position of resistance to the popular norm by representing itself, again ironically, as holding on to the now vanishing but then dominant values of the past. I would like to say that I see Faulkner offering a third option, a way out of the play of oppositions, the cycle of dominance and resistance. I'm not sure that I can.

I would like to suggest, however, that Faulkner's fictions both represent and to a certain extent analyse the question of resistance in the South by encoding that question in terms of sexuality. Although it would be appealing to look at specific narratives involving sexual resistance or its absence, I have something rather duller in mind. I will suggest that a careful look at the specific sexual *cultures* that come into conflict in Faulkner's work can serve both as an example of the ways in which resistance fails in his work, or at best differs from the hopeful expectations set by romancing "resistance" in cultural studies criticism, and as an explanation for that failure. By sexual "cultures" I mean something perhaps closer to "discourses": a set of representations, in various media, that construct a more or less coherent understanding of what human sexuality is and means. By "resistance," then, I mean not resistance to literal sexuality, but resistance to the set of values and meanings implied by a "culture" of sexuality. Certainly questions concerning the meanings of resistance to *literal* sexuality (such as, how do those meanings differ with gender? race? class?) are an important aspect, but only an aspect, of a given "sexual culture." But, again, that will not be my specific subject for the remainder of this essay.

To repeat, I will be interested in Faulkner's negotiation of meanings in two specific cultural contexts. One is the traditional sexual culture of privileged white Southerners, that is, of paternalism. The second is the emerging national and international popular culture of (Western) sexuality available to Faulkner in books, films, magazines, and the like. This national culture of sexuality—despite its self-contradictions, which we will touch on in a moment—endorsed a sexuality that challenged Southern culture at key points. Faulkner's texts can be read as sites of contestation between modern popular and traditional paternalist "cultures of sexuality."

We will look briefly at both the regional and the national (and international) "cultures of sexuality" that pervaded Faulkner's world in order to ascertain those sites of contestation in his literary texts. What was it that made it impossible for Faulkner's writing either to fully resist traditional Southern sexual values by endorsing the values of the national/international culture of the twenties and thirties, or to fully resist popular sexual culture by sticking with Southern tradition? What is the relation of "resistance" to gender and sexuality? Does resistance make men? If so, what made resistance in Faulkner's South feel at times not manly but feminine, like a virgin, like boundary diffusion, category confusion, and displacement? And how did Faulkner—when he did—write his way out of these difficulties?

First, a closer look at those two cultures of sexuality.

Two Cultures of Sexuality

The sexual ideology of Southern culture emerged historically as a sort of unhappy marriage between Victorianism and slavery. Most readers are no doubt familiar with its tenets: black women "have" sexuality, privileged white women do not; black men have almost uncontrollable sexuality, white men. . . . Here the ideology blurs, and in the place of an answer concening white men's sexuality, we have the white man's job as protector of the helpless and sexless white woman, who is eternally vulnerable to black men's sexual advances, indeed rape. In *Killers of the Dream*, Lillian Smith begins to fill in these blurry parts by describing the paths from the big house to the back yard: white men's sexuality, according to her analysis, could be found in the slave cabins if not in the cultural ideology.[22] Faulkner's "The Bear" captures this evanescent aspect of culture, of course, in Ike's search through the family records that unearths a history of his family's sexual exploitation of female slaves, and the pregnancies and suicide that resulted.[23]

Towards white women, white men's sexuality seems equally obscure and complex. A century earlier than Faulkner, Louisa McCord, arguing as strenuously as she could against the enfranchisement of women in the South, used as her clinching point white women's fear of *violence* from white as well as black men. As long as we stay on the pedestal, she wrote, they will have to protect us; as soon as we step down to vote, we will be vulnerable not only to black violence but to violence from (our own) white men.[24] To Faulknerians, "Dry September" may come to mind again: McLendon's wife disobeys his orders and McLendon, having just taken violent revenge for the supposed violation of another white woman, responds to his own wife's disobedience by hitting her across the room. Of course Southern marriages in fact were various, as letters and diaries show; many were tender and sexual. But as a cultural category, Southern white womanhood has been marked by fear of male violence and yet dependence on male authority, by male adulation as "better than human" and male degradation as "less than man." In the white South, in short, the cultural divide between the sexes, as Ted Ownby has shown in *Subduing Satan*, was deep and wide, however successful individual men and women could be at bridging it.[25] Such is the sexual heritage of Southern paternalism.

We are all at least vaguely aware of the supposed sexual emancipation that emerged nationally and internationally after the First World War: jazz, speakeasies, smoking, and flappers variously represent the new sexuality. According to historians of American sexuality John d'Emilio and Estelle Freedman, the titles in successive editions of a chapter in Emily Post's *Etiquette* suggest those changes (a bit wistfully, perhaps): a chapter called "Chaperons and Other Conventions" in 1923 became in 1927 "The Vanishing Chaperon and Other New Conventions" and, in 1937, "The Vanished Chaperon and Other Lost Conventions." "Fully a third of the women born before 1900 usually remained clothed during sex," they tell us; "among those born in the 1920s, the figure was 8 per cent. Kinsey's data for female orgasm are similar; women born before the century turned were frequently unaware of its possibility."[26] Theodore Van de Velde's *Ideal Marriage* [1930], that extraordinarily popular marriage manual, made it plain that wives were capable of pleasure, and that husbands were responsible for making it happen, opening the way for assumptions like Hawkshaw's about Minnie Cooper.

In another popular but more radical book of marital advice, *Companionate Marriage* [1927], the author, Judge Ben Lindsey of the Juvenile and Family Court of Denver, tells story after story from his experience as a judge. He appears to have been a judge who preferred to resolve issues outside of court, and whose gifts as a counselor were great. His values were simple but dangerous: people, not genders, are differently constituted sexually and thus have differing needs and desires. Meeting those needs and desires should be a private matter of mutual consent, so long as no one else's rights are damaged. Further, the judge tells his readers, no one has a right to another person; in particular, he reiterates, women are not property and hence male sexual jealousy is inappropriate and should not be legally indulged.

The emerging popular culture of sexuality in the post–World
War I period was at odds with Southern sexual culture in several
key and perhaps obvious points. Most important, the new sexuality
challenged the desirelessness and sexual helplessness of the Victorian lady by representing the normal middle-class woman as having active sexual desire and, to a limited extent, the ability to take
care of herself. The new sexuality encoded these changes by combining cultural signs of "bad" women such as short skirts and long
legs, and cultural signs of "good" masculinity such as short or
bobbed hair, or having serious nonsexual interests, such as art,
writing, or holding a job, and using these combinations to resignify
the middle-class woman. The flapper—invented, interestingly, by
Southerner Zelda Sayre, whose father was a judge—served as a
symbol for these radical shifts in the understanding of privileged
and bourgeois white female sexuality. A large organization of white
Southern women, the Association of Southen Women for the Prevention of Lynching, took advantage of the emerging national ideology of woman to organize an ideological campaign against
lynching black men primarily by arguing that they and their
friends were not being raped and were not even afraid of being
raped by black men. If Minnie Cooper did circulate the story, the
rumor, whatever it was, about Will Mayes, then, she did so in
defiance of the Association of Southern Women for the Prevention
of Lynching.[27]

Although the more visible recontextualizations of sexuality in
this national discourse were for women, the new national sexual
ideology had serious implications for men and manhood as well. If
wives now had their own sexual desire, husbands had to pay attention to their wives' sexual needs in addition to their own. I have
written elsewhere about the implications of the work of Van de
Velde's sex manual *Ideal Marriage,* which went into reprints for
decades.[28] As the old national Victorian ideology merged and conflicted with the new, writers like Van de Velde tried to recuperate
male authority by telling husbands not only that they should honor
their wives' desire but that they should teach them how to enjoy
it. "The wife must be *taught*, not only how to behave in coitus,

but, above all, how and what to feel in this unique act! . . ." he wrote. "And the teacher is her husband."[29] Van de Velde urged on the one hand that experimenting with new sexual positions was a great thing—woman astride in particular was, he said, a position of greatest pleasure for women. However, he added, one should indulge in this position only very rarely for, and again I quote, "the main disadvantage in . . . frequent practice of the astride attitude lies in the complete passivity of the man and the exclusive activity of his partner. This is directly contrary to the natural relationship of the sexes, and must bring unfavorable consequences if it becomes habitual."[30] Clearly the new sexual culture carried a risk of feminizing men. If Southern ladyhood was in direct danger from these new ideas, what about Southern manhood?

Far more than manhoods elsewhere in the U.S.A., Southern white and black manhoods had been marked by paradoxes of violent resistance and violent defeat, independence and conformity to group norms, control and helplessness. Southern white men had been attacked in popular culture as female, weak, cowardly, unwilling or unable to resist, most famously perhaps in the cartoons of Jefferson Davis escaping Yankees disguised in woman's clothing.[31] And of course white Southern men lost a war.

In an essay called "The Poet as Woman," Faulkner's contemporary John Crowe Ransom argued that man differed from woman by intellect, that a real man was an intellectualized woman, and yet that an intellectual woman was a contradiction in terms.[32] The feminized man, as Ransom portrays him, is not a danger but an ideal—as long as the masculinized woman remains a freak. To construct a man who *deliberately* appropriates femininity, as Ransom urges, is to take the dominant position not only over women but over the feminine within oneself, not by *resisting* femininity but by allowing it, and then controlling it, within. This is a risky business, in some ways similar to Van de Velde's effort to control women's desire with male authority, but still riskier because it allows the "other" to enter the male subject, something Van de Velde sees as unnatural. It is especially risky in a culture in which (men's) territory of various sorts has historically been entered against their will—that is, where men have already been culturally "feminized." Faulkner narrates the failure of this strategy, as we saw, in the story of Quentin Compson, a male whose desire for and identification with the feminine resolve in his decision to allow it to overwhelm him, as liquidity pours over and into him in the River Charles, and in the story of Joe Christmas, whose agonies about his sexual identification, though less obvious than those about his race, resolve in his feminizing death.

But this Southern cultural phenomenon of the manly womanly man points us back again to the problematic of resistance in the South and its relation to masculinity. As we saw, resistance in the South historically has joined violent rebellion with failure and loss, whether slave rebellion or Civil War, and resistance through other means with racism and the right. To resist may not be noble; it may not even be smart. The Japanese concept of *amae*, an adult continuation of pre-Oedipal identificatory bonding, comes closer to explaining Southern manhood. *Amae*'s strategy is not to resist the other, but to incorporate it.[33]

Following this logic, it would make sense for the new national sexual culture's womanly man to meet with less resistance from Southern men than they feel for its new manly woman. The contest for consent between emerging national and traditional Southern sexual cultures, when it is staged in Faulkner's texts, then, we might expect to allow some oneway crossovers as long as men appropriated femininity under the control and aegis of manhood. The relation between national and regional sexual cultures will not be simply oppositional. Simplistic assumptions about the value of resistance, or of parody, or of gender performance will fall to pieces when they confront Southern cultural history.

This contest between a traditional Southern culture of sexuality and an emerging national and international culture shaped numerous Southern literary texts during Faulkner's lifetime, particularly those written by women, who had more to gain from the new ideas but who, as Southerners, differed with certain assumptions about the meanings of those gains. Frances Newman shocked the world with her two twenties novels, *The Hard-Boiled Virgin* and *Dead*

Lovers Are Faithful Lovers. In both novels, the contest becomes a focus of narrative interest—in the first, the loss of virginity, so important to Southern womanhood, is exposed as relatively meaningless, and in the second the reader is invited to sympathize with both a married woman and her husband's librarian mistress.[34] Lillian Smith's analysis of Southern culture in *Killers of the Dream* exposes the dependence of Southern racism on shoving white privileged women up onto a pedestal where they wither and dry up. Katherine Anne Porter's "Old Mortality" shows how male narratives of competition and violence circulate around a Southern woman's sexual choices.[35] In short, Southern literary women, like the women of the Association for the Prevention of Lynching, were beginning to use the cultural base offered by national texts about sexuality to resist and revise the sexual assumptions with which they had been raised.

What about Faulkner? I want to suggest that Faulkner was entirely familiar with the same national cultural base, and, like the women, used it to resist Southern tradition. But for Faulkner, whose investments lay finally, I believe, with the traditional power of manhood, such resistances were complicated and curtailed. Faulkner (perhaps deliberately, perhaps not) counterposed these sexual cultures—traditional Southern and emergent if conflicted modern—in novels like *Sanctuary* and *The Wild Palms*.

Faulkner's Resisting Readings

Although Faulkner did not have Van de Velde's or any other marriage manual in his library, according to Joseph Blotner's guide, it would have been impossible for him to have missed its meanings.[36] He may well have read that other extremely popular text of the twenties, Judge Ben Lindsey's *Companionate Marriage*. As Noel Polk reminded me, Cla'ence Snopes suggests in *Sanctuary* that Temple Drake has run away in "one of them companionate marriages."[37]

If Faulkner didn't read *Companionate Marriage*, he obviously knew the title and almost certainly knew about its sexual values.

Indeed, passages from his own fictions seem to be direct rejoinders to—resistances to—specific narratives of the Judge. See if this story sounds familiar. It is taken from Lindsey's 1927 volume, where Lindsey uses it to illustrate the virtue of transcending sexual jealousy:

> Archie . . . is a very fine boy, steady, hardworking, effective in all he does, well balanced, and gifted with a kindliness of nature which is a part of his stable and dependable make-up. In him Esther had picked a winner. . . . And yet [after she married him] she fell in love with Bob.
>
> Archie presently took note of the fact that she was very largely in Bob's company. They found this and that excuse to be together. Bob was often at the house.
>
> At last Archie said to her, "Esther, do you think you'd be happier with Bob than with me?"
>
> She admitted that she would.
>
> "All right," said Archie, "get a divorce from me and marry him. In the meantime, do as you please."
>
> In due time she brought suit for divorce. They got by without the collusion being detected, and without otherwise betraying the fact that they were in cahoots. At last the interlocutory decree was granted. The final decree was to follow six months later—another senseless obstacle.
>
> In the meantime, Esther and Bob had been living together secretly, though with Archie's knowledge; and when the final decree was granted, Esther was already pregnant by Bob. I married them a few months later.
>
> Shortly before the birth of this baby, Archie gave a dinner party to his divorced wife Esther, now very obviously on the verge of motherhood. . . . It was a thoroughly amicable occasion.[38]

The "Wild Palms" section of *If I Forget Thee, Jerusalem* explores and questions just such a narrative. Yet if Faulkner did read Lindsey's text, he certainly seems to have read it resistingly, if we can judge by the outcomes in "Wild Palms." Instead of a happy pregnancy and a new marriage, Charlotte dies unwed (by choice) of an abortion. Harry ends up in jail. Oddly, however, Faulkner seems to have accepted the role of Archie without question, in his creation of the otherwise (at least to me) inexplicable Rat, who like Archie entertains his wife's future lover in his home, supports her decision to leave him, and talks it all over with Harry. Despite his continuing love for his wife, Rat is "in cahoots" with Charlotte and Harry as they "live together secretly, with [Rat's] knowledge." Faulkner's version of Archie is even willing to raise as a single parent the children Charlotte leaves behind.

What can we make of Faulkner's "revision" of Lindsey? Most obviously, the saccharine rationality of Lindsey's narrative disappears with the violence Faulkner locates as a consequence of Charlotte's and Harry's desperate search for a love that transcends all sorts of law. Here, it seems plain that Faulkner resists the simple minded emotional logic evident in the Judge's didacticism. But perhaps too Faulkner ultimately rejects—despite the sympathy of his exploration of it—the values endorsed by Lindsey's narrative as well. He not only does not allow the search for "companionate marriage" to succeed without pain; he does not allow it to succeed at all. Harry is left, in prison, thinking of a lonely gesture that nevertheless links language, writing, the past, and the body. He tells of masturbating himself into remembering, remembering into masturbation: "It was there, waiting, it was all right; it would stand to his hand when the moment came. . . . But after all memory could live in the old wheezing entrails: and now it [the memory/ the entrails] did stand to his hand, incontrovertible and plain, serene, the palm clashing and murmuring dry and wild and faint and in the night but he could face it, thinking. . . . *So it is the old meat after all. . . . Because if memory exists outside of the flesh it wont be memory.*"[39] What survives is only half the memory—"*when she became not then half of memory became not*"—and the surviving half is "grief."[40] Clearly Faulkner's vision is countertranscendent; where Lindsey wafts his vision above the pain of heart and flesh, Harry unequivocally limits history itself within the bounds of the body.

Still, there is Archie/Rat. If Faulkner's and Lindsey's narratives explore Oedipal fantasies with very different outcomes, their vision of the kindly father seems surprisingly similar. In this respect, Faulkner does not resist the "national sexual culture" represented by Lindsey. How can we account for this? Following my reasoning about Southern manhood, I would guess that the tradition from which both draw this sacrificial father is consistent with traditional Southern sexual culture, indeed, more so than with traditional "American" sexual models as described by Anthony Rotundo or David Leverenz.[41] Denial, sacrifice, and loss characterize the most heroic of Southern cultural figures; Robert E. Lee's cultural heritage models the dignity of losing well. The Faulkner character who comes closest to this tradition is perhaps Ike McCaslin, who like Rat turns loss into a virtue. Judge Lindsey's Archie likewise is able to know a lost cause when he sees one, and provides a model for Lindsey's readers of the gracious and rational mode of behavior (if not feeling) that can be chosen where falling "in love" cannot be rationalized away. Perhaps Lindsey draws here on Southern traditions; in any case, Faulkner's resistance to Lindsey's popularized sexual culture stops here with Archie. Archie is acceptable.

Here next is Judge Lindsey on Millie, "one of the most completely fascinating little personalities it has been my fortune to meet with in the flapper world" (124). Millie has come to discuss her parents' failing marriage. In the judge's words, "She sat back and listened with a comically judicial air, her knees crossed, her short skirt carelessly drawn back exposing her bare knees, and legs ditto half way from knee to hip. . . . I . . . reflected on the fact that a few minutes earlier another girl had sat in that chair, who was a very wild specimen, indeed; and that she had been garbed precisely as Millie was garbed, and had displayed her person with the same apparent unconsciousness of doing it."[42] Judge Lindsey makes up his mind to find out about Millie's sexual values and experience.

Millie almost immediately makes it clear that she is a virgin. "I guess you'll think I'm pretty hard-boiled for a girl that's never let a boy do more than kiss her; but I know all about these things [sex]. You see Dad shot the whole works at me a couple of years ago. Told me he hoped I'd go straight, but that if I didn't, he wanted me to know the ropes—*all* about it; how to take care of yourself and all that. So I was wise" (125).

Later the judge asks her directly: " 'You meant it, did you, when you said you had never had sexual relations with any boy'?" " 'Sure I did,' " says the flapper, and explains herself. " 'I won't have those half-grown kids . . . that I don't care beans about, pawing me over and kissing me and—all that, much less going the limit. There's no kick in it if you've got any judgment, Dad says. . . .' " Now some day " 'I'm going to meet a fellow I really like—you know what I mean. . . . And . . . I'll fall in love with him. And . . . believe me, when I fall in love I'm not going to be stingy. . . . Then, if we cared for each other enough to want to stick, we'd get married and have some babies' " (127).

The Judge returns to the signifying effects of Millie's clothing, or lack of it: " 'That other girl, who is a pretty wild one, sat in that chair—just the way you do.' Millie was plainly not disturbed by my remark. 'This doesn't mean a darned thing,' she said, coolly pulling her short skirt an inch higher and placidly eyeing her comely leg. 'It's more comfortable and freer, that's all. It's like the short skirts. *Good* people finally got used to them, and even took to wearing them, after they had talked themselves to death against the 'bad' people who started them. Then they bobbed their hair— after saying that bobbed hair was unwomanly. After awhile these birds will learn not to undress in the dark.' "[43] Millie leaves, thanking the judge for letting her speak what was really on her mind. Once again our judge, through his persona as a sort of idealized therapist, uses his narrative to teach his audience the new sexual meanings. The clothes are not reliable signifiers: they don't make the woman, in any sense, we are to believe. Further, it is possible, with strong family values and female self-respect, to locate a sexual faith somewhere between promiscuity and premarital virginity. Millie plans to be strong enough to handle herself rationally when she finally "falls in love"; perhaps the only retrogressive sound in the story is her use of "stingy" to suggest that her sexuality is not for herself but a gift to someone else.

Here is Faulkner's description of Temple Drake as three town boys watch her getting into Gowan Steven's car: "Three of them watched Temple and Gowan Stevens come out [of the dance], into the chill presage of spring dawn. Her face was quite pale, dusted

over with recent powder, her hair in spent red curls. Her eyes, all
pupil now, rested upon them for a blank moment. Then she lifted
her hand in a wan gesture, whether at them or not, none could
have said. They did not respond, no flicker in their cold eyes. They
watched Gowan slip his arm into hers, and the fleet revelation of
flank and thigh as she got into his car. It was a long, low roadster,
with a jacklight.

'Who's that son bitch?' one said.

'My father's a judge,' the second said, in a bitter, lilting fal-
setto."[44]

I like to think that Faulkner's decision to make Temple Drake's
father a judge was inspired by Judge Ben Lindsey. Be that as it
may, it is clear that Faulkner again revises the tale Judge Lindsey
so hopefully tells. There is no healthy Millie here, no all-American
girl who wears her flapper clothes because they are "comfortable."
Temple's makeup, her clothes, her manner, and even her "spent
red curls" suggest ill health, a false front, decadent sexuality. If
Millie is the flapper, Temple is the vamp; Faulkner's descriptions
suggest a turn-of-the-century femme fatale dissipation, hardly a
bouncy twenties energy. For Temple to wait for the right man, to
flout sexual convention only in a serious and hopeful relationship,
seems unlikely, as of course the narrative will show. Indeed, if
there is any subjectivity in this snapshot of Temple as femme fatale, it is invisible, dampened, or dead. Judge Lindsey's efforts to
popularize a new national sexual culture would have to wait for
the 1960s for anything like public success; Faulkner counters
Lindsey's wolf in sheep's clothing, his radical liberation of female
sexuality into female control, with a traditional association of female sexuality with male danger, male risk, and, consistently, the
need for male control.

Instead of a happy second marriage, a full term pregnancy, and
a birth celebrated by both her husband and her lover, Charlotte
Rittenmeyer dies with a man who hates the very thought of becoming a husband and who terminates his lover's pregnancy and
her life with his too late botched abortion. Instead of a sexually
inexperienced yet confident young woman who enjoys frank talk

with adult men and thinks exposing her thighs means nothing, Temple Drake is represented as a sexually experienced yet insecure girl who is by turns nervous, placating, and childlike with adult men, and thinks exposing her thighs means everything. Faulkner's narratives use Judge Lindsey's material against his arguments; they resist the Judge by recontextualizing his stories.

I submit that Faulkner's recontextualizing the sexual narratives of the emerging national culture like these of Ben Lindsey occurs not only because as a traditional Southern white man he sees a darker outcome for female sexual freedom, but also for a different and more difficult, more subtle reason. Faulkner's sexual logic remained deeply binary but not essentialist, lodged in a cultural conviction of the necessity for gender opposition linked, as I have argued elsewhere, with the associations between penetration and manhood. This did not mean that sex determined gender; on the contrary, it is clear that numerous Faulkner characters cross the boundaries that their sex would dictate. Charlotte, says Harry, is not only a better man than he but a better gentleman as well. Drusilla makes a fine soldier and laborer, dressing and thinking like a man during and after the war. Joanna Burden lives alone and runs her business like a man. Even Temple's desire for and behavior with Red is, like Joanna's for Joe Christmas, arguably gender transgressive in its force and aggressivity. What Faulkner's commitment to gender binarism meant instead was that crossing those boundaries, "penetrating" in its various meanings, would be possible, but fatal—for most women. Emily in "A Rose for Emily" succeeds at her eminently subversive game precisely because she plays exactly by the rules of Southern womanhood. I'm not sure that Faulkner could imagine very clearly a world of female desire, assertiveness, and competence that was not a world of manly women with tragic outcomes.

On the other hand, he was—like so many other Southern writers—quite able to imagine a womanly man who could appropriate femininity without losing his manhood and without dying in the end: the Archie-Harry man. The model for such a man in *The Unvanquished* is Bayard Sartoris, who appropriates the Biblical

"Thou shalt not kill" that Granny Millard has taught him and uses it to resist and revise a dominant form of violent and retributive masculinity. I've argued elsewhere that Bayard's success is deeply imbricated with the story of writing that is embedded within the novel's plots. In revising the *Saturday Evening Post* short stories for novel publication, Faulkner made a change that is crucial here. He inserted into the story "Raid" a long passage having to do with the boys' being so swept away by Drusilla's story of the locomotive race that they felt it was reality. It is reminiscent of Quentin's conjuring of the figure of Thomas Sutpen as Rosa begins to tell him the story in the first chapter of *Absalom, Absalom!* In both cases the power of storytelling belongs to women; Bayard and Quentin listen. Then in *The Unvanquished*, as in *Absalom, Absalom!*, two young men compete and collaborate as they learn to narrate from older women, Drusilla, Granny, and Rosa. But where Quentin and Shreve make a happy if not companionate marriage of speaking and hearing, Ringo and Bayard emerge loser and winner: Bayard's voice survives and prevails while Ringo's is reduced in "Odor of Verbena"—a story also added for the novel version of *The Unvanquished*—to silence and servanthood. Moreover, even as Bayard, energized by her death, adopts his grandmother's Biblical teaching in order to renovate masculinity, he represses a woman who threatens him more, and Drusilla leaves the text like an evanescent odor if not, in Charlotte's words, a bad smell. By the same token, Rosa Coldfield's death—or the written notice of it—arguably energizes Quentin to tell his narrative and complete his feminization of manhood, however despairing and deadly it turns out to be.

Indeed, not infrequently Faulkner's male characters' femininity threatens to overwhelm them. Horace Benbow both of *Flags in the Dust* and of *Sanctuary* comes to mind; so do Harry Wilbourne and Joe Christmas. And when it does, the results are fatal. But when it does not, when a man can make matters "stand to his hand," the incorporation of femininity allows both male control and writing itself. In short, when Faulkner's women move into the norms of popular national sexual culture—when they cross gender boundaries into masculinity—they have a tendency to die, disappear, and otherwise lose narrative control; when Faulkner's men cross into femininity—think of Horace with his shrimp as the sexually compliant husband in an "Ideal Marriage" of the twenties—they generally find some way to rescue traditional manhood. That rescue comes, as noted, by the hand and by the word, both metonyms for writing. When Harry Wilbourne cuts an incision in Charlotte, the novel's context forces us to see it as a form of sculpture; Bayard and Ringo of course bring back the hand of Grumby; and Horace Benbow, like Bayard, turns to words and the Word as a way out of a sticky situation with a woman. Joe's incision in Joanna is his writing on her flesh, cutting off her male head, just as surely as Percy inscribes Joe's body with his meanings. Perhaps this is the real reason for Granny Millard's death: she wrote men's letters with a man's hand.

Where the gender that should follow the male body fails to do so, *writing* the male body—the hand—will recuperate masculinity, will allow the feminine to take its proper and subservient place in a hierarchy of identities. Why?

Let me conclude with some even more speculative thoughts about the anxieties that may lie on the cusp that connects popular and Southern sexual cultures for Faulkner. It's my sense that, of all the aspects of "femininity" that Faulkner so willingly attributed to his male characters, the worst, the most frightening, was the possibility of a loss of all boundaries altogether, of a symbiotic merger with the all. Harry Wilbourne leaves the lake when he becomes aware that he has lost the boundaries that define time, that he is in effect merging with timelessness. Horace leaves Belle when he feels his identity has been submerged in her liquidity and turned into little drips of shrimp juice. Bayard resists Drusilla's seductive erotics fearing a swoon, succumbing to an odor. Quentin succumbs to honeysuckle and ultimately to liquid; he is most shamed by the occasions when he faints away. Loss of consciousness, loss of control, are linked then with the loss of boundaries and distinctions, with liquidity and timelessness.

It seems entirely reasonable to me that a culture whose boundaries have themselves been famously invaded and whose men have resisted bravely but unsuccessfully would have particular anxieties about masculinity insofar as masculinity has had to do culturally with marking, controlling, and penetrating boundaries. A man marks and writes; he is not inscribed. A man controls; he is not out of control or in someone else's control. A man penetrates—indeed creates new boundaries by penetrating—he is not the object of penetration.

Yet these were just the values and practices that the new sexual culture seemed to urge. Women with sexual freedom, no longer under even a husband's control; women who showed their legs but stopped there—these cultural representations would therefore have to be renarrativized, resisted by telling stories that were less appealing, perhaps, and certainly less hopeful. Men who honored women's voices and minds, men who allowed women to make crucial decisions about their lives—these men had to be shown femininity's proper place, well regulated whether in a man's body or a woman's.

For Faulkner, resistance to a dominant national culture thus could eventuate not, as cultural theory might hope, in radical inversions and deconstruction of hierarchies, or in social revolution. Instead, Faulkner's resistance of texts like Lindsey's and Van de Velde's—a resistance that acknowledged the sexual revolution's presence—offered a way of recuperating new material into old paradigms, and thus of allowing continuity in apparent change, persistence of the old values in the image of the new. No surprise then that in the South the dominant culture would both try to preserve the abyss between the genders and try to remotivate a history of perhaps unwillingly feminized men by actively appropriating femininity. His response to the anxieties about being overwhelmed by the other, even or especially by the other that is already within, anxieties stimulated by the prevalence of new and popular national sexual cultures, was to reinstitute the dominance and sexual divisions of traditional masculine culture finally by making the pages stand to his hand.

Temple Drake's resistance to traditional masculine culture,

though its form and shape are (as Diane Roberts has shown) understandably more indirect than Drusilla's, or Granny Millard's, or Joanna Burden's, or Rosa Coldfield's, or Charlotte Rittenmeyer's, or Caddy Compson's, or Mrs. McLendon's, is, like theirs, a lost cause. Propped up by her father and brothers, she no longer tells her own compelling story, but lies and thus no longer resists the judge's law. She becomes part of an ancient masculine text as, next to her father in Paris, she politely hides her yawn and studies her appearance in a compact, surrounded by gray statues of dead queens in the "embrace of the season of rain and death."[45] As she is written into the dominant cultural text, so are Drusilla (who disappears, reduced to an odor of verbena for Bayard), Granny ("all the little sticks had collapsed in quiet heap on the floor"[46] enabling Bayard's accession to manhood), Joanna (silenced by beheading), Rosa (whose death provides Quentin with his text), Charlotte (whose death provides Harry with his), Caddy (vanished into prostitution and a photo), and Mrs. McLendon, pushed out of McLendon's narrative. There is no doubt that the tones of these stories are greatly various; as so many critics have argued so well, Faulkner writes out his resisting women with great empathy. But it seems impossible for him to imagine a conclusion that is not, however agonizing it may be, tragic for these women who resist the Southern patriarchal sex-gender system. Where the new sexual culture emerges with a new, womanly man, there is less conflict for Faulkner, as we saw. But where a Judge Lindsey or a Theodor Van de Velde edges toward female subjectivity and sexual autonomy, Faulkner's hand revised the new sexuality into some old sad songs: under his hand, their resistance lost its romance.

NOTES

1. Raymond Williams, *Keywords: A Vocabulary of Culture and Society,* rev. ed. (New York: Oxford University Press, 1985), 87.

2. Raymond Williams, *Culture and Society, 1780–1950* (New York: Anchor Books, 1960).

3. Cleanth Brooks and Robert Penn Warren, *Understanding Poetry* (New York: Harcourt, Brace, & Co., 1938).

4. John T. Matthews, "Faulkner and the Culture Industry," in *The Cambridge Compan-*

ion to William Faulkner, ed. Philip M. Weinstein (Cambridge: Cambridge University Press, 1995), 53.

5. See Walter Benjamin, *Illuminations* (New York: Schocken, 1979).

6. The title of this year's Faulkner and Yoknapatawpha Conference, "Faulkner in Cultural Context," can be read as a committee's compromise between these two positions. On the one hand, it introduces the anthropologists' idea of culture, acknowledging the importance of Faulkner's historical world to understanding the man and his writing. Still, it retains the privileged centrality of the Faulknerian "text," surrounded as it is, etymologically, by the (mere) *context* of culture.

7. For an excellent example of such an analysis of Faulkner's work, see Lawrence H. Schwartz, *Creating Faulkner's Reputation: The Politics of Modern Literary Criticism* (Knoxville: University of Tennessee Press, 1989).

8. Matthews, "Faulkner and the Culture Industry," 59–60.

9. Lora Romero, "Bio-Political Resistance in Domestic Ideology and *Uncle Tom's Cabin*," *American Literary History* 1 (Winter, 1989): 715–34; Diane Roberts, "Ravished Belles: Stories of Rape and Resistance in *Flags in the Dust* and *Sanctuary*," *Faulkner Journal* (Fall 1988/Spring 1989): 21–35. For a Gramscian reading of the Agrarians' "resistance" to the expanding American federal state beginning in the 1930s, see Paul Bové, "Agriculture and Academe: America's Southern Question," *Boundary 2*, 169–95.

10. See Eugene Genovese, *Roll, Jordan, Roll: The World the Slaves Made* (New York: Vintage Books, 1976), for a Gramscian analysis of slave resistance.

11. William Faulkner, *Collected Stories of William Faulkner* (New York: Random House, 1950), 169.

12. Minrose Gwin, *Faulkner and the Feminine: Reading (Beyond) Sexual Difference* (Knoxville: University of Tennessee Press, 1990); Diane Roberts, *Faulkner and Southern Womanhood* (Athens: University of Georgia Press, 1994).

13. William Faulkner, *Sanctuary* in *Novels 1930–1935* (New York: Library of America, 1985), 279. " 'Now, now,' Miss Reba said. 'I bled for four days, myself. It aint nothing. . . . That blood'll be worth a thousand dollars to you, honey.' " Although she never says it directly, Miss Reba seems to be referring to (1) her own loss of virginity (surely not her own corncob rape), (2) Temple's presumed loss of virginity, and (3) the market value of a virgin in Miss Reba's business. But Miss Reba only assumes Temple's virginity—as she seems to assume the blood comes from sex with Popeye, not rape—and Temple neither confirms nor denies it.

14. Faulkner, *Sanctuary*, 218–19.

15. Among the lyrics to Madonna's famous song:

> I was beat incomplete
> I'd been had, I was sad and blue
> But you made me feel
> Yeah, you made me feel
> Shiny and new
> Chorus: Like a virgin
> Touched for the very first time

Madonna's song, offered from the point of view of the woman whose virginity is the issue, expresses a feeling of *emotional* virginity; her "heart beat[s]/ For the very first time," she feels, because—regardless of how much sexual activity she has experienced—she has felt "scared and cold" until now. This is a very different point of view, and point, from mine concerning Temple, whom one can—sadly—hardly imagine thinking these thoughts even for Red. My point rather is that Temple is "like a virgin" *for others*. No one, not even the narrative, cares much about her point of view or her interior life.

16. See William Faulkner, *The Sound and the Fury: The Corrected Text.* (New York: Random House, 1984), 78, 177.

17. Florence King, *Southern Ladies and Gentlemen* (New York: Stein and Day, 1975).

18. Michèle Barrett, *The Politics of Truth: From Marx to Foucault* (Stanford: Stanford University Press, 1991), 154.

19. Ibid., 146.

20. Barrett is citing Descombes on Derrida's "critique of, and alternative to, the entire framework of assumptions and conventions in which such epistemological problems have got stuck." Barrett, 160.

21. It is important to be cautious here; Gandhi's and Martin Luther King Jr.'s forms of "passive resistance" seem to offer exceptions to these generalizations. In both cases, unlike the case of Gramsci, the notion of resistance does not entail desire for hegemonic control, at least as Gramsci seems to have envisioned it. It would be interesting, however, to explore these and other alternative forms of resistance in some detail. Kaja Silverman's analysis of T. E. Lawrence's masochism, to be found in *Male Subjectivities at the Margins* (New York: Routledge, 1992), is useful in thinking about the difficulties of constructing a nondominant masculine subject position.

In my view, the history of "everyday" American literary critical practice—I exclude the groundbreaking works of theory and practice—has been marked precisely by historical changes in the efficacy of critical "keywords." Who now regularly uses parentheses to point out the internal jostlings in a word? How long will "privileged" last? How long will "representations" be sexy? My hope here is not to quarrel with the rapid changes in literary fashions, which we should all enjoy as fully as any other changeable pleasures. Instead, it is to acknowledge that this practice of romancing terms like "resistance" *is* a bit like infatuation. I hope that to throw some cold water on the term may yield not an end to romance but a more sober, complex, and resilient relationship with the words that we need and want to use.

22. Lillian Smith, *Killers of the Dream* (New York: Norton, 1949).

23. William Faulkner, "The Bear," in *Go Down, Moses* (New York: Vintage International, 1985).

24. Louisa McCord, "On the Enfranchisement of Women," in Michael O'Brien, ed., *All Clever Men, Who Made Their Way: Critical Discourse in the Old South* (Athens: University of Georgia Press, 1992).

25. Ted Ownby, *Subduing Satan: Religion, Recreation, and Manhood in the Rural South, 1865–1920* (Chapel Hill: University of North Carolina Press, 1990).

26. John d'Emilio and Estelle B. Freedman, *Intimate Matters: A History of Sexuality in America* (New York: Harper & Row, 1988), 258, 268.

27. See Jacquelyn Dowd Hall, *Revolt Against Chivalry*, 2nd ed. (New York: Columbia University Press, 1979).

28. Theodore H. Van de Velde, *Ideal Marriage: Its Physiology and Technique*, trans. Stella Browne, introd. J. Johnston Abraham (New York: Random House, 1957 [1930]). Louis D. Rubin Jr., found a copy in his parents' attic and read it at the age of 13. Conversation, New Haven, May 1995. Anne Goodwyn Jones, "Desire and Dismemberment: Faulkner and the Ideology of Penetration," in *Faulkner and Ideology*, ed. Donald M. Kartiganer and Ann J. Abadie (Jackson: University Press of Mississippi, 1995), 129–71.

29. Van de Velde, 262.

30. Ibid., 223.

31. Nina Silber, "Intemperate Men, Spiteful Women, and Jefferson Davis," in *Divided Houses: Gender and the Civil War*, ed. Catherine Clinton and Nina Silber (New York: Oxford University Press, 1992), 283–305.

32. John Crowe Ransom, "The Poet as Woman" [1936], in *The World's Body* (Baton Rouge: Lousiana State University Press, 1968), 76–110.

33. See Takeo Doi, M.D., *The Anatomy of Dependence*, trans. John Bester (Tokyo: Kodansha International, 1981). Doi's discussion of guilt and shame in Japan will also be of interest to students of Southern honor.

34. Frances Newman, *The Hard Boiled Virgin* [1926] and *Dead Lovers Are Faithful Lovers* [1928] (Athens: University of Georgia Press, 1994).

35. Katherine Anne Porter, "Old Mortality," in *Collected Stories* (New York: Harcourt, Brace & Jovanovich, 1972).

36. Blotner, Joseph, comp. and intro., *William Faulkner's Library: A Catalogue* (Charlottesville: University Press of Virginia, 1964).

37. " 'When it come out in the paper folks thought she'd run off with some fellow. One of them companionate marriages,' " says the Senator to Horace Benbow. Faulkner, *Sanctuary*, 301.

38. Judge Ben B. Lindsey and Wainwright Evans, *The Companionate Marriage* (New York: Boni & Liveright, 1927), 83–84.

39. William Faulkner, *If I Forget Thee, Jerusalem*, in *Novels: 1936–1940* (New York: Library of America, 1990), 715.

40. Ibid.

41. See Anthony Rotundo, *American Manhood: Transformations in Masculinity from the Revolution to the Modern Era* (New York: Basic Books, 1993) and David Leverenz, *Manhood and the American Renaissance* (Ithaca: Cornell University Press, 1989).

42. Lindsey, *Companionate Marriage*, 124–25.

43. Ibid., 129–30.

44. Faulkner, *Sanctuary*, 199.

45. Ibid., 398.

46. William Faulkner, *The Unvanquished*, in *Novels: 1936–1940* (New York: Library of America, 1990), 423.

The Social Psychology of Paternalism:
Sanctuary's Cultural Context

KEVIN RAILEY

Faulkner's *Sanctuary* has traditionally been discussed as an exploration into evil and more recently as a text delineating the cultural significances of the Oedipal conflict.[1] In this discussion I want to move away from humanistic and Freudian analyses to a historically grounded approach that recognizes ideology as the link between social formations and subjectivity. Recognizing the productive function of ideology, I want to investigate not just how the dynamics of Horace Benbow's world set the conditions for Temple Drake's story, as John Matthews has suggested, but also how *Sanctuary*'s narrative perspective highlights the cultural context forming and guiding Horace and Temple's world, namely paternalism.[2] Through the depiction of Horace we get a close look at someone who is identified by that context, a look at the social psychology characteristic of an upper-class, aristocratic paternalist male mentality; through the depictions of Narcissa, Temple, and Popeye we get to see how this social psychology is projected onto those in society who are not upper class aristocratic men. The logical pattern of evil, thus, becomes the logic of paternalism's social psychology.

Horace Benbow and Paternalism

Since the 1981 publication of Faulkner's original version of *Sanctuary* and the subsequent comparisons to the first-published, revised version, this seemingly uncharacteristic Faulkner novel has come to be closely linked to Faulkner's other works of the period 1927–1931. Articulating the critical consensus, Noel Polk has written: "It seems to me obvious that there are ways in which all the texts of these years form a single intertext which holds important meanings for the study of Faulkner's work."[3] If this insight is true, and I think it is, then Faulkner's comments about *Flags in the Dust*, which he wrote during this period, can apply to *Sanctuary* as well: "nothing served but that I try by main strength to recreate between the covers of a book the world as I was already preparing to lose and regret . . . and desiring, if not the capture of that world and all the feeling of it as you'd preserve a kernel or a leaf to indicate the lost forest, at least to keep the evocative skeleton of the dessicated [sic] leaf."[4] Though no one would argue for a commemorative celebration in *Sanctuary*, "the world" to which Faulkner refers remains the same in this novel as it is in *Flags* and *The Sound and the Fury*: the aristocratic paternalist, noblesse oblige world associated with the Old South.

Faulkner points to Horace Benbow's association with this world by labelling him a "gentleman." Like Quentin Compson, a very similar type of character who receives the label "cavalier," Horace receives a label identifying him with the cavalier, paternalist ideology stemming from Old South social formations (and enjoying considerable revival during the 1920s). Horace underscores his identifcation with this label when he comments, "God is foolish at times, but at least He's a gentleman," and Faulkner reiterates the association when he has Clarence Snopes call Horace a "southron gentleman."[5] Further, Horace's motivation for leaving his wife, Belle—the motivation for the novel itself—stems from his desire to return to his patrilineal home in order, it can be argued, to claim his father's paternalist status as well as to attain a sanctuary from the present society.

What this society has become is indeed a bourgeois, middle class one with which Horace feels no kinship. Faulkner clearly indicates this situation in a revealing scene in the original version of the novel. Late in the story Horace considers Temple's surprise entrance into the courtroom where she will testify: "He realised now that it was too late, that he could not have summoned her; realised again that furious homogeneity of the middle classes when opposed to the proletariat from which it so recently sprung and by which it is so often threatened" (*SO* 260).[6] Though the class-specific vocabulary is unusual for Faulkner, and the reference to middle *classes* and the mistaken pronoun reference seem strange, these thoughts can be seen to explain some of the novel's social dynamics. First, Horace recognizes that Judge Drake, Temple's father, has cooperated with the District Attorney only for the purposes of the trial; second, Horace distances himself from the kind of "low-class" legal chicanery forced on Judge Drake for the D.A.'s political purposes—that is, Horace distances himself from the lower of the middle classes; and third, Horace senses that these two men, the DA and Judge Drake, are from different classes in some way—that is, Judge Drake is from the higher of the middle classes. Horace's lack of identification with these "middle classes" points to an affinity with some other class—as I have argued, the upper, aristocratic paternalist class, and he senses that Judge Drake, except in this one instance, is closer to him than to the DA. Even though the Jefferson society in this book can be associated with the bourgeois, middle class, the novel's narrative perspective—Horace's perspective—has more to do with that of an aristocratic paternalist.

To clarify the connection between Horace and Judge Drake and to indicate that Horace's status as gentleman is not purely a description of personal behavior but a social class designation, Faulkner also makes definite connections between Horace and the title "judge." In a few places in both texts, Faulkner has Clarence Snopes call Horace "Judge Benbow" (*SR* 182). More than a simple mistake, Snopes persists in using this designation even after Horace corrects him, indirectly connecting Horace to his father—Judge Will Benbow—and the social position his father held in a different type of society. Considering also the prominence of Temple's refrain, "My father's a judge," Faulkner clearly links Horace to Judge Drake in a rather direct manner. A real connection exists, then, between the personal, descriptive label of gentleman and the social, class designation of judge. What John Irwin says about various Faulkner characters is true for both these men: each is "a twentieth-century descendant of an aristocratic Southern family . . . a descendant who personified, if not the South, then the Southern ruling class at a certain point in this century."[7]

Klaus Theweleit has analyzed in detail the fantasies of upper class, aristocratic men within patriarchal social formations. His volumes of *Male Fantasies* are wide-ranging analyses of the patriarchal (paternalist) male mentality as it was exhibited in the writings of the pre-fascist Freikorpsmen of post–World War I Germany.[8] However, though his specific subject is the writing of these men, he is more broadly concerned with the correlations between these extremists and patriarchy in general. In fact, a constant theme of Theweleit's books is how the fascist's psychosocial reality reveals, in more intense ways, tendencies existing in all patriarchies. Barbara Ehrenreich enumerates this point in her introduction; as she explains: "the point of understanding fascism is . . . because it's already implicit in the daily relationships of men and women. Theweleit refuses to draw a line between the fantasies of the Freikorpsmen and the psychic ramblings of the 'normal' man."[9]

But beyond this explanation that Theweleit's books put into vivid relief otherwise less extreme forms of patriarchal masculine behavior, there are some direct, general areas of connection between his subject matter and Faulkner's. The Freikorpsmen were all heirs to the European aristocratic tradition. All considered themselves part of the highest civilization; all considered themselves gentlemen. Most of them had been soldiers, and all of them felt the defeat of Germany in World War I as a crushing loss of their hopes and dreams, their pride and sense of self. Their very formation into the Freikorpsmen was dependent upon a shared sense that civilization was being threatened by unruly and chaotic forces with which it was their duty to contend. They saw their roles as defenders of culture and preservers of law, and order, in the face of threats from a new class of people wanting to take power and from the so-called lower orders of society trying to rise above their station.

These defining characteristics can certainly be related to the Southern paternalist tradition and its legacy after the Civil War, and to an extent after World War I, with which Faulkner was so familiar and in which he was so immersed. Southern paternalists believed that materialistic and vulgar hordes from the North were descending upon them, ruining their way of civilized life in the creation of a New South which was not the South. They felt that this way of life would unleash destructive forces from the lower orders and they sought to maintain the status quo in the name of justice, law, and civilized (Southern) life. In *Sanctuary*, this fear and its realization are embodied in the way Faulkner describes the Old Frenchman's Place as being taken over by the lower elements of society who have allowed it to revert back to some jungle status; meanwhile, the descriptions of the Old Frenchman's place parallel descriptions of Horace's patrilineal home, both of which lack the hand of husbandry and which have reverted to a primitive state.[10] Horace's attempts to reinvigorate his old home parallel his attempts to bring the principles of "law, justice, and civilization" to bear on Lee Goodwin's trial—both are attempts to reassert paternalism. Ultimately, though Theweleit analyzes extreme versions of this aristocratic mentality, comparisons between the social psychology of those men and various Faulkner characters—in this case, Horace Benbow—seem not only entirely plausible but especially relevant.

In coming to understand these men, their behavior, and the rhetoric of images guiding their fantasies Theweleit offers an avenue of departure from Freudian analyses that have come to dominate discussions of *Sanctuary*. In his explanations Theweleit emphasizes that what these aristocratic men seem to repress is not incestuous desire, as Freudian interpretations would have it, but desire itself. In the works he analyzes Theweleit finds ample evidence that these men never really experienced warm, close relationships with their mothers. Never having experienced this kind of relationship, these men have both a desperate yearning for and a desperate dread of love and sex, of intimacy with women, and the fusion of human beings that these entail. This tension can only be released in violence—an action which combines both the need and the dread in one culminating and explosive moment. This lack of relationship with the mother also leads to the inability to draw boundaries between self and other and increases the fear of dissolution of the ego when coming close to other people. Theweleit explains that the motivation for the patriarch's fantasies and behavior stems not so much from a wish for incestuous union with the mother but from a wish to rid himself of all those maternal qualities of warmth, intimacy, sensuality—and the deep-felt emotions they engender—which could be called mother.[11]

As if Theweleit and Faulkner observed similar phenomena but presented their observations in different media, Faulkner identifies the origins of Horace's psychological reality in a way parallel to Theweleit's descriptions. Horace's memory of his own mother reveals this similarity: "mother . . . had been an invalid so long that the one picture of her he retained was two frail arms rising from a soft falling of lace" (SO 62). Rather than reveal, as Polk claims, that Horace was mothered his whole life, this memory indicates that Horace had no real relationship with his mother at all.[12] The effects of Horace's inability to relate, to connect to all that is his mother, are recorded throughout the entire novel.

The initial effects of this nonrelationship between Horace and his mother are revealed in a series of images that at first seem rather bizarre; in the context of Theweleit's theories, though, the logic of Horace's dream imagery reveals the foundation of the paternalist's psychosocial world. Just prior to Horace's memory of his mother he imagines the following: "After a while he could not tell whether he were awake or not. . . . but he was talking to his mother too. . . . Then he saw that she wore a shapeless garment of faded calico and that Belle's rich, full mouth burned sullenly out of the halflight, and he knew that she was about to open her mouth and he tried to scream at her . . . But it was too late. He saw her mouth open; a thick, black liquid welled in a bursting bubble . . . and he was thinking He smells black. He smells like that black stuff that ran out of Bovary's mouth when they raised her head" (*SO* 60). Importantly, Horace's pleasant fantasies of a presexual state of childhood are here annihilated by the black liquid erupting from the woman—who is both mother and wife. The reference to black liquid, associated with the lower-class, sexually deviant Popeye, and the description of Belle's mouth as rich and full charge this scene with unmistakable sexual energy. This energy causes the horror Horace feels, horror associated with wife and mother. Thus, this vivid and bizarre scene reveals that Horace becomes repulsed by both mother and wife because they are together associated with sexuality and the lower class. (As we will see, this repulsion is a constant in Horace's behavior.) In other instances, Horace's less nightmarish fantasies involve prepubescent or asexual women, namely his step-daughter, Little Belle, and his sister, Narcissa. These women do not conjure the same repulsion in Horace precisely because they are presexual or asexual. Like the men Theweleit studied, Horace's lack of relationship with his mother causes a fear of fusion, of losing the boundaries of self, of real, intimate relationships with other people, especially women. This fear manifests itself primarily as a reaction against the supposedly innate sexuality women are seen to possess.

The foundation of paternalism, then, directly connects to an aversion to sexuality—an act of fusion which is seen as self-destructive rather than life-affirming. The images in this scene, moreover, link mother to sexually active wife and sexually deviant Popeye; thus, like the men Theweleit analyzes, Horace's reactions to the "low and base" emotions are connected to reactions to "low and base" people. *Sanctuary* implies that Horace's psychological fixations connect directly to images of women and the lower class—as if paternalist fantasies get projected outward onto society. Like Theweleit's insights, then, Faulkner's novel implies that the paternalist's psychological reality has definite social ramifications. Thus, we need to investigate how Faulkner's novel explores both the psychological root of these paternalist, masculinist fantasies and the social effects of them.

Masculinist Fantasies

1. *Paternalism and Female Sexuality*

When discussing his reasons for leaving Kinston, his wife's hometown, and returning to Jefferson—the very motivation for the plot of the novel, Horace stresses that the "flat and rich and foul" country had gotten him "upset," and he needed to get away from feeling emotionally agitated: "I thought that maybe I would be all right if I just had a hill to lie on for awhile" (*SR* 16). The specific reasons for his departure he explains as follows: "it wasn't Little Belle that set me off. Do you know what it was? . . . It was a rag with rouge on it" (*SR* 16). A bit later, in answer to Ruby's question about why he left his wife, Horace responds: "Because she ate shrimp. . . . And I still dont like to smell shrimp. But I wouldn't mind the carrying it home so much. I could stand that. It's because the package drips. All the way home it drips and drips" (*SR* 18).

A careful reading of this rhetoric of images reveals that in reacting to the reported foulness of the rich, fertile homeland of his wife Horace makes direct associations among women's bodies, the earth, and sexuality (which parallel the description of Belle's mouth as rich and full noted earlier). Somehow the literal threat of a flood across the Kinston plain becomes associated with a flood of emotions which he desires to escape, and this flood becomes associated with Belle. His description of the dirty handkerchief can be seen to represent a function of the female body which disgusts Horace. And his odd overreaction to the dripping of the shrimp seems to indicate an aversion to getting his hands wet, here associated with Belle and indirectly to the foulness of her homeland and her sexuality. These images link together in a pattern associating dirt, fluids, and female sexuality, and this sexuality with an overwhelming emotional agitation which Horace wishes to avoid. Thus, though critics have focused on Horace's journey *to* Narcissa, *to* his incestuous desire for Narcissa and Little Belle, and *into* evil, these particular motivations for Horace's departure seem important in terms of what he flees *from*. In fact, Horace seems to flee from evil, that is, from female sexuality as embodied by Belle.[13]

André Bleikasten has noted this and other patterns of bizarre images in *Sanctuary*; however, he does not attempt to link the rhetoric of images to the novel's narrative perspective.[14] In order to make some sense of the images in relation to the novel's socio-historical perspective we need to turn to Theweleit, who explains the manifestations of the paternalist's psychological reality in ways corroborating Faulkner's vivid depictions. Theweleit explains that paternalists' fear of sexual women often manifests itself in a dread of fluidity, motion, anything that flows or streams. This dread manifests itself in physical ways as negative reactions to getting one's hands wet or dirty, to being immersed in water and wet substances; it manifests itself in psychological ways as reactions against emotions and feelings, that which flows inside. These men always attempt to maintain an attitude and pose of tight, rigid control, of order and stasis; they wish to maintain erect and firm in a whirlwind of chaotic forces or to place a distance between themselves and the impulses that lead to chaotic feelings.

Here we find a way to understand Horace's desire to reach the top of a hill, to find a distant and therefore safe spot that is dry and away from his wife. We also discover a link between the images associated with Horace and those associated with Judge Drake and his sons. Late in the novel, Faulkner describes Judge Drake and his sons waiting for Temple to step down from the witness stand and be returned to their safe hands: "the old man erect beside her. . . . Four younger men were standing stiffly erect. . . . They stood like soldiers" (*SO* 279–80; *SR* 304). These descriptions indicate a degree of sexual tension, as others have noted, but they also reveal a dread of releasing that tension, a stiffening of the defenses against all the sexuality associated with Temple. Like the very "soldier-males" described by Theweleit, these men's postures reveal both desire and the intense inhibition of desire. Horace and the Drakes need somehow to protect themselves from Belle and Temple, respectively, that is, from all they come to represent in this novel—sexuality, intimacy, a loss of self. These can only be pre-

vented by maintaining firm and erect or by distancing one's male
self from the threat.

Nowhere is this need to avoid chaotic emotions and sexuality,
as well as the loss of self they imply, more evident than in the now
infamous scene where Horace falls into his bathroom and vomits
his coffee. Several aspects surrounding this scene are significant
for my discussion of the novel. First, Horace has just returned
from Memphis where he listened to Temple recount her horrific
experiences at the Old Frenchman's place. That story does not
make Horace feel sick, nor does it cause a sexual fantasy involving
himself and Temple. No; rather, Temple's tale of vicious violation
causes Horace to feel a cruel pity: he thinks she would be better
off dead. Indications of Horace's sexual desire for Temple, a key
point in Freudian interpretations, seem nonexistent. Second, Temple's story leads Horace to think about Little Belle's sexuality and
her eventual sexual initiation; these fantasies cause the reaction
and the rather strange psychic interlude where Horace refers to
himself as "she." Here's the interlude: "he gave over and plunged
forward and struck the lavatory . . . while the shucks set up a
terrific uproar beneath her thighs. Lying with her head lifted
slightly . . . she watched something black and furious go roaring
out of her pale body. She was bound naked on her back on a flat
car moving at speed through a black tunnel, the blackness stream-
ing in rigid threads overhead" (*SO* 220).

Significantly, Horace does not imagine himself *with* Little Belle
in this scene but imagines himself *to be* Little Belle during a sexual
encounter.[15] Identifying with that plight causes a violent physical
reaction. The very shift in pronouns during the scene symbolizes
Horace's wish to remove his male self from the act of sexuality; the
linguistic shift fulfills the function of shielding him from unwanted
contact with both liquids and sexuality—as if the black liquid (the
coffee) does not really roar out of his body. Listening to Temple's
story of violent rape had moved Horace little; thinking of his presexual step-daughter experiencing sex causes a violent repulsion,
an experience Horace must literally purge from his body.

Moreover, being repulsed by sexuality, wanting to avoid sexuality, and shielding others from sexuality become repetitive behaviors for Horace throughout the novel. He recalls having tried to convince Narcissa not to get married, arguing that they both should avoid sexual relations; he constantly tries to stop Little Belle from getting involved with boys; and whether Miss Jenny mentions sex in reference to Narcissa's marriage or Ruby mentions it in terms of payment for legal services, Horace overreacts with strong feelings of aversion and repulsion. As his specific advice to Little Belle, "Not to soil her slippers," reveals, he also links sexual relations to images of dirt, and the book is filled with numerous instances of Horace removing himself from areas of dirt and/or dirty liquid: he moves from train cars in which men spit; he avoids Ruby's baby who spits up; and he avoids becoming "soiled" at any expense. In whatever form it erupts into his psychic ramblings and into his day-to-day life, Horace constantly seeks to avoid coming into contact with sexuality. Like that black liquid he purged from his body, Horace attempts to purge sexuality from his life.

As the very basis of the paternalist's psychic world, this aversion also comes to explain other aspects of Horace's personality: his rejection of sexuality, the "low and base," becomes revealed through his admiration for the "high and lofty"; his rejection of the material body mirrored by his fascination with ideals and idealization; his rejection of manual labor, of "getting his hands dirty," connected to his aristocratic association. These characteristics—the enjoyment of the high and the lofty, the pursuit of ideals—show that paternalists' neuroses become socially accepted, even venerated qualities, thus, indirectly, how the neuroses of the powerful are never simply "private." No, not at all. The polite front that Horace, and all paternalists, show the world, based as it is on the rejection of physical and emotional intimacy, has dire consequences for society at large.

2. *Paternalism and Masculinity*

As the direct connection between the black liquid and Popeye indicates, Popeye comes, in some way, to represent what Horace represses. As the opening scene of the revised version reveals, where Horace and Popeye sit across a pond from one another for hours, the two are fractured mirror images of one another. Distancing myself again from Freudian analyses, I do not want to say, however, that Popeye enacts Horace's incestuous sexual desire. The specific way Popeye performs his violation of Temple seems anything but sexual; it seems more rooted in a desire to punish than to have sexual relations. This behavior, the specific ways in which Popeye becomes described in the novel, and the juxtaposition of Popeye and Horace indicate the more general attitudes toward manliness and sexuality caught up in definitions and actualizations of paternalistic masculinity.

The version of masculinity associated with Horace and the term gentleman obviously relates to the idealistic, chivalric aspect of paternalistic masculinity—the side that treats all women like ladies and that Horace epitomizes almost in caricature. Men identifying with this version of masculinity struggle with the act of sexuality to some extent because men who are supposed to treat all women like ladies find it difficult to have sexual relations with ladies. Thus, in order to have sexual relations at all, something Horace seems perfectly willing not to do, men identifying with this definition of masculinity unconsciously need to project women as inherently sexual, creatures who are dirty and who are seen to bewitch men into having sexual relations. Even here, men will have "to steel" themselves for the experience, refusing any intimate relation or any shred of human feeling for the event or the woman. This is the aspect Popeye represents.[16]

Of course, for a long time the social structure of the South allowed upper class men to maintain this perverse attitude toward women and sexuality. They had their lady in the big house, safely ensconced, and their "dirty women" in the city or in the slave quarters, always available. As the social structure changed, however, men found it more difficult to maintain this situation, both in personal and social terms, and had more and more to face both aspects of their masculinity—their gentlemanly side and their manly side, so to speak.[17] The social world of *Sanctuary* resembles this world; the two sides of paternalist masculinity cannot exist in the same man any longer. But the narrative perspective itself highlights that of paternalism, and Horace and Popeye, like the fractured mirror images they are, embody the dual aspects of paternalist masculinity.

A key aspect of this definition of masculinity is the objectification of women. Horace objectifies women into ladies for whom he can fight the good fight, denying their sexual presence, praising them as if they were statues, goddesses—ladies on the pedestal. These attitudes are revealed in the way he treats Ruby, Lee Goodwin's common-law wife, refusing to see her as anything else but a damsel in distress, and in his attitudes toward Narcissa, who becomes identified as "heroic statuary" (*SR* 110). Popeye's objectification takes the form of making women simply dirty objects to be used and thrown aside: to him, all women are whores. Both these attitudes derive from the same paternalist impulse not to see women as flesh and blood human beings with whom their natural human drive for sexuality, intimacy, and fusion can be consummated.

Another key aspect of this version of masculinity, however, is the objectification of men themselves. For Horace this objectification denies precisely the close association indicated by two people's entwining their lives together in marriage. Intimacy and the concomitant loss of psychological isolation cause Horace to yearn to be "counsellor, handmaiden, and friend" (*SO* 19)—anything but intimate husband and lover. A platonic, idealistic relationship—that is, a nonmaterial one—with women is Horace's goal precisely because it does not involve sex, that "dirty business." On the other hand, as the projection of the sexual side of the paternalist masculinity, Popeye's is precisely that "dirty business," and his actions reveal what that entails for men. The use of the corncob in the rape scene represents the dire need of the paternalist to remain as detached as possible from the sexual act. Paternalists never want to get themselves "dirty," and Popeye's specific behavior—using a corncob and blaming Temple—symbolize this wish. Moreover, descriptions of Popeye throughout the novel indicate that he is

less human than machine: "His face had a queer bloodless color
. . . he had that vicious depthless quality of stamped tin" (*SR* 4); his
"eyes looked like rubber knobs" and he looked "like a modernist
lampstand" (*SR* 6); he also seems part of his car when the door
opens without any movement on his part. As symbolic embodiment of the sexual side of the paternalist, Popeye comes to reveal
how paternalistic men had to objectify themselves, to make themselves into inhuman machines in order to partake in sexual relations. He epitomizes the effects on men within this version of
masculinity—the mechanization of the male body.

Indeed, Popeye's treatment of Temple symbolizes, in an extreme and exaggerated manner, the way paternalist men approach
women. Their actions have nothing to do with pleasure, but with
violence and punishment. Punishment for sexual women must be
enacted through violence on the female body, and men will do
anything to avoid contact with this body. This aspect of Horace is
not revealed for the most part because he remains so much in
control, so safe from the impulses which would conjure these reactions from him. In an imagined scene in the original version of the
novel, however, Faulkner reveals the connection between Horace
and Popeye, gentleman and rapist. When Horace's repressed, true
nature becomes revealed, we see the killer within the gentlemanly
exterior, the beast in the jungle that comprises part of the paternalistic masculine identity. Horace's fixation about cleanliness becomes a vicious comment on women.

In this scene Horace has become sick of the trial and thinks
about how he could end it and go to Europe. He explains, "The
first thing would be to clean up the mess. He would sub-poena
Temple; he thought in a paroxysm of raging pleasure of flinging
her into the courtroom, of stripping her: This is what a man has
killed another over. This, the offspring of respectable people. . . .
Stripping her, background, environment, all" (*SO* 255). Though
often read as an indication of Horace's sexual desire for Temple,
this scene implies punitive, violent desires rather than sexual ones.
Horace wants to clean away all that might hide what Temple truly
is—a woman, to strip her down to the bare essential—her body.

He wishes, that is, to reveal that her body contains the fault, holds the blame, and certainly is not worth one man killing another. Horace does not want to clean up the mess Temple has made but the mess her body is in and of itself.

Ultimately, then, Horace and Popeye feel the same way about Temple. Any woman who behaves the way Temple does is inherently dirty and should be punished harshly. In fact, if a woman does not control herself and behave cleanly, "Better for her if she were dead" (*SR* 232), as Horace says about Temple. Popeye does indeed enact what Horace represses, and these two characters symbolize two aspects of the same ideology. As both men reveal, the consequences of this ideology are dire for the paternalist demeanor is one of controlled violence and repression, his nature deadly. Attempting to "kill off" the need for physical intimacy and emotional closeness in himself, the paternalist becomes an armored death machine, enacting both suicide and murder. Needing to avoid his twisted dread of these same human essentials, he becomes a repressive, control-oriented robot enjoying punishment rather than pleasure. Faulkner's novel thus becomes part of a discourse revealing and struggling with a masculinist death vision. From locking "madwomen in the attic," to worshiping frozen images of women which they do not touch; from armoring themselves for either competitive or deadly battle with one another, to using "mother earth" for their own purposes, paternalists represent a death-in-life principle.[18]

The Social Psychology of Paternalism

As has been indicated throughout this discussion, within a world or a novel dominated by a paternalist perspective, paternalist psychological fantasies do not simply have psychological effects. Paternalist ideology works to create a social world and individual subjects that fulfill the paternalist's psychic needs. Thus, masculine fantasies can be said to become projected outward onto social reality. Because of the way in which paternalist men need to define their relation to the world, repressing all that flows, social power becomes equated with control, cleanliness, order, stasis—a near pristine state that denies affection and intimacy, sexuality and emotion, as well as change, mobility, motion. Because women become the embodiment of both the desire for and the dread of sexuality and intimacy, paternalist fantasies project two different types of women. The image of woman that permits the paternalist to maintain the image he has of himself and thus to maintain his social power Theweleit has labelled "the white woman." The image that threatens the paternalist's need for control, stasis, and sterility and thus shakes the structure of his psychic world and threatens the social reality it upholds he has labelled "the red woman." In blunt terms, these types of women are the lady/sister/ wife, and whore, respectively.

As Theweleit explains, the white woman remains the safe woman; clothed in her white uniform or dress, almost it seems already in her sepulchre, this woman inspires men to leave her to perform great deeds for her benefit—or so the men say. This woman is glorified and deified, always in absentia; her image looms significantly, her body ignored completely. She helps the paternalist maintain his control and calm by shunning sexually explicit clothes, language, and behavior; she mollifies his combined need for and dread of sexuality and intimacy by allowing him to play the role of counsellor and friend. The red woman, on the other hand, does not accept or fulfill these roles. She shakes off the constraining white garments, in any number of ways, revealing both her own and the men's needs and desires. In asserting this type of subjectivity, this woman threatens the men's ability to control themselves. Always in a state of constant tension due to their perpetual repression of needs and desires, these men read these women's behavior as a threat to their very being and world. As the men see it, she has "only one thing on her mind," and, as we have seen, they often punish her.

In *Sanctuary* Narcissa Benbow can easily be seen to represent the proper role, image for women, especially upper class women, within paternalism. Narcissa lives in "the home of her husband's people" (*SR* 24), walled in and protected by their name and heritage. She always dresses in white, and she remains one of the "sheltered chaste women" (*SR* 121). She lives with no man and has only nonsexual relations with men; she is inviolable and impenetrable. She need not be controlled by men because she has so definitely accepted her role and controls herself. She is safe: she will have no impure thoughts and she will cause no unwanted emotions. Narcissa is indeed the idealized woman on the pedestal—statuesque, frozen in time, the proper state for women within paternalism.

Clearly, the most prominent aspect of Narcissa's character is the absolute quiet that surrounds her. There is never a rushed movement, never a spontaneous outburst; in all descriptions of her she retains a stillness. This state indicates, and her actions reveal, that she will never be moved from her position as the white woman. In this role, she is appalled by Horace's actions: she sees his leaving Belle as the actions of "a nigger" (*SR* 112), and she refuses to allow him to offer Ruby a room in their old house: she does not see Ruby as a lady in distress but as a whore. She is also horrified by Horace's involvement in the trial of people who are "not his people," that is, who are below him. Revealing how her subjectivity has been defined by the paternalist social order, Narcissa's reactions oppose sexuality—the low and base emotions, oppose associating with those "below" one's social station, and oppose the upheaval of the social order.

These attributes are heightened by the contrast between Narcissa and the other significant women characters: Ruby and Temple. Both Ruby and Narcissa are housekeepers and mothers of children, yet, while we see Ruby cook, clean, and change her child's diapers, we never see Narcissa involved in similar activities. As an upper class woman Narcissa never gets her hands wet or dirty, while Ruby, who is "common," is associated with fluids, liquids, dirt, and sexuality. Within the masculinist fantasy world, and the social reality it works to create, this is as it should be. Both characters reveal female roles defined by paternalism. If these characters seem "real," it is because paternalism still has influence on the ways in which American society defines roles for women according to class. Not at all connected to universal definitions of women, which do not exist, both characters embody rather projections of the real that paternalist fantasies place onto the social definitions of women. When the novel focuses on the story of Temple Drake, however, it confronts a woman who threatens to topple these limited definitions. In her actions, Temple reveals she has not accepted, yet, the role prescribed to her by the paternalist ideology dominating the novel's perspective. In her attempt to define herself, to define her own subjectivity, Temple is a threat to this perspective and is thus the perfect personification of the red woman.[19]

Though when we first meet Temple she is not associated with fluids as Belle is, she most definitely becomes associated with fluidity and motion. She has "long legs blonde with running" (SR 29), and throughout the novel she constantly moves, runs, darts, whirls, spins, and writhes. In fact, this fluidity of motion defines her entire subjectivity as she hardly ever stays still: she never stays with one boy, always drives around to different places, her favorite activity is dancing. Within this narrative perspective, this very "running around," Temple's mobile subjectivity comes to represent her defiance of the role of the white woman (or lady) which she is supposed to occupy by virtue of her class. Unlike Narcissa, Temple refuses to sit still and mollify the twisted forces of desire and repression charging the masculine world around her. She expects to be treated on her own terms. That, however, cannot be tolerated.

As the narrative makes clear, Temple's very "running around" leads to her rape. As Gowan's comment indicates, "Look out . . . you're getting all that stuff stirred up in me again" (SR 54), and Ruby's reiterates, "If she'd just stopped running around where they had to look at her" (SR 169), Temple's constant motion leads people to think she should be manhandled, that in fact she wants to be. From the paternalist perspective of the novel, it does not matter that almost all of Temple's movements indicate resistance and flight; it does not matter that they indicate independence and agency rather than desire; movement, motion, fluidity—anthing that flows or streams—is read as seductive and threatening. We should not be surprised that Temple paints her mouth "boldly scarlet" (SR 38) or that she has red hair, for, from the novel's paternalist perspective, she stands in direct opposition to Narcissa and represents the "the red woman." By filling the expectations of that role, Temple becomes threatening; she must be punished, "put down," as it were.

The first time Temple is still for any duration occurs during the rape scene itself. Finally, her motion has been stilled; her identity "pinned down," importantly, *for her*. The red woman has been punished. Within the patriarchal social conditions in this novel, Temple's rape represents the culmination of a sick and perverted logic: Temple's constant motion defined her as a red woman; Popeye has been emasculated by the social system—Faulkner takes pains in the revised version to explain his background—and thus feels the most pressure to exert some power over her. This action does serve as a punishment, of sorts, in that it curtails Temple's mobililty; at the same time, this punishment is not the proper one for Temple from the perspective of the paternalists for it only releases the wild, chaotic forces which they think always lurk in women. Temple obviously needs further treatment, from their perspective, in order to be restored to her proper place—frozen on the pedestal. Likewise, the lower class needs to be shown its proper place.

The need to return Temple to the position of lady and to punish the lower class represents how the paternalist's need to repress sexuality connects to the way he must repress all associated with sexuality in society. As Theweleit explains, the way in which patriarchs want to control emotions from flooding their psyche and causing a whirlwind within the order of their subjective identity parallels the way in which they wish to control the lower elements of society from "rising up" and causing a threat to the social order. As they must repress the "low and base" elements of their psyches, they must repress the same elements of society. In *Sanctuary* Faulkner clearly links female sexuality to the lower class. We have already seen the associations among images of dirt, liquids, and female sexuality and how all of these become related to the figure of Popeye through the one, repeated image of the black liquid. Specific images related to female sexuality are connected to the lower class in other ways as well: Pap constantly spits into a hand-kerchief, reminding us of Belle's handkerchief, which disgusted Horace; Popeye also has a handkerchief, a soiled one, reminding us of Horace's request that Little Belle not soil her shoes by associ-ating with the wrong type of boys; the men at the Old French-man's Place always spit, reminding us of the dirty liquids with which sexual women are generally associated. The threat of female sexuality, then, becomes directly connected to the paternalist's fear of threat from the lower class. After Temple's experiences with Popeye and Red, the perspective of the novel demands that a "foul and filthy" aspect of both the personal psyche and the social order must be controlled, punished, "set straight." The desired state of psychological calm demands a state of social calm.

That these two threats to paternalist social order are the signifi-cant concerns of the novel, rather than the specific events sur-rounding Temple's rape, becomes dramatically revealed in the trial. Ironically enough, Lee is not on trial for rape but for murder, both having been committed by Popeye. For the paternalists, though, the point is not to find Tommy's murderer or Temple's rapist. It is, on the one hand, to punish the lower class, to set an example so none step over the boundaries again, and, on the other, to rescue Temple from this class and from the raging demons within her. To them, the crime is not the physical attack on the individual woman: since women are seen to cause sexual feelings in men, that can scarcely be a crime at all. Rather, the crime is the threat to the dominant order. Both Lee and Popeye die, both for crimes they didn't commit; no matter, their deaths serve as re-minders to others. Meanwhile, Temple is taken away from Popeye and Red, and returned to "these good men, these fathers and hus-bands" (SR 299).

Short of the death Horace wished for her, Temple experiences a living death after the trial. In their cooperation with this process, the Drakes show their (class) allegiance to Horace's unspoken pu-nitive desires. They allow Temple to be condemned publicly and to serve as an example of what happens to girls who behave as she did. Returned to the control of father and brothers for another, hopefully more long-lasting lesson in discipline, Temple's agency is voided and she is returned to her role of lady. Represented by the statues of dead queens at which she gazes at novel's end, Temple's position now is one of stasis, stillness; like Narcissa's state of heroic statuary, Temple is now back where the paternalists want her.[20]

Interestingly enough, though Temple is in the proper state of immobility and stasis at novel's end, she is not in the state of Mississippi; she is in Europe. Her physical removal seems to indicate the increasing lack of power these paternalists have over the social world of Jefferson. Though the novel's perspective has been dominated by paternalism, Horace's own failures to revive his patrilineal heritage or to bring the principles of "law, justice, civilization" to bear on Lee Goodwin's trial also point directly to an absence of paternalism's power in the current social world. These failures signal the passing of paternalism in a manner very much like Quentin Compson's suicide indicated a similar passing in *The Sound and the Fury*. Thus, the perverse duality of paternalism's definition of masculinity no longer has a social structure that can support its continuation either, and the novel shows that the representations of that masculinity must change: Horace returns to his wife and Popeye accepts execution. Now, the bourgeois world of Jefferson itself, represented by the District Attorney, the church ladies, and the men who hang Goodwin, will ascend, and different definitions of masculinity and femininity will develop to some extent as will different relationships to sexuality. As shown by the D.A.'s association with Judge Drake and by the attitudes of the men outside the jail, these different definitions will not be completely new, however: they certainly will maintain some definitively patriarchal attitudes.

Reading *Sanctuary* from a perspective seeking to integrate psychological fixations with social reality, recognizing ideological formations as the link between the personal and the social, allows us to understand this novel as part of the ideological, cultural history

with which Faulkner was intricately involved—the intensely complicated transition from one kind of world, the Old South, to another. *Sanctuary* reveals in vivid detail the ways in which this
transition touched even the most personal aspect of people's lives,
how attitudes toward sexuality and intimacy are linked to the ideological formation with which characters are identified, and how
the ideological perspective guiding this world was rooted in a
twisted web of desire, fear and dread. Perhaps, as Noel Polk has
hinted, *Sanctuary* reveals all these so dramatically because Faulkner was so "close" to the matrix of forces shown in *Sanctuary*.
Unlike Horace, though, who could not decipher the logical pattern
of evil because he was so immersed within its tangled strands,
Faulkner seems able to depict both the inner psychological root of
paternalism as well as its dire consequences and social ramifications. Ultimately, *Sanctuary* seems to indicate that the only embrace left for people within paternalism is "the embrace of the
season of rain and death" (*SR* 333) into which Temple falls at novel's end. Horace's sanctuary was an idealization of the past, but
Faulkner's novel reveals that the past, unfortunately, is not everything he might have wanted it to be.

NOTES

1. Until very recently when feminist readings of *Sanctuary* have begun to surface,
Freudian analyses have been the most convincing and stimulating discussions of this novel.
Perhaps the best one is John T. Matthews's, "The Elliptical Nature of *Sanctuary*," *Novel*
17 (1984): 246–66. Another very good psychoanalytical reading is John T. Irwin, "Horace
Benbow and the Myth of Narcissa," *American Literature* 64.3 (1992): 543–66. For a feminist
reading see Diane Roberts, "Ravished Belles: Stories of Rape and Resistance in *Flags in
the Dust* and *Sanctuary*," *Faulkner Journal* 4.1, 2 (1988/1989): 21–36 and her extended
discussion in *Faulkner and Southern Womanhood* (Athens: University of Georgia Press,
1994).
2. My understanding of the productive nature of ideology stems from Louis Althusser
and Terry Eagleton. Eagleton summarizes Althusser's contribution to the theory of ideology
when he states: "Ideology is now not just a distortion . . . a screen which intervenes between ourselves and reality. . . . It is an indispensable medium for the production of human
subjects. Among the various modes of production in any society, there is one whose task is
the production of forms of human subjectivity" (148). And as Althusser states, "ideology
interpellates concrete individuals as concrete subjects" (173). In other words, what allows
individual human beings to become social subjects is ideology; thus, whether one's behavior gets associated with the social subject of "lady" or "whore" or "gentleman" or "man"
has everything to do with ideology. Louis Althusser, "Ideology and Ideological State Apparatuses," *Lenin and Philosophy and Other Essays*, trans. Ben Brewster (New York: Monthly

Review Press, 1971), 127–86. Terry Eagleton, *Ideology: An Introduction* (London: Verso, 1991).

3. Noel Polk, "The Space Between *Sanctuary,*" *Intertexuality in Faulkner* (University Press of Mississippi, 1985), 34.

4. Joseph Blotner, *William Faulkner: A Biography* (New York: Random House, 1974), 531–32.

5. These quotations appear in the revised version of the novel, pages 295 and 280, respectively. Throughout the article I quote extensively from both versions of the novel, seeing them as two parts of an extended text as suggested by Noel Polk. All subsequent references to these texts are cited parenthetically: *Sanctuary: The Original Text*, ed. Noel Polk (New York: Random House, 1981), cited as *SO*; *Sanctuary: The Corrected Text*, ed. Noel Polk (New York: Vintage Books, 1987), cited as *SR*.

6. Horace Benbow and his world have been labelled bourgeois by many critics. When used, though, this label seems to have less to do with the name for historically specific class formation or with relationships to a specific society than it does with a description of behavior or qualities that the individual critic seems to dislike. Bourgeois can be associated with relying on appearance over reality as in Donald Petesch, "Temple Drake: Faulkner's Mirror for the Social Order," *Studies in American Fiction* 7.1 (Spring 1979): 37–48, or with effeminate, superficial qualities, as in Noel Polk. Here, I use it as a description of a class with its own ideology, usually called liberalism; this class and its ideology are very different from a plantocratic society and its ideology, paternalism.

7. John T. Irwin, "Horace Benbow and the Myth of Narcissa," *American Literature* 64.3 (1992): 543.

8. Klaus Theweleit, *Male Fantasies, Volume 1: Women, Floods, Bodies, History* (Minneapolis: University of Minnesota Press, 1987) and *Volume 2: Male Bodies: Psychoanalyzing the White Terror* (Minneapolis: University of Minnesota Press, 1989).

Theweleit's work has come to have an influence on various scholars' work. Within Faulkner studies, Anne Goodwyn Jones has compared his ideas to the depictions of men within Faulkner's war stories. See "Male Fantasies? Faulkner's War Stories and the Construction of Gender," *Faulkner and Psychology*, ed. Donald M. Kartiganer and Ann J. Abadie, (Jackson: University Press of Mississippi, 1994), 21–55.

9. Barbara Ehrenreich, "Foreword" to *Male Fantasies, Volume 1*, xv.

10. Descriptions of the Old Frenchman's Place read as follows: "The house was a gutted ruin rising gaunt and stark out of a grove of unpruned cedar trees. . . . gardens and lawns long since gone back to jungle" (*SR* 8). Descriptions of Horace's patrilineal home read: "The house was of red brick . . . in the uncut grass that year after year had gone rankly and lustily back to seed. . . . The cedars needed pruning too, their dark tips . . . breaking on against the house itself in a fixed whelming surge" (*SO* 61).

11. For a further discussion of these ideas see Anson Rabinbach and Jessica Benjamin, "Foreword," *Male Fantasies, Volume 2*.

12. Polk, 27.

13. Roberts, 27. Roberts discusses here and in her book as well how in Faulkner's canon evil is a code word for female sexuality. I agree. There are many similarities between the way Roberts and I read both the South's sexual politics and *Sanctuary*, though our insights come from different avenues of investigation.

14. André Bleikasten, "Terror and Nausea: Bodies in *Sanctuary,*" *Faulkner Journal* 1.1 (Fall 1985): 17–29.

15. Other critics have assumed that Horace's identification in this scene is with Temple, that he "becomes" Temple, primarily because of the reference to the shucks. I believe, however, that the movement of Horace's thoughts is away from Temple to envisioning Little Belle in a scene like the one Temple experiences. Earlier in the book, Horace remembers his trip on a train with Little Belle, and this horrific scene seems to place her back on a train without Horace, that is, unescorted, as was Temple. Her deflowering seems to be enacted in Horace's nightmare.

16. In relation to this point, we can recall Quentin Compson's remarks to his sister, Caddy, when she discovers him fooling around with Natalie in the barn. He calls Natalie

"a dirty girl." William Faulkner, *The Sound and the Fury: The Corrected Text*, ed. Noel Polk (New York: Vintage, 1984), 134.

17. That Horace is undergoing this implicit conflict is indicated in a couple of places in the novel. After he tells Ruby that God might be foolish but at least He's a gentleman, she tells him that she always thought He was a man. Later, in conversation with Horace, Lee comments, "What kind of man are you?"—implying that Horace is no kind of man at all. In this new world, this new social structure, all that had maintained Horace's definition of masculinity is in the process of fading.

Gowan's situation also indicates a struggle between definitions of gentleman and man. Gowan overtly attempts to decipher whether Temple is either a lady or a whore so that he will know how to treat her. However, as his embarrassment about getting drunk and vomiting and his interactions with both Narcissa and Temple reveal, he more covertly struggles with whether he is a gentleman or a man. In his treatment of Narcissa, Gowan seems to want to adopt all the trappings of the Southern gentleman courting the lady. In his treatment of Temple he seems to want to prove he is a man by "having his way with her." He never seems to resolve any of these conflicts; thus, he can also be said to show that both aspects of paternalist masculinity cannot exist in the same man in this new social world.

18. This definition of masculinity slips into some people's criticism of Faulkner as well. Polk comments: "Doubtless part of [Horace] admires the Negro's neat, simple, passionate solution to his marital troubles [that is, cutting off his wife's head], and perhaps in his *fantasies* he wishes he were aggressive enough, *masculine* enough, passionate enough, to solve his own problems so completely" (21; my emphasis). To identify this kind of behavior with masculinity is an ideological statement influenced by an historically specific version of masculinity. Theweleit offers the best response: "The sexuality of the patriarch is less 'male' than it is deadly" (I, 221–22).

19. All the cases discussed in this section of my article reveal just how much the novel's perspective does derive from that of paternalism as well as how much this novel exposes the social ramifications of masculine fantasies. The subjectivities or personalities revealed by Narcissa, Popeye, Ruby, and Temple all derive from the ideology of paternalism. These are positions through which this ideology works to identify individuals. (In Temple's case, the holders of this ideology had to work harder than in the other cases.) That Temple *would* be treated by poor, out-of-work men the way she is in *Sanctuary* is no more "true" than if she subdued them via kung-fu and brought them to the authorities; or if she fell in love with one boy there who returned her home and was rewarded by the father with money to attend college. All of these stories *could* occur, depending on the perspective the writer takes to tell the tale: if Temple's explorations into sexuality were narrated by Kate Chopin, say, we would probably read a very different story. Likewise, to depict reactions to a rape the way they are depicted here, as if this experience would unleash raging lust, seems particularly, and even absurdly, the perspective of a paternalist.

Even if we can find people in our world who do behave in the way these characters do, we cannot deny the perspective from which this book depicts the behaviors of its characters. Like the real people they might represent, these characters reveal the operations of an ideology on the subjects it seeks to create—to some extent, exactly what *Sanctuary* is about.

In this context, my view parallels Minrose Gwin's claims that looking for examples of "authentic female subjectivity" (64) in Faulkner is a fruitless activity. Rarely, if ever, does one find women in Faulkner who are not essentially projections of male fear and/or desire. Minrose Gwin, "Feminism and Faulkner: Second Thoughts or, What's a radical feminist doing with a canonical male text anyway?" *Faulkner Journal* 4.1 and 2 (Fall 1988/Spring 1989): 55–66.

20. In "Desire and Despair: Temple Drake's Self-Victimization," *Faulkner and Women*, ed. Doreen Fowler and Ann J. Abadie (Jackson: University Press of Mississippi, 1986), 112–27, Robert Moore argues that Temple's passivity after her rape reveals her complicity with evil. But, Temple has already been taught that activity, on her part, *is* dangerous; how else can she behave? To blame her is to assign blame to the wrong party.

X Marks the Spot: Faulkner's Garden

DAWN TROUARD

"As a literary critic [woman] might fabricate strategic 'misreadings.' . . . She might, by the superimposition of suitable allegory, draw a reading out of the text that relates it to the historico-social differential of the body. This move should, of course, be made scrupulously explicit."

GAYATRI SPIVAK, "DISPLACEMENT AND
THE DISCOURSE OF WOMAN"

"And [Thalberg's] sense for 'the pulse of America' was well expressed when he dismissed an assistant's protests about a scenario that called for a love scene in Paris to be played against a backdrop of a moonlit ocean. The assistant brought him maps and photographs to demonstrate that Paris is nowhere near any ocean. 'We can't cater to a handful of people who know Paris,' said Thalberg, refusing to make any change in the script."

OTTO FRIEDRICH, *City of Nets*

1. "I threw myself on a bench and began to wonder if there was anything better in the world worth doing than to sit in an alley of clipped limes smoking, thinking of Paris and of myself." George Moore, *Memoirs of My Dead Life*

One of the righteous vanities of Faulknerians is that we know the woe of genealogy—from textual production to McCaslin ledgers. Those who were drawn into Jim Hinkle's *Reading Faulkner* project[1] for the University Press of Mississippi in the mid-1980s now live with the ghost, not just of Jim, but the project itself (and the five solid inches of correspondence that Jim generated from its inception until his death in December of 1990). The authors of the series share with the press editors (who probably want these

volumes published, not because they hope to buy a chair but because the editors may, nearly a decade after all of the editors of
the series signed the agreements, *must have* begun to feel as if
they invented Jim, or maybe they [the press editors] suspect that
it must have taken Jim to invent the authors, and so want some sort
of special editorial revenge on those deadline-missing demons) a
desire to rake up as many rag-tag and bob-ends of history as possible in order to overpass to readings of Faulkner's novels that could
make them accessible enough.

In the process of working so closely and for so long on *Sanctuary*, pursuing Jim's charge to fill in all the blanks and catalogue all,
I have in this reading perhaps been seduced by the serendipitous
at the expense of the comfortably speculative. My plan is to arrive
in *Sanctuary*'s Paris, with embarkation from Ohio, since the spon-
sors of this trip are some students, almost all Generation Xers, the
likes of whom any Faulkner teacher has probably found in recent
classes.[2] In the course of my journey, I will discuss the actual
Parisian gardens that served as site for *Sanctuary*'s and press connections between Gustave Flaubert and Marie de Medicis, acknowledged presences in the Luxembourg Gardens, but forces, I
believe, in Faulkner's conception of that final image of Temple in
the garden.

Prompting more than its fair share of critical attention, *Sanctuary*'s complications do not stop with its apocryphal origins. It was
a scandal in its own time—the corncob rape of an abducted coed,
a Southern lynching, a touch of sodomy, Memphis brothels—
fueled by the provocative comments of its author writing at the
peak of his form and already savvy about throwing people off his
track. For a long time, Faulkner's disingenuous claims misdirected
readers: "To me it is a cheap idea, because it was deliberately
conceived to make money. . . . I took a little time out, and specu-
lated what a person in Mississippi would believe to be current
trends, chose what I thought was the right answer and invented
the most horrific tale I could imagine and wrote it in about three
weeks."[3]

Later Faulkner also claimed that he paid for the privilege of

rewriting *Sanctuary* so it wouldn't shame his other books, specifically *The Sound and the Fury* and *As I Lay Dying*.[4] Given what we
know about the intensity of Faulkner's desire to achieve literary
greatness, I am not sure why his crass disclaimer so appealed to
readers; but unlearning it, even with the help of evidence accumulated by critic Noel Polk, has proven hard. Polk's edition of *Sanctuary: The Original Text* makes it clear that even in *Sanctuary's*
earliest incarnations it was far more than a cheap idea. Faulkner's
painstaking revisions confirm that he was hardly tossing off any
slick piece of fiction. Polk notes that on top of Faulkner's usual
deletions, additions, and minor stylistic emendations, Faulkner
pasted long passages scissored from other, earlier pages, sometimes two or three such passages per page. Nearly all the pages
were shifted during the writing. One page bears twenty-two different page numbers indicating Faulkner continued shifting materials
almost obsessively, throughout revisions.[5] Polk has tried forever to
move Faulknerians to this next improbable level: to read *Sanctuary: The Original Text* as seriously as we have managed to read the
1932 Modern Library edition and its spawn[6] to see how they read
as companions, to see the craft of revision, to see at least two
novels.

   Perhaps Faulkner's claim about his artistic intention was merely
an indicator of his intense desire to be artistically unsponsored,
impervious; maybe it offered no clue to the value he placed on the
book, but was rather something he said to keep the public at bay.[7]
Even when *Sanctuary* managed to escape the tincture of Faulkner's dubious assessment, however, it suffered the other fate: it
entered "the canon," hazarding the cultural blight reserved for
works of genius. The novel was fixed in and by its greatness. [8]
Once great, it warranted attention and justified its institutional
commodification through its critical yield. *Sanctuary* has prompted
critics to debate Temple's rape, Faulkner's view of dysfunctional
families, the theme of voyeurism, Southern myths, its pop cultural
connections, Faulkner's misogyny, and impotency—the law's and
Horace's. By the early 1980s there were already sumptuous foot-
notes summarizing *Sanctuary's* critical heritage and preparing the

reader for yet-another-new-study-of-Why-Temple-Lied. In "Be-wildered Witness: Temple Drake in *Sanctuary*," Elisabeth Muh-lenfeld's first footnote captures the prototypical critical and historical assumptions generated by *Sanctuary*: "Attempts to ex-plain Temple (and *Sanctuary* in general) in psychological terms have been made since the earliest analyses of the novel."[9] She proceeds to round up the usual suspects from Lawrence S. Kubie to Olga W. Vickery.

Each year since 1986 brings more essays to thicken the end-notes, fill in spaces, and locate significant absences.[10] Even when these critics intend to disrupt the status quo, the canonical order continues stable; more specifically, the dead queens in the final paragraph never budge.[11] Still more curious is the significant con-sensus in what critics select from the text—even when they are on their way to radically different conclusions about what the evi-dence "leaves so little doubt about."[12] Critics looking at the end of *Sanctuary* have offered a particularly false stability. Muhlenfeld again serves as a standard. She concludes: "Temple is not bitter, not guilt-ridden, but 'sullen and discontented and sad' (379–80). Her sadness is the appropriate response to the world of *Sanctuary*. Although we like her even less at the novel's close than we ever have, we share that sadness. Faulkner's Temple Drake has been diminished by the world around her and by her own smallness."[13] Muhlenfeld claims this diminishment reduces us all—as readers, we shrink with Temple.

I would like to pose another way to think about the end(s) of *Sanctuary*, to ask the questions about why Faulkner decided to have Temple's journey end in the Luxembourg Gardens.[14] My pur-pose is not to retravel the circuits already plenty well negotiated, if not resolved, by previous guides. I don't want to tamper with any of the established approaches. Instead, I prefer to excavate some elements submerged in the text which I think shaped Faulk-ner's sense of self at this juncture in his career. This reading per-mits another possibility for Temple and deepens Faulkner's debt to Flaubert. Refusing to discover *other* possibilities for Temple has trapped critics in a false binaryism: good girl or bad girl; nightmare figure or realistic 1920s coed; existence meaningful or not.[15]

Faulkner's own misogynistic comments are probably most responsible for some of the rigid readings of Temple's character:
"women are impervious to evil. . . . How she sat there on a bench,
so quiet and serene? And just as if none of those horrific things
that happened to her in the old house and the corn crib or in the
whore house with Popeye and her lover, Red, even occurred. She
wasn't demoralized or touched by any of it. All of it was like water
falling on a duck's back and sliding right off."[16] Such a depiction
encouraged critics to find Temple an agent of evil and the instrument of the novel's horrifically dark vision. This version of Temple
harmonized naturally with Horace's bleak summary of defeat:
"Spring . . . [y]ou'd almost think there was some purpose to it."[17]
More sympathetic, feminist readings have attempted to see in
Temple's behavior the broken victim of a culture which exploits
the powerless, objectifies and consumes women, and abuses justice.[18] Yet, whether the critics found Temple to be pure evil or a
traumatized survivor, nearly all commentary on *Sanctuary* includes the novel's lush finale in the Gardens where critical opinion
achieves surprising unanimity. Faulkner fostered this certitude by
a letter he wrote to his mother:

> I have come to think of the Luxembourg as my garden now. I sit and
> write there, and walk around to watch the children, and the croquet
> games. I always carry a piece of bread to feed the sparrows. . . . I have
> just written such a beautiful thing that I am about to bust—2000 words
> about the Luxembourg Gardens and death. It has a thin thread of plot,
> about a young woman, and it is poetry though written in prose form. I
> have worked on it for two whole days and every word is perfect . . . a
> jewel.[19]

With amazing accord, critics assent to the view that this jewel
became in the revised *Sanctuary* the final scene which so pleased
its ratty-faced author.[20]

2. "Paris is now the capital of limbo." Janet Flanner,
"Paris Germany"

Sanctuary's images of the Gardens are precisely borne out by
the descriptions in the 1924 *Baedeker for Paris and Its Environs.*

Faulkner took a train from Geneva to Paris on Sunday 16 August
1925.[21] There is no way to know for certain whether he carried any
guide to Paris with him when he made his way to the city that
the expatriates had chosen as the site "to create the twentieth-
century."[22] If he did, the *Baedeker* confirms for tourists that the
fountains "play" daily from 1 April to 30 September; water reaches
the Gardens through an aqueduct modeled on a Roman one;
model yachts can be hired for use on the octagonal pond; the military bands play under the trees; and "the gardens consist chiefly
of clumps of trees and playgrounds provided with benches and
adorned with sculptures." The *Baedeker* further notes several
points of interest which have special bearing on *Sanctuary*: "On
the terraces overlooking the basin are twenty marble statues of
famous French women and in a Southeast part of the garden a
monument to *Gustave Flaubert.*" The guide also directs readers,
by the way, to various tributes to Balzac, Stendahl, Berlioz, and
George Sand.[23]

In the first battery of his letters from Paris (13 August 1925 to 22
September 1925) included in Blotner's *Selected Letters,* Faulkner
mentions the Luxembourg Gardens in ten of the twelve. He uses
the Gardens to mark his arrival in the first hotel, "not far away
from the Luxembourg gardens" (*SL* 11) near the Louvre and the
Seine, and Notre Dame. Three days later, he has been to the Bastille, Père Lachaise (to see Oscar Wilde's tomb), and he waxes
eloquent about the Gardens, the children sailing boats, the boat
rental man, and the yacht races. On 18 September Faulkner is
installed in a new hotel at 26 rue Servandoni (11 francs a day) on
a street which runs nearly into the Gardens where he has already
established a sense of place—writing and watching children, admiring everything—but especially the way everything in the Gardens is set up for children: "the beautiful way the French love
their babies. They treat children as though they were the same age
as the grown-ups—they walk along the street together" (*SL* 13).
He has met a real painter who won't go to exhibitions and prefers
to go to the Luxembourg Gardens and watch "children sail their
boats" (*SL* 13), and Faulkner agrees with him.

By 26 August, Faulkner has discovered the all-day croquet games in the Gardens and the chance to bet on them. He goes to the galleries only if it rains; otherwise he is euphoric with his writing. Four days later, in his 30 August letter, Faulkner elaborates all the same ingredients—the boats "well made, of fine wood, and all flagged and pennoned like big ones. Think of a country where an old man, if he wants to, can spend his whole time with toy ships, and no one to call him crazy or make fun of him" (*SL* 15). He elaborates the croquet information and he rhapsodizes again about the beauty of French adults and their children. He plans, he tells his mother, to go the next day to Marie Antoinette's "hangout" (*SL* 16).

By 6 September he has written the ecstatic letter, observing in it that he has been unable to sleep "for two nights, thinking about it, comparing words, accepting and rejecting them, then changing again. But now it is perfect—a jewel" (*SL* 17). In this same letter, Faulkner reveals that he has become hooked on bus rides, and he also recounts his thoughts on French culture beyond the Gardens: "In almost every house there is a picture of Saint Genevieve, the patron saint of Paris, staring out over Paris at dusk. There is a beautiful one by Puvis de Chavannes in the Pantheon, where the unknown soldier's grave is" (*SL* 18). In the abridged versions of his life directed to his great-aunt, Faulkner reports spending all his time in the Gardens playing with children and helping them sail their boats. About the beautiful passage, he tells his great-aunt that "when he finished it," [he] "went to look at [himself] in the mirror" (*SL* 20).

In the letter postmarked 10 September, Faulkner tells about the near loss of his good knife in the Gardens and how everyone helped him to find it (*SL* 21). The arrival of relatives with a guidebook and the smugness of Americans on tour, however, prick his magical interlude; Faulkner declares he is getting tired of Paris and plans to travel. In the letter of 22 September, he describes the bandstand in the grove of chestnut trees in the Gardens and the sounds and sights from the Belgian Military Orchestra playing Chopin, Berlioz, and Wagner and he notes how the laborers and

the Senators and the children all stop to listen. This letter is relatively full of Faulkner the tourist; he reports on Rodin's museum,
the art he has seen, the Tuileries, and the Moulin Rouge. He's
even prompted to note that "[a]fter having observed Americans in
Europe I believe more than ever that sex with us has become a
national disease" (*SL* 24).

3. "There is never an ending to Paris." Ernest Hemingway,
A Moveable Feast

In *Sanctuary: The Original Text*, Temple sitting in the Luxembourg Gardens is not quite *the end* of the book. In this version,
Faulkner moves directly from Popeye's request to have his hair
adjusted at his execution into the description of the Gardens.
Faulkner concludes the Gardens scene, a line break follows, and
then occurs the italicized, *"Sure, the sheriff said, I'll fix it for you;
springing the trap."*[24] This arrangement, where Temple's gaze into
her compact is juxtaposed with Popeye's concern for his death
"do," is a culmination of the novel's thematic narcissism, a motif
linking characters like Temple and Popeye (and Horace) from early
chapters in both versions of the novel. Impotency and virility,
murder and execution, irony and justice, jails and public gardens,
dying and the vanity of human wishes converge, however disrup-
tively, in this final set of juxtapositions rendered through incident
and character. Though the prose of the Luxembourg Gardens
scene jars with the exceedingly naturalistic cadences of Popeye's
case history, the tonal anomalies have nonetheless served to affirm
for most critics the novel's coherence rather than disturb any of
the entrenched readings of *Sanctuary's meaning.*

In the revised *Sanctuary*, Faulkner first has Popeye ask for his
hair to be fixed, the trap opens, and then Faulkner's readers fall
into the Gardens. The novel ends with the imagery of rain and
death. It's easy to see how this second bleakness, so rhetorically
overwrought, would likely exceed the recommended daily needs
of nearly any critic in search of a high modernist text. But what
if the description of the Luxembourg Gardens—reserved for the

end—offers more than mere despair? What if the demands of modernistic irony require an alternative possibility: a defiance of despair simultaneously embedded in the scene? Suppose high modernism's jutting angles and vitiated seasons are only what tourists who pay the general admission price get to see on a critical tour?

Neither *Sanctuary: The Original Text* nor the revised version comes even close to the 2,000-word count Faulkner claims in his 6 September 1925 letter—though critics have discussed the passage as if it is one and the same. If the novel's two excerpted paragraphs—the 344 words—are in fact the euphoric passage he wrote to his mother about, no one is telling what became of the nearly 1,700 missing words.[25] Nor have readings accounted for Faulkner's radical shift in tone: why attach jeweled poetry to the end of such a bleak story about Temple Drake, Popeye, and Horace?

Though they are marble rather than jewels, the stained statues noted in the Paris guidebook provide figurative and literal connections to my reading of Faulkner's strategy. *Sanctuary*'s obvious debt to the actual Gardens, the statues, for instance, is enriched by subtle homages Faulkner was paying; these twenty marble statues of French women are in proximate location to two other garden habitués: Flaubert and Marie de Medicis. By setting *Sanctuary*'s final scene in the Luxembourg Gardens, Faulkner keeps Flaubert tacitly present. The French author's allusive appearance in the novel's opening scene is recalled when Horace notes Popeye "smells black . . . like that black stuff that ran out of Bovary's mouth and down upon her bridal veil when they raised her head."[26] Horace will shortly declaim on Little Belle, sexuality, and the female Trap of Nature.[27] However, Flaubert's monument so near signals more than a lone reinforcement of an isolated debt to *Madame Bovary*.

Faulkner's explicit tribute to *Madame Bovary* in *Sanctuary* highlights other affinities between the two authors. Both men shared kindred hostility for the bourgeoisie. Flaubert described it: "I am doing my best to rub their noses in their own turpitudes."[28] Similarly Faulkner's own sense that his hand held genius was matched by Flaubert's self-regard: "[w]hen I think of what it can be I am dazzled. But then, when I reflect that so much beauty has been entrusted to me, I am so terrified that I am seized with cramps and long to rush off and hide—anywhere."[29] Each man believed the author's personality should be erased from the art. According to Flaubert, the "ideal of Art demands that the artist show none of this, and that he appear in his work no more than God in nature. The man is nothing, the work is everything."[30] Compare this to Faulkner's famous "maybe what I think is humility is really immitigable pride. I would have preferred nothing at all prior to the instant I began to write, as though Faulkner and Typewriter were concomitant, coadjutant and without past on the moment they first faced each other at the suitable (nameless) table" (*SL* 222).

Faulkner's conflicted desire to connect with the masters—and to exceed them—is fundamental to Faulkner biography and criticism. These aesthetic points of contact between the artists inevitably made me wonder about what it must have been like for Faulkner to sit in *that* garden in *that* city. In *Faulkner in the University*, when he was asked about the expatriates in Europe, he used the metaphor of the writer getting lumber for his edifice, but he stressed that he didn't think of himself as a writer then: "I was a tramp, and I didn't—I wasn't interested in literature nor literary people. . . . I knew Joyce, I knew of Joyce, and I would go to some effort to go to the café that he inhabited to look at him. But that was the only literary man that I remember seeing in Europe in those days."[31] Like Temple, Faulkner lied.

4. "to be famous, on display in all the book shops, constantly mentioned in the newspapers, known all over France." Gustave Flaubert, *Madame Bovary*

We know Faulkner was reading—he claims to have worn out the books he brought to Europe, reading them "at least five times" while waiting to cash the $200 personal check he'd received from Liveright.[32] He would later refer to the reading from this period as "delayed repercussions like summer thunder [when] I discovered the Flauberts and Dostoievskys and Conrads."[33] Like everyone else who has read *Sanctuary*, I want that unidentified book in Horace's back pocket to be *Madame Bovary*. But I think the book was in Horace's pocket to do more than trigger the black smell given off by the black man. I think Flaubert was present for Faulkner in more ways than critics have even begun to acknowledge.

André Bleikasten, for instance, is one of the foremost commentators on the Emma Bovary connections to *Sanctuary*. Bleikasten's reading—along with those others who have named that black smell in two notes, four notes, in every note I have encountered—has satisfied the aesthetic quotient for thematic exquisiteness by tracking *Sanctuary*'s motif of disgorgement, a nausea compatible with a misogynistic reading of the novel. All of Faulkner's best critics have noted the nausea, the vomit, the smells of rankness permeating the book. Bleikasten states: "It is also worth noting that this is the only literary allusion to be found in Faulkner's novel and, as far as I know, the only reference to Flaubert's work in the whole Faulkner corpus."[34] This provocative claim attempts to fix the book through an intertextual focus: Horace's nausea evokes Emma's disgorgements. Indisputably, Horace and Popeye, who smells "like the black stuff that ran out of Bovary's mouth," blur.[35] Bleikasten notes, however, that Temple, despite her various predicaments, never vomits. If Faulkner's debt to Flaubert extends beyond the allusion to the black smell and the bridal gown, then Temple's connection to Flaubert could be far more inflected than Horace—who is wrong about most things—and Bleikasten have allowed. I suspect Flaubert offered Faulkner other fictional secrets beyond nausea.

Unfortunately the black smell in *Sanctuary* is so potent, it has obliterated other connections to Flaubert's work. For instance, could the clubfooted Eustace Graham have been inspired by Hippolyte Tautain, the clubfooted stableboy and victim of Dr. Charles Bovary's disastrous surgery in *Madame Bovary*? Or when Horace leaves Belle "[b]ecause she ate shrimp"[36] could Faulkner have been remembering Rodolphe and his justification for choosing

Emma as his mistress, displacing Virginie because, "She is so fin-ikin with her pleasures; and, besides, she has a mania for prawns."[37]

What if Flaubert in monument, in fact, served as another "liter-ary" man who was waiting in the bushes teaching craft to Faulk-ner, the young writer? What if Faulkner was, for hours, in his own way, doing the literary version of the "professor" thing (the profession, according to Popeye, of anyone caught with a book)? Ruby's question as to what it was Horace was doing in the woods remains one of the unsolved mysteries for critics of *Sanctuary*. And had we asked for an answer about what Faulkner did in the Gar-dens when he had wearied of admiring the children and betting on croquet, we, like Ruby, might have been told: "I don't know. I never thought to ask. Maybe to read the book."[38]

By the time Faulkner found himself sitting in the Luxembourg Gardens, more than 150 essays and articles in easy access maga-zines had already appeared on Flaubert. From the *Atlantic Monthly* and the *New Republic*, to the *Yale Review* and the *North American Review*, Flaubert was in the air and in print, as well as in the Luxembourg Gardens. While conceding that the clues in Faulkner's library are no guarantee of what he read or when, based on Blotner's *William Faulkner's Library: A Catalogue*, Faulkner did own Flaubert's *The Complete Unabridged Novels*.[39] In the records that track the distribution of Flaubert in English by 1921, even George Sand's and Flaubert's letters had been published (by Boni and Liveright) and available "to subscribers" by MW Dunne as early as 1904 and excerpted in the *Nation* by 1884.[40]

It must have seemed serendipity to the man who put the "U" in his own name to learn (as he probably did) that when Flaubert saw his name advertised for the first time for *Madame Bovary*, the author's name was spelled "Faubert."[41] Flaubert's *The Complete Works* in ten volumes were in translation by 1923. In the 11 March 1957 interview, Faulkner characterizes Flaubert's approach to lan-guage: "[it] was almost the lapidary's, that he was . . . a man who elected to do one book perfectly, in the characters, and in the method, in the style."[42] Faulkner sees the lavish ability to do both in *Salammbô* and *The Temptation of St. Anthony*. Like Flaubert, Faulkner claimed he didn't want to have to choose between the truth about people and the truth about a chalice.

Over the years, Faulkner registered his admiration for Flaubert. But it is in the "absolute manner of seeing things," the style, where Flaubert seems to haunt Faulkner.[43] Though I accede to the utter hazard of surmising what version Faulkner had access to in translation, and I acknowledge fully that the illustration I now offer is utterly vulnerable, I still beg indulgence for this stylistic comparison.

> It was a bright, soft day, a wanton morning filled with that unbelievable soft radiance of May, rife with a promise of noon and of heat, with high fat clouds like gobs of whipped cream floating lightly as reflections in a mirror, their shadows scudding sedately across the road. It had been a lavender spring. The fruit trees, the white ones, had been in small leaf when the blooms matured; they had never attained that brilliant whiteness of last spring, and the dogwood had come into full bloom after the leaf also, in green retrograde before crescendo. But lilac and wisteria and redbud, even the shabby heaven trees, had never been finer, fulgent, with a burning scent blowing for a hundred yards along the vagrant air of April and May. The bougainvillia against the veranda would be large as basketballs and lightly poised as balloons, and looking vacantly and stupidly at the rushing roadside Temple began to scream.

Compare with this passage from *Madame Bovary*:

> It was the beginning of April, when the primroses are in bloom, and a warm wind blows over the flower-beds newly turned, and the gardens, like women, seem to be getting ready for the summer fêtes. Through the bars of the arbour and away beyond, the river could be seen in the fields, meandering through the grass in wandering curves. The evening vapours rose between the leafless poplars, touching their outlines with a violet tint, paler and more transparent than a subtle gauze caught athwart their branches. In the distance cattle moved about; neither their steps nor their lowing could be heard; and the bell, still ringing through the air, kept up its peaceful lamentation.[44]

Faulkner, by praising *Madame Bovary,* appears to have focused, and so circumscribed, critical attention on Flaubert's most famous novel. But Faulkner's brief stay in Paris seems infused with Flaubert. Faulkner left Paris and sent a postcard from Rouen dated 22 September with the news that he had purchased a good second-hand bicycle and was on his way (*SL* 26). Having been close to Flaubert's monument each time he went to the basin, Faulkner's pilgrimage to the author of *Madame Bovary*'s home would seem an appropriate excursion for an artist-in-waiting who also shared with Flaubert the inability to sleep at night following the excitement of culling words all day. Even with responsible dose of caution, in context, I think it is likely that Faulkner's trip to Rouen may have also have been a young tramp's own version of going to the literary mountain.

But one needn't go as far as Rouen to collect evidence of such buried treasure. As proof I offer another piece of travel speculation. The index entry on Flaubert in the 1924 *Baedeker* sends a traveler to two places—to the Luxembourg Gardens on page 317, and to page 81 where a discussion of boulevards states: "The following boulevards, with their small shops and cafes are uninteresting. The Boulevard du Temple (Pl. R, 27; III) is named from its proximity to the old Temple quarter . . . . Gustave Flaubert lived at No. 42 from 1856 to 1871, and here 'Salammbô' and 'Madame Bovary' were written."

If Temple is a boy's name, and *Madame Bovary*, c'est Flaubert, then isn't it reasonable that Faulkner saw something like Flaubert's scratch on the wall in Paris and figured out what a young artist needed to know about starting off behind somebody else's scratch?

And of course there may be no connection at all.

5. "She wished at the same time to die and to live in Paris."
Gustave Flaubert, *Madame Bovary*

Like so much else in *Sanctuary*, we do not know the when or why of Temple's trip to Paris. Faulkner offers no clue as to why, or even if, Temple chose Paris: has she read Henry James's fiction after the trial? Or has she remained silent and simply been trans-

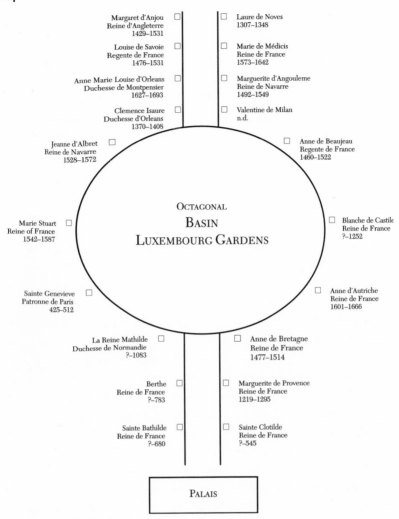

Margaret d'Anjou
Reine d'Angleterre
1429–1531

Louise de Savoie
Regente de France
1476–1531

Anne Marie Louise d'Orleans
Duchesse de Montpensier
1627–1693

Clemence Isaure
Duchesse d'Orleans
1370–1408

Laure de Noves
1307–1348

Marie de Médicis
Reine de France
1573–1642

Marguerite d'Angouleme
Reine de Navarre
1492–1549

Valentine de Milan
n.d.

Jeanne d'Albret
Reine de Navarre
1528–1572

Anne de Beaujeau
Regente de France
1460–1522

OCTAGONAL
BASIN
LUXEMBOURG GARDENS

Marie Stuart
Reine of France
1542–1587

Blanche de Castile
Reine de France
?–1252

Sainte Genevieve
Patronne de Paris
425–512

Anne d'Autriche
Reine de France
1601–1666

La Reine Mathilde
Duchesse de Normandie
?–1083

Anne de Bretagne
Reine de France
1477–1514

Berthe
Reine de France
?–783

Marguerite de Provence
Reine de France
1219–1295

Sainte Bathilde
Reine de France
?–680

Sainte Clotilde
Reine de France
?–545

PALAIS

francs needed to subsidize the Renaissance corner were acquired, according to one Paris guide, when Marie de Medicis drove around to the Bastille and robbed it—twice—from the war chest maintained for future wars.[47] In 1612 when she bought the chateau and grounds of Duc de Pincy-Luxembourg, Marie de Medicis wanted, but did not get, a replica of the Pitti Palace and its Boboli Gardens of her childhood. Humiliated by her husband, Henri IV, and repaid for much of her diplomatic skill by exile, she lived in

ported behind soundproof glass to Paris? The Gardens as 1
renders them are lush with indulgent ennui. Temple wears
new hat and she and her father have walked to the spo
they finally sit and she checks herself in the compact.

The water in the basin and the wavelike and dissolving i
of *Sanctuary*'s final scene have been slighted in favor of
preferences for chastisements of Temple. To most critics, s
pears to have resumed her life of pure surface, yawning and
dering her nose, fresh from the wanton destruction of on
Goodwin. (Critics cross with Temple are curiously indiffere
other dimensions of Lee as dad and victim.) Though one re
has even been dedicated to demonstrating that Temple, a
disembodied, has been taken to Paris by her father in a new
tage situation, most criticism insists that she has become *li*
dead tranquil queen, with emphasis on the stained marble, ra
than the musing. Even Muhlenfeld's largely sympathetic es
concludes by closing ranks: "we like her [Temple] even less at
novel's close."[45]

But why should we like her less? Evidence that Temple has ev
been jaded is in short supply; a flirt, certainly, pretentious, willf
and sly to be sure. She was not ready for what happened to h
when she stepped off the train, and no critical case has demoi
strated a capacity for evil. As a survivor, she can be viewed atavist
cally as a winner in an unsympathetic world. But why would thi
make a critic like her less? A fuller knowledge of the Luxembour
Gardens, viewed as a strategy of historical exploitation, jams this
view.[46] The queens authorize, in fact insist on, a different reading
of Temple's presence among them.

Marie de Medicis did not will her fate either. The Gardens
where Temple and her father sit are the result of Marie de Medicis's desires. Even if he read no guides to discover the historical
significance of the Luxembourg Palace, Faulkner would still have
passed the Fontaine de Medicis near the rue de Medici, a Renaissance fountain designed by the garden's architect, Salomon de
Brosse, the architect hired by Marie de Medicis. Nearby is a Fontaine de Léda and the river gods have a corner as well. The 90,000

the house then called Palais-Medicis as a prisoner rather than a Queen.[48] Her life testifies to brilliant strategies of recuperation where one *appears* to have power yet must inhabit a world where the signs and trappings of justice are ever an affront to your own experience.[49]

Marie de Medicis is one of the twenty famous statues. A snippet of her life is included in some of the guidebooks, but the lives of the other famous women are not in most travel and historic litera- ture. The omission of the stories, another reduction of Marie de Medicis's own struggle, testifies to the female erasure enacted in *Sanctuary*. Not only was it impossible to assemble a complete list of the names of the women celebrated by monuments, one of the guidebooks merely dismisses the unnamed monuments to the twenty famous women as "mediocre statuary."[50] The *Blue Guide* gives names to only nine members of the sorority: Bertha, the mother of Charlemagne, St. Genevieve, Mary Queen of Scots, Margaret of Anjou, Blanche de Castille, and Anne of Austria. Mar- guerite de Valois, the guidebook notes, was "beautiful, elegant, witty and a total libertine." Jeanne d'Albret was a strong-minded queen who, by instituting freedom of worship in her dominions, taught the virtue of tolerance to Henry IV. With the exception of Anne of Brittany, the French queens at best are recalled as better mothers than wives.[51] Marie de Medicis is one of them.

The ability to turn oneself into something so powerful one can't be hurt is one of the core desires in *Sanctuary*. When Temple tells Horace about the night in the Old Frenchman place, she reports trying to turn herself into a boy and then a gray-haired school teacher; she even improvised a chastity belt: "something used to lock the queen up. . . . maybe it would have long sharp spikes on it" to teach men to let women alone.[52] In the novel, on the night of the assault, Faulkner describes Temple with "her hands crossed on her breast and her legs straight and close and decorous, like an effigy on an ancient tomb."[53] Dying, especially for women, has been traditionally privileged as an alternative to violation.[54] Yet other available routes to inviolation for women are not imaginable in *Sanctuary*. Much of the novel's shock and outrage stems from

Temple's survival. Among the most frequently asked questions
about *Sanctuary* is why Temple does not leave the Old Frenchman
place. The companion interrogatory is why Ruby promises to abet
in an escape and then doesn't: " 'Listen. If I get a car for you, will
you get out of here?' she said. Staring at her Temple moved her
mouth as though she were experimenting with words, tasting
them. 'Will you go out the back and get into it and go away and
never come back here?' " Later, in Reba's house Temple learns
that as Popeye's chosen girl she will "wear diamonds." She has
previously longed for queenly paraphernalia: an iron belt "like a
king or something used to lock the queen up in when he had to go
away . . . if [she] just had that."55

The Luxembourg Gardens' monuments to the women do not
appear to serve as sites of instruction. Normally, monuments mark
heroic acts and individuals. But if these statues were intended as
way stations of feminist possibility, not finding them in the guides
makes it harder to discover messages in their lives. Unless the one
lesson they all offer is that one can be known, a queen, and erased.

The twenty famous women surround the basin on the Eastern
terrace. Faulkner may have exclusively boated with the children
on this basin, but Temple and her father walk into position near
the statues. When circumnavigating the basin, walkers are forced
to go near the statues. Regardless of one's aesthetic assessment of
these sculptures, no one can walk near the queens without appreciating how imposing the figures are. Contained and muted, the
statues are still overpowering. A visitor willing to accept that the
pond is not just a pond with boats, but a landscape artist's strategy
to force visitors around and under and close to these enormous
figures, finds another possibility for the end. The enormous stained
and silent queens help me unleash a different reading of the ending. When Temple and her father are seated, they are nearby Flaubert's monument, the basin, and the women who preside in this
garden. In some ways, this garden scene inverts the opening of
Sanctuary: The Luxembourg Palace and Gardens marks the spot
where the Old Italian woman place could launch an Old Frenchman place. By setting the end of *Sanctuary* in these gardens,

Faulkner captures the territory that he, during that brief autumn in Paris, came to regard as his own.

Though the autumnal rain has set the tone for most readings of *Sanctuary*, the other fluids should not go unnoticed. The basin itself in the Luxembourg Gardens deserves attention, for if readers attend to all the fluids in *Sanctuary*, and not just the two images dominating the criticism (the dripping shrimp and vomit), there can be interesting disruptions. Even the sound of dry shucks can be drowned out by the music of Massenet, Scriabin, and Berlioz. The garden glistens like Pound's metro station: "twilight *dissolved* in *wet* gleams. . . . Rich and resonant the brasses crashed and died in the thick green twilight, *rolling over* them in rich sad *waves* . . . she seemed to follow with her eyes *the waves* of music, to *dissolve* into the dying brasses, across the *pool*" (emphasis added).[56] The liquid images create an Irigarayan site for resistance in the dark male world of *Sanctuary*. If the masculine imaginary relies on re-capture by the solid economy, then Luce Irigaray suggests women (fluids) must escape to an "elsewhere," a location necessary for the emergence of women's language and pleasure.[57] The route to Irigaray's "exterriority" has not been mapped. Temple's story is a culturally perverse one : she is successfully transformed, but apparently unchanged. She has escaped. It does not, of course, purely illustrate what Irigaray means when she says women are not permitted to speak their own pleasure. Temple had already ventured the strictly forbidden. She claimed her own pleasure in grotesque mimicry with Red in the Grotto. Though she has performed the masquerade of femininity for Eustace Graham, she tells, nonetheless, her story from two lips moving together Yes Yes Yes. Note that later when Temple recounts the details of her night at the Old Frenchman place, Horace is most appalled by her "bright chatty monologue."[58]

She has survived much. With Popeye executed, Lee lynched, Horace safely caged in Belle's Kinston lair, and her Daddy in tow, she knows considerably more than she used to. She has had an unsentimental education. She has not succumbed to despair or opted for romantic death with arsenic or train. A thoroughly mod-

ern girl, she has returned, in touring metaphor, from the Coliseum
without the fever. Significantly, readers have never had less access
to her.

The yawn is not Temple's final act, nor is her look into the mirror. Sitting beside her father, she elects to look not at him—but
somewhere else. The narration asserts that she only "seemed to
follow with her eyes the waves of music.[59] It is autumn (the season
of rain and death to be sure), but it is a book which has done much
to hammer away at the notion of spring. Literally, the book has
foregrounded all kinds of springs. Besides the famous ones, there
are twenty-seven other references to "spring" in *Sanctuary: The
Original Text*, including springing, springs, and sprang. The revised text uses the word spring thirty-four times. The novel begins
in the spring(s) with Popeye in a stare/squat-off with Horace, and
it takes readers to an altogether different "spring," the opening of
the hangman's trap. As readers, we have passed literally through
spring—the wanton spring when Temple rides screaming and
bleeding to Memphis.

Sanctuary ends in the fall. If I were Temple, I would be glad it
was not the spring. She sits among queens and powerful women
like Joan of Arc and the Annes—of Brittany, of Provence, of Austria, and of Beaujeau. Those women excluded and diminished by
official history remind us of difference. This silence tells a tale of
the stories that have not been told. Temple told a tale in Jefferson.
Her last speech in Mississippi "parrots" the language needed to
satisfy the legal system in a Jefferson courtroom.[60] In playing the
role of a raped judge's daughter who lived to tell a chatty tale, she
settles the score(s) and fulfills her script. In so doing she joins
Caddy and Miss Quentin who escaped the boundaries of Jefferson.[61] She will no longer be in Jefferson where the men protect
girls in case they need them for themselves.[62]

Irigaray acknowledges the difficulties of resistance, the complications of survival, and the remoteness of the "elsewhere": "If she
can play that role so well, if it does not kill her, quite, it is because
she keeps something in reserve with respect to this function. Because she still subsists, otherwise and elsewhere than there where

she mimes so well what is asked of her. Because her own 'self' remains foreign to the whole staging."[63] I think it is crucial for feminist readers of treacherous modernist texts to claim space however perversely, look for opportunities for emancipation. The tranquil queens are company fit for Temple as she muses. She is in the Luxembourg Gardens. Emma Bovary wanted to live in Paris. She married and died instead. Marie de Medicis lived in Paris and died betrayed and outcast. Temple is in Paris. She is not in Oxford and she is not in Memphis. Readers should not miss the possibility. This time the girl in Faulkner lives.

NOTES

1. Jim Hinkle—a San Diego State University teacher, father of seven, who wore nearly exclusively his son Lon's hand-me-down golf clothes—loved facts and Faulkner and Hemingway. When he discovered literary conferences, the computer, and publishing, Jim for roughly the next six years was everywhere—talking, checking things out, and enlarging a notecard collection that ultimately traveled like Addie's coffin to its final resting place, full of its facts on mule prices, railroad schedules, and as yet unanswered questions. These new questions were intended not to undermine the slickest of academic performances at conferences, but to reveal that there was a piece of data that no one, least of all the speaker, had bothered to ask much less investigate. So it was Jim's doom, ever listening at every session, clutching his head as if in agony to pass notes correcting local pronunciations and telling speakers that had they bothered to check a map of voting districts in 1932, they'd know as well as he did that Faulkner could not possibly have intended—. Mostly Jim wanted to learn what other people knew.

This bit of biography serves to show that Jim had officially proposed the production schedule for his nine books in a series on *Reading Faulkner* 21 September 1986. By his estimates seven of the books were to have been in print by August of 1990—four months before Jim unexpectedly died and three years before even the first one had ever emerged from the press.

The correspondence I have from Jim, like Jim in life, is full of direction: "turn off your right justification" (11 March 1989); "instruct your computer to print the citation itself in bold"; "if it turns out that any co-author is not chiefly responsible for at least one-quarter of the work, his name should not appear on the title page or cover as co-author—although he would still receive his pro-rata share of the royalties and be credited prominently in the preface" (28 February 1986). In the same letter he sent a "relevant digression" on the sales figures for Random House Vintage editions "since the time they got a computer about fifteen years ago." The list dissolves into a Hinkle rant: "The man at Random House who compiled this list for me didn't know anything Faulkner. He told me that *Sartoris* was out of print and didn't realize *Flags* was its replacement—so I have no figures for either one. . . . He didn't know the names of the various titles for the short story collections and so gave me the misleading figure of 66,000, which is just for the Vintage *Collected* (or *Selected*—he didn't know which) *Stories.*" Though some of the correspondence, densely typed, was generically addressed to all the Faulkner Glossarians—(roughly sixteen individuals Jim had booked for strange passage), a frightening portion of these missives, I realized as I reviewed them recently, were letters to me about *Sanctuary*—the book he'd assigned to Edwin [Chip] Arnold (Appalachian State University) and me—because Chip would get it right and I would save it from being stodgy. And what I know to be true is that he was writing as feverishly on an individual basis to almost all of his glossarians as he was to me. He asked questions, noted some nuance he'd discovered somewhere that I needed to know, forever refining and distilling what he wanted the collection to be. On 12 February 1986 he sent two paragraphs—no salutation. It erupts on the subject of how far the series should go in trying to make the glossaries also serve beginning students:

> Everybody is ganging up on me and I guess I have to back down. One person said about my glossing the Colonel's old chair as "the one he used to use, not necessarily an old one": "It seems absurd to offer to explain that 'old' can mean 'former.' At that level of illiteracy one ought long ago to have give up all hope of making Faulkner even minimally accessible!" I am afraid I have to agree with that. Even if we should use two different type fonts, I concede that the lower end of the lower one should not extend as far down as I had originally envisioned. I will probably persist in urging some of you to have greater consideration for the needs of the less-than-already-expert than you might normally be tempted to show, but I am now persuaded that it is a fool's mission to try to make Faulkner understandable to every idiot in the back row. There are degrees and degrees, and I promise to be reasonable on this point if you will be.

Jim was never reasonable in any conventional sense of the word. But for nearly a decade I lived in close proximity to *Sanctuary* and his way of thinking about words and books. The small details this essay pursues, I believe, would have pleased Jim.

2. The students who galvanized my initial work on this essay were enrolled in a Faulkner seminar at the University of Akron in Spring 1995. One student, named for my purposes here only as Chip, returned a homework assignment where I'd asked for plausible theories on why *Sanctuary*'s final scene might have been set in the Luxembourg Gardens. His reply: "Luxembourg had been neutral in the War." While this response confirmed for me the absolute tragic necessity of Jim Hinkle's whole venture, it also set me to wondering how much more about Paris and Faulkner's response to the Garden could be discovered. The connections I propose extend the safe but ritualized standard fare about Faulkner's use of "season of rain and death." *Generation X* sprang from the title of Douglas Coupland's 1991 novel subtitled *Tales for an Accelerated Culture* (New York: St. Martin's Press, 1991). Its ironic and savvy take on pop culture stamped the market with the vocabulary and style of the grunge-chic/post-baby-boomer generation. Gen Xers typically work at "McJobs," go to the Spa de Luxembourg, and practice "o'propriation" ("the inclusion of advertising, packaging, and entertainment jargon from earlier eras in everyday speech for ironic and/or comic effect" [107]).

3. William Faulkner, Introduction, *Sanctuary* (New York: Modern Library, 1932), v–viii.

4. Ibid.

5. See Noel Polk, Afterword, *Sanctuary: The Original Text*, by William Faulkner (New York: Random House, 1981), 294–95. According to Harry Levin, Flaubert's process of revision of the 3600 manuscript pages of *Madame Bovary* was similarly agonized with a single passage revised through as many as twelve versions. See "*Madame Bovary*: The Cathedral and the Hospital," *Madame Bovary* (New York: Bantam, 1989), 363.

6. Including the Vintage International, eight versions of *Sanctuary* are listed in *Books in Print*.

7. See Philip Cohen, "'A Cheap Idea . . . Deliberately Conceived to Make Money': The Biographical Context of William Faulkner's Introduction to *Sanctuary*," *Faulkner Journal* 3.2 (1988): 54–66.

8. Charles Altieri, *Canons and Consequences: Reflections on the Ethical Force of Imaginative Ideals* (Chicago: Northwestern University Press, 1990). See especially the chapter "Canons and Differences," 49–79. See also Gerald Graff, *Literature Against Itself* (Chicago: University of Chicago Press, 1979).

9. Elisabeth Muhlenfeld, "Bewildered Witness: Temple Drake in *Sanctuary*," *Faulkner Journal* 1.2 (1986): 43. Muhlenfeld's first footnote states:

Attempts to explain Temple (and *Sanctuary* in general) in psychological
terms have been made since the earliest analyses of the novel. See, for example, Kubie (218, 224–26); Guerard (215–31). Guerard offers a good recent
re-examination of the artistry of the novel. Mythic treatments may be found
in Adams, Brylowski, McHaney, and Williams. Williams, for example, contends that on "the fundamental level of the unconscious," Temple "draws
the male world towards annihilation" (145). (Williams, however, sometimes
reaches a bit too far for allusion. In a note, he contends that perhaps the Old
Frenchman is, symbolically, the Marquis de Sade [225].) Critics who find
Temple a symbol of moral decay or evil include Vickery, Page, Mason, and
Brown.

10. See Noel Polk, "The Space Between *Sanctuary*," in *Intertextuality and Faulkner*, ed.
Michel Gresset and Noel Polk (Jackson: University Press of Mississippi, 1985), 16–35. See
also John T. Matthews, "The Elliptical Nature of *Sanctuary*," *Novel* 17.3 (1984): 246–65.

11. See Kenneth Gross, *The Dream of the Moving Statue* (Ithaca: Cornell University
Press, 1992); and William H. Gass, "Monumentality/Mentality," *Oppositions* 25 (1982):
127–44.

12. See Thomas L. McHaney, "*Sanctuary* and Frazier's Slain Kings," *Mississippi Quarterly* 24.3 (1971): 227. McHaney asserts that "there can be little doubt that Faulkner's
"sanctuary" refers to Diana's shrine at Nemi or that he borrowed the word from Frazer
[sic] who uses the word eleven times in the first seven pages of *The Golden Bough* to
describe it."

13. Muhlenfeld, 55.

14. Noel Polk has also addressed the scene in his speech, "Faulkner: The French Connection: Faulkner in the Luxembourg Gardens," delivered in Rennes, Spring 1996. Authors
like Gertrude Stein, Iris Murdoch, and Henry Miller have used the Luxembourg Gardens.
Ernest Hemingway captures the autumn in the following: "I can remember the Jardin du
Luxembourg well. I can remember afternoons with the boats on the lake by the fountain in
the big garden with the trees. The paths through the trees were all gravelled and the men
played bowling games off to the left under the trees as we went down toward the palace.
In the fall, the leaves came down and I can remember the fall best . . . the way the gravel
was dry on top when everything was damp and the wind in the trees that brought the
leaves down." See Mary Ellen Jordan Haight, *Walks in Gertrude Stein's Paris* (Salt Lake
City: Peregrine, 1988), 84. Alfred de Musset recasts his affair with George Sand also using
the Gardens as his setting: "The appearance of the avenues of the Luxembourg made my
heart leap; every other thought vanished. How many times, playing truant in these little
knolls, I had stretched out in the shade, brimming with wild poetry. For alas! this was the
scene of my childhood debaucheries. Among the leafless trees and the withered plants of
the flower-beds I found all these memories again." See Ian Littlewood, *Paris: A Literary
Companion* (New York: Harper, 1988), 134.

15. See Michael Millgate, "Undue Process: William Faulkner's *Sanctuary*," in *Rough
Justice: Essays on Crime in Literature*, ed. M. L. Friedland (Toronto: University of Toronto
Press, 1991), 157–69.

> To be thus committed to the law was to become the more sensitive to its
> abuse, and Faulkner seized almost inevitably upon the unique reticulations
> of the legal system—its constant institutionalized interactions between the
> powerful and the powerless, the socially gracious and disgraced—as provid-
> ing narrative materials and sources of symbolic reference precisely suited to
> writing about the sickness of specific societies or about the universal experi-
> ence of human mischancing, the failure of things to be or to turn out as they
> should. If, in *Sanctuary* and elsewhere, Faulkner's world seems structured
> upon the relationship—at once intimate and distant—between the panoply
> of the court-house and the squalor of the jail, that is perhaps only another
> element of his fundamental recognition of the necessary co-existence and

countervailing polarity of human (and especially societal) aspiration and human (especially individual) defeat (167).

16. See Joseph Blotner, *Faulkner: A Biography* (New York: Random House, 1984), 294.

17. William Faulkner, *Sanctuary. The Corrected Text. William Faulkner: Novels 1930–1935* (New York: Library of America, 1985), 381.

18. See Joseph R. Urgo, *Novel Frames: Literature as Guide to Race, Sex, and History in American Culture* (Jackson: University Press of Mississippi, 1991); Laura E. Tanner, *Intimate Violence: Reading Rape and Torture in Twentieth-Century Fiction* (Bloomington: Indiana University Press, 1994); Homer B. Pettey, "Reading and Raping in *Sanctuary*," *Faulkner Journal* 3.1 (1987): 71–84; and Diane Roberts, "Ravished Belles: Stories of Rape and Resistance in *Flags in the Dust* and *Sanctuary*," *Faulkner Journal* 4.1–2 (1989): 21–35.

19. Blotner, *Faulkner: A Biography*, 164.

20. Joseph Blotner, ed., *Selected Letters of William Faulkner* (New York: Vintage, 1978), 20. Further references cited in the text as *SL*.

21. Blotner, *Faulkner: A Biography*, 158.

22. Descriptions of the Luxembourg Palace have appeared in travel literature about Paris beginning in the 1640s. See Deborah Marrow, "Maria de Medici and the Decoration of the Luxembourg Palace," *Burlington Magazine* 121 (December 1979): 783–91. See also Oliver Millar, "An Exile in Paris: The Notebooks of Richard Symonds," *Studies in Renaissance and Baroque Art Presented to Anthony Blunt on His Sixtieth Birthday* (London: Phaidon, 1967), 157–64. Gertrude Stein is the source for this assessment of Paris as "the background for this period." See Haight, 82.

23. Karl Baedeker, *Paris and Its Environs* (Leipzig: Karl Baedeker, 1924), 316.

24. Faulkner, *Sanctuary: The Original Text*, 291; *Sanctuary*, 398.

25. See Faulkner, *Sanctuary: The Original Text*, 25; and *Sanctuary*, 184.

26. See Faulkner, *Sanctuary: The Original Text*, 14, 19; *Sanctuary*, 188.

27. Polk, afterword, 293–306. Faulkner, *Sanctuary*, 188. Both Popeye and Lee have been treated in the criticism as casualties of Temple's female trapping ability.

28. Gustave Flaubert, *The Selected Letters of Gustave Flaubert*, ed. Francis Steegmuller (New York: Vintage, 1953), 214. Faulkner claimed he gave the public what it wanted in *Sanctuary*: "guts and genitals." See Blotner, *Faulkner: A Biography*, 234.

29. Steegmuller, *Selected Letters*, 128.

30. Ibid., 247.

31. Frederick L. Gwynn and Joseph L. Blotner, ed., *Faulkner in the University* (Charlottesville: University of Virginia Press, 1959), 58.

32. James G. Watson, *Thinking of Home: William Faulkner's Letters to His Mother and Father, 1918–1925* (New York: Norton, 1992), 230.

33. Meriwether, "Faulkner Lost and Found," 7, qtd. in Blotner, *Faulkner: A Biography*, 319.

34. See André Bleikasten, "'Cet affreux goût d'encre': Emma Bovary's Ghost in *Sanctuary*," *Intertextuality and Faulkner*, ed. Michel Gresset and Noel Polk (Jackson: University Press of Mississippi, 1985), 36.

35. Faulkner, *Sanctuary*, 184.

36. Ibid., 191.

37. Gustave Flaubert, *Madame Bovary*, trans. Eleanor Marx Aveling (New York: Modern Library, 1900), 151. Thanks to Peter Alan Froehlich who suggested this specific lead after my presentation at the 1995 Yoknapatawpha conference. For more critical comparisons of the two texts see Steegmuller, *Selected Letters*, 214, 128, 247. See also Bleikasten, "'Cet affreux gout d'encre'" and "Terror and Nausea: Bodies in *Sanctuary*," *Faulkner Journal* 1 (1985): 17–29. See also Margaret Yonce, "'His True Penelope Was Flaubert': *Madame Bovary* and *Sanctuary*," *Mississippi Quarterly* 29 (1976): 439–42.

38. Faulkner, *Sanctuary*, 185.

39. Joseph L. Blotner, *William Faulkner's Library: A Catalogue* (Charlottesville: University Press of Virginia, 1964), 94.

40. Ernest Jackson, *The Critical Reception of Gustave Flaubert in the United States* (Paris: Mouton, 1966), 122.

41. See Francis Steegmuller, *Flaubert and Madame Bovary: A Double Portrait* (Chicago: University of Chicago Press, 1977), 315.

42. Gwynn and Blotner, 55–56.

43. Ibid., 56; for Flaubert's view of Pure Art, see Steegmuller, *Selected Letters*, 126.

44. Faulkner, *Sanctuary*, 274; Flaubert, *Madame Bovary*, 129. Eleanor Marx Aveling's translation of *Madame Bovary* was the likeliest available version when Faulkner went to Paris.

45. Muhlenfeld, 55.

46. According to Luce Irigaray, "jamming" has as its goal the complete disruption of the theoretical machine by "suspending its pretension to the production of a truth and of a meaning that are excessively univocal" (*This Sex Which Is Not One*, trans. Catherine Porter [Ithaca: Cornell University Press, 1985], 78). Irigaray continues: "An interim strategy for dealing with the realm of discourse (where the speaking subject is posited as masculine), in which the woman deliberately assumes the feminine style and posture assigned to her within this discourse in order to uncover the mechanisms by which it exploits her" (220). If pretending to be hard and cold is seen as an assigned role *assumed by* Temple to cope with all that has happened and all that is expected of her, then her transformation to this "ideal status" is a strategy, a way of "jamming the works of the theoretical machine" (107).

47. See Ian Littlewood, *Paris: A Literary Companion* (New York: Perennial, 1989), 133–34. Vincent Cronin, *The Companion Guide to Paris* (New York: Harper, 1963), 98–99.

48. This is distilled from *Heroic Deeds and Mystic Figures* by Ronald Forsyth Millen and Robert Erich Wolf (New Jersey: Princeton University Press, 1989). See also Rosalys Coope's *Salomon De Brosse and the Development of the Classical Style in French Architecture from 1565 to 1630* (University Park: Pennsylvania State University Press, 1972); see Cronin;. and Helen W. Henderson, *A Loiterer in Paris* (New York: George H. Doran, 1921). The touchstones and setbacks in Maria de Medicis's life include the house arrest, expulsion from Paris, exile at the Chateau de Blois, betrayals by trusted confidantes, including Richelieu, agonizing death in poverty, and shabby burial in Saint-Denis where she had once enjoyed glorious coronation.

49. See Julia Pardoe, *The Life of Marie de Medicis: Queen of France*, vol. 6 (New York: Pott, 1905), 200. This volume concludes with the wretched circumstances of the Queen's death:

> Surely history presents but few such catastrophes as this. The soul sickens as it traces to its close the career of this unhappy and persecuted Princess. Whatever were her faults, they were indeed bitterly expiated. As a wife she was outraged and neglected; as a Queen she was subjected to the insults of the arrogant favourites of a dissolute Court; as a Regent she was trammeled and betrayed; the whole of her public life was one long chain of disappointment, heart-burning, and unrest; while as a woman, she was fated to endure such misery as can fall to the lot of few in this world.

50. See Findlay Muirhead and Marcel Monmarche, *Paris and Its Environs* (London: Macmillan, 1921). (Series title *The Blue Guides*)

51. Noel Polk provided the complete list of statues and the names for the chart (see p. 114). James B. Carothers writes about "The Dead Tranquil Queens," but the focus in this essay is on the sculptors and sculpture in Faulkner's fiction. See " 'The Dead Tranquil Queens': Sculptors and Sculpture in Faulkner's Fiction," in *The Artist and His Masks*, ed. Agostino Lombardo (Rome: Bulzoni Editore, 1991), 65–79. Not a single queen is identified.

Emily Searcy, the research assistant who dived into the wreck for this project, served as private eye investigating the various women who surround the basin to see what could be known about them. *The Catholic Encyclopedia* proved a faithful source, as well as Duc de Castries, *The Lives of the Kings and Queens of France*, trans. Anne Dobell (New York: Knopf, 1979). The diction tells the tale. Anne of Austria, for instance, is described as "one of France's most interesting queens: virtually ignored by her husband, she adopted a reserved and dignified bearing" (Castries 184). Margaret of Provence managed "to die piously" despite her resentment of authoritarian mother-in-law, Blanche of Castile (Castries 77). One account notes that Mary Stuart "took pleasure in gazing on the hanged men by torchlight" (Castries 160). A short biography of Anne-Marie-Louise D'Orleans, known as La Grande Mademoiselle, is preserved in Thérèse Louis Latour, *Princesses, Ladies, and Adventuresses of the Reign of Louis XIV* (New York: Knopf, 1924). In pursuit of a partner of appropriate rank, La Grande Mademoiselle is forgiven by her biographer: "Considered from this point of view—and it is the correct one—the actions . . . became in a way divested of that sense of the grotesque which is necessarily invoked by her exaggerated ideas as to her own importance as compared with her utter indifference to the feelings of ordinary people" (18). For more information about the queens see Fr. Funck-Brentano, *The National History of France: The Earliest Times*, trans. E. F. Buckley (New York: Putnam, 1927), and Frederic J. Baumgartner, *France in the Sixteenth Century* (New York: St. Martin's, 1995).

52. Faulkner, *Sanctuary*, 329.

53. Ibid., 228.

54. See Dawn Trouard on Eula Varner's suicide in "Eula's Plot: An Irigararian Reading of Faulkner's Snopes Trilogy," *Mississippi Quarterly* 42.3 (Summer 1989): 281–97.

55. Faulkner, *Sanctuary*, 220, 280, 329.

56. Thanks to Jay Watson who pointed me to the dissolution of this passage. See his essay "The Failure of Forensic Storytelling in *Sanctuary*," *Faulkner Journal* 6.1 (1990): 47–66.

57. Irigaray, 157; and Dawn Trouard, "Faulkner's Text Which Is Not One," *New Essays on "The Sound and the Fury*," ed. Noel Polk (Cambridge: Cambridge University Press, 1993), 23–69.

58. Faulkner, *Sanctuary*, 219.

59. Ibid., 398.

60. But in Temple's parroting, I found a rather wonderful allusion. In Rouen, there is a statue of Flaubert, and, if Julian Barnes's *Flaubert's Parrot* (New York: Knopf, 1985) is as faithful to certain fact, there are stuffed and certified parrot(s) in the Museum of Rouen vying to be Loulou in Flaubert's *Un Coeur Simple* (17). Flaubert checked them out of a museum. Though there are no parrots in *Madame Bovary*, the Rouen parrots bring the Luxembourg Gardens into Mississippi and link Temple yet again with Marie de Medicis, who dies destitute at sixty-seven leaving her pet parrot to Richelieu, the man who betrayed her. See Millen and Wolf, 19.

61. Trouard, 53–54.

62. Faulkner, *Sanctuary*, 385.

63. Irigaray, 152.

The Guns of *Light in August:* War and Peace in the Second Thirty Years War

WARWICK WADLINGTON

1

In five days we will mark an unthinkable light in August. For most, memory will not really believe, though knowing will remember, that in this month fifty years past it seemed that the sun had suddenly fallen on Hiroshima and Nagasaki. The day of the first nuclear bombing was also a commemoration. In traditional Christian belief, August 6 is the feastday of the Transfiguration, when Jesus's "face shone like the sun."[1] According to the synoptic gospels, as Jesus was miraculously joined on a mountaintop by Moses and Elijah, a transforming supernatural brilliance verified that his teaching fulfilled the law and the prophets, the law that was to mark the prophesied reign of the peace that passes understanding. An incredible act of war coincides with a visionary Judeo-Christian law of peace, nuclear sun with sunlike transfiguration, in this challenge to memory's belief on a day layered with cultural memory, fifty years ago.

It might be seen as a terribly fitting end, even a Faulknerian end, to what Winston Churchill called another Thirty Years War. These were the thirty-odd years in which Faulkner wrote, or which provided a significant basis for, his most important work. These years left their print on Faulkner the fabulist and on Churchill the statesman and historian, as these writers left theirs on an era that taught many, then and now, how to think about themselves.

In choosing thirty years as the actual length of the war, Church-

ill, always one for defining ends and beginnings, was taking another August light as his starting point. He was evoking what
Barbara Tuchman was to call the guns of August that had lit the
sky across Europe in 1914 to open the Great War. As an agent of
culture like his fellow candidate for the Nobel Prize for Literature
in 1949, William Faulkner, Churchill was putting a name to what
others felt during and after the period he marked off. He was saying that there was in reality a continuing gigantic struggle between
August 1914 and August 1945, including two officially designated
world wars and the official twenty-year peace between them.[2]

We can see what is at stake when Churchill names this entire
period a war: what counts as war and what counts as peace? To
put it another way, at stake here is the cultural selective building
of what *counts as* a cultural context. This broadest sense of the
word *culture* I invoke here came into popular use at the socially
self-conscious time we survey. Cultures in this meaning are what
teach humans the powers to interpret and otherwise to perform
peace and war. That is, culture is the necessary basic empowering
of human beings. It comprises all the innumerable acquired
knowledges and practices required to supplement and develop
what the human body is born knowing how to do. Culture's highly
selective contexts define and enable our actions and nonactions
alike. But measured in ethical or political terms, this fundamental
"anthropological" empowering may be disempowering in an another sense.

Churchill meant to teach a cultural lesson about disempow-
erment, and it was encapsulated in the period-name he chose. The
advocate of peace through military strength and the early, forceful
confrontation of Hitler's initial aggressive acts, Churchill argued
that following World War I Britain and its allies had disempow-
ered themselves by cultures of peace advocating pacifism, disar-
mament, and "appeasement." They had failed to recognize that
despite the appearance of peacetime, long, ongoing war menaced
them.

However one stood, or stands, on this particular issue, Churchill
had grounds for his striking redefinition of a defining time in this

century. The term *thirty years war* historically connotes more than a given length of combat; it connotes a particularly confusing, many-sided conflict. In the twentieth-century version, diverse military cultures dictated politics and warfare with frequent appeals to national glory, honor, and security, beginning with the century's early widespread romanticizing of war, which was integral to the competing imperialisms aimed at Africa and Asia. After the First World War came a bewildering sequence: the postwar invasion of Bolshevik Russia by U.S. and other allied forces; the postrevolution Russian civil war; the Graeco-Turkish War; the rise of facism, with the military theatrics of Mussolini in Italy and Hitler in Germany, and the military party in Japan; the Italian invasion of Ethiopia; the Japanese invasions of Manchuria and China; the civil wars in China between the forces of Mao Tse Tung and the Kuomintang; the Spanish Civil War, which drew support for the Republican side from Faulkner and many other American writers and intellectuals; and the German annexation of Austria, Czechoslovakia, and other territory leading up to World War II.[3]

For our purposes, we may add to these examples the international submilitary yet militant atmosphere of real and imagined revolutionary acts and the sometimes violent strikes of the period, met with counterviolence such as the Palmer Raids in the U.S. or the General MacArthur–led assault on the World War I veteran Bonus Marchers; and the flareup of white Southern lynchings of blacks, including black military veterans, as well as the assaults on black people North and South in twenty-five urban riots that followed upon wartime-inspired black migration; and, on an immense scale, the Soviet "liquidation" of millions of its people as enemies of the state as well as the Nazi German "final solution" by a holocaust of further millions of Jews, Slavs, and other perceived enemies of its state.

All these events may be seen as the products of diverse international militant cultures confident and unapologetic in their opposing or converging militance. Yet as weighty as this list is, a good case can be made for not relegating the entire period to the nomenclature and memory of war. The production of peace accompanied all this staggering conflict. The first salvos of the Great War erupted in what was from all accounts a summer of unusual beauty and serenity, that offered a paradigmatic memory of true reality in comparison to which the protracted war seemed unbelievable. The war's unprecedented combination of size, ferocity, and length, astounding to everyone at the time, resulted largely from the extensive interlocking alliances that were widely thought to be the best guarantee of peace. The very incredibility of this trench war's deadliness and seemingly endless irresolution arose from two further, related cultural constructions of peace as context.

The first is the assumption that gentle peace is the natural, normal state of affairs, so much taken for granted as to be imperceptible, Horace Benbow thinks in *Flags in the Dust*, without the distancing perspective of war.[4] The second reason for the contemporary incredulity at the protracted, stalemated Great War was the assumption that while war is unusual, it does *settle* matters. By its very nature it was supposed to be decisive, a final solution that returns things to their normal peaceful state—with that finality Faulkner's people seek but find illusory.[5] So in *Absalom, Absalom!* the guns of the Civil War's national fratricide re-sound in Henry Sutpen's shooting of his brother Charles Bon and, as Rosa Coldfield notes, reverberate tediously, without resolution.

Let us recall further, then, that working into and against the thirty-year products of militant cultures were diverse and unprecedentedly ambitious peace cultures. They were actuated by such motives as hopeful utopian conviction, fear of another devastating war, further war preparations under the camouflage of peace, and a business strategy of beating swords into bankshares. The peace-culture products comprise not only the many conventional treaties and arms limitations such as the punitive Versailles agreement of 1919 and the Washington conference pacts of 1921. More ambitious were the Wilsonian idea that the Great War was a war to end all wars and the League of Nations that was to institutionalize global peacekeeping; and the pre- and post–Great War peace movements, including socialist and feminist international initiatives; and the American citizens campaign to outlaw war, leading to the signing of the Kellogg-Briand Pact renouncing war by almost all major nations in August 1928; and the opposition of most Americans to entering European conflicts again, right up to the eve of Pearl Harbor; and the plan for an international peacekeeper United Nations that accompanied the Allied conduct of World War II.[6]

2

Faulkner's work emerges at a key intersection of regional, national, and international cultures of war and peace. His novel *Light in August* was written and is set at roughly the midpoint between the cannon flash of one August and the nuclear blaze of another. It is one of a series comprising, in all but title, a mutivolume Faulknerian *War and Peace* for the second Thirty Years War. The series includes, but is not limited to, *Soldiers' Pay, Flags in the Dust, The Sound and the Fury, As I Lay Dying, Light in August, The Unvanquished, Pylon, Absalom, Absalom!, Go Down, Moses, Knight's Gambit, A Fable*, and a sizable collection of short stories, reviews, and movie scripts.

Read in this and the larger context that I have been outlining, the 1932 novel can be seen to follow the narrative logic of World War I and its aftermath. It opens with the evocation of a peaceful summer seemingly outside of time, embodied in the "inward-lighted" tranquility of a lone pregnant woman safely traveling Alabama and Mississippi roads for weeks.[7] But she "traverses the ranked battery of maneyes" (27), encounters a woman who looks and acts like "generals who have been defeated in battle" (16), and wages a "mild battle" within herself (27). She travels accompanied by "slow and terrific" sounds, a series of "dry sluggish reports carrying for a half mile" (8) across the August silence in a "kind of rhythm," a wagon's "outraged wood one with the slow afternoon" (13). If the novel is subtly pregnant with battle in the opening chapter, however, it delivers it to the reader as a convulsion at times unforeseeably fierce and repeated. This violence bears the features of wars old, new, and to come, yet features also curiously unmilitary and domestic.

Gail Hightower's Civil War grandfather dies in two different ways. In the first, as Hightower remembers it, the grandfather is shot off his galloping horse in the conventional military fashion corresponding to pre–Great War martial romanticism. In the second, later surprisingly introduced and eccentrically romanticized by Hightower, he is killed by a woman outraged that he is stealing her chickens, who shoots him with a bird-hunting gun. Comparably, we see Joe Christmas "shot" twice, though the first is a misfire. With an old Civil War pistol recalling the peacetime assassination of her grandfather and brother by the local war hero John Sartoris, Joanna Burden pulls the trigger on her lover Joe Christmas, who has refused to play the role of black man for her any longer. He in return almost decapitates her with a stereotypically Southern black weapon, a straight razor, ordinarily an instrument of peaceful routine.

Colonel Sartoris in his time, and ironically, Joanna Burden in hers, were trying to keep black people in their white-designated place. So to keep black men in their place away from white women, Percy Grimm, local First World War hero manqué, shoots the supposedly black Christmas to death with an automatic pistol as Joe crouches behind a kitchen table. Grimm castrates Christmas with a butcher knife, homely instrument of peace, to make Christmas harmless to white women "even in hell" (464). Then there follows an apotheosis of Christmas: a remarkable prophecy of a memory coalescing airwar and a peace passing understanding, a rocket to a deifying transfiguration and an actual but unbelievable warning siren:

> For a long moment [Christmas] looked up at them with peaceful and unfathomable and unbearable eyes. Then . . . from out the slashed garments about his hips and loins the pent black blood seemed to rush like a released breath. It seemed to rush out of his pale body like the rush of sparks from a rising rocket; upon that black blast the man seemed to rise soaring into their memories forever and ever. They are not to lose it, in whatever peaceful valleys, beside whatever placid and

reassuring streams of old age. . . . It will be there, . . . not fading and not particularly threatful, but of itself alone serene, of itself alone triumphant. Again from the town . . . the scream of the siren mounted toward its unbelievable crescendo, passing out of the realm of hearing. (464–65)

We will see that this scene of terrible transfiguration fulfills the old law of peace in the new.

I have cited but the most obvious instances of the guns of *Light in August* and their coexistence with the peaceful. This novel, after all, with irony aforethought requires a commentator to conjoin, as I have just done, the peace-on-earth feastday name *Christmas* with multiple acts of unsettling violence given and received. I will continue to trace a contextual circuit around this novel. My aim is to suggest how much not only it but Faulkner's writing generally can be understood as the cultural production of the second Thirty Years War and its peculiarly intense hybrid of war and peace.

As in the phrase "agent of culture," I intend the preposition "of" in "cultural production of" to point in both directions. It indicates that agency and writing are both complexly shaped and empowered by the larger cultures, and also shape and empower them. The roughly thirty-year period we survey, as we know and remember it, produces and is produced by, among others, William Faulkner. And I not only acknowledge but stress that the period Churchill named and Faulkner helped to imprint, carries here a simplifying metaphorical name. But I will ask it to do work different from Churchill's. For all its useful connotation of confusion and loose ends, the designation *second Thirty Years War* in a sense arbitrarily carves out the beginning, middle, and end of a narrative from an ongoing flux of heterogeneous acts. In the pages to follow, we will need to trace some of the complicating U. S. and Southern cultural history from which the cultural history of these thirty-odd years comes.

War-as-literal-armed-combat rarely occurs in Faulkner's fiction. But then, too, in the words of *Light in August*, pure "Peace is not that often" (289) either in Faulkner's world. Criticism has treated

Faulkner on war and, less often, Faulkner on peace; more relevantly to my essay, elsewhere I have examined peace thematically, rhetorically, and contextually in *Light in August*.[8] Though I took account of the interworking of peace and violence there, I have since become convinced that the most fruitful context to study now is not peace or war singly, but their relationship. The issues that preoccupy Faulkner's writings are largely forged when the two world wars of this century could be seen as continuous with the officially demarcated peace between them. Powerful movements of both pacifism and militarism sweep the world, as war is fearfully or gladly foreseen and hopefully or strategically renounced, all in the most dramatic terms.

In Faulkner's representation, it is a time when cultures of war try to fashion peace, and a culture of expansionist, acquisitive peace "comes indeed into its own in war."[9] In well-known Faulkner shorthand, a time of both Sartoris and Snopes. A time too of those such as Horace and Narcissa Benbow, Quentin Compson, Gavin Stevens, Lena Grove, young Sartoris Snopes, General Gragnon and the unmartial old Marshall in *A Fable*, and many others who manifest, seek, and subvert, in Horace's phrase, "the meaning of peace" (177, 184). Peace "was all I wanted" (331) says violent Joe Christmas, deserter from the Army, in the mixture of longing and deception that intricate regional, national, and international cultures fashioned from 1914 to 1945.

3

When *Light in August* was published, in 1932, the Great Depression had reached its lowest point, but it was to continue until the Second World War economic boom ten years later, just as the First World War–inspired twenties boom had preceded the Depression. After a series of such dramatic reversals over thirty years, the U.S.A. in 1945 was described as the most powerful nation on earth, amid popular claims that this was the American Century. About thirty years before, the first Southern President in a long time, Woodrow Wilson, had symbolized American reunification after the

Civil War, not only in his person but in his policies. After successfully campaigning for office on a peace platform, he had staked a claim for a major U.S. role in the Great War and the peace to follow by reluctantly asking Congress to declare hostilities against Germany. In famous words, Wilson put this construction on his act: "It is a fearful thing to lead this great, peaceful people into war."[10] To understand something of the construction of the U.S.A. as a great peaceful people and the preceding regional and national history that brought it into its own during the second Thirty Years War, we can begin by returning to our two key words.

War and Peace are a captivating pair, with the lure of the self-evidently good or bad—or so it usually seems. These terms are ready-made reifications, false concretions that appear to dichotomize something tangible and self-evidently evaluatable. They are, in other words, a perfect ideological couple. Seeming to bear their meaning and value on their faces universally and naturally, outside specific historical, cultural contexts, they invite uncritical political attitudes and action. Who would not say that Peace is better than War?

Some thought about context, of course, tells us that things aren't this simple. Except, I suppose, for absolute pacifists, arguably there are wars and there are wars, peaces and peaces, with a myriad of aspects to be weighed. There are, arguably, just wars and unjust peaces, defensive wars and aggressive wars, praiseworthy revolutions and tragic absences of revolt. There is the peace in which masters wish to keep their slaves and the wars that free them; and there are the wars many freed African Americans thought of as the opportunity to gain full citizenship in a white-dominated nation. W. E. B. Du Bois supported American entry into World War I on just these grounds. On a comparable gender basis, many women leaders supported the war because it gave new opportunities to women in the workplace.[11]

It is politically crucial to establish what counts as war and peace, and how it counts, and when, why, and for whom. There is war which is not, but police action; and there is police action which is not, but war. There is cold war; there are trade wars, wars on poverty, class wars, race wars, gender wars, culture wars, wars to end war, and the peaceloving peoples who wage them.

And there were long peacetimes, only occasionally interrupted by officially designated war, in which the expanding United States, like its predecessor European empire-builders here and such predecessor indigenous imperialists as the Aztecs, engaged in what Faulkner in *Go Down, Moses* calls *dispossession*—a term from the protest language of the 1930s.[12] In this peace, the United States acquired its territory from the people already occupying the land by taking whatever it could, just about any way it could, as did all the other European-derived nations of North and South America. And also did this, in the final "Indian Wars" in the 1870s and '80s, with the considerable help of "buffalo soldiers," enlisted blacks recently freed from *their* long peace of dispossession.

With further irony, it was this national war that in the 1860s had taken many regular federal troops away from the frontier, and so unleashed the settlers of peaceful name. Freed from the relative restraints of Regular Army rules of engagement, and sometimes, in Percy Grimm style, as volunteers using military uniforms and equipment, the settlers intimidated, raided, massacred, and drove off Native peoples and so facilitated huge land-grabs and "settlement."[13]

In 1795, President George Washington had warned Congress that the provisions for "the protection of the Indians from the violences of the lawless part of our frontier inhabitants are insufficient. . . . [T]hese violences can now be perpetrated with impunity. And . . . unless the murdering of Indians can be restrained, by bringing the murderers to condign punishment, all the exertions of the Government to prevent destructive retaliations by the Indians will prove fruitless." Prophetic message.[14]

Obviously, one need not imagine that the typical Euro-American male or female settler was a murderer of Indians, and indeed, she or he might well have deplored such killing. Comparably, the decent white Southern man or woman in the first decades of the twentieth century might deplore the violence of vigilantes and lynchers, the rebirth of the KKK in 1915, or borderline-official killers like deputized Percy Grimm. But the white men and women of Yoknapatawpha and the whites of both South and North nevertheless took and held onto what they perceived as the benefits of others' policing of the color line by force and the threat of force.

So too for centuries similar unremitting "low-intensity" killings made possible the settlers' steady takeover of tribal lands, in a taking and keeping very much at issue in *Go Down, Moses.* Terrorizing violence, but one element of dispossession, was supplemented by massive deportations, deadly epidemics, outright swindling, one-sided bargaining by white laws, language, and money, consistently broken treaties, thieving laws, and other peacetime means. It is altogether characteristic of this history that Helen Hunt Jackson's widely read *Century of Dishonor* (1881), which shamed her nation for its mistreatment of Native peoples, resulted in a calamitous law, the Dawes Act, ostensibly meant to help them by requiring them to turn to the peaceful, civilizing pursuits of family farming—like their civilized settler neighbors, who immediately plundered immense quantities of tribal lands further under the law's provisions. General Sherman, for all his demeaning of Native peoples, aptly defined a reservation as "a parcel of land inhabited by Indians and surrounded by thieves."[15] Peace could be hell too.

War, Clausewitz famously said, is the extension of national policy by other means. John Keegan, in his recent *A History of Warfare*, seeks to correct this formula by arguing that, although much of the history of warfare has nothing to do with national policy, wars are always the extension of the cultures that wage them. Just as Keegan shows there are many cultural styles of warfare, so, I think, there are cultural styles of peace—or peacefare, if you will. The American historical style is low-profile dispossession, not a war but a peace of attrition. It would appear, then, to be the use of peace as an extension of national war by other means.

This is the serious point of Faulkner's comic story "Lo!," written shortly after *Light in August* and extending its themes. In this story Francis Weddel, leader of the Mississippi Chickasaws, conducts a peace campaign to turn the tables on President Andrew Jackson, renowned Indian-fighter and Supreme Court-defying "author" of the infamous Indian removals, the deadly Trail of Tears. Jackson advertised these deportations as necessary to reestablish Eastern tribes far away from their rich homelands in order, at the nation's own expense, to protect the tribes from the supposedly inevitable waves of civilization rolling westward.[16]

Chief Weddel leads his people peaceably in the reverse direction, from Mississippi to Washington. In a similar reversal, he petitions to have his nephew tried by Jackson in Congress itself on the charge of murdering a white man, as George Washington's message to Congress reminds us that white men were rarely tried at all for the murdering of Native Americans. Snopes-style, the white man had set up a profitable toll station on his small piece of strategically located property within Chickasaw land. Weddel pointedly encamps his people around and in the White House as self-invited guests in winter time, inconveniencing themselves, one explains, for the white man's sake and honor, and in the process dispossessing the President with bland courtesy. There follows a farcical sequence of desperate Jacksonian legal charades to exculpate the nephew. The story ends with Jackson's casting off the cloak of paternal President to happily resume the soldier's plan of naked force. Chief Weddel is to be forcibly prevented from conducting further polite campaigns that travesty and unmask peaceable dispossession and legal show about benefitting Indians.

Americans had mostly come from Europe in search of land on which to settle in peace. They indeed settled in peace what they did not need to settle in war—active for centuries in indefatigable routine dispossession on the homefront. After pacifying the Native peoples by the end of the nineteenth century, Americans turned to secure a further empire from other dark-skinned people in the Philippines in a bloody antiguerilla pacification, and later sent military forces to establish domestic tranquility for American business in the Caribbean and Latin America—so that, for example, Nicaragua and Haiti became effectively U.S. protectorates.

It was to these cultural sons and daughters of the pioneers, then, that Wilson referred in 1917: "It is a fearful thing to lead this great, peaceful people into war." Exactly so. It was fearful enough to lead this peaceful people as it conducted peace. Its benefits were so great that Wilson had to wage a huge propaganda campaign to have his compatriots see that this war was consistent with the national way of peace.

The cultural history sketched here I think illuminates and is illuminated by, among other Faulkner texts, *A Fable*, which was begun as the U.S. entered World War II and which recounts a failed mass soldiers' strike for peace in the midst of World War I. This novel searingly enumerates the ordinary secular and religious political-cultural networks of democratic America, no less than its allies, "which control by coercion or cajolery man's morals and actions . . .—all that vast powerful terror-inspiring representation which, running all democracy's affairs in peace, comes indeed into its own in war, finding its true apotheosis then" (232).

4

For a white Southerner, there were additional grounds for understanding how this style of peace could come into its own in war. When Percy Grimm takes on his National Guard title of Captain, organizes a patrol to keep order, and then fatally attacks and mutilates a purportedly black man for sleeping with and killing a white woman, the novel recalls and constructs a context beyond the immediate reference to World War I. Obviously Grimm and his followers are staging a replacement for the experience of war Grimm missed because he was too young. Combined with this is a more subtle replacement of a missed peace-experience. Military titles such as *Captain* and *Colonel* usually associated with the traditional South far preceded the Civil War. As Joel Williamson has pointed out, they were used in peacetime slavery days because all Southern white males were expected to serve in militias to keep the peace. That is, they organized into regular patrols to prevent free movement by slaves and to punish on the spot, sometimes with terrorizing mutilations, any suspected sexual or other infringement. The militias got their greatest impetus from the rebellion Nat Turner led in August 1831, one hundred years before Grimm punishes Christmas.[17]

The militarism of these militias was thoroughly integrated into ordinary Southern life. It was crucial to the region's self-depiction as a land of easeful, gracious serenity—the South as the very meaning of peace in a bustling nation that had elsewhere lost the old reposeful ways. This picture of the old South revived in the 1920s and especially the Depression 1930s, with the popular nostalgia for a haven of ease that had *Gone with the Wind*.[18]

This Southern peace had to be carefully defined to distinguish it from torpor and vulnerability. It had to be an armed, vigilant peace guaranteed by dangerous men whose ease and courtesy were not to be mistaken for weakness. The cultural guarantee went far beyond militias, as does the Percy Grimm scene. In *Reading Faulknerian Tragedy* I drew partly on Bertram Wyatt-Brown's study of the traditional Southern cult of honor to argue that a strongly developed honor-shame culture empowers Faulkner's people and his rhetorical relationship with his readers.[19] What one learns in this culture is that being dangerous is attractive, magnetic. Whatever behavior most evokes or walks the thin line between being excitingly provocative and insultingly outrageous is most attractive—except when it challenges *the* line, the line of color.

This means that social bonds of peace—ties of family, sex, friendship, economics, politics—are formed and sustained by provocative behavior that binds those that it really or potentially outrages. Like Bayard and John Sartoris, Horace and Narcissa Benbow, Quentin and Caddy Compson, Henry Sutpen and Charles Bon—or better, like these entire families—Joe Christmas and Joanna Burden can bond precisely because they deeply provoke, and can destroy, each other. This is why the novel suggests a bond, a doubling, between Christmas and his destroyer Percy Grimm.

In short, in this culture as Faulkner produces it, critiques it, and is produced by it, all forms of tranquility and violence are tightly interdependent. Calm mutuality and mutual outrage are fraternal if not identical twins. So Hightower's pulpit preaching of martial glory and death, though it estranges his congregation by crossing the line, is only a serious, unconscious parody of his people's Southern Calvinist Christianity. As Hightower and the narrative voice later combine to describe it, this religion is the perversion of "that peace which is the promise and the end of the Church" by a violence leading them to find cathartic peace in *"crucifixion of themselves and one another"* (367–368). Joe Christmas's violent death and transfiguration into a perceived supernal peace makes sense in exactly these terms.

Given these cultural dynamics, discerning what gestures count as offense or alliance, war or peace, is constantly at stake at every level beginning with interpersonal politics and extending to politics at large. An indispensable complement is the highly developed capacity for not noticing, for selective attention to what seems conducive to one's honor and peace, though these may be in contradiction. One knows and one does not really believe, one believes and yet does not know, one knows and one does not quite know, many things. It is no accident that *Light in August* is populated by obsessives; that tunnel vision makes characters appear in each other's line of sight with apparitionlike suddenness; or that Lena Grove is both quite sincerely and quite cannily oblivious to the contradiction between her mental pictures of Lucas Burch, at once faithful lover and scoundrel.

5

"Memory believes before knowing remembers. Believes longer than recollects . . ." (*Light in August* 119). Before and after remembering it, white Southerners believed a further lesson in the national style of conducting peace.

Colonel John Sartoris in *Flags in the Dust*, frank about the dubious ancestral pride he nevertheless honors, says that "in America . . . only what a man takes and keeps has any significance . . . and the only house from which we can claim descent with any assurance, is the Old Bailey [prison]" (96). The history of rapacity, to use one of Faulkner's favorite words for such taking and keeping, bleeds through the present of his work in this period. (And vice versa: Faulkner has Colonel Sartoris killed in 1876 by his former business partner on August 4, the August date marking the Great War's beginning.) But it is not only the settler and the slaveholder ethos that is described in Sartoris's words. It is also, from the standpoint of many white Southern Democrats of Faulkner's generation and earlier, the rapacity of the Reconstruction and the subsequent decades of Northern colonization of the South, primarily under Republican party rule. For white Southern Democrats to hold on to their property in the face of this plunder sanctioned in Washington was in their eyes a considerable achievement. This kind of tenacity is what McCaslin Edmonds praises in the ruthless ancestor, old Carothers McCaslin, in order to dissuade young Isaac McCaslin from repudiating his inherited property because Isaac sees in it the unjust dispossession of others driving American history as it has most history.

Isaac has learned from Sam Fathers an ethos deriving from Fathers's version of his part-Native heritage. His vision of a dispossessed Native American people who still hold the land by right, communally, is reinforced by discovering his grandfather's incest with his slave daughter. Isaac comes to think his Western culture's way of continuing family ownership is wrong, cursed by God, though the Indians who thought the land was theirs to sell incurred the curse before encountering whites. He argues this position at the same time, the 1880s, that Helen Hunt Jackson's book and her subsequent popular novel, *Ramona*, prompted in many a desire to make amends for U.S. possession of tribal land. As we just recalled, however, the result was a law abolishing communal ownership for those Native peoples who practiced it and disastrously forcing them overnight into exactly the individual family ownership Isaac rejects.

In opposition to Isaac, Edmonds advocates a *realpolitik* of peace. He reminds Isaac that old Carothers "bought the land, took the land, got the land no matter how, held it to bequeath, no matter

how, out of the . . . wilderness of wild beasts and wilder men . . .
for his descendants' ease and security and pride" (256). McCaslin
Edmonds in effect also praises himself here, since at the time he
and Isaac argue in the 1880s, the elder cousin Edmonds doesn't
even need to say that he too has held the property, held it against
Republican rapacious opportunism in the South during Reconstruction and continuing at the moment they speak (298). Textual references to Federal Army pensions (Fonsiba's impractical husband
holds one), "Tariff," and "Silver" indicate directly and indirectly
three principal economic policies of patronage and favoritism white
Southern Democrats complained of as post-Reconstruction Republican strategies to continue plundering the South (275, 284). John
Dent wrote in 1883 that these policies aimed "to change the Government from a Republic to one of a money power aristocracy creating a class of Rulers and Imperialists."[20]

Dent was referring to schemes such as President Grant's design
to annex the Dominican Republic (Santo Domingo) to serve as a
safe haven for Southern blacks. White Southerners like Dent saw
such efforts in the Caribbean and elsewhere as part and parcel of
the imperialism directed at them. It is no wonder that *Flags in
the Dust* complains of economic colonization of Mississippi in the
twenties by Northern timber interests (400–401) and that among
Jefferson's serene lawns that inspire Horace Benbow's musings on
peace is "an astonishing clump of stunted banana palms and . . . a
lantana with its clotted wounds" brought back from the Caribbean
in 1871 (178).

But the Spanish-American war and especially the First World
War provided occasions for the South to reestablish itself as an
essential part of patriotic America, martial but peaceful. Thus Captain Percy Grimm, by virtue of the National Defense Act of 1920—
"the new civilian-military act" (450)—is calmly confident that he
represents Uncle Sam, though others, remembering a somewhat
older history, protest against getting Washington involved in Jefferson's affairs.

So, too, part of the ironic postwar soldiers' pay that Faulkner
tallies in his first novel (1926) is "the hang-over of warfare in a

society tired of warfare. [The Great War veterans are] [p]uzzled and lost, poor devils. Once Society drank war, brought them into manhood with a cultivated taste for war; but now Society seemed to have found something else for a beverage."[21] Beginning with the giant binge that opens the novel, these young men, thus encul- turated, are paid with a hangover peace. The imagery and action of the novel, heavily laced with war and peace, display and culti- vate two things at once. One is a taste for a sober peace that re- mains elusive, despite the exceptional capacity for kindness several characters show in helping the wounded pilot Donald Mahon. The other is a taste for a drink of war that remains as imminent as the next predictable shift in cultural beverage in Pro- hibition U. S. A.

Or in the words of the 1930 story "Ad Astra," peace is "the suspension, the not-quite-believing, not-quite-awakened night- mare, the breathing spell of the old verbiaged lusts and the bun- tinged and panoplied greeds."[22] In Faulkner's world of violence dreaming after tranquility and calm thirsting after rampage, peace is not infrequently just such a suspension and breathing spell of war's panoplied and verbiaged rapacity. Actually, neither war nor peace are quite believed or quite awakened from.

In *Flags in the Dust* Horace Benbow epitomizes this state of affairs when he says of the Great War veterans: "they've just gone through . . . an experience that pretty well shook the verities and the humanities, and whether they know it or not, they've got an- other one ahead of 'em that'll finish the business" (176–77). Sus- pended between predicting a follow-up war and/or a postwar disillusionment at verbiaged lusts and acquisitiveness, Horace's statement makes peace and war one smooth arc of devastation. The effect is compounded as Benbow gazes at the fine homes that "emanated a gracious and benign peace": " 'Perhaps this is the reason for wars,' he said. 'The meaning of peace' " (177).

Economically, politically, and psychologically, this war and this peace are mutually implicated strange bedfellows. Violent, war- fixated Bayard Sartoris and serene, gentle Narcissa Benbow are mutually attracted into marriage. Virginia Dupre, scathing on the subject of masculine martial vainglory, still teaches its culture in several ways, including telling stories of Civil War gallantry and attacking martial vanity with a bellicose violence. As Narcissa recognizes, Miss Jenny is trying to enlist her too in the cultivating of doomed warriors, to make Narcissa's son "just another rocket to glare for a moment in the sky, then die away" (410).

6

It's not hard to see that Faulkner's writing is open to the same charge of transmitting a culture of war's "glamorous fatality" (*Flags in the Dust* 433) with all those doomed pilots and their kindred spirits in several novels, stories, and movie scripts. What an attractive challenge of theatrical danger they present, these damaged and driven people! And this too perhaps although, or because, the fictions sometimes scathingly unmask such glamor—Jiggs's puncturing of the reporter's romantics in *Pylon* is a good example—and demonstrate the desirability of peace. As shown in *Flags in the Dust* and elsewhere, Faulkner knows just how deviously the psychology of such cultural transmission works. So in *Knight's Gambit* Gavin Stevens half-sardonically admires "that way of living . . . which could not only accept war but even assimilate it in stride by compromising with it; with the left hand so to speak, without really impeding or . . . even compelling the attention of the right hand still engaged in the way's old prime durable business."[23]

With a similar selective attention, Faulkner himself with one hand participates in a revived expansionist mood in the U.S. as it enters the Second World War, and with the other hand he repudiates it. The story "Shall Not Perish," in praising the entry into the war, ends with a vision of the pioneering of America right out of Manifest Destiny by way of Southern dangerous honor: "the men and the women who . . . tamed the wilderness and overpassed the mountains and deserts and died and still went on as the shape of the United States grew and went on. . . . [T]he men and women still powerful seventy-five years and twice that and twice that again afterward, still powerful and still dangerous and still coming,

North and South and East and West, until the name of what they did and what they died for became just one single word, louder than any thunder. It was America, and it covered all the western earth" (114–15). This jingoistic foreshadowing of a United States covering all North and South America links the meaning of peacetime and of war in expansion, but this time only to celebrate it. During the same brief period, Faulkner's other hand works differently. It writes a counter history of dispossession in *Go Down, Moses*. And it begins *A Fable*, which sees such jingoism as tragic, though inevitable, as are the dialectical counterforces of peace.

Granted Faulkner's complex, ambivalent militarism. But to disclose as he does the intertwined operations of a specific warfare and peacefare on the homefront is to offer one possibly effective means of removing the glamor of exoticism from combat on special battlefields. It resembles the strategy advocated by Kenneth Burke in an essay reviewing the 1933 controversy between Archibald MacLeish and Malcolm Cowley over the problem of how to represent war without making it attractive, either as an openly titillating glory or as a repellent horror that tacitly poses a compelling challenge.[24] Published in the same year as *Light in August*, John Dos Passos's novel *1919* deploys a similar technique of deflating war while deflating the vast network directing both peace and war that *A Fable* later also describes.

In a sense I agree with Anne Goodwyn Jones's recent essay that Faulkner is trying to write a peace narrative.[25] What is distinctive about *Light in August* is that it takes an interesting step toward doing just that, beginning with revising the plot of fatal attraction between war and peace Faulkner used elsewhere. For example, this time the Narcissa Benbow character of serenity, Lena Grove, doesn't even meet, much less marry or carry the child of, the violent war-type, Bayard Sartoris/Joe Christmas, whose (explicit) war connections are parcelled out to Hightower and Grimm. Considering the force of this fatal magnetism, however, the great problem for Faulkner's novel is to show that its peace narrative is not some abstract Peace. In other words, the problem is to show that its narrative acts in contradistinction to—not War—but the culturally specific mixtures that help to empower the narrative itself. These are empowering and disempowering intricacies of war and peace within what Churchill, and in his own way Faulkner, was to teach as the second Thirty Years War.

7

A closing note on theory.

The phrase "culture wars" might be thought redundant considering the practice of some of the most influential analyses of culture today. For this theory and practice, typically war is simply the secret truth of things, and peace the name dupes are taught to misname the secret so they may be the more easily conquered and exploited. In this critical narrative, culture *is* war because culture is about the imposition of power and its resistance or subversion by counterpower. I have no doubt that war (*understood in certain forms and aspects*) offers a valuable frame of analysis, and I have no wish to dispense with it, as this essay in part should make clear. But taken as the only or the privileged model of understanding and cultural critique, War becomes the new essentialism. This is as reductive as assuming Peace to be the essential norm of life, and arguably more dangerous for the human present and future. In light of this century's bellicose history and, less obviously, the national history of peacefare, we should not be surprised at the pervasiveness and persuasiveness of the model—or of the difficulty of thinking in alternative terms. By the same token, we need not relegate all culture to the nomenclature and memory of war any more than we should the period 1914–1945. Faulkner's representative efforts and problems in *Light in August* and elsewhere indicate the challenge that remains.

One way to state the challenge then and now is this: to develop narrative and analytical discourses that draw upon the war paradigm as one among several linked frames of reference that qualify and transform each other without in effect collapsing into false concretions such as War and Peace. During the period we have remembered here, Burke in the U.S. and Bakhtin in the U.S.S.R.

were among those who sought to develop such styles of talking, writing, thinking, and otherwise acting, Burke with his studies of symbolic action "toward the purification of war" (*Ad bellum purificandum*, the motto of *A Grammar of Motives*) and Bakhtin with his concept of dialogism incorporating struggle but not reducible to it. The memory of Faulkner within that time and among such efforts may help to teach us to meet that challenge.

NOTES

1. Matthew 17:2; John Garvey, "Light in August: The Transfiguration and Hiroshima," *Commonweal*, September 1991, 535.

2. Winston Churchill, *The Gathering Storm* (Boston: Houghton Mifflin, 1948), iii; Barbara Wertheim Tuchman, *The Guns of August* (New York: Macmillan, 1962).

3. For Faulkner and the Spanish Civil War, see Joseph Blotner, *Faulkner: A Biography*, rev., 1 vol. (New York: Random House, 1984), 411.

4. William Faulkner, *Flags in the Dust* (New York: Vintage, 1974), 177, 184. All subsequent references are to this edition.

5. For a critique of the assumption that war is fundamentally decisive, see John Keegan, *The Face of Battle* (New York: Barnes and Noble, 1976), 54–62 and *A History of Warfare* (New York: Knopf, 1993), 57.

6. I have found especially useful Paul Fussell, *The Great War and Modern Memory* (New York: Oxford University Press, 1974); David M. Kennedy, *Over Here: The First World War and American Society* (New York: Oxford University Press); Gabriel Kolko, *Century of War* (New York: Free Press, 1990); and Robert S. McElvaine, *The Great Depression: America, 1929–1941* (New York: Times Books, 1993).

7. *Light in August*, The Corrected Text, Vintage International Edition (New York: Random House, 1990), 18. All subsequent references are to this edition.

8. *Reading Faulknerian Tragedy* (Ithaca: Cornell University Press, 1987), 131–69; cf. my discussion of *A Fable* in "Doing What Comes Culturally: Collective Action and the Discourse of Belief in Faulkner and Nathanael West" in *Faulkner, His Contemporaries, and His Posterity*, ed. Waldemar Zacharasiewicz (Tubingen: Franke, 1993). I am grateful to Donald Kartiganer for allowing me to read his paper, " 'So I, Who Had Never Had a War,' " which deftly weaves aesthetic, cultural, biographical, and psychological strands to account for the scarcity of combat scenes in Faulkner.

9. *A Fable* (New York: Modern Library, 1966), 232. All subsequent references are to this edition.

10. *In Our First Year of War: Messages and Addresses to the Congress and the People March 5, 1917 to January 8, 1918* (New York: Harper, 1918), 25.

11. David Levering Lewis, *W. E. B. Du Bois: Biography of a Race 1868–1919* (New York: Henry Holt, 1993), esp. 525–32, 551–52. See also Du Bois on African American military service in the Civil War: "Nothing else made Negro citizenship conceivable, but the record of the Negro soldier as a fighter," *Black Reconstruction in America* (New York: Russell and Russell, 1963), 104; and Bernard C. Nalty, *Strength for the Fight: A History of Black Americans in the Military* (New York: Free Press, 1986). On American women and the Great War, see Kennedy, *Over Here*, 30–31, 284–87.

12. *Go Down, Moses* (New York: Vintage, 1973), 257–58. All subsequent references are to this edition.

13. Alvin M. Josephy Jr., *The Civil War in the West* (New York: Knopf, 1991), esp. xiii, 227–316.

14. *George Washington: A Collection*, ed. W. B. Allen (Indianapolis: Liberty Classics, 1988), 503. This was a recurrent topic of Washington's letters and addresses.

15. For the juxtaposition of Helen Hunt Jackson and General Sherman's statement, I am indebted to Peter Matthiessen, *In the Spirit of Crazy Horse* (New York: Viking, 1983), 17.

16. To some degree these policies preceded Jackson's administration. See Ronald N. Satz, *American Indian Policy in the Jacksonian Era* (Lincoln: University of Nebraska Press, 1975). As Lewis M. Dabney points out, the story also evokes the bonus marches and other mass movements of the early thirties: *The Indians of Yoknapatawpha: A Study of Literature and History* (Baton Rouge: Louisiana State University Press, 1974), 43.

17. *The Crucible of Race: Black-White Relations in the American South since Emancipation* (New York: Oxford University Press, 1984), 15–43; see also Bertram Wyatt-Brown, *Southern Honor: Ethics and Behavior in the Old South* (New York: Oxford University Press, 1982), 402–34.

18. Especially relevant here is the background in Williamson, *Crucible*, 475–82.

19. Wyatt-Brown, *Southern Honor*; Wadlington, *Reading*, 50–64 and passim.

20. Quoted in Charles L. Flynn, Jr., "Procrustean Bedfellows and Populists: An Alternative Hypothesis," in *Race, Class, and Politics in Southern History*, ed. Jeffrey J. Crow (Baton Rouge: Louisiana State University Press, 1989), 86.

21. *Soldiers' Pay* (New York: Liveright, 1926), 198–99.

22. *Collected Stories* (New York: Random House, 1950), 413. All subsequent references are to this edition.

23. *Knight's Gambit* (New York: Random House, 1949), 245.

24. "War, Response, and Contradiction," *The Philosophy of Literary Form*, 3d. ed. (Berkeley: University of California Press, 1973), 234–57. For related recent criticism, see Lynne Hanley's critique of memorializing war predominantly in terms of male battle experience and John Limon's differing argument that all male war writing is not shaped around a knowledge closed off to women and common experience. Hanley, *Writing War: Fiction, Gender, and Memory* (Amherst: University of Massachusetts Press, 1991); Limon, *Writing after War: American War Fiction from Realism to Postmodernism* (New York: Oxford University Press, 1994).

25. "Male Fantasies?: Faulkner's War Stories and the Construction of Gender," in *Faulkner and Psychology*, ed. Donald M. Kartiganer and Ann J. Abadie (Jackson: University Press of Mississippi, 1994), 21–55.

Light in August: A Novel of Passing?

GENA MCKINLEY

1

In the early part of the century, around the time that *Light in August* was published, many black writers, mostly in the North, were dealing with the same racial issues that Faulkner addressed in his works. In fact, throughout the twenties and thirties, a number of these writers published short stories in the same journals in which Faulkner's stories were published.[1] Given that they were concerned to expose and dramatize the same failures of the American system of race, and given that they were writing and publishing at approximately the same time, it is curious that there have been few, if any, comparisons of Faulkner's works with those of writers who were associated with what is now called the Harlem Renaissance. By rereading Faulkner within this sociopolitical and literary context, we might begin to create a critical dialogue that has long been absent both among the writers themselves and in academic scholarship devoted to these works. My immediate aim in this essay is to reexamine Faulkner's *Light in August* alongside James Weldon Johnson's *Autobiography of an Ex-Colored Man,* one of the many (and possibly the earliest) "novels of passing" that came out of the Harlem Renaissance.[2] Though originally published in 1914, *The Autobiography* was not popular until its reintroduction in 1928, at the height of a movement that found it surprisingly undated. Because it is the story of an orphaned male of mixed racial background who wanders from place to place, it bears many important resemblances to Faulkner's tragedy. Perhaps most significantly, both employ a version of the "tragic mulatto" character, a literary figure that was used first by abolitionists as a way to gain sympathy for slaves, then by racist white writers who exploited fears of miscegenation, and ultimately by writers of the Harlem Renaissance who were motivated by an agenda of racial uplift. We will see that Faulkner's creation in *Light in August* is both a product of and a reaction to this broad legacy.

Throughout its history, the figure of the mulatto[3] in literature has served as "America's metaphor," to use Judith Berzon's phrase. That is, the character, whether intentionally or unintentionally, has exposed the "tragic dichotomy between the promise of the American dream and the grim reality of life in America for the marginal member."[4] For antebellum writers of abolitionist novels such as Harriet Beecher Stowe, the light-skinned, educated, and refined slave seemed most capable of arousing the sympathy of a predominantly white middle-class readership. Though they were successful in increasing antislavery sentiment, one racist implication of these novels was that blacks were worthy of moral standing only insofar as they resembled members of the white middle class. Positive character traits such as virtue, intelligence, and chastity (along with "European" physical features such as straight hair, streamlined facial features, and light skin) were depicted as being inherited from the white father, while the opposite characteristics were "blamed" on the mother. After the Civil War, the function of the mulatto character in literature by white writers altered in theme and purpose: the openly propagandistic novels of abolitionism gave way to the novels of the Reconstruction period in which the "tragic mulatto" was still a stock figure but was used now not to arouse antislavery sentiments, but to warn against what many feared would be the harmful consequences of miscegenation. Even those writers who were not operating from a white supremacist ideology continued to depict mulattos stereotypically. Whether a beautiful, mysterious, and passionate female or a gallant, educated, and spirited male, the mulatto character was portrayed as being tormented by a dual lineage, exiled from both races, and doomed to psychological or bodily destruction.[5]

Earlier, black novelists borrowed many of the stereotypical depictions of blacks from white-authored fiction, but they also began to shape these conventions to meet their own narrative needs. Throughout the second half of the nineteenth century and in the early part of the twentieth century, black writers began to explore the theme of blacks who "pass" for white in order to gain liberties still unavailable to those with darker skin. The trend toward responding to the tragic mulatto stereotype by reversing or altering it continued into the twenties and thirties—a time when the leaders of the "New Negro" movement were calling for an end to the caricaturization of blacks, announcing that "the popular melodrama has about played itself out."[6] The objectives were to "repair a damaged group psychology and reshape a warped social perspective." Writers of fiction associated with this movement found that one way of challenging the racist stereotypes and repairing the psychological damage was to dramatize the importance of maintaining one's "true" racial identity. Most often, the mulatto character in these novels would vacillate between the two strands of his or her genealogy, but would ultimately remain loyal to the black community. Those who chose to cross the color line permanently were depicted as traitors to their race.

If we are going to look at *Light in August* in the context of novels written during the Harlem Renaissance, we must remember that although Faulkner was not working under the pressures of a racial agenda, he was writing from within and about the same overall social system that could produce both a Joe Christmas and an Ex-Colored Man. Because he shared their culture, Faulkner was far from immune to the stereotypes and myths that black writers themselves sought to overcome but that still often influenced their own works. Increasingly, however, in the works of black and white writers alike, the mulatto figure became less a symbol of the dangers of miscegenation and more an emblem of the arbitrariness and irrationality of classification according to skin color. By not fitting neatly into either of the only two available categories, the mulatto stood as a powerful indictment of racial dualism and came to represent the abstractness of the concept of race in general.

Donald Kartiganer recognized the importance of Joe Christmas as such an emblem when he wrote that "[a]t the center of *Light in August* is the mulatto—more important, the imagined mulatto."[7] What Kartiganer suggests here but does not fully explore is that Faulkner has taken to its extreme the idea of race as a social construct. By electing to leave Christmas's parentage undefined, Faulkner lays bare the extent to which society's definition of race is grounded in fiction rather than biological fact. Though the definition rests theoretically on a difference in skin color—or a genealogy that somewhere down the line can point to a difference in skin color—neither of these is a useful criterion for determining the race of Joe Christmas. In the traditional novel of passing, the character's racial ambiguity is presented as a rather well-defined problem of dual identity. In the paradigm case, the mulatto has one black parent and one white parent and must choose which racial heritage he will adopt. Because Christmas is an orphan whose parentage is uncertain, his race is entirely a fiction, one that begins when the children at the orphanage start calling him "nigger." Although Doc Hines is almost certainly to blame for planting these initial seeds of racism, ultimately it does not matter *why* he is labeled this way. Once he is convinced of the truth of their accusations, Christmas is black in the only sense that matters—that is, he *believes* himself to be black.

None of what I have said is meant to suggest that, were Christmas depicted in the novel as actually being the offspring of an interracial union, we should be any less outraged by the way in which his society condemns him. Nor does Faulkner, I think, mean to create a more sympathetic character by leaving open the possibility that the community has "misread" him. He is not more tragic because there exists the possibility that the town has lynched a "white" man. Rather, by giving us someone who merely believes himself to be black and whose life is wholly and tragically altered because of this belief, Faulkner can reveal more fully the horrifying power of society to shape an individual's identity according to its own perverse distortions.

Perhaps in an effort to interpret Christmas as a character that comes out of the "tragic mulatto" tradition, critics of *Light in Au-*

gust have focused on him as a bodily challenge to the artificial division of race into two mutually exclusive categories. They have, somewhat inaccurately I think, characterized him as someone who chooses to reject society's insistence that he identify with one race or the other: "At the center of *Light in August* is the mulatto— more important, the imagined mulatto. This is the role that Christmas, never being sure of what his origins are, has chosen. Able to "pass," to choose a single identity, Christmas chooses instead his doubleness."[8] "Christmas is a walking oxymoron and its negation: both white and black, and neither. He might choose, he could 'pass,' yet he chooses not to choose, refuses to settle for either of the ready-made identity patterns urged upon him by Southern society."[9] "Living at once as a black man and as a white man brings Joe Christmas close to the symbolic possibility of racial amalgamation expressed in Faulkner's later novels. That he fails is both the result of his own personality and of social and environmental pressures. Joe is free to choose his race, but he must in fact choose—choose or face destruction."[10]

In each of these passages, there is explicit in the language of "choosing" the assumption that Christmas, poised on the edge of two racial paths and aware of the consequences of each, is ultimately free to decide his own course. They all suggest that Christmas is somehow dissatisfied with his limited options and so rejects, through his not taking one of the paths, the dualism that his society insists upon. Certainly these critics are speaking metaphorically on one level: of course, there is no definable moment when Christmas announces his intention to "choose his doubleness" or makes the decision not to pass; nevertheless, the language of "choice" is misleading in his case for reasons that I hope to make clear with the following comparison.

In contrast to Christmas, it would not be misleading to speak of Johnson's hero as being in a position to choose: he actually thinks of himself as having rejected a life among his "mother's people" for the life of "an ordinarily successful white man who has made a little money." His famous, final words—"I cannot repress the thought that, after all, I have chosen the lesser part, that I have sold my birthright for a mess of pottage"[11]—reflect the extent to which he considers his categorization as a "white man" to be a direct result of the decisions he made in life. This is not to suggest that the Ex-Colored Man had more freedom than Christmas or that he was operating within an environment that was any less tolerant of racial ambiguity. In part, the difference is simply a result of the fact that Johnson wrote with an admitted agenda of heightening racial awareness among his readers. He pointedly juxtaposes the nearly unlimited opportunities available to middle-class "white" men in this country with the very restricted life available to those who were labeled "black," and his stated goal in the preface is to make the reader more aware of a growing "prejudice against the Negro" that was "actually and constantly forcing an unascertainable number of fair-complexioned coloured people over into the white race."[12] Also, because the novel is written as a first-person narrative, we witness firsthand the psychological struggle to choose between these two rather well-defined, but unsatisfactory options.

Such is not the case with Joe Christmas. The passages I quoted above and other critical analyses of *Light in August* retain the vocabulary of choice that, while appropriate to novels in which the character actively vacillates between passing for white or not, is somewhat inaccurate as a means of characterizing Joe Christmas's situation. In part, we can attribute the absence of a similar psychological battle to the distance Faulkner places between the reader and the mind of his hero. Kartiganer rightly recognizes Christmas as the "impenetrable center" of the novel—"[a]s remote from us and his author as he is from the society around him."[13] Most of the information we get about the content of his thoughts is speculative: "Perhaps he thought of that other window which he had used to use and of the rope upon which he had to rely; perhaps not."[14] Throughout the novel, Faulkner uses this technique to attribute thoughts or beliefs to his hero. Still, we might infer from what we see Christmas do, rather than what he thinks, that he struggles to choose between "whiteness" and "blackness." We know, for example, that when the white prostitute infuriates him by not reacting

more strongly to his "admission," he turns to the black community
and lives "as man and wife with a woman who resembled an ebony
carving."[15] Yet, in this same scene, Faulkner leaves no doubt about
the repulsion that Christmas feels toward blacks and the confusion
he has about his own racial identity:

> At night he would lie in bed beside her, sleepless, beginning to
> breathe deep and hard. He would do it deliberately, feeling, even
> watching, his white chest arch deeper and deeper within his ribcage,
> trying to breathe into himself the dark odor, the dark and inscrutable
> thinking and being of negroes, with each suspiration trying to expel
> from himself the white blood and the white thinking and being. And
> all the while his nostrils at the odor which he was trying to make his
> own would whiten and tauten, his whole being writhe and strain with
> physical outrage and spiritual denial.[16]

In Freedman Town, his reaction is similar—once again the suffo-
cation and disgust is associated with blackness and femaleness:

> He was standing still now, breathing quite hard, glaring this way and
> that. About him the cabins were shaped blackly out of blackness by
> the faint, sultry glow of kerosene lamps. On all sides, even within him,
> the bodiless fecundmellow voices of negro women murmured. It was
> as though he and all other manshaped life about him had been re-
> turned to the lightless hot wet primogenitive Female. He began to
> run, glaring, his teeth glaring, his inbreath cold on his dry teeth and
> lips, toward the next street lamp.[17]

In both scenes, it might seem that Christmas thinks of himself as
a white man (his "white chest" and the language which was "not
his") who tries unsuccessfully to "choose his blackness." But it is
precisely because Christmas already believes himself to be black
that he is filled with self-hatred. His agony and frustration are not
over indecision about what racial life he will lead, but a result of
his belief that race is not a matter of choice. He can recognize that
outward manifestations of difference (in language or skin color)
might separate him from the people of Freedman Town or from
the "ebony"-skinned woman, but because he accepts the racist
ideology that there is a biological, "blood" difference between
blacks and whites he must classify himself as irreversibly black.

The only fact that would change his perception of himself would be if he were to discover that he did not have "black blood." But it is not possible for him to know for sure, and he knows that it is impossible, so he must not take any chances.[18] When Joanna Burden asks, "How do you know . . ?", his response is: "I don't know. . . . If I'm not, damned if I haven't wasted a lot of time."[19] From this it is clear that Christmas has lived his life *as if* he were sure of his "blackness."[20] Like the Ex-Colored Man, Christmas is aware of the dualisms that govern society, but his story is not one of the struggle to choose between them any more than it is the story of one who chooses to live outside the established framework. Unlike the Ex-Colored Man, Christmas shares the racist views of his persecutors, resulting not only in self-hatred but also in the resignation that he cannot change his condition merely by choosing between his lineages.

With the speech he gives Gavin Stevens at the end of *Light in August*, Faulkner even mocks the "battle of blood" that traditionally characterized the tragic mulatto stereotype:

> Because the black blood drove him first to the negro cabin. And then the white blood drove him out of there, as it was the black blood which snatched up the pistol and the white blood which would not let him fire it. And it was the white blood which sent him to the minister, which rising in him for the last time, sent him against all reason and all reality, into the embrace of a chimera, a blind faith in something read in a printed Book.[21]

What Faulkner seems to ridicule in this passage is the absurdity of the very notion of "mixed blood." By making Christmas's anguish a matter of biology, Gavin Stevens exposes his complicity in a racial division irrationally grounded in skin color and genealogy. It is this racist ideology—that there is a "blood" difference between blacks and whites—that Christmas also accepts and that finally destroys him.

2

I have argued that Christmas is not engaged in the kind of psychological dilemma that drives the narrative of characters like the Ex-

Colored Man. For Christmas, the combination of his racism and his belief that he is black (according to the definition of his society) leave him with no choice of the kind we find in novels of passing. Now I would like to shift the focus of the argument in a way that might seem to run counter to what has come before. Even though Christmas does not see race as a matter of choice, he does frequently "pass" for white and, like the Ex-Colored Man, wanders from place to place desperately seeking a single identity. This, however, is in no way incompatible with Christmas's belief that he is black. He frequently allows others to think otherwise when there is something (like sex, or a job) to be gained by it. And yet, Christmas's primary source of dissatisfaction is the guilt he feels as a black man who "passes" for white and the hatred he has both for himself and for those who are not outraged by his "transgression"—the transgression of a racial code that he himself believes in. I will also try to show how Christmas's racial guilt is inextricably linked to his sexual guilt and his loathing of all things physical.

Characters who consciously adopt personae that will identify them with the white middle class are engaged in what I call "active" passing. Angela Murray, the heroine of Jessie Redmon Fauset's *Plum Bun*, for example, moves to New York, changes her name to Angele Mory, and refuses to associate with her darker-skinned sister for fear of being "exposed."[22] Similarly, in Nella Larsen's *Passing*, Clare Kendry rejects the black community by marrying a racist white man from whom she actively conceals her background.[23] The characters in these novels recognize the irrationality of a biological-based classification of race, but they choose to live as "white" because it affords them a power that they know should have never been denied them in the first place. On a date with a young man who is both wealthy and white, Angela thinks to herself, "Here I am having everything that a girl ought to have just because I had sense enough to suit my actions to my appearance."[24] In contrast, Christmas accepts the categorization and, perhaps because of this, does not actively pursue a life as a white man. But neither does he always inform others that he is "black" when he knows that they believe him to be "white." This is what I will call "passive" passing, the situation in which we find Christmas when we first meet him in chapter 2. When he arrives in Jefferson, he appears to be close to starvation and so probably passes for white in order to obtain employment. Though he does "a nigger's work" at the planing mill, his fellow employees are white and he makes no effort to alter their belief that he is "white" like them. In fact, he comes across as something of a dandy, a role that we find out later he adopted from the white men at Max's diner: "He looked like a tramp, yet not like a tramp either. His shoes were dusty and his trousers were soiled too. But they were of decent serge, sharply creased, and his shirt was soiled but it was a white shirt, and he wore a tie and a stiffbrim straw hat that was quite new, cocked at an angle arrogant and baleful above his still face."[25] Critics have often cited this passage as further evidence that Christmas cannot decide whether to be black or white. I think, rather, that although he wants (and often sorely needs) many of the advantages that being white allows one to have, his belief that he is black prevents him from taking full advantage of his ability to "pass." This is not to say that he would prefer not to be "white." Like Angela and Clare and the Ex-Colored Man, he realizes that if he had been born white, his life would have been much easier, safer, and more peaceful; but unlike them, he does not believe that he can choose membership in a race that is as distant to him as the black race is repulsive. After fleeing Freedman Town, Christmas passes through a white neighborhood, looks wistfully at the people on the "lighted veranda . . . the white faces intent and sharp in the low light, the bare arms of the women glaring smooth and white above the trivial cards" and thinks "That's all I wanted. . . . That dont seem like a whole lot to ask."[26] This passage is significant in its uncharacteristic poignancy and represents one of the few times in which Christmas actually expresses his innermost longings. To him, being white would mean, at the very least, having time and energy for something as "trivial" as a card game on the porch of a nice house, just as for Angela it would mean having the leisure to go to the cinema or date whomever she likes. But Christmas does not allow himself the full benefits of a white man; in fact, his "passing" is interrupted repeatedly by his guilt-driven need to "confess" his "blackness."

Much of the guilt Christmas experiences can be attributed to his Puritanical upbringing at the hands of the brutally strict McEachern. Christmas associates whiteness with pleasures of the flesh (beginning with the toothpaste incident)—pleasures that McEachern would have him renounce completely but that he nevertheless pursues, partly out of spite, partly out of pure desire. Rebelling against McEachern's ascetic religiosity, Christmas buys a new suit, begins to drink, and attends dances. But his pleasure is tempered by the residue of Puritanism that has left its mark on him, causing him to respond violently to the discovery that women are afflicted with "periodical filth." That Christmas vomits in reaction to Bobbie Allen's news is clearly reminiscent of the scene in the dietitian's office, and much has been made of the connections between these two formative events in Christmas's twisted sexual awakening and his consequent association of sex with guilt and disgust. There is certainly even more to be said on the topic, but my point is concerned, more particularly, with the fact that Christmas's cycle of "passing" and "confessing" is almost exclusively associated with his sexual experiences.

When he recovers from the shock of what he perceives to be Bobbie Allen's biological flaw (the flaw of womanhood), Christmas accepts her in spite of it and is moved to share with her his own, dark secret:

> "You noticed my skin, my hair," waiting for her to answer, his hand slow on her body.
>
> She whispered also. "Yes. I thought maybe your were a foreigner. . . ."
>
> ". . . You cant guess?"
>
> "What? How more different?"
>
> "Guess."
>
> Their voices were quiet. It was still, quiet; night now known, not to be desired, pined for. "I cant. What are you?"
>
> His hand was slow and quiet on her invisible flank. He did not answer at once. It was not as if he were tantalising her. It was as if he just had not thought to speak on. She asked him again. Then he told her. "I got some nigger blood in me."[27]

Up until this point Christmas had been "courting" Bobbie Allen in a manner that, in his mind, would have accorded with white, middle-class codes of behavior. He brings her candy and naively assumes that her intentions are as "pure" as his. He even introduces himself to the "men of the house" as Joe McEachern in what comes across as a pitiful, even laughable, attempt to appear the respectable boyfriend. Earlier, however, he had revealed to Bobbie Allen his true name, and he continues, now as her lover, to confide in her in hopes of being accepted for what he believes himself to be. The scene is a variation on the stock "confession scene" of passing novels, almost always a highly sentimentalized or melodramatic moment when the protagonists risk rejection for performing what they perceive to be their "duty" to confess their "blackness." Compare Faulkner's scene to the one in *The Autobiography of an Ex-Colored Man*:

> I felt her hand creep to mine, and when I looked at her, her eyes were glistening with tears. I understood, and could scarcely resist the longing to take her in my arms; but I remembered, remembered that which has been the sacrificial altar of so much happiness—Duty; and bending over her hand in mine I said: "Yes, I love you; but there is something more, too, that I must tell you." Then I told her, in what words I do not know, *the truth* [my italics]. I felt her hand grow cold, and when I looked up, she was gazing at me with a wild, fixed stare as though I was some object she had never seen. Under the strange light in her eyes I felt that I was growing black and thick-featured and crimp-haired.[28]

The salient difference between the two passages is that Johnson's is highly melodramatic while Faulkner's is matter-of-fact in tone but marked by a peacefulness (a tenderness even) uncharacteristic of Joe Christmas. And, while the narrator of Johnson's novel cannot even repeat the words of his "confession," Christmas bluntly and unhesitatingly refers to his "nigger blood." For reasons I discussed earlier, I think it matters very little that Christmas qualifies his claim by admitting that he is not certain of his racial status; what the Ex-Colored Man characterizes as the unspeakable "truth" is just as "true" for Christmas. Because Christmas himself is so committed to this truth, he cannot bear to leave it buried. His guilt over engaging in sex mingles with his guilt over "passing" as the white lover of a white woman, forcing him to "own up to" the only identity he knows—one that he abhors but is unable to escape.

More interesting than the differences between these two passages, however, are the telling similarities. During their confessions, both heroes are acutely conscious of certain physical features ("my skin, my hair" and "black and thick-featured and crimp-haired") that society has led them to believe stand as outward evidence of their "negritude." In both cases, we get the sense that by "confessing" they are preempting the feared scenario in which their lovers guess their race by "reading" these features, as Ike McCaslin "reads" Jim Beauchamp's granddaughter when she comes into his tent in "Delta Autumn."[29] This same fear surfaces when the "gaze" of the white woman transforms the Ex-Colored Man into a black man; in the "confession" scene, she represents the distorted vision of white America and the power of its racism to shape an individual's self-perception. It is a powerful force, indeed. While throughout *The Autobiography* the narrator attacks the biological-based foundations of racist ideology, under the disapproving eye of his lover he (and Johnson, too, I think) lapses into the very discourse that condemns him: "This was the only time in my life that I ever felt absolute regret at being coloured, that I cursed the drops of African blood in my veins and wished that I were really white."[30] The irony is that, while the central polemical goal of the novel is to attack a racial system invested in maintaining that there are "blood differences," the narrator falls victim to this rhetoric during a moment of weakness. When the person he most hoped would not be affected by the artificial difference reveals that she is, his self-perception is radically altered in accord with her racism.

Although Faulkner does not give us a hero who is quite so articulate, we are left with little doubt that Christmas, too, "wishes he were white" at times. Unlike the Ex-Colored Man, however, he is never without the belief that his biology is what makes him different and that the "blood" difference is a real one. In a sense, this makes Christmas's own loss of love even more painful. When McEachern crashes the dance and Bobbie Allen turns on Christmas—"you nigger bastard!"—she expresses (though more crudely) the same racism expressed by the Ex-Colored Man's girlfriend who begins to cry at the news. With this incident, Christmas's only hope of love is shattered, and it is in the aftermath of its violence that he begins his lonely trek down "the street which was to run for fifteen years."

This decade and a half, along with Christmas's youth, passes fleetingly before us in a mere three pages. Like the Ex-Colored Man, Christmas takes on one role after another ("he was in turn laborer, miner, prospector, gambling tout"),[31] always a stranger wherever he goes, so that he can maintain (vehemently now) his cycle of "passing" and "confessing." We sense that during this time, as later when he works at the planing mill, the "passing" takes place on the job while the "confessing" is confined to the bedroom. When he nearly beats to death a prostitute who reacts to his "confession" with complete indifference (and even refers to previous black "patrons"), we are shocked into realizing how much hatred Christmas has for himself and for his race. His belief that blacks are inferior to whites requires him to be "punished" for "passing"—especially when, as a "black" man, he sleeps with a white woman. It is the fear and hatred of this same taboo that drives Christmas into the arms of Joanna Burden, and then leads, finally, to his murder of her.

When Christmas first enters Burden's place through the window, he already knows that she is a middle-aged white woman (as the young boy tells him, "Miz Burden aint old. Aint young neither")[32]—the ultimate challenge in his series of sexual conquests and, yet, the ultimate threat to his life. Like many writers, Faulkner is guilty of having in his stock of characters the stereotype of the widowed or spinstered woman in her thirties or forties whose sexual fantasies often include encounters with young, black males (historically depicted by racist white writers as having extraordinary sexual prowess). In "Dry September," an innocent man is lynched because of the careless accusation of a white woman ("thirty-eight or thirty-nine" in age) whose testimony, despite its dubiousness—"This aint the first man scare she ever had. . . . Wasn't there something about a man on the kitchen roof, watching her undress, about a year ago?"—is all the community needs to justify their murder of Will Mayes. In Johnson's novel, the rich "widow" represents a cosmopolitan version of the stereotype that we find in Faulkner, and her violent death sheds light on some of the same fears and anxieties that lead to Burden's murder.

The Ex-Colored Man meets the widow, "an exceedingly beautiful woman of perhaps thirty-five" . . . with . . . "very white skin" whose companion was a "well-set-up, very black young fellow," at a nightclub in Harlem.[33] After several overtures made by the woman, the narrator joins her for a drink in the club, an act that ends, not in his death, but in hers. Her black companion enters, with an "ugly look" and, "instead of striking her, he whip[s] out a revolver and fire[s]; the first shot [goes] straight into her throat."[34] In a passage that reveals the Ex-Colored Man's own fears, he recalls: "but still I could see that beautiful white throat with the ugly wound. The jet of blood pulsing from it had placed an indelible red stain on my memory."[35] Both the widow and the narrator are white-skinned outsiders in Harlem, subject to the hatred of "blacks" who might not be able to tell that the narrator is "really" black like them. Lying just beneath the melodramatic surface, however, is the narrator's real fear: that he will be caught in the company of a white woman, pretending to be white and, thus, failing both as the competent black male lover and as the white male who would "protect" her from the violence of "black" men like himself. At a very basic level, he sees in her death his own potential destruction at the hands of a lynch mob, like the one led by Percy Grimm or John McLendon. The fear that exists merely in the (not unfounded) paranoia of the narrator's imagination is realized in the story of Joe Christmas.

Critics have long recognized a similar "doubling" in the characters of Joe Christmas and Joanna Burden: their names are alike; they are both outsiders, loners whose genealogies are "tainted" by miscegenation, but whose skin is white; and they are both depicted as having craven sexual appetites. To the extent that they bond with each other, however, it is not through sex but through the long talks they have, especially the very lengthy discussion in which Burden reveals to Christmas her entire past—a past that, like his, includes tales of secrets and bigotry and violence. During this interlude, Christmas listens and reacts with a pathos that is distinctly uncharacteristic of him. Faulkner puts words into his mouth that we would be more likely to find in Johnson's novel: "Just when do men that have different blood in them stop hating one another?" he asks.[36] Christmas sees in Burden's past his own future—his murder and castration at the hands of Percy Grimm—another instance of hate that keeps on going even after the object of hate has been destroyed.

Christmas's identification with Burden, however, ends when she begins to remind him of their difference and of what both believe to be his lower place in the racial hierarchy. It is then that all his fears and guilt and hatred begin to reemerge. He is reminded of his status as an "impostor," a black man who is passing for white and sleeping with a woman who not only is not outraged by his "blackness," but who prefers it. Like the widow, Burden's sexual fantasy is fulfilled by Christmas because he is, to her, a "Negro" who is indebted to her for her philanthropic contributions to "his race." For the widow in Johnson's novel, the young black male is even more of a commodification: "I learned that she paid for his clothes and his diamonds. I learned, too, that he was not the only one of his kind."[37] Not unlike the widow who "purchases" the "services" of her black lovers by financially supporting them, Joanna Burden wants to "buy" Christmas and mold him to her specifications. Her work for the "negro colleges" represents the paternalistic attitude that often accompanied white support for these institutions. But because they were financially dependent, the schools were forced to submit, just as Christmas is urged to submit to Burden's plan—one that would require him to attend "a nigger school." It is this paternalism of Burden's that unleashes Christmas's deepest fury and resentment. He retaliates by striking where he might offend her as much as she has offended him: "You're old. I never noticed that before. An old woman. You've got gray in your hair. . . . You just got old and it happened to you and now you are not any good anymore. That's all that's wrong with you."[38] He "reads" her hair and skin in the way that he fears others might read him or his offspring. The physical features that society points to in justification of its irrational race categories are the same features (hair and skin) that, in part, divide young from old. In an unconscious appeal to the dualist society that victimizes him, Christmas finds a way to make Burden, too, feel like the "Other."

Burden's response to Christmas's "blackness" stands in extreme opposition to the reaction of those whites who share (and are responsible for) Christmas's own racism. Rather than react with horror, disbelief or even indifference to his "confession," she welcomes his presence as an opportunity to expiate her own guilt—the burden of "every white child that ever was born and that ever will be born."[39] Her pity, however, is the most intolerable of all reactions because it assumes his inability to survive on his own, without the charity of "white folks." It seeks to deprive him of the one thing that he is capable of—existing, alone, but in a manner that he thinks is honest, passing only "passively," but always "confessing," and forcing his society to face up to the irrationality of a color-coded classification of race that he hates but does not repudiate.

NOTES

1. Nella Larsen's "Sanctuary," for example, was published the same year (1930) as Faulkner's "A Rose for Emily" in a later edition of the *Forum*.

2. In these novels, the protagonist is a light-skinned black capable of passing for white.

3. I employ the term grudgingly because of its etymological roots. It derives from the word "mule," the barren animal that results from the union of a horse and a donkey. In the nineteenth and early twentieth centuries, it was rumored that the offspring of an interracial union would, like the mule, be barren.

4. Judith Berzon, *Neither White Nor Black: The Mulatto Character in American Fiction* (New York: New York University Press, 1978), 52.

5. It is interesting to note that while Faulkner deviates significantly from the "tragic mulatto" stereotype in his creation of Christmas, he later embraces it as a model for Charles Bon.

6. Alain Locke, ed., *The New Negro: Voices of the Harlem Renaissance* (New York: Macmillan, 1925), 8–9.

7. Donald Kartiganer, "The Meaning of Form in *Light in August,*" in *William Faulkner's Light in August,* ed. Harold Bloom (New York: Chelsea House, 1988), 10.

8. Ibid.

9. André Bleikasten, "Light in August: The Closed Society and Its Subjects," in *New Essays on "Light in August,"* ed. Michael Millgate (Cambridge: Cambridge University Press, 1987), 83.

10. Thadious M. Davis, *Faulkner's "Negro": Art and the Southern Context* (Baton Rouge : Louisiana State University Press, 1983), 137.

11. James Weldon Johnson, *The Autobiography of an Ex-Colored Man* (New York: Hill and Wang, 1988), 211.

12. Ibid., xii.

13. Kartiganer, 91.

14. William Faulkner, *Light in August* (New York: Random House, 1932), 216.

15. Ibid., 212.

16. Ibid.

17. Ibid., 107.

18. His attitude is not so different from that of the sheriff, whose response to Joe Brown's accusation of Christmas represents a similar caution: "You better be careful what you are saying, if it is a white man you are talking about," 91. According to the sheriff (and the community that he stands for) the greatest crime one can commit is to accuse a white man of being black. Christmas's belief (also shared by the community) seems to be that it is equally criminal to pass for white when one is "really" black.

19. Faulkner, *Light in August,* 241.

20. Although I disapprove of his terminology, I agree with Lee Jenkins who claims that "any discussion of whether or not Joe actually possesses black blood is immaterial, since he believes, and thus behaves, as if he did," *Faulkner and Black-White Relations: A Psychoanalytic Approach* (New York: Columbia University Press, 1981).

21. Faulkner, *Light in August,* 424–25.

22. Jessie Redmon Fauset, *Plum Bun: A Novel Without a Moral* (Boston: Beacon Press, 1990).

23. Nella Larsen, *Quicksand and Passing,* ed. Deborah McDowell (New Jersey: Rutgers, 1986).

24. Fauset, *Plum Bun,* 123.

25. Faulkner, *Light in August,* 27.

26. Ibid., 108.

27. Ibid., 204.

28. Johnson, *The Autobiography of an Ex-Colored Man,* 204.

29. "Now he understood what it was she had brought into the tent with her, what old Isham had already told him by sending the youth to bring her in to him—the pale lips, the skin pallid and dead-looking yet not ill, the dark and tragic and foreknowing eyes. . . . He cried, not loud, in a voice of amazement, pity, and outrage: " 'You're a nigger!' " William Faulkner, "Delta Autumn" in *Go Down, Moses* (New York: Random House, 1940, Vintage Books, 1973), 360–61.

30. Johnson, *The Autobiography of an Ex-Colored Man,* 205.

31. Faulkner, *Light in August,* 211.

32. Ibid., 214.

33. Johnson, 108.

34. Ibid., 124.

35. Ibid., 125.

36. Faulkner, 236.

37. Johnson, 108.

38. Faulkner, 262.

39. Ibid., 239.

Faulkner and Proletarian Literature

JOHN T. MATTHEWS

I had hoped my title to seem a little odd, a little strained. I thought I could pique your interest with a whiff of class conflict, the sort of topic not very popular in Faulkner criticism, one most unfashionable in the post-Soviet world, and one that current Newtonian physics has so reversed that we now take seriously the "problem" of protecting the rights of the ruling class. On July 4, however, I opened the *Boston Globe* to a front page story entitled "Sound and fury arising over Elvis at Ole Miss."[1] Bill Ferris was quoted as saying that the resistance in some quarters of Oxford to a Presley Conference has a "class-based tension at [its] heart" (8). This present "class cleavage" stems from Faulkner's affiliation with the "privileged, educated elite" of the state, while Elvis, representing the "working class," could never realize his dream of attending Ole Miss and majoring in football. As a result, presumably, Elvis had to give up his Labovian potential and settle for worldwide fame, outlandish wealth, and the burden of spending his life filming beach movies and murmuring love lyrics to millions of adoring fans. Faulkner, meanwhile, for most of his life became a connoisseur of those rarest of life's pleasures: professional obscurity, the enmity of those who knew him best, and financial desperation. For the sake of fairness in this comparison I have not mentioned Elvis's arguable immortality, at least in the aisles of K-Mart. I'm all for putting Count No 'Count and the King cheek by jowl, so to speak, but I am a little skeptical of strict class oppositions. An era of mass culture, consumption, and publicity has pretty much made simple wealth and fame the only marker of class in our society. The American elite need no longer pretend to lineage, cultivated taste, and secluded power. Indeed, stars like Elvis helped shake that all up. And what prestige the academy used to accord high cultural icons has disappeared before the leveling motives of popular culture studies. In Don DeLillo's novel *White Noise*, a new faculty member at the College-on-the-Hill confides his academic dream to his successful older colleague, who has instituted on campus his own first-of-a-kind research center in the nation: "I want to do for Elvis what you've done for Hitler."[2] So we begin with Faulkner newly repoliticized, under the sign of a cultural class struggle.

My paper investigates the relations between Faulkner's writing of the thirties and arguably the foremost cultural enterprise of the decade, the widespread effort of artists and intellectuals to imagine and instigate a class revolution in the United States. We all know that Faulkner explicitly repudiated the sort of fiction that subordinates the particular stories of individuals to the illustration of abstractions about society: "if one begins to write about the injustice of society, then one has stopped being primarily a novelist and has become a polemicist or a propagandist."[3] The novelist must, he goes on to say, write about "people, not about the injustice or inhumanity of people" (177).

Concentrating on the significant individual helps Faulkner register his antipathy to the diminishment of personal stature associated with the modern age: Mr. Compson describes the South's epic age as populated by figures "integer for integer, larger, more heroic . . . not dwarfed and involved but distinct, uncomplex".[4] The political valence of Faulkner's writing seems set by his general lamentation over the passing of a social and cultural order that, no matter how deeply flawed, seems destined to be supplanted by a worse. The broad outlines of Faulkner's relation to the transformation of the South into a modern society suggest a reluctant but eventually compliant observer. Dating roughly from the New Deal's reconstruction of Southern economic ways, and leading ultimately to the destruction of social forms like segregation, modernization transformed the cotton belt into the sunbelt between the 1930s and the 1970s.[5]

Faulkner hardly welcomed these changes with revolutionary fervor. "Slow" was his watchword. When he came round to writing in a vein more favorable to desegregation, for example, in *Intruder in the Dust* (1948), he had already spent two decades elaborating less the suffering of victims than the psychic trauma debilitating the guilty heirs of corrupted Southern ideals. Faulkner's modernist aesthetic suits such interests. Experiments in narrative temporality reflect the experience of subjects like Quentin Compson, Horace Benbow, and Gail Hightower for whom change means only anxiety over lost bearings. Stream-of-consciousness technique intricately reproduces the effort of a single mind to unify at least an interior world. Perspectivism isolates individual ways of looking and reinforces the uniqueness of subjectivities. Abstractionism substitutes the manipulation of form for the description of a world. All of these modernist effects have been criticized as politically reactionary; they tend, as Lúkacs complained, to attenuate the representations of social reality and to exaggerate the individuality of the bourgeois subject.[6]

Contrast this view of high modernism with the familiar attributes of proletarian fiction. Prescriptions for successful proletarian novels often called for depictions of the living conditions and labor of the working class, the portrayal of class conflict, plots that led to the protagonist's awakened class consciousness, and a manner of presentation that was readily comprehensible and preferred communication to artistic effect. Raised to the level of cultural warfare, as declared by Mike Gold, the editor of the communist *New Masses* magazine, such principles revile what most of us care about in Faulkner and many other great writers. Gold insisted that literature portray "real conflicts" of "the suffering of hungry, persecuted and heroic millions," not "the sickly mental states of the idle Bohemians," as in the case of the scorned Proust, "mastermasturbator of the bourgeois literature."[7] Gold ridiculed other modernists for being "verbal acrobats," acrobatics being "only another form for bourgeois idleness" ("Proletarian Realism" 207).

Gold's smashmouth criticism established the base line for proletarian judgments of twenties modernists: he called Hemingway a "white collar poet" who "describes the same material as do tabloids, and his sole boast is his aloofness, last refuge of a scoundrel."[8] In perhaps his most inflammatory moment, Gold accused Thornton Wilder of seeking to restore "a pastel, pastiche, dilettante religion . . . that centers around Jesus Christ, the First British Gentleman."[9] Wilder, concludes Gold, is our "Emily Post of culture" ("Wilder" 202).

Given this sketchy opposition, Faulkner's writing looks to have little to do with the central ambitions of proletarian literature. I begin with this version of the received opposition between a politically conservative modernism and a revolutionary social realism because I wish to question it. Not only did political and aesthetic positions prove more provisional and changeable than we commonly appreciate, but the proletarian movement itself housed widely discrepant opinions and artistic practices. This was so even before the mid-thirties, when the Communist Party's Popular Front strategy reached out to "fellow travellers" of various leftist stripes in opposing fascism.

Revising our view of the radical writing of the thirties matters to our understanding of Faulkner because his fiction treats so many issues central to proletarianism, and does so with at least a keen sense of the injustices suffered by individuals under plantocratic and later mercantile capitalism. Sylvia Jenkins Cook observes that "Faulkner is as acutely class-conscious as any Marxist and as prone to patterns of economic sympathy and class allegiance."[10] But Faulkner parts ways with Marxist representations of class, Cook argues, in his refusal to identify class exploitation as responsible for the plight of Yoknapatawpha's poor. For example, Cook argues that Faulkner partially reinforces the stereotype of the longsuffering poor in *As I Lay Dying* and *The Hamlet*, in which poverty ennobles its victims and charity obscures fundamental economic injustice. In a work like *Sanctuary*, Cook continues, Faulkner sees good and evil manifested as attributes of individual characters and distributed across class lines; underworld thugs and middle class hypocrites earn equal censure, and the only sources of moral hope reside in Horace and Ruby, both "relics of a nobler age" (47). Even in stories like "Wash" and "Barn Burning," where class resentment drives the plot, Cook sees Faulkner's disinclination to secure his protagonists' class identification, the principal objective of prototypical proletarian novels like Gold's own *Jews Without Money* (1930) and Jack Conroy's *The Disinherited* (1933). Wash acts within the aristocratic ideal to "fix" Sutpen's degradation of it, while Sarty rejects his father Ab's violent guerrilla warfare against the injustice of tenancy.

Readings like Cook's of the outcomes of these stories of redneck resentment concentrate on what has been produced by the gestures of defiance. In the case of "Wash," poor white rage combusts into apocalpytic violence. Wash cannot believe that Sutpen does not intend to marry Milly, the granddaughter who has just borne a child to his hero. Surely the Colonel, who is the very "apotheosis" of Wash's unrealizable dreams, will "make hit right."[11] When Sutpen insultingly repudiates mother and infant—"too bad you're not a mare. Then I could give you a decent stall in the stable" (535)—he unambiguously destroys Wash's delusion that he and the Kernel might work together to rebuild the South after the Civil War. When Wash realizes that Sutpen and his "kind," though temporarily reduced to storekeeping and consorting with Joneses, wish to preserve the plantocratic ideal that assures their domination, he can think of no recourse but suicidal assault. Striking down Sutpen, killing his granddaughter and her child, then rushing furiously but also silently into the gunbarrels of "Sutpen's own kind" (547), Wash makes good on his despairing realization: *"Better if his kind and mine too had never drawn the breath of life on this earth"* (548).

No proletarian plot would end this way, one must agree with Cook. Wash arrives at no sense of class affiliation, no glimpse of practical collective redress, no alternative to the Southern myth he now realizes to be flawed. Yet Faulkner's mild aesthetic complications in this otherwise realistic short story suggest a residue not wholly absorbed by Wash's act of futility. In the first place, Faulkner complicates the question of class before Wash defines it as simply an issue of "kinds" of men. The story appeared originally in *Harper's* in 1934; it was one of several versions of the Sutpen material that Faulkner eventually used in *Absalom*. In the novel's version of this episode, Sutpen repudiates Milly's child because it is a girl and Sutpen wants sons. Many readers assume this explains the action of "Wash" too.[12] But the story shows Sutpen insulting Milly *before* he learns of the child's gender; after refusing Milly so much as a decent stall, and after reporting to Milly's black nurse that one of his mares foaled that morning too, Sutpen asks "What's this?" She answers, "That un's a mare, I reckon" (535).

The confusion arises from more than Faulkner's recasting of this scene into *Absalom*'s preoccupations with dynasty. Later in the story, Wash goes over the events of the morning, struggling to accept the fact that Sutpen awakened early only to check on his thoroughbred, not to look after "me and mine" (544). Wash remembers Sutpen passing him on the way into the Jones shack, and recalls saying proudly, " 'Hit's a gal, Kernel. I be dawg if you ain't as old as I am—' until Sutpen passed him and entered the house" (544). Wash discovers that the Colonel never did mean to listen to him and his kind. But the doubling back in narrative time locates Wash's embryonic class consciousness within the larger frame of multiple social relations established between narrator and reader by the first page.

The opening tableau of "Wash" allows no Southern mythology, no dynastic schemes to veil Sutpen's blunt exercise of prerogative. Instead, the story stages a moment of masterly assertion that expresses indivisible domination over the poor white, over women of both races, and over a black servant. Subtly, Faulkner suggests the entanglement of race and gender relations with class structure in the South. It is the black slaves who ridicule Wash's airs and call him "white trash behind his back" (536). In the post-Reconstruction South, the ideology of race guarded against the affiliation of blacks and whites with common economic interests. Sutpen must uphold class differences because they secure the color line, just as he must be free to use white women as reproductive vessels or sexual outlets at will. The relatively modest wrinkle in narrative temporality spreads vastly into the experimentalist narrative of *Absalom, Absalom!*, of course, partly for the same reasons. The narrators' efforts to tell everything at once, or repeatedly with different explanations, expresses Faulkner's multivariant analysis of the South's system of exploitation. Faulkner's fiction refuses to isolate class relations in the modern South from a mythology and a history that binds them to other peculiar social relations.

To the extent that Wash's recognition of the hopelessness of class division does not exhaust the *text*'s insights, we may also note that Wash's violent resolution does not entirely settle questions raised by the moment of crisis. Wash approaches his granddaughter in the dark to murder her. Their brief exchange suggests the story's untold underplot:

> "Who is it? Light the lamp, grandpaw."
> "Hit won't need no light, honey. Hit won't take but a minute," he said, kneeling, fumbling toward her voice, whispering now. "Where air you?"
> "Right here," she said fretfully. "Where would I be? What is . . ."
> His hand touched her face.
> "What is . . . Grandpaw! Grand . . . ." (549)

Faulkner's imagination, too, fumbles toward the voices of rejected women lying in the dark. Touching their faces before the stroke of annihilation, catching their cries just as they vanish—these become a spectral ambition in *Absalom, Absalom!* By reposing the narrative partially in the mouth of Rosa Coldfield, another of Sutpen's casualties, Faulkner at least gestures toward what has been left out of the simple story of class conflict between white males. That story's unassimilated remnant persists in Milly's unanswered questions, in what *Absalom* calls "the weary voices of murdered women and children homeless and graveless" (204), voices marginal but meaningful.

"Barn Burning" also suggests that the simple plot of class consciousness and conflict fails to cover the multiplicity of exploitative forms in the South. Ab understands his economic situation as a tenant farmer to be a straightforward case of class disadvantage.

He explains to his son Sarty that their new landlord DeSpain will begin "tomorrow owning me body and soul for the next eight months" (9) and that the white mansion he occupies has been built with "sweat. Nigger sweat. Maybe it ain't white enough yet to suit him. Maybe he wants to mix some white sweat with it" (12). However, Sarty cannot share his father's willingness to commit arson in order to protest his unfair treatment. Sarty wishes DeSpain might simply forget the judgment against Ab for ruining his rug, just as earlier he wishes his father might absorb the "peace and dignity" symbolized by the planter's mansion and give up his violent ways.

When Sarty cannot prevent his father from torching DeSpain's barn, he alerts the landlord, setting off a confrontation that he thinks costs his father's life. Yet Sarty does not simply betray his father's class and identify with DeSpain's. Instead, he rejects bankrupt forms of class warfare as an era of new opportunities dawns. It is true that Sarty remains partially under the spell of the planter ideal, admiring DeSpain's house and boasting (mistakenly) of his father's service to the Confederate army. But he also keenly feels the injustice of his father's treatment at the hands of DeSpain and the judge. "Barn Burning" appeared in 1939, when it had become clear that tenancy would be replaced by wage labor and that mechanization would finally prevail in Southern agriculture. Sarty feels as if he is *"being pulled two ways like between two teams of horses"* and wishes it could all be *"gone, done with for ever and ever"* (17). Sarty is just old enough to inherit the legacy of hostility between rednecks and aristocrats, "the light weight of his few years, just heavy enough to prevent his soaring free of the world as it seemed to be ordered but not heavy enough to keep him footed solid in it, to resist it and try to change the course of its events" (9). The model of blackmail and revenge, based on an ethos of clan and individual dignity, Sarty intuits to be irrelevant to the future. Even in his assault on his oppressor, Ab remains indebted to outmoded ways: he dresses for arson in "the hat and coat, at once formal and burlesque as though dressed carefully for some shabby and ceremonial violence" (20).

Sarty finds himself suspended between orders, the old founded on blood, the new uncertainly based on the commodification of all relations. In the opening scene of the story, Sarty sees that the path to justice for his class in the future will lead through a store. The child registers the transition between two regimes. He knows he can smell actual cheese, but he also "could see the ranked shelves close-packed with the solid, squat, dynamic shapes of tin cans whose labels his stomach read, not from the lettering which meant nothing to his mind but from the scarlet devils and the silver curve of fish" (3). Sarty's response to the advertising age signals Southern modernization. Like the goods for sale, Ab looks like he is "cut from tin" (8), and he makes a figure on DeSpain's carpet that writes his own doom: "scoriations resembling the sporadic course of a lilliputian mowing machine" (14). Sarty understands that he occupies a point of transition: "it was as if he had swung outward at the end of a grape vine, over a ravine, and at the top of the swing had been caught in a prolonged instant of mesmerized gravity, weightless in time" (5). The instant of weightlessness frees Sarty from Ab's gestures, stiffly grounded in the past. It will be up to Sarty's older brother Flem, unburdened by even nominal ties to the plantocracy, to realize revenge in the marketplace. But Sarty has his eyes on the future, too; the closing words of the story are "He did not look back" (25), a resolve that prepares for *The Hamlet*'s "Come up."

Faulkner indulges in a little modernist playfulness when he incorporates Ab's story into *The Hamlet*. If we believe with Sarty that DeSpain has killed Ab and his older son, we may be surprised to see their return in the novel. In fact, it is Sarty who is missing. Sarty disappears because he represents a futile longing for some inexpressible revision of oppressive ways. His confusion argues the need for new languages of both ambition and resistance. Faulkner captures this quest for revised forms in Sarty's speech; the child often breaks off sentences that portend some solution to his father's predicament: "'He won't git no ten bushels neither. He won't get one. We'll . . .' until his father glanced for an instant down at him" (19). Sarty's behavior reserves a space not covered by the rigid lines of class warfare.

In examining Faulkner's writing in the context of proletarian literature, I am proposing that his fiction rejects an explicit revolutionary vision for reasons more important than his own often confused conservatism. Since Faulkner's texts almost invariably possess more complex, nuanced, and critical thinking about social and historical problems than Faulkner ever displayed in public remarks, my inclination is to trust the writing—particularly writing from an individual who wished he could obliterate everything but the books themselves. Faulkner's imaginative descriptions of the people of Yoknapatawpha often overlap with central features of proletarian writing about the poor in the era of the Great Depression and the destruction of the South's "rural worlds."[13] But his insider's grasp of a region's history and mythology discovered in modernist aesthetics a way to represent the complexities of his material in the complexities of form. Faulkner formalizes social reality in his art and in so doing reserves social and imaginative possibilities not scripted by discourses dominating the thirties: communism, progressive reform, and regressive reactionism.

The opposition between the literatures of social engagement and formal experimentalism in many accounts of American writing between the wars rests on questionable assumptions: to the extent a work possesses political or social interests of representation, its devotion to aesthetic form seems somewhat beside the point; and to the extent the modernist work revels in its apparent formal autonomy, its interest in social or cultural contexts seems marginal. A certain ideology of modernism shapes the critical treatment of literary art from the thirties, then, but if, under the pressure of proletarian debates, we adjust our estimation of the radical possibilities for modernist aesthetics, we may be able to see Faulkner *as modernist* working much closer to the projects of social and economic critique so central to the proletarian movement.

Barbara Foley's recent book on the radical literature of the American thirties presents a deliberately complicated account of proletarianism.[14] She demonstrates that many of the accepted be-

liefs about the movement derive from Cold War-era reconsidera-
tions of the so-called Red Decade. The list of those repudiating
their former participation in revolutionary activities grew long by
the 1950s. Even by the late thirties, when the Hitler-Stalin nonag-
gression pact stunned American communists, all the more in the
wake of growing suspicions of Soviet domestic brutality, the re-
formist successes of Roosevelt's New Deal, and the greater
urgency of combating fascism, many American artists had disaffil-
iated themselves. Foley, however, returns to the hopeful confu-
sions of the early thirties, showing that the major phase of
proletarianism stimulated remarkable creative and critical vitality.
Authors contributed all manner of works to the cause, while critics
debated exactly what the subgenre of the proletarian novel com-
prised. The mainstream press reviewed proletarian literature
largely with enthusiasm, and many reviewers explicitly denied that
the works' artistic integrity was marred by propagandism.

The proletarian novel emerged under a variety of definitions:
some saw it as the authentic expression of writers born into the
working class. Jack Conroy, a factory worker who composed his
novel *The Disinherited* by night, stood as the prototype. Other
theorists argued for the criterion of audience, although a famous
survey by Louis Adamic revealed that the working class tended to
read Westerns and other popular literature while it was the middle
class who read novels about working class life. The genre was also
defined by subject matter; if a book described class relations, especially if it used representative types, it could produce the desired
results. Such a view made room for works that dissected the cor-
ruptness and inauthenticity of middle class existence. Finally, a
novel might be legitimately proletarian if it subjected whatever
material it treated to a "proper" perspective, that is, one that by
its analysis of behavior and conditions led the reader toward the
left.

Like the question of definition, other features of the genre allowed for differences. Foley describes substantive disagreements
over the place of race and gender in the proletarian movement.
Earlier accounts of proletarianism suggest the preoccupation of

communist policy with class issues, and certainly some of the best proletarian novels by African Americans and women explore the incompatibility of rival practical programs. William Attaway's powerful novel about the Great Migration, entitled *Blood on the Forge* (1941), follows the efforts of three black brothers to integrate their experiences as exploited steel workers with the activities of white trade unionism. They fail when the models of white ethnic community and European immigrant history marginalize them. Likewise, Agnes Smedley's somber *Daughter of Earth* (1929) shows the ultimate placelessness of the female protagonist who will not surrender her ambitions for gender equality to the demands of male-dominated communist party solidarity. Yet Foley insists that it was under proletarianism that women and blacks were invited to express their own experiences, and that the movement must be credited at least with providing space for the discussion of such emancipatory longings, even if they never achieved a secure place in the communists' immediate agenda.

One of the questions the proletarian writers debated most vigorously was the role of literary experimentalism. Gold's vicious assaults on Proust, Eliot, and others notwithstanding, he and his collaborator on the *New Masses*, Joseph Freeman, attempted to reconcile modernist poetics and left politics.[15] Foley cites the example of one communist journal of the period called *The Left*, the masthead of which subtitled it "A Quarterly Review of Radical and Experimental Art," and the manifesto of which spoke of the belief "that new forms and techniques must be hammered out to express the fresh substance, the faster tempos and rhythms of the new world order and encourage that experimentation" (56). Dos Passos's *U.S.A.* predictably earned praise, but other works such as Clara Weatherwax's *Marching! Marching!* were also lauded for combining "formal experimentalism with party politics" (56–57). Foley concludes that for many proletarian writers, "the impulse to rebel against the social order is aligned with the impulse to transgress inherited forms. The charge that the majority of American literary proletarians repudiated literary innovation simply does not stand up under the evidence" (57).

Before I suggest further some of the ways we can see social and aesthetic experimentalism coincide in Faulkner's fiction, I must allow Foley to add one caveat about the consequences of perforating the opposition between experimentalism and proletarianism. Foley does not want to be taken as implying that revolutionary writing amounts to no more than one variety of a strictly artistic rebellion against outmoded literary forms. The "literary proletarians were *part* of modernism," she insists, but only if we understand modernism to encompass the effort to portray "a new and vivifying experiential basis for art" (62).[16] While the "postwar hegemony of Trilling, Rahv, and other anti-Stalinists" rewrote the history of modernism as exclusively the "high modernism" of Eliot, Joyce, and Pound, other writers sought to realize radical social visions in radical aesthetic form. Precisely upon this common ground may one distinguish "the political differences dividing the proletarians from their bourgeois experimentalist contemporaries" (62).

Though Faulkner's politics would never qualify him for inclusion among the proletarians, I contend that his *textual politics* equally disqualify him for ready enlistment among the "bourgeois experimentalist[s]." For all his pursuit of genteel prosperity, few writers have shown greater loathing for their own kind than Faulkner does in his fiction; we may think of Quentin Compson as the exorcised demon of a suicidal hater of the South, but surely his creator destroys his own world novel by novel as he surveys the ruination of a society founded, as the narrator of *Absalom* puts it, on "a soil manured with black blood" under "two hundred years of oppression and exploitation" (202).

These last words from *Absalom, Absalom!* refer to the Haiti in which Sutpen gets his start. Faulkner reserves some of the novel's harshest language about the history of New World slavery for the episodes involving the slave insurrection on a sugar plantation. According to modern historians, Haiti at the end of the eighteenth century was, for its slaves, "the worst hell on earth."[17] The sugar, coffee, cotton, and indigo plantations of the French colony of Saint-Domingue produced immense wealth for France, especially from the 1760s to the 1790s. World record production for sugar and coffee cost a staggering number of slave lives; in some years more than 400,000 new African slaves arrived on the island ("Afterword" 188). Quentin remembers General Compson describing it as

> a theatre for violence and injustice and bloodshed and all the satanic lusts of human greed and cruelty . . . the halfway point between what we call the jungle and what we call civilization, halfway between the dark inscrutable continent from which the black blood, the black bones and flesh and thinking and remembering and hopes and desires, was ravished by violence. . . . (*AA* 202)

One widely admired proletarian novel deals with the historical slave rebellion on Saint-Domingue which began in August 1791. Guy Endore's *Babouk* (1934) fictionally recreates the career of an actual rebel leader named Boukman. French sources available to Endore recounted Boukman's role in inciting an armed uprising in the northern province. Boukman was captured and decapitated in the first phase of the rebellion. Eventually, however, the slaves' determination resulted in French capitulation to rule by blacks; the celebrated Toussaint Louverture governed Saint-Domingue until 1802, when Napoleon attempted to restore direct French authority. Though many black leaders died and Louverture was exiled to France, the rebels finally repulsed the French. Jean-Jacques Dessalines won the victory, declared the country's independence in 1804, and restored the Indian name of Haiti ("Afterword" 188–89).

Endore's novel animates a previously neglected chapter in the history of capitalist oppression. C. L. R. James would not publish his *Black Jacobins* until 1938; most of the extant histories of the Caribbean colonial islands represented European historiography. Endore wanted to recreate with immediacy the historical event of an oppressed people's violent uprising, but he also wished through fiction to fill in the gaps of the historical record. Endore's narrator sharply rebukes traditional history for concentrating on the fortunes of the elite: "For it is not history until the rich man suffers"

(96). Other experiences, other voices vanish, but *Babouk*'s narrator makes a promise to his subject:

> Your voice is lost in the past. Your wavering voice is lost in the steaming field of Saint-Domingue. It is lost both in time and space. And yet it cannot be lost altogether, Babouk. It cannot die in a void. Oh, no. All the wavering voices of the complaining Negro, be they of the dead or of the living, of Africa, or America, yet they will some day be woven into a great net and they will pull that deaf master out of his flowery garden and down into the muddy, stinking field. (97)

Endore's fiction must bear witness to the distortions of official history: "My pen is not so delicate; it can say, and it will never cease to say: not over a thousand or so of whites were killed in this reign of terror, while the legal and protected slave trade killed over a hundred thousand Negroes a year" (168).

Not only does the novel seek to remedy the biases of European historiography, it also demonstrates the crucial role storytelling plays in a culture. History by the dominant represses and silences; counternarratives by the dominated remember and incite. Babouk springs to power on the wings of his eloquence. He tells creation fables that insist upon the black man's priority; he presents allegories of revenge, invents lies to console, tells jokes proving whites are no different under the skin than blacks, and even produces utopian fantasy that helps inspire the slaves to insurrection. A work like *Babouk*, which is in effect a proletarian historical novel, had to confront the discursive consequences of social and economic exploitation. Controlling the means of representation, as Endore and Faulkner both knew, matters vitally to the prospects for change.

A second thrust of Endore's critique of slavery aims at the contradiction between the myth of European enlightenment and the practice of brutality. Conrad bares this horror graphically a generation before; perhaps Endore and Faulkner derive the language of "satanic lust" from that common source. Endore recounts how white slave traders chain the masses of Africans into pairs, then call out, "Line up men! . . . Right by two's" (22). "But these are ignorant savages," the narrator observes sarcastically, "They do not think or act in straight lines" (22). The power of abstraction undergirds European assumptions of cultural superiority: "Ah, if these blacks, huddled together, some still in chains, others free, but all under the close surveillance of armed guards, but knew that they represented European culture in its first stage, how justly proud they might be" (7).

European reason denies the reality of slave humanity, of the empirical evidence of common feeling. The novel captures such brutal folly in an historical vignette, in which a group of planters arrange for the first balloon ascension on Saint-Domingue. An emblem of "this new victory of mind and science over the limitations placed upon man by flesh and nature" (128), the balloon receives its passengers, a cock and a pig, then lifts off splendidly. But Endore follows the crew aloft, where he overhears a conversation in which the pig, gazing down at the island, wonders why the numerous blacks own nothing, when only a handful of whites, clearly outnumbered, own everything, including the Africa over which they are to fly.

One of Endore's most powerful rebukes to the brutality of abstraction involves the novel's permeation by senses other than sight. The odor of crops and fields and laboring bodies culminates in a ghastly aroma, that of the roasting flesh of three black criminals burning in the town square. The "sharp odor of singed hair and nails" (50) accompanies the "loud greedy crackle" (48) of the flames and the unearthly singing of one of the victims, which penetrates the roar of the chanting mob. Endore brilliantly creates the obdurate presence of slave flesh, of the bodies themselves that refuse to disappear into the ratiocination of plantation production. The novel introduces the idea with the description of a bizarre ritual in which slave traders employ a "nigger-taster," a man whose "genius" enables him to appraise each lot: "out came his tongue, his marvelously trained tongue, and licked each Negro under the chin. There was a brief, critical gathering of saliva, then he spat the contents of his mouth into the Negro's face. And he pronounced judgment" (2).

The narrator periodically drops the historical screen to reveal targets in contemporary society: "But that's another matter and hardly worth going into, seeing that it would lead us astray into the whole subject of whether it's right or wrong to punish a Negro for a crime he did not commit, for example, to lynch a nigger who did or did not rape a certain white girl" (53). Like these "anachronist slips" (53), most of Endore's experiments with form depart only modestly from realism. The novel's conclusion attempts to sound out the rising, only partially intelligible rhythms of underclass revolution. The body of language reproduces the claims of exploited, obliterated flesh:

> Dum didi dumdum. Dum didi dumdum.
> And from the distant wall of smoke and fire came a strange echo:
> Tom-tom. Tom-tom. Tom-tom. (180)

By the last page of the novel the rhetoric has risen to peroration, calling for the black man to "arise" and for Europeans and Americans to "beware." Endore and Babouk merge across an historical divide. Interestingly, they also merge across a racial divide.

Guy Endore was a white man, a Brooklynite born in 1901. He majored in Romance languages at Columbia College and wrote several other novels, one about Joan of Arc, another about Alexander Dumas. In the mid-thirties he went to Hollywood to write film scripts; in the fifties he suffered blacklisting because of his ties to the Communist Party. I have not learned whether Faulkner knew Endore. They worked in Hollywood during the same years, and at the time of his death Faulkner did own a copy of Endore's book on Dumas. *Absalom, Absalom!* obviously does not share *Babouk*'s revolutionary agenda, but its concerns overlap strategically, and do so in ways that highlight the distinct role a modernist casting of social critique might contribute to a corrective imagination of history.

Readers of *Absalom* have long appreciated that Sutpen's moral innocence involves some fatal variant of the flaw of abstract reasoning. His approach to his ambition, like his response to his misstep with Eulalia, possesses an inhumanly cold logic. For a moment I would like to think of this less as the manifestation of individual character or even of a certain Western tragic *hubris*, though both frames fit. Instead, I propose connecting Sutpen's behavior to the founding principles of capitalist domination, which at their roots may be seen as implicating an entire logic. I am drawing on the Frankfurt School's critique of enlightenment reason to guide this approach, but let me find the emblem for the analysis in Faulkner's text. When Sutpen subdues the revolting Haitian slaves, Quentin imagines them "turning in horror and fleeing from the white arms and legs shaped like theirs and from which blood could be made to spurt and flow as it could from theirs and containing an indomitable spirit which should have come from the same primary fire which theirs came from but which could not have, could not possibly have" (205). Put another way, Sutpen's design denies the particularity of flesh; it sublates it into "indomitable spirit" that seems unworldly to those it masters.

Capitalism depends on the logic of equivalence. Intrinsically different goods—objects that have been made, crops that have been raised, labor to be performed—must be converted into some common measure in order to be exchanged. According to Horkheimer and Adorno in *Dialectic of Enlightenment*, this power of abstraction is related inseparably to the capacity for abstract thought.[18] Ideas distill essences and eliminate particularity. A kind of violence governs this process; Horkheimer and Adorno want to trace the inner dynamic of brutality within the project of rational enlightenment, ultimately to try to explain how Western culture could have produced the barbarity of the Holocaust. In the case of another genocide, New World slavery, Faulkner helps us see that "the peculiar institution" did not simply prove a helpful instrument to Southern plantation agriculture. Rather, the brutal mastery of humans grotesquely magnifies a logic that depends upon commodification.

Sutpen reasons to himself after Pettibone's insult in a language that conveys the violence at the heart of equivalence making: "If you were fixing to combat them that had the fine rifles, the first thing you would do would be to get yourself the nearest thing to a fine rifle you could borrow or steal or make" (192). Sutpen's design involves two distinct but indivisible habits of mind: one insists on assigning economic value to every experience, the other adheres to a confidence in reason. Sutpen invariably explains his behavior in economic terms: Eulalia and her father deceived him because he had "accepted them at their own valuation" (212). Quentin describes the grand design as just "getting richer and richer" (209), but the language of acquisition, payment, and credit saturates all of Sutpen's doings. Correspondingly, his scheme advances by "logical steps" (212); whenever Sutpen arrives at an impasse, he resorts to what the novel repeatedly calls his "formal logic" (216). By intertwining the economic practices of the self-made agrarian capitalist with the epistemology that founds it, Faulkner conducts his search for the South's fatal flaw in a sphere occupied by writers to his left.

Sutpen's logic and his moral code prove inseparable, "the old logic, the old morality which had never yet failed to fail him" (224). They constitute an instrumental reason that insults everything it touches by sucking it into an abstraction. Property itself constitutes the initial act of abstraction, and so it is for Sutpen, who, when he falls down the mountain into Tidewater Virginia, cannot believe that the country is "all divided and fixed and neat because of what color . . . skins happened to be and what [people] happened to own" (179). The concepts of class and race organize a hierarchy, one Sutpen can imagine combating only through seizure. The insult of this logic ripples outward in the novel—in Sutpen's repudiation of wife and son, in the proposal that Rosa first satisfy his design, in Milly's instrumentalization by Sutpen, even in Eulalia's and the lawyer's use of Charles to perfect revenge.

The failure of Sutpen's logic and morality indicts nineteenth-century capitalism, but it also reaches toward a fundamental critique of an attendant epistemology. How does Faulkner's novel respond to this state of affairs? I want briefly to suggest that Faulkner—through the means afforded by a modernist aesthetic—formalizes ways of thinking and experiencing that shake or deconstruct this economic logic. To begin with: the body of *Absalom*'s language. Stylistic excess itself rebukes abstraction. Faulkner's language possesses all the uniqueness of an individual body; its tics, folds, scars, weight, articulation compose an unmistakable identity. We would know it anywhere. Notice how Rosa voices that language in a moment when the idea of racial difference collapses as white flesh touches black. Rosa and Clytie *"glare at one another not as two faces but as the two abstract contradictions which we actually were"* (111). But then:

> Then she touched me, and then I did stop dead. Possibly even then my body did not stop, since I seemed to be aware of it thrusting blindly still against the solid yet imponderable weight (she not owner: instrument; I still say that) of that will to bar me from the stairs; possibly the sound of the other voice, the single word spoken from the stairhead above us, had already broken and parted us before it (my body) had even paused. I do not know. I know only that my entire being seemed to run at blind full tilt into something monstrous and immobile, with a shocking impact too soon and too quick to be mere amazement and outrage at that black arresting and untimorous hand on my white woman's flesh. Because there is something in the touch of flesh with flesh which abrogates, cuts sharp and straight across the devious intricate channels of decorous ordering, which enemies as well as lovers know because it makes them both:—touch and touch of that which is the citadel of the central I-Am's private own: not spirit, soul; the liquorish and ungirdled mind is anyone's to take in any darkened hallway of this earthly tenement. But let flesh touch with flesh, and watch the fall of all the eggshell shibboleth of caste and color too. (111–12)

Sutpen's victims long for the touch of flesh that might negate abstraction. Love, thinks Rosa, is *"best of all . . . the actual living and the dreamy flesh itself"* (119), just as the *"substance of remembering* [is] *sense, sight, smell: the muscles with which we see and hear and feel—not mind, not thought"* (115). Bon wants from Sutpen only one sign of recognition: "the living touch of that flesh warmed before he was born by the same blood which it had bequeathed him to warm his own flesh with" (255). It is no surprise that when Wash Jones finally brings his "apotheosis" to ground, he and Sutpen exchange these final words: " '*Stand back. Dont you touch me, Wash.'—'I'm going to tech you, Kernel'* " (151).

So much of *Absalom, Absalom!* defies the logic of economics and the economics of logic. Narrative playfulness, extravagant repetition in style and plot, the span of sentences that make the lungs wince, the sensuous tumble of words all but abandoned by intelligibility, refusals to conclude, assertion through negation all create a novel with the "logic- and -reason-flouting quality of a dream" (15). When Philip Rahv reviewed *Absalom* for the *New Masses*, he objected to its style as a form of "mystification," an "ideological dream": "The material is not explored objectively to provide the vision; it is manipulated to illustrate and fit the vision, which is preconceived. Thus the language becomes a function of the author's metaphysics, of spiritual relations, and of reverie: it no longer sticks to the object, but to the author's idea of the object."[19] Given the amount of uncomfortable truth Faulkner's novel belabors, one might rather understand its language as tonic for a rationalized view of history, whether left or right. Sutpen practices class consciousness by emulating his oppressors, Wash eventually by declaring war on them; but the narrator asserts that, after all, the morality of the two was a good deal the same (230). Faulkner turns his aesthetic into an embodiment of all that has been left out, overpassed. Shreve understands that this has been a story of the remainder:

> "So it takes two niggers to get rid of one Sutpen, dont it? . . . Which is all right, it's fine; it clears the whole ledger, you can tear all the pages out and burn them, except for one thing. And do you know what that is? . . . You've got one nigger left. One nigger Sutpen left." (302)

The mixture of flesh contradicts Sutpen's abstract purity, the debit left prevents historical justification of the books, the howl in the night disrupts the confidence of reason.

If we look at Faulkner's writing in the context of proletarian literature with the questions only of content and personal politics in mind, we are likely to reinforce the idea that modernist aesthetics cared more for technical experimentation for its own sake, psychologism, and the aura of the art work's autonomy. Such an understanding generally governed radical left reviews of Faulkner's work in the thirties. In addition to Rahv, Granville Hicks complained in the *New Masses* that *Pylon* demonstrates Faulkner's inability to respond to anything other than immediate stimulus, the more violent the better. Consigning the novel to the school of sensibility associated with Eliot, Hicks concludes that the novel is "pure melodrama" and does nothing with the plight of the oppressed fliers it portrays.[20] Likewise, Oakley Johnson writes in the *Modern Quarterly* that crime in Faulkner's *Sanctuary* proves strictly pathological, not the product of a social system.[21] The main exception to this sort of treatment of Faulkner's explicit purposes predictably involves *The Wild Palms*. Edwin Berry Burgum, reviewing it for the *New Masses*, appreciates the novel's illustration of middle class neurosis and "the contrasting virtues of the proletarian" class.[22]

In this paper I have been more concerned to bring another dimension of the proletarian context to bear on Faulkner's writing, the cultural function of modernist social critique. Until its possibilities were short-circuited by the urgencies of the ideological wars against fascism in the forties and communism in the fifties, this strain of modernism might have established a more vigorous dissident imaginative tradition. Faulkner himself suggests the continuity of thirties and fifties leftism in *The Mansion* (1955), which complicatedly respects communist determination to work for justice.

The complementary phase of my project here would be to consider Faulkner's and other modernists' influence on proletarian writers. Richard Wright's admiration for Faulkner and Gertrude Stein is well known; he absorbed them even as the communist John Reed Club of Chicago was encouraging the early stories that became *Uncle Tom's Children* (1938). A tantalizing connection to Faulkner appears in Tillie Olsen's *Yonnondio: From the Thirties*. Olsen began this novel of a working class girl's childhood in 1932 and worked on it for several years. Unfinished, it was laid aside until the early seventies, when Olsen arranged and published the work in fragmentary form. Olsen relies on passages of stream of consciousness to alternate with a realistic depiction of her characters' suffering and realization of their class oppression. The mosaic

this produces reads a little like *As I Lay Dying*, with its ventrilo-
quistic expression of simple people's complex feelings. Even more
intriguingly, Olsen surrounds Mazie with several siblings, including a younger one whose innocence registers the pain and trauma
of those with little. Often pictured hurt and weeping, he is mothered by the whole family: "What's the matter, Benjy, did you hurt
yourself?"[23]

I am encouraged to argue for a greater fluidity between intellectual projects in the thirties in part by recent scholarship on the
period. Cary Nelson's and Walter Kalaidjian's books on revolutionary and avant-garde poetry reveal diverse cultural energies dedicated to social change in the period between the wars.[24] Ann
Douglas's new book on American modernism argues for a much
greater area of shared interests among high art and low entertainment, and among various ethnic traditions.[25] In his recent book on
the cultural history of the American novel, David Minter places
Faulkner's fiction as the "culmination of both the formal preoccupations of literary modernism . . . and of the thirties' engagement
with poverty and violence as social problems."[26]

In trying to describe the means by which this combination
might take place in a few Faulknerian instances, I am also motivated by a consideration that arises from the present day context
of reading, teaching, and writing about Faulkner. Intellectuals interested in keeping the historical and current failures of democratic capitalism before the eyes of a public initially mesmerized
by the triumph of American Wayism and the New World Order
may take inspiration from recent attempts to imagine the preservation of marxism after the death of Soviet communism. A conference at the University of California at Riverside two years ago
debated the question, "Whither Marxism?" Derrida gave the key-
note address, since published as *Specters of Marx*.[27] In it he argues
that the dead end of Soviet communism need not mean the end of
a vital marxist social criticism or political practice. According to
Derrida, marxist revolutionism from the outset had to confront the
nonpresence of its object. Before revolution, the future is haunted
and hollowed out by the past which must be overthrown; after

revolution, the present is haunted and hollowed out by the incompleteness of political transformation, as in the case of Stalinism. Derrida argues that marxism must adjust to post-Cold War realities by forming what he calls a New International. Such a movement would operate "without organization, without party, without nation, without State, without property" (29). The role for marxism would be to foster emancipatory promise in two forms: the idea of justice, associated with a messianism (a "weak" messianism, without religion); and the idea of democracy (though one substantially different from that of present Western capitalist states). Derrida wishes to retrieve the spirit of marxism from its historical incompleteness, a project that has much to say to current efforts to reassess the revolutionary writing of the American thirties. If more instrumental versions of proletarian literature sought a class revolution in no uncertain terms during this decade, perhaps Faulkner's texts kept alive another kind of spirit—a spirit devoted to the incessant questioning of history and social forms, a spirit nourished by art's formal negation of social reality, a spirit alive to almost unthinkable changes in the world he had inherited.

NOTES

1. Curtis Wilkie, "Sound and fury arising over Elvis at Ole Miss," *Boston Globe*, 4 July 1995, 1, 8

2. Don DeLillo, *White Noise* (New York: Viking, 1985), 11

3. William Faulkner, *Faulkner in the University*, ed. Frederick L. Gwynn and Joseph L. Blotner (New York: Vintage, 1965), 177.

4. William Faulkner, *Absalom, Absalom!* (New York: Vintage International, 1990), 71.

5. See Bruce Schulman, *From Cotton Belt to Sunbelt* (New York: Oxford University Press, 1991; Duke University Press, 1994), for an account of this transformation.

6. Georg Lúkacs, *The Meaning of Contemporary Realism*, trans. John and Necke Mander (London: Merlin Press, 1963).

7. Mike Gold, "Notes of the Month," *New Masses* (September 1930); reprinted and excerpted in "Proletarian Realism," in *Mike Gold: A Literary Anthology* (New York, 1972), 206.

8. Mike Gold, "Review of *Men Without Women*," *New Masses* (March 1928), as reprinted in "Hemingway—White Collar Poet," in *Mike Gold: A Literary Anthology*, 160.

9. Mike Gold, "Wilder: Prophet of the Genteel Christ," *New Republic* (22 October 1930), as reprinted in *Mike Gold: A Literary Anthology*, 200.

10. Sylvia Jenkins Cook, *From Tobacco Road to Route 66: The Southern Poor White in Fiction* (Chapel Hill: University of North Carolina Press, 1976), 39–40.

11. William Faulkner, *Collected Stories of William Faulkner* (New York: Random House, 1950), 538, 542.

12. For a recent example of such an interpretation of "Wash" see Joel Williamson, *William Faulkner and Southern History* (New York: Oxford University Press, 1993), 243–44.

13. The phrase is Jack Temple Kirby's, from his study of the South's modernization, *Rural Worlds Lost: The American South 1920–1960* (Baton Rouge: Louisiana State University Press, 1987).

14. Barbara Foley, *Radical Representations: Politics and Form in U.S. Proletarian Fiction, 1929–1941* (Durham: Duke University Press, 1993).

15. See James D. Bloom, *Left Letters: The Culture Wars of Mike Gold and Joseph Freeman* (New York: Columbia University Press, 1992).

16. Foley is quoting from Marcus Klein, *Foreigners: The Making of American Literature, 1900–1940* (Chicago: University of Chicago Press, 1981), 140.

17. David Barry Gaspar and Michel-Rolph Trouillot, "Afterword: History, Fiction, and the Slave Experience," in Guy Endore, *Babouk* (New York: Monthly Review Press, 1991; Vanguard Press, 1934), 184.

18. Max Horkheimer and Theodor Adorno, *Dialectic of Enlightenment*, trans. John Cumming (New York: Continuum, 1987).

19. "Review and Comment" [Review of *Absalom, Absalom!*], *New Masses* (24 November 1936), 20–21.

20. Granville Hicks, "Melodrama" [Review of *Pylon*], *New Masses*, (14 May 1935), 25.

21. Oakley Johnson, Review of *Sanctuary*, *Modern Quarterly* 6 (Winter 1931–32): 122–23.

22. Edwin Berry Burgum, "Faulkner's New Novel," *New Masses* (7 May 1939), 23. Burgum's position anticipates Pamela Rhodes's and Richard Godden's interpretation of the novel as all but producing authentic class consciousness in the Tall Convict, and forcing Harry to confront the prison of bourgeois respectability ("*The Wild Palms*: Degraded Culture, Devalued Texts," in *Intertextuality in Faulkner*, ed. Michel Gresset and Noel Polk [Jackson: University Press of Mississippi, 1985], 87–113. Michael Grimwood, however, offers a well-informed, if strident, refutation of this left reading of the novel; he argues that Faulkner appropriates Depression-era subjects, imagery, and generic conventions only to parody them (*Heart in Conflict: Faulkner's Struggles with Vocation* [Athens: University of Georgia Press, 1987], 87–134).

23. Tillie Olsen, *Yonnondio: From the Thirties* (New York: Dell, 1974), 57.

24. Cary Nelson, *Repression and Recovery: Modern American Poetry and the Politics of Cultural Memory, 1910–1945* (Madison: University of Wisconsin Press, 1989) and Walter J. Kalaidjian, *American Culture Between the Wars: Revisionary Modernism and Postmodern Critique* (New York: Columbia University Press, 1993).

25. Ann Douglas, *Terrible Honesty: Mongrel Manhattan in the 1920s* (New York: Farrar, Straus, and Giroux, 1993).

26. David L. Minter, *A Cultural History of the American Novel* (Cambridge University Press, 1994), xi.

27. Jacques Derrida, *Specters of Marx: The State of the Debt, the Work of Mourning, and the New International*, trans. Peggy Kamuf (New York: Routledge, 1994).

If I Forget Thee, Jerusalem and the Great Migration: History in Black and White

CHERYL LESTER

Addressing the national mass readership of *Time* magazine in 1939, Robert Cantwell presented William Faulkner as a latter-day Mark Twain and called the "Old Man" portion of Faulkner's new novel *The Wild Palms* "a pulsing, racing story, a kind of hysterical *Huckleberry Finn*."[1] The hysteria Cantwell perceived in Faulkner's 1939 novel, which was originally entitled *If I Forget Thee, Jerusalem*, is symptomatic of Faulkner's ambivalent recognition of the contradictions most urgently haunting the Jim Crow South.[2] Having remained a resident of Oxford, Mississippi, for the better part of his life, Faulkner was unable to escape these contradictions, which he examined in all his writings. His disturbed and disturbing depictions of the contradictory place that was his "home" attracted a national and even international readership, but it irritated most white Mississippians. "Mr. Faulkner a great writer?" Moon Mullen wrote in the *Oxford Eagle* on 26 January 1939, acknowledging the Southern cultural nerve Faulkner touched, "Well, they sure wouldn't hire him to write a Chamber of Commerce booklet for the town."[3]

Faulkner's writings burst with revelations of conflict and contradiction, emerging not only in tortured themes but also in notably complex and disjointed literary structures. *If I Forget Thee, Jerusalem* went so far as to alternate two abruptly disparate narratives; the five chapters of the novel that compose "Old Man" alternate with the five chapters that compose "Wild Palms." With its frontierlike setting, exaggerated adventure and misadventure, and misogynistic protagonist, "Old Man" is easy to situate within the framework of Faulkner's Yoknapatawpha County writing. "Wild Palms," however, with its ill-fated Northern migration, awkward urbanity, and dogged effort to depict and foreground a powerful female, is difficult to locate within the context and idiom of Faulkner's Southern county. Consequently, readers most often situate "Old Man" and "Wild Palms" in different contexts and, while recognizing their common thematic dimensions—especially regarding the meaning and pursuit of "freedom"—judge them on their own, prying them apart like the clasped hands of star-crossed lovers.

Insofar as the conflicts and contradictions expressed by the text informed Faulkner's own subject position as a white Jim Crow Southern male, they could reach expression, as Cantwell suggested when he called "Old Man" "hysterical," only indirectly or by way of symptoms. Because Western logic mandates and Westerners believe that contradictory propositions cannot both be true, social contradictions and conflicts are typically expressed in indirect roundabout ways. By acknowledging contradiction through such feelings as ambivalence, confusion, guilt, and shame, we can admit what propositional logic and the commonsense positivism that devolve from it cannot. Yet even these feelings are difficult for subjects, like Faulkner, positioned on the profitable side of inequitable social relations, to acknowledge let alone bring to clear expression. Unwilling to call their own privileges into question, such individuals rarely and grudgingly subject themselves to self-scrutiny, except, as Faulkner's writings demonstrate, in complex, nonpropositional, indirect, and negative fashions that are difficult to decipher.

Imagine the two narratives of *If I Forget Thee, Jerusalem* as the nonpropositional revelation of contradictions that Faulkner felt strongly but could declare only at the cost of all he possessed as a subject. The two tales are carefully demarcated from one another even though Faulkner sometimes allowed one, through a common theme or image, for example, to spill over its boundaries into the other. I want to demonstrate that the disparate dramas of "Wild

Palms" and "Old Man" rest on common ground. Set during the Great Mississippi River Flood of 1927, a disaster that displaced 185,000 Mississippians, nearly 80 percent of whom were African American, "Old Man" concentrates on the brief and paradoxical emancipation of a convict from Mississippi's legendary state penitentiary Parchman Farm.[4] Set in 1937, "Wild Palms" charts the strangely hollow romantic emancipation of Harry Wilbourne and Charlotte Rittenmeyer, who abandon discontented lives in New Orleans and embark upon a migration adventure that begins in Chicago, as had the migration adventures of hundreds of thousands of black Southerners who had left the South since 1915.

Faulkner could not disclose the ground these narratives rested upon because this ground was unspeakable and unspoken territory, the territory of African American experience colonized by European Americans. *If I Forget Thee, Jerusalem* breaks or breaches this ground by fashioning it as a unsolved puzzle, whose ill-fitting pieces challenge the pretended seamlessness, linearity, and uncontestability of univocal narratives of the Southern past. As opposed to the narrative of the South set forward, for example, by Malcolm Cowley's anthology *The Portable Faulkner*, *If I Forget Thee, Jerusalem* demonstrates Faulkner's habitual depiction of the past as an irreducible multiplicity of settings, events, themes, characters, and viewpoints.[5] By emphasizing the stubborn hybridity of kindred narratives, Faulkner challenges the reductive presentations of the past offered by univocal, linear narratives.

If I Forget Thee, Jerusalem characterizes such continuist narratives as fairy tales, which create the illusion of continuity by posing artificial beginnings, middles, and ends. "Old Man" begins with a prickly invocation of one of the best-known tropes of the fairy tale, the "once" of "Once upon a time": "Once (it was in Mississippi, in May, in the flood year 1928) there were two convicts." "Old Man" immediately challenges the vague and timeless temporality of "once," however, by parenthetically providing the detailed markers of time and place more typical of journalism or historiography. "Old Man," therefore, is simply posing as a fairy tale, the better to expose its "timeless" narrative of human endeavor and endurance as a tale mired in historical time and space. As the modernist Irishman James Joyce might have said, "Old Man" was no fairy tale; rather, it was the nightmare [of history] from which Faulkner was trying to awake.

Like other modernist texts, the troubled unity of *If I Forget Thee, Jerusalem* suggests that something obstinate and disruptive haunted Faulkner's conscious experience of everyday life, something he could neither set aside nor explain away. As good as the promise of its title, *If I Forget Thee, Jerusalem* held fast—albeit in the blurry, disturbed, and disturbing form of nightmare . . . or of testimonies to nightmarish lived experience—to the obstinate something it quietly evoked.[6]

With the distance of half a century, Toni Morrison, Faulkner's most astute interlocutor, has begun giving recognizable shape to this historical nightmare. Something akin to the ghost of Morrison's *Beloved* already haunted Faulkner's writings, most visibly incarnate and insufficiently mourned as Joe Christmas in *Light in August* and Charles Bon in *Absalom, Absalom!*[7] Representing the historical experiences excluded from mainstream American history and collective memory, this ghost haunts us still. We are currently convulsed with the problem of reconciling American pluralism with representations of American identity, a problem at the heart of controversies recently flaring in the names, for example, of "political correctness," "diversity," and "multiculturalism," problems that have traditionally raged in the name of democracy. As evidence of contradictions that still haunt American history and collective consciousness, Faulkner's discontinuous narrative puzzles urge us to interrogate issues that remain pressing and unresolved in American history and life.

*   *   *

Although inextricable from American history and life, African American historical experience and cultural traditions have nevertheless been marginalized, distorted, and overlooked. The very same processes are at work in Faulkner, whose writings minimized, distorted, and omitted African American historical and cultural life. In a brilliant essay titled "Twentieth-Century Fiction and the Black Mask of Humanity" (written immediately following World War II but not published until 1953), Ralph Ellison described and demonstrated what he called the "insidious and least understood form of segregation." As Ellison argued, this segregation is difficult to see, understand, and combat, because it inheres in the word, infecting all verbal forms, "from the proverb to the novel and stage play."[8] Therefore, he concluded, the representation of blackness in the fiction of Twain, Hemingway, and Faulkner should be grasped as more than

> the mere verbal counterpart of lynching or segregation. Indeed, it represents a projection of processes lying at the very root of American culture and certainly at the central core of its twentieth-century literary forms, a matter having less to do with the mere "reflection" of white racial theories than with processes molding the attitudes, the habits of mind, the cultural atmosphere and the artistic and intellectual traditions that condition men dedicated to democracy to practice, accept and, most crucial of all, often blind themselves to the essentially undemocratic treatment of their fellow citizens.[9]

Like most of Faulkner's writings, *If I Forget Thee, Jerusalem* reveals not simply Faulkner's representative blindness to nondemocratic practices but also exposes the processes that produce or mold "the attitudes, the habits of mind, the cultural atmosphere and the artistic and intellectual traditions" that support and reinforce cultural blindness. Symptomatic of the prevalence of such processes, Ellison noted, is what Richard Wright described as a battle between black and white Americans over the nature of reality.[10] Another soldier in this battle, James Baldwin also turned to Faulkner in an effort to expose and explain the mystified depiction of African Americans in American history, literature, and life.

> Faulkner's portraits of Negroes, which lack a system of nuances that, perhaps, only a black writer can see in black life—for Faulkner could see Negroes only as they related to him, not as they related to each other—are nevertheless made vivid by the torment of their creator. He is seeking to exorcise a history which is also a curse. . . . One may

see that the history, which is now indivisible from oneself, has been full of errors and excesses; but this is not the same thing as seeing that, for millions of people, this history—oneself—has been nothing but an intolerable yoke, a stinking prison, a shrieking grave. It is not so easy to see that, for millions of people, life itself depends on the speediest possible demolition of this history, even if this means the leveling, or the destruction of its heirs. And whatever this history may have given to the subjugated is of absolutely no value, since they have never been free to reject it; they will never even be able to assess it until they are free to take from it what they need, and to add to history the monumental fact of their presence.[11]

In *If I Forget Thee, Jerusalem*, the monumental fact of the African American presence is reduced to a "faint plinking," discernible in "Old Man," for example, only through such details as the cameo appearance of a young black male with no more property than lean hips and a guitar. "The sound of the guitar had not ceased and now the convicts saw him—a young, black, lean-hipped man, the guitar slung by a piece of cotton plow line about his neck. He mounted the levee, still picking it. He carried nothing else, no food, no change of clothes, not even a coat."[12] While the narrative of "Old Man" seems to say next to nothing about African American experience and life, this image reveals a supersensitive and even hysterical awareness of the meanings and values of racialized identities, particularly the fluctuation in values that was currently underway. As was evident, for example, by the successful commodification of the blues, which both demonstrated and elevated the cultural capital of black identity, the historical dispossession of black Southerners and corresponding entitlement of white Southerners were undergoing an inversion. Sensing the erosion of their privileged racial capital, white Southerners were confronted with the difficulty of imagining advantageous or even tolerable identities. In other words, transformations on the level of political economy were producing crises on the level of personal identity-formation, self-representation, imagination, and idealization.

Because the inversion of racialized cultural capital posed so profound a threat to them and because, with the mass migration that began in 1915, this inversion was held less in check, most white

Southern males surrendered themselves to such defensive processes as projection and denial. Thus, Ellison proposed that "we
view the whole of American life as a drama acted out upon the
body of a Negro giant, who, lying trussed up like Gulliver, forms
the stage and the scene upon which and within which the action
unfolds."[13] In "Wild Palms" this drama is acted out upon the body
of Charlotte Rittenmeyer who, "lying trussed up like Gulliver,
forms the stage and the scene upon which and within which the
action unfolds." Her body serves as the object of fascination and
denial to the provincial doctor whose narrative frames the body of
the text. Beginning to suspect that he has *"live[d] forever behind a
barricade of perennial innocence like a chicken in a pen,"* the doctor becomes increasingly hysterical as he approaches Charlotte,
whose body has come to rest, as if by chance, virtually in his back-
yard, staining with blood "the bed in which his wife said she would
not ask a nigger servant to sleep."[14] The doctor's association of this
scandalous body with the black body of a "nigger servant" is far
from insignificant. It offers a commentary on the doctor's growing
resistance as he nears Charlotte, about to bear witness to an un-
welcome revelation: "the veil was going now, dissolving now, it
was about to part now and now he did not want to see what was
behind it."[15] Faulkner's writings both approach and avoid this captive body, and we should not read past the casual details that figure
its yoke, prison, and grave.

"Wild Palms" begins its tale of transgression from a point of
view of "provincial and insulated amazement," that is, from the
focal perspective of a character who has never dared to venture
beyond his narrow experience and cultural bounds. Living out his
life well within customary limits and boundaries, the middle-aged
Protestant doctor "married the wife his father had picked out for
him and within four years owned the house which his father had
built and assumed the practice which his father had created."[16]
The doctor's complacent acceptance of these limits corresponds to
the exaggeratedly large zone of danger that lurks at their fringes.

Having never ventured forth from his prescribed identity, the
doctor is fiercely guarded against, or in other words, hysterically

reactive to any experience or evidence that challenges or reflects critically on the choices he has made. The doctor's view, like the flashlight's beam by which he guides himself down the dark steps of his house to the rental cottage next door, or like the gap in the oleander bush through which he peeps at the unmarried couple renting the cottage, takes in a highly restricted range of information. Although professionally trained to read the body, his powers of observation and analysis are limited by his personal beliefs, by the narrow spectrum of what he can allow.

"Separated from the truth . . . by a veil," the doctor recognizes that to see beyond this veil would be to confront evidence in contradiction with the principles that ground his personal identity and life course. Faulkner describes the doctor's choice to see no farther than this veil as a retirement into "pure morality."[17] Rashly concluding that Charlotte's hemorrhage was the symptom of a lung malady—by suppressing the thought that it might involve sexuality and other illicit practices, such as adultery, fornication, and abortion—the doctor is forced to recognize his dilemma, namely, that his vision as a doctor is clouded by his beliefs as a Protestant.

Recalling the famous veil offered by W. E. B. Du Bois in *The Souls of Black Folk* to represent the double consciousness of black Americans, Faulkner uses the trope of the veil to suggest the divided and self-contradictory consciousness of the white Southerner.[18] Like the protagonists in Richard Wright's prizewinning *Uncle Tom's Children*, which was published just as Faulkner began writing "Wild Palms," the doctor remains faithful to one aspect of his identity only by betraying another.[19]

Because the doctor has so little purchase on material he perceives as illicit, the text must find a way to bypass the doctor. Hence, it shifts its point of view, getting as close to Harry and Charlotte as indirect free-style narration permits, moving back to an earlier point in time and introducing a different setting and cast of characters, with different hopes, dreams, limits, and bounds. From this point on, the narrative of "Wild Palms" presumes to fill us in on everything the provincial doctor was unwilling or unable to see. By brandishing its power to move beyond the doctor's limitations as an observer, the text encourages us to forget that it cannot readily move beyond Faulkner's limitations, that it will not show us what the author himself could not allow or allow himself to see. "It is only what people see that shocks them," Faulkner wrote Robert Haas, "not what they think or hear."[20]

"Wild Palms" represents the doctor's narrow limits and bounds primarily in terms of romantic passion, desire, and sexuality; curiously, it does not explicitly examine the doctor's opinions with regard to racial identity or the racialized history of the South. This should strike readers of Faulkner as a puzzling omission, which is not adequately explained by relegating this and other racially silent texts to the customary marginalized category of non-Yoknapatawpha or simply nonmajor writings. We need not and should not confine ourselves to the customary limits that bound Faulkner's powers of discernment and governed his judgment or imagination.

In spite of its self-interested biases, distortions, and omissions, Charlotte and Harry's migration narrative falls squarely within the range of widespread debates about the expectations and consequences of black migration. For black Southerners, the leverage offered by the opportunity to leave the Jim Crow South provoked an inspired and inspiring debate; for white Southerners, the threat represented by the possibility of losing an exploited labor force provoked frustration and embarrassment. Agitated by the very approach of the topic, Faulkner's emphasis on the doctor's hysteria enabled him to deflect some measure of his own, long enough at least to construct a migration narrative in spite of his own resistance to the phenomenon of black migration.

From the doctor's narrow perspective, we learn that the transient couple renting his cottage is jobless, childless, penniless, ill-clad, and probably adulterous, and that Charlotte is hemorrhaging. From the third-person indirect free-style narrative that composes the body of the text, we learn the history of this pair from the perspective of Harry. He and Charlotte had left the South by train, as had more than a million black Southerners since 1915, disrupting lifelong routines, affiliations, and responsibilities. In search of liberty and fulfillment, they had fled the security of familiar worlds, often to encounter dissatisfaction, rejection, exploitation, deception, impoverishment, death, and imprisonment.

Having failed to remake himself, Harry's migration is figured as an economic and spiritual failure. His only victory, which is to admit and endure his loss, comes at the cost of Charlotte's life. Worse still, the untimely passing of Charlotte (and Harry's part in it) takes the place of what white Southerners perceived as the untimely migration of masses of black Southerners to the North, a migration that left them with complex feelings of loss. In *If I Forget Thee, Jerusalem*, then, Faulkner disguised this loss, depicting the mass departure of more than one and a half million African Americans and its impact on the South as the particular and preposterous tall tales of a few individual characters, not even represented as black. By dint of this *quid pro quo*, Faulkner was able to minimize and obscure the factors that pushed African Americans out of the South, the courage of masses of individual black migrants, and the sustaining social institutions that kept black migrants from swiftly returning South, as Harry and Charlotte do.[21]

As "Wild Palms" moved away from the viewpoint of the provincial doctor to that of Harry Wilbourne, it intensified its inquiry into the underlying processes of cultural blindness discussed by Ralph Ellison. Habits of mind like denial, avoidance, hysteria, passivity, and fear are Harry Wilbourne's characteristic *modus operandi*. Just at the point of embarking on a new unforeseeable life with Charlotte, Harry figured his professional identity as the veil, costume, blanket, or mask whose security he is about to relinquish. Anxious to flee his own desire, he wished to return to the hospital, where, he reasoned, "*I can hide behind my white jacket again, draw the old routine up over my head and face like niggers do the quilt when they go to bed.*"[22] Once again, another wild and unexpected comparison to black experience and the black body emerges from this text, jumping out at us like a haunt. Hovering over this text like a spirit or a bad smell, such casual details lead us to a vast and threatening territory that Faulkner never fully grasped and that most of Faulkner's readers have still left unexplored.

"Old Man" betrayed the monumental fact of the African American presence when it depicted the transport of the convicts from Parchman Farm, "packed like matches in an upright box . . . shackled by the ankles to a single chain," to aid during the rescue operation.[23]

> The truck passed a negro cabin. The water was up to the window ledges. A woman clutching two children squatted on the ridgepole, a man and a halfgrown youth, standing waist-deep, were hoisting a squealing pig onto the slanting roof of a barn, on the ridgepole of which sat a row of chickens and a turkey. Near the barn was a haystack on which a cow stood tied by a rope to the center pole and bawling steadily; a yelling negro boy on a saddleless mule which he flogged steadily, his legs clutching the mule's barrel and his body leaned to the drag of a rope attached to a second mule, approached the haystack, splashing and floundering. The woman on the housetop began to shriek at the passing truck, her voice carrying faint and melodious across the brown water, becoming fainter and fainter as the truck passed and went on, ceasing at last, whether because of distance or because she had stopped screaming those in the truck did not know.[24]

A casually developed image of the racist discrimination that characterized rescue operations in the Jim Crow South, the fading image and faint sounds of the distressed family are left behind as the truckload of convicts drives through a business district, where "a man in hip boots emerged knee-deep in water from a store, dragging a flat-bottomed skiff containing a steel safe."[25] Here, "Old Man" flagrantly if quietly reveals everyday facts of Jim Crow that it just as flagrantly and quietly conceals. The racialized injustice remarked here in passing can serve as an example of Faulkner's nonassertive manner of representing contradiction. The African American family threatened with losing their lives as well as their livestock was posed in mute, unacknowledged, disavowed contradiction with the well-equipped [white] man who was dragging his accumulated capital to safety.

Although the tall convict of "Old Man" is not figured as black, his marginal status in relation to the community and his experience of the flood code him black. From the outset of the narrative, the convicts of Parchman Farm identify with the circumstances of black Southerners. Listening to newspaper stories about the flood, for example, the convicts were "actually moved" when they heard "stories of men, even though they were negroes, being forced like themselves to do work for which they received no other pay than coarse food and a place in a mudfloored tent to sleep on—stories, pictures, which emerged . . . [of] the mudsplashed white men with the inevitable shot-guns, the antlike lines of negroes carrying sandbags, slipping and crawling up the steep face of the revetment to hurl their futile ammunition into the face of a flood and return for more."[26] The identification is taken even further when "Old Man" suggests that the convicts may have awaited the "approach of disaster" "with that same amazed and incredulous hope of the slaves." Naturally, Faulkner did not allude to African Americans in slavery but to those slaves "who watched the mounting flames of Rome from Ahenobarbus' gardens."[27] Later, however, the mounting flames that served to mark the destruction of Rome and Roman slavery reappear in the image of "a burning plantation house": "Juxtaposed to nowhere and neighbored by nothing it stood, a clear steady pyre-like flame rigidly fleeing its own reflection, burning in the dusk above the watery desolation with a quality paradoxical, outrageous, and bizarre."[28]

However Faulkner tried to suppress the thought, "Old Man" expressed his anxiety about the potential decline of racialization in Southern political and libidinal economy at the same time as it depicted the guilty image of white businessmen rescuing their securities and forcing "a chain of negroes" to carry their household goods to shelter—a "jumble of beds and trunks, gas and electric stoves, radios and tables and chairs and framed pictures"—while black families and their little bits of property were stranded and endangered on rooftops and haystacks in steadily rising waters.[29]

A white refugee in "Old Man," marked by "an old terror, an old blending of fear and impotence and rage," voiced the fury of a generation of white Southerners who watched masses of black Southerners leaving for the promise of safety and a better life: " 'I saw that launch and them boats come up and they never had no room for me. Full of bastard niggers and one of them setting

there playing a guitar but there wasn't no room for me! A guitar!'
he cried; now he began to scream, trembling, slavering, his face
twitching and jerking. 'Room for a bastard nigger guitar but not
for me—'."[30]

Such hysteria—the screaming, trembling, slavering, twitching,
and jerking—emerged as a defense against material evidence that
threatened to destabilize (hemorrhage or flood) the racialized limit
on which white Southern privileges were based. Hysteria typically
marks the places where Faulkner treads on the customary boundary lines of Southern cultural identities.

In the wake of World War II, Ellison spoke of the "moral awareness" awakened in white Americans in times of crisis. "During
periods of national crises, when the United States rounds a sudden
curve on the pitch-black road of history, this moral awareness
surges in the white American's conscience like a raging river revealed at his feet by a lightning flash. Only then is the veil of anti-
Negro myths, symbols, stereotypes and taboos drawn somewhat
aside. And when we look closely at our literature it is to be seen
operating even when the Negro seems most patently the little man
who isn't there."[31] Immediately following the 1927 flood, Faulkner
wrote *The Sound and the Fury*, reproducing its tumult in his depiction of experience and acknowledging the scandal of its revelations in his depiction of the idiocy, fatality, and stubborn tenacity
of white Southern male supremacism. Embarking with this novel
on the so-called major phase of his literary career, in which his
sensitivity to racism and racialization reached a peak, Faulkner
began his halting approach to something he preferred not to see,
that is, the black hands whose steady flight both exposed and dispossessed Jim Crow. Throughout and beyond this phase of his
writing practice, and particularly in *If I Forget Thee, Jerusalem*,
we have to look carefully at the text to see that the processes of
denial are operating, especially when "the Negro seems most patently the little [person] who isn't there."

*   *   *

One and a half million black Southerners, like Charlotte Ritten-meyer and Harry Wilbourne, left the South in search of less con-fining and more fulfilling lives. Between 1915 and 1942, the fact of mass migration suggested without directly asserting the fact of racist injustice in the Jim Crow South. The significance of the African American presence to Southern political economy became particularly vivid during the Great Mississippi Flood of 1927 and the Ohio River Flood of 1937. These disasters made it especially difficult to deny the systematic devaluation of African Americans in the Jim Crow South, where they were considered not as people but as inexpensive labor.

Mass migration of black Southerners out of the rural South began during World War I, when declining immigration and rising war production stimulated the need for labor, and urban industri-alists, particularly in the North, began recruiting black workers from the South.[32] From 1916 to 1930, one and a half million Afri-can Americans left the South, repudiating the advice offered by Booker T. Washington in his famous 1895 Atlanta Exposition Ad-dress. In the late nineteenth-century context of urbanization, in-dustrialization, and (as Anglo-Americans described the high rate of immigration) "mongrelization," the aging founder of Tuskegee Institute offered Southerners the following practical advice: "Cast down your bucket where you are." Accept "the fact," he enjoined black Southerners, "that the masses of us are to live by the produc-tions of our hands," and recognize that "whatever other sins the South may be called to bear, when it comes to business, pure and simple, it is in the South that the Negro is given a man's chance in the commercial world."[33]

Cast down your bucket among the eight million Negroes, he advised white Southerners,

> who have, without strikes and labour wars, tilled your fields, cleared your forests, builded your railroads and cities, and brought forth trea-sures from the bowels of the earth. . . . As we have proved our loyalty to you in the past, in nursing your children, watching by the sick-bed of your mothers and fathers, and often following them with tear-dimmed eyes to their graves, so in the future, in our humble way, we

shall stand by you with a devotion that no foreigner can approach, ready to lay down our lives, if need be, in defence of yours, interlacing our industrial, commercial, civil, and religious life with yours in a way that shall make the interests of both races one. In all things that are purely social we can be as separate as the fingers, yet one as the hand in all things essential to mutual progress.[34]

Washington's benign appeal to mutual cooperation, that is, to self-interest, assumed a more threatening urgency, however, when he turned to the matter of Justice, Human and Divine. "There is no escape through law of man or G-d from the inevitable: 'The laws of changeless justice bind/ Oppressor with oppressed;/ And close as sin and suffering joined/ We march to fate abreast.' Nearly sixteen millions of hands will aid you in pulling the load upward, or they will pull against you the load downward."[35]

Twenty-one years later, a million feet walked away from the South within some 1,000 days, that is, at the net rate of about 1,000 feet per day. Some two million more followed on their heels over the course of the next decade. Whereas 90 percent of the African American population still lived in the South in 1910, that percentage decreased to 85.2 by 1920 and to 78.7 by 1930.[36] Whereas 87 percent of Afro-Mississippians still lived in Mississippi in 1910, that percentage fell to 80.3 by 1920 and to 76.5 by 1930.[37] Owing to rural-urban migration, which these percentages do not reflect, Mississippi's urban black population almost doubled between 1910 and 1940. Rural Mississippi increasingly felt the scarcity of black hands.

The monumental fact of African American migration has been treated as a footnote in mainstream narratives of twentieth-century American history and culture. Even the transformation of the post-World War I South was seen primarily in terms of modernization, urbanization, and economic and political restructuring, rather than in terms of demographic shifts and their impact on racialized identities throughout the nation. Long recognized as an important topos in African American narrative, mobility and its impact on racial identity have gone largely unnoticed in European American narratives until quite recently. Long before it became commonplace, Faulkner recognized whiteness as a historical and cultural construction rather than as a natural phenomenon.[38]

*   *   *

Within the wide spectrum of the language used to describe migration—which has historically included tides, waves, flights, herds, trains, exodus, etc.—flooding has continued to occupy a privileged place. Black migrants have long been described as "flooding" out of the South and "inundating" the North, and floods have long been seen as one of the "natural" push factors of black migration. In July 1994, for example, the influx of Haitian refugees seeking asylum in the United States was described as "a raging flood," just as the flight of refugees from war-torn Rwanda, at the rate of 10,000 per hour, was described as a "human wave" moving through "an open floodgate." However commonplace, a flood is not an apt metaphor for human migrations, which do not actually occur as continuous flows but, as McMillen has pointed out, as a great number of individual stops and starts.[39]

The treatment of black Southern refugees during the Great Mississippi River Flood of 1927 was not simply the product of a natural phenomenon but rather the byproduct of numerous social, political, historical, cultural, and moral forces.[40] An international spectacle because of its sheer magnitude, the complexity of the rescue and relief operations, and the vexations of trying to "reconstruct" the Deep South, the 1927 flood became a focal point of condensation. The flood gave high visibility to the racialized pattern of Jim Crow life, which marked everything from discriminatory rescue operations to guarded concentration camps, established and maintained to prevent black sharecroppers, tenant farmers, and leased convict laborers from using the flood as an opportunity to flee debt and seek a better life. It demonstrated the injustice of Jim Crow land tenure and labor law as well as the differential consequences of flood control for the primarily white land owner, banker, and merchant, on one hand, and for the primarily black sharecropper, on the other.

Addressing the nation, Secretary of Commerce Herbert Hoover, who engineered the rescue and relief effort, described the 1927 Mississippi River Flood as the worst peacetime calamity the United States had ever seen. Affecting seven states, it flooded over 16.5 million acres of land and cost $300 million in damages, including $102.6 million in crop losses. It left an estimated 608,000 people homeless. Hardest hit were the large plantations in Arkansas, Mississippi, and Louisiana, which were worked primarily by African American sharecroppers, tenant farmers, and debt peons. As a consequence, 555,000 of the 608,000 refugees were African Americans. In Mississippi, 142,000 of the 185,500 refugees were African American. Eighteen Red Cross camps in Mississippi, the largest of which were in the Delta, gave emergency aid to 70,000 refugees; outside the camps, another 88,000 flood victims received aid.

Like the Jubilee of 1913, the flood served as a benchmark of African American progress in the South, a glaring indication of the fact that the South had by no means offered black Southerners "a man's chance in the commercial world." The 1927 flood proved that black hands still reaped little fruit from their labor. Officially at risk in the flood were not black hands but white capital; hence, black laborers were rescued and relieved during the flood only insofar as they would be necessary to the preservation and reproduction of capital. White capital's greatest concern for these systematically exploited black hands was that many of them might disappear altogether from the South. African American migration had increased steadily since 1916, and no one knew at the time that net migration out of state would decline during the Great Depression. In short, the greatest hope of many black refugees was white capital's worst nightmare.

Landlords took every possible measure to prevent black laborers from "flooding" from their plantations. They ordered labor agents to keep away from the dispossessed black workers and forced tenants to stay on the plantations or nearby levees for as long as possible, sometimes at the cost of their lives. From the perspective of the landlords, the lives of a few laborers were cheap. If the laborers were permitted to evacuate, what earthly power would be able to convince them to return? And if they were good and gone, whose sweat and tears would replant and rebuild the devastated fields and towns?

The heightened fears of white landowners encouraged local authorities to act as swiftly and harshly as Pharoah to reassert their grip on the people who worked their land and secured their mortgages. African American refugees who could not be put to immediate work on the levees or in the rescue operation were herded in barges and taken to special relief camps. Many of the 154 camps operated and maintained by the Red Cross and the National Guard became special "concentration camps" holding black refugees hostage. In Mississippi, such camps existed, for example, at Greenville—where William Alexander Percy was chairman of the local Red Cross and where Faulkner's friend and former editor Ben Wasson was raised—as well as Vicksburg, Yazoo City, and Cleveland.[41]

As early as 7 May, the *Chicago Defender* began printing stories that exposed the abuses taking place during the rescue and relief operation. Following a tour of the Southern flood area, Walter White, assistant secretary of the NAACP, announced to the Associated Press the fact that black refugees were being "released only to their landlords and sent back against their wills to the plantations from which they came." This information appeared in a small news item on page 7 of the Saturday *New York Times* on 28 May 1927. The following day, the Sunday *Times* announced that Hoover had created the Colored Advisory Commission, which was charged "to work with the rehabilitation organization in connection with the relief of negro victims of the flood." At the same time, Hoover "denounced a statement printed in the North that negroes are being brutally treated in refugee camps as being absolutely without foundation. . . . 'They are being splendidly treated and cared for' said Mr. Hoover." In both Walter White's article in *The Nation* and an NAACP investigation published in *Crisis*, it was argued that local authorities interned African Americans in refugee camps because of the fear that black refugees would sooner migrate than return to the plantations. Both the *Crisis* and the *Chicago Defender* reported that refugees in these camps were tagged like items of property, forced to work for little or no remuneration, and, with few exceptions, could leave the camps only when "reclaimed" by their landlords or overseers. Thus, although the flood might have offered many refugees the opportunity for a fresh start, "the flood situation," as Walter White wrote in the *Nation*, only "strengthen[ed] their chains."

Overdetermined as it was, the 1927 flood received wide and frequent if hugely varied attention, not only from local and federal agencies, activists, newspapers, newsreels, and the business world, but also in music, poetry, fiction, photography, motion pictures, and painting. A burgeoning market in "race records," for example, readily absorbed the half dozen blues flood songs released between April and August 1927 by such well-known blues singers as Ma Rainey, Bessie Smith, Sippi Wallace, Charlie Patton, and Blind Lemon Jefferson. Sterling Brown treated the flood in poems collected in *My Southern Road*, including the well-known poem about Ma Rainey's performances of "Backwater Blues."[42] In 1937, when there was another devastating flood and when Faulkner began writing *If I Forget Thee, Jerusalem*, Pare Lorentz filmed *The River*, Richard Wright published "Down By the Riverside" in *Uncle Tom's Children*, and Zora Neale Hurston published *Their Eyes Were Watching God*. Three years later, Jacob Lawrence exhibited his "Migration Series," which included the image of floods, along with trains and lynchings, as a key figure of black migration.[43]

In spite of all the attention the flood received, however, the monumental fact of African American experience was still ignored or minimized in the mainstream. Nonetheless, the 1927 flood made it difficult to deny the fact that hundreds of thousands of African Americans had flooded out of the South and into the North over the past twelve years and that hundreds of thousands more were likely to follow. By 1939, when Faulkner published *If I Forget Thee, Jerusalem*, black migration had been exerting its complex and widespread cultural effects for nearly a quarter of a century;

second-generation migrants were already coming of age. Issues of
African American cultural memory, transmission, and survival
were acutely felt and widely debated.[44]

*   *   *

In a much-cited letter to his editor Robert Haas, written on 8
July 1938, Faulkner claimed that, having written the novel under
physical and emotional duress, he was in no position to judge it.
"I have lived for the past six months in such a peculiar state of
family complications and back complications that I still am not
able to tell if the novel is all right or absolute drivel."[45] Faulkner
attributes his lack of distance from the novel to recent complications in his personal life, pointing specifically to his "family" and
"back." He attributes his inability to pass judgment on the novel
to the period of senselessness he experienced as he wrote it. "To
me, it was written just as if I had sat on the one side of a wall and
the paper was on the other and my hand with the pen thrust
through the wall and writing not only on invisible paper but in
pitch darkness too, so that I could not even know if the pen still
wrote on paper or not."[46] Separated from the paper by a wall and
writing in pitch darkness, it is almost as if Faulkner, like the protagonists of each of the narratives, had been composing the novel
from a prison cell.[47]

Confronted with the riddle of this novel, we can deny it, answer
it, or do our best to spell it out. Weary of the time I myself have
spent noting the denials, challenging the answers, and trying to
spell out the riddle, I am ready at this point to hazard an answer—
one that also suggests why the riddle cannot be foreclosed. Although *If I Forget Thee, Jerusalem* is certainly informed by what
Faulkner called personal "complications," we have always had a
narrow picture of what these complications were; furthermore,
whatever the personal complications at issue, these were linked to
broader social complications, facts of Southern historical and cultural experience that could neither be reconciled with the rendi-
tion of Southern history and life that was then in dominance nor
even readily spoken.

Thus, when I speak of the riddle of *If I Forget Thee, Jerusalem*, I am attempting to speak of a breakdown of sense and the senses whose origins reach through the personal into our social and cultural consciousness. What occupies this realm that exceeds sense and confuses the senses are broad areas of experience, areas that fall outside cultural limits and bounds. It is not simply an imaginary place but rather a location of material breakdown, to which we relegate all that is wild, frightening, disreputable, worn out, forgotten, or ignored. Insofar as customs and limits are requirements of meaning and sense, we cannot eliminate these dangerous places. From time to time, however, we need to redefine the zone of safety, respectability, and empowerment. When binding customs enhance our own particular interests and remove us from the danger zone, we run the risk of accepting them complacently. When they run contrary to our own welfare and place us in harm's way, however, we cannot afford this luxury and are obliged to undertake the arduous and dangerous battle for reform.

Complacent or not, most of us have one way or another suffered a radical upheaval of our customary world. Minor personal or major social accidents and catastrophes can take us far beyond our accustomed bounds.[48] Even the ordinary course of experience can teach us that the familiar world is bound to time and space, cannot be held fast, and is simply bound to vanish. Thus we learn the lessons of the uncanny, what it is to be dislocated, out of step, out of bounds, or out of reach. Most everyone can testify to the fragility of the familiar world, which can at any moment give way to unfamiliarity, incomprehension, and mayhem. On the other hand, such disruptions of the familiar sometimes represent the hope of salvation, an end of suffering, justice. This depends, of course, on where one stands with respect to binding customs and limits.

Despite such knowledge of the fragility of the customary world, people accustomed to privilege are typically as reluctant to relinquish their privileges as to admit that they enjoy them at someone else's expense. To enjoy privilege, we have to forget, ignore, or deny the struggles and suffering of others less fortunate than ourselves. It is difficult to admit that we do this, that we go on with our own trivial pursuits in the face of suffering and injustice, that we fail to drop whatever we are doing to organize and lead collective protest. Today, as in 1938, when Faulkner was writing *If I Forget Thee, Jerusalem*, there are 20 million reasons why we should all stop what we are doing. However, as millions of others find themselves on the nether side of some preposterous limit, prey to massive and unspeakable suffering, we go on with business as usual, more or less haunted by what we do not wish to see.

*   *   *

This is a propitious moment for returning to *If I Forget Thee, Jerusalem*, the original title of the novel published as *The Wild Palms*. The words of the title are drawn from Psalm 137, *The Mourning of the Exiles in Babylon*, a famous prayer that at once mourns Jewish captivity and begs for vengeance on Israel's enemies, the Babylonians and the Edomites, who destroyed Jerusalem in the 6th century B.C. Listen to the psalm's terrible sense of loss and terrifying demand for retribution. "By the rivers of Babylon,/ there we sat down, and there we wept, as we remembered Zion./ We hung our harps upon the willows in her midst./ For there they that carried us away captive required of us a song;/ and there they that conquered us required of us mirth, saying/ Sing us a song of Zion./ But how can we sing our Savior's song in a strange land?/ If I forget thee, O Jerusalem,/ let my right hand forget her cunning./ If I do not remember thee,/ let my tongue cleave to the roof of my mouth;/ If Jerusalem be less than my greatest joy./ Remember, G-d, the sons of Edom/ in the day of Jerusalem!/ who said, strip her, strip her,/ strip her bare./ O daughter of Babylon, for your treachery,/ blessed be he, who repays you for what you've done to us./ Blessed be he who seizes and dashes/ your little ones against the rocks."[49] What is most puzzling about Faulkner's invocation of this psalm is the psalm's point of view.

Psalm 137 speaks from the perspective of the Jewish exiles in captivity, who grieve for their homeland and denounce their captors. As a trope for the sufferings of exile and slavery as well as the hope of retribution, this psalm has not typically served as an expressive vehicle for Anglo-American historical experience. On the contrary, the psalm is invoked with some frequency in the sermons, poetry, and songs of Africans in the diaspora. Because Faulkner's novel appears to have little or nothing to say about black Southerners and their historical experience, it is very curious that Faulkner chose to invoke it, reminding us that Southern history and life make very little sense without encompassing both black and white hands. Nevertheless, Southern history remains primarily a narrative of white experience, unable to comprehend black experience. Often divided by irreducible differences, the inextricable histories of black and white Southerners, like a pair of clasped hands, resist simple incorporation into narratives of the Southern past.

Faulkner's allusion to this psalm offers us a way to think about its two distinct narrative threads. Focussing on historical wrongdoing, the psalm emphasizes the suffering of the vanquished and their hope that justice will one day be done. Living in the midst of glaring social injustice, Faulkner calls forth a commonplace set of correspondences, that is, between Jewish and African diaspora, exile, and captivity; between Babylon and the Jim Crow South; and between Babylonians and white Southerners. Is it not the entirety of this historical drama, as replayed in the American South, that Faulkner vows, through his invocation to the psalm, never to forget? If I forget, let my right hand lose her cunning and my tongue cleave to the roof of my mouth. Even if I cannot come to terms with the inextricability and irreducibility of black and white Southern experience, and my part in it, I must not forget to try. . . . Remember that *If I Forget Thee, Jerusalem* is immediately preceded by *The Unvanquished* and almost immediately followed by *Go Down, Moses,* both of whose tenacious efforts to remember this muddled and muddied past surmount the indirection of this novel, steeped as it is in the effort—begun long ago and pursued in *Absalom Absalom!* and *Pylon*—to understand the powerful mechanism of denial and its obstructive role in processes of mourning.

Thus, like the psalm from which it takes its title, *If I Forget Thee, Jerusalem* vows to remember the long and troubled history of the South and Faulkner's own hand in it. Both "Old Man" and "Wild Palms" map out cultural responses—especially psychic defense mechanisms, such as denial—that enable privileged subjects to live with and profit from their positions within structures of dominance. However, in addition to mapping out patterns of cultural denial, the text also involuntarily enacts them by obscuring the black hands that it reveals.

*   *   *

At issue since the Middle Passage, migration remains a key element of life in the African diaspora. African Americans were drawn to the Hebrew Bible's account of the Jewish diaspora and thus to a rich and ancient discourse of nomadic or deterritorialized subjectivity on its way to nationhood or territorialized collective identity. According to this account, the Flood was something like the Divine Deletion of G-d's first draft: "Nasty work," G-d declared, arrogating nearly all creation to a "*.jnk" file. Like an African American sorrow song, *If I Forget Thee, Jerusalem* uses richly historicized and overdetermined topoi—diaspora and the flood, suffering and judgment, remembering and forgetting, home and exile—to bear witness to unspeakable and unspoken injustices.

The experience and meaning of the flood diverged widely, particularly along the valence of race, and the racial perspective of *If I Forget Thee, Jerusalem* is difficult to tease out, particularly insofar as the text seems to have little or nothing to do with race. As I hope to have demonstrated, however, the topics foregrounded in the text are inextricable from African American experience and from the cultural construction of racialized difference.

*   *   *

In "Faulkner and Desegregation," Baldwin argued that few people are courageous enough to undertake the risk and the agony of genuine self-transformation.

Any real change implies the breakup of the world as one has always known it, the loss of all that gave one an identity, the end of safety. And at such a moment, unable to see and not daring to imagine what the future will now bring forth, one clings to what one knew, or thought one knew; to what one possessed or dreamed that one possessed. Yet, it is only when a man is able, without bitterness or self-pity, to surrender a dream he has long cherished or a privilege he has long possessed that he is set free—he has set himself free—for higher dreams, for greater privileges. All men have gone through this, go through it, each according to his degree, throughout their lives. It is one of the irreducible facts of life. And remembering this, especially since I am a Negro, affords me almost my only means of understanding what is happening in the minds and hearts of white southerners today.[50]

In its presentation of precisely such a collapse of identity and material well-being, "Wild Palms" almost seems to pantomime Baldwin's essay. Harry would not or could not imagine himself as a deracialized subject, any more than the hysterical old man of "Old Man" could feature a subject with no more property than lean hips and a guitar. Like that furious old man, Harry figured himself as almost completely annihilated, almost suffocated by the oppressive weight of the "black wind" and the "black sand" that filled his lungs. "[A] tremendous silence . . . roared down upon him like a wave, a sea, and there was nothing for him to hold to, picking him up, tossing and spinning him and roaring on, leaving him blinking steadily and painfully at his dry granulated lids."[51] Toward the end of "Wild Palms," Wilbourne answers to any name—Webster, Watson, and, oddly enough, Morrison—but in the end he grasps for the refuge of identity. Crushed by "blackness," Harry sought his identity in "grief," that is, in what he knew or thought he had known, possessed or dreamt he had possessed, lost or imagined he had lost. While *If I Forget Thee, Jerusalem* seems to admonish both Harry and the tall convict for failing to reinvent themselves, it also suggests that they achieved some modest success. Each survived the dissolution of earlier ideals, which was after all the task, according to Baldwin, of white Southerners, who would have to let go of everything they knew and had and wished for.

NOTES

1. Robert Cantwell, *Time* (23 January 1939); William Faulkner, *The Wild Palms* [1939] (New York: Random House, 1966). For a discussion of Robert Cantwell's review of *The Wild Palms* and feature story on Faulkner, whose picture also appeared on the cover of the "middle-brow magazine of mass circulation," that is, *Time*, see Joseph Blotner, *Faulkner: A Biography* (New York: Random House, 1974), 404–6.

2. Although an edition of the "original text" has not yet appeared, Noel Polk encouraged me to refer to this novel by its original title, a stunning and, in the context of the novel as traditionally read, inexplicable allusion that I also prefer to remember and acknowledge.

3. Blotner, *Faulkner: A Biography*, 406.

4. See David M. Oshinsky, *Worse Than Slavery: Parchman Farm and the Ordeal of Jim Crow Justice* (New York: Free Press, 1996).

5. *The Portable Faulkner*, ed. Malcolm Cowley (New York: Viking Press, 1946).

6. On testimony, memory, and narrative form, see, for example, Lawrence L. Langer, *Holocaust Testimonies: The Ruins of Memory* (New Haven: Yale University Press, 1991).

7. Toni Morrison, *Beloved* (New York: Penguin, 1988), William Faulkner, *Light in August* [1932] (New York: Vintage, 1985), and William Faulkner, *Absalom, Absalom!* [1936] (New York: Vintage, 1986).

8. Ralph Ellison, *Shadow and Act* [1953] (New York: Random House, 1972), 24.

9. Ibid., 26–27.

10. Cited in Ellison, *Shadow and Act*, 26.

11. James Baldwin, *The Price of the Ticket: Collected Nonfiction, 1948–1985* (New York: St. Martin's Press, 1985), 473.

12. Faulkner, *Wild Palms*, 74.

13. Ellison, *Shadow and Act*, 28.

14. Faulkner, *Wild Palms*, 19.

15. Ibid., 16.

16. Ibid., 4.

17. Ibid., 280.

18. W. E. B. Du Bois, *The Souls of Black Folk* [1903] (New York: Penguin Books, 1989).

19. Richard Wright, *Uncle Tom's Children* [1936, 37, 38] (New York: Harper Perennial, 1993).

20. *Selected Letters of William Faulkner*, ed. Joseph Blotner (New York: Random House, 1977), 106.

21. For an analysis of Faulkner in the context of African American narratives of ascent and immersion, see Craig Werner, *Playing the Changes, From Afro-Modernism to the Jazz Impulse* (Urbana: University of Illinois Press, 1994), 27–62, to whose work I am greatly indebted.

22. Faulkner, *Wild Palms*, 51.

23. Ibid., 61.

24. Ibid., 63–64.

25. Ibid., 65.

26. Ibid., 29.

27. Ibid.

28. Ibid., 70.

29. Ibid., 66.

30. Ibid., 79.

31. Ellison, *Shadow and Act*, 29.

32. Representations of black migration from a variety of perspectives are steadily rising. For a survey of current historical research on the topic, see *Black Exodus: The Great Migration and the American South*, ed. Alferdteen Harrison (Jackson: University Press of Mississippi, 1991) and *The Great Migration in Historical Perspective: New Dimensions of Race, Class, and Gender*, ed. Joe William Trotter Jr. (Bloomington: Indiana University Press, 1991). For a sense of its cultural impact, see *Up South: Stories, Studies and Letters of This Century's African-American Migrations*, ed. Malaika Adero (New York: New Press, 1993),

Farah Jasmine Griffin, *"Who Set You Flowin'?" The African-American Migration Narrative* (New York: Oxford University Press, 1995), and Lawrence Rodgers, *The Afro-American Great Migration Novel* (dissertation, University of Wisconsin, Madison, 1989. Forthcoming, University of Illinois Press). On Mississippi black migration in particular, see James Grossman, *Land of Hope: Chicago, Black Southerners, and the Great Migration* (Chicago: University of Chicago Press, 1991) and Neil R. McMillen, *Dark Journey: Black Mississippians in the Age of Jim Crow* (Urbana: University of Illinois Press, 1989).

33. Booker T. Washington, *Up From Slavery* [1901] (New York: Penguin, 1986), 220–21.

34. Ibid., 221–22.

35. Ibid.

36. Charles Johnson, *Shadow of the Plantation* (Chicago: University of Chicago Press, 1934), 28, 143; Daniel M. Johnson and Rex R. Campbell, *Black Migration in America* (Durham, North Carolina: Duke University Press, 1981), 73.

37. McMillen, *Dark Journey*.

38. See, for example, Bell Hooks, *Black Looks: Race and Representation* (Boston: South End Press, 1992), Ruth Frankenberg, *White Women, Race Matters: The Social Construction of Whiteness* (Minneapolis: University of Minnesota Press, 1993), and David Roediger, *The Wages of Whiteness: Race and the Making of the American Working Class* (New York: Verso, 1991).

39. McMillen, *Dark Journey*, 269–70.

40. On the 1927 Mississippi River Flood, see Pete Daniel, *Deep'n As It Come: The 1927 Mississippi River Flood* (New York: Oxford University Press, 1977) and William Howard, "Richard Wright's Flood Stories and the Great Mississippi River Flood of 1927: Social and Historical Backgrounds," in *Southern Literary Journal* 16 (Spring 1984): 44–62.

41. For a startlingly different white Southern perspective on the flood, see William Alexander Percy's *Lanterns on the Levee: Recollections of a Planter's Son* (New York: Knopf, 1941), published just a couple of years after *If I Forget Thee, Jerusalem*.

42. Sterling Brown, *Southern Road* (New York: Harcourt Brace, 1932).

43. On cultural responses to the 1927 flood, see William Howard, "Richard Wright's Flood Stories," and Michael Grimwood, *Heart in Conflict: Faulkner's Struggles with Vocation* (Athens: University of Georgia Press, 1987). For the broader framework of cultural responses to black migration, see Griffin, *"Who Set You Flowin'?"* In a longer version of this paper, I elaborate further on these other constructions of flooding, black migration, and Jim Crow.

44. For an introduction to the "racial consciousness" provoked by black migration, see *The New Negro: An Interpretation*, ed. Alain Locke [1925] (New York: Atheneum, 1992).

45. *Selected Letters*, 106.

46. Ibid.

47. For a general discussion of the text and of Faulkner's life circumstances as he wrote it, see *Selected Letters*, and David Minter, *William Faulkner: His Life and His Work* (Baltimore: Johns Hopkins University Press, 1980). Blotner notes that Faulkner returned to Mississippi from Los Angeles without Jill's nanny of three years, Narcissus McEwen, and without Jack Oliver. Both Afro-Southerners had accompanied the family to California in July 1936. When Faulkner went home in August 1937, however, they determined to stay in Los Angeles. To my knowledge, nothing further has been published about McEwen or Oliver.

48. In this context, I cannot fail to mention Deletha Word, who was thrown or forced to her death from the Belle Isle Bridge on Saturday, 19 August 1995. As a consequence of a minor automobile collision, she was torn from her car, brutalized, and killed. A crowd of 50 some spectators, who failed to come to the rescue of Deletha Word, witnessed this brutality. What will be the testimony of such witnesses? What kind of tragic forgetfulness (*lethe*) informed their moral failure and how will they put it into words?

49. Freely adapted from the *Anchor Bible* and *King James Bible*.

50. Baldwin, *The Price of the Ticket*, 147.

51. Faulkner, *Wild Palms*, 307.

Faulkner and the Frontier Grotesque: *The Hamlet* as Southwestern Humor

PETER ALAN FROEHLICH

I would like to begin with a confession: I hate the title of this essay. It's not just that it's unimaginative—what bothers me is its tone of self-assurance and the overdeterminacy of its claims. It suggests a tidy project of contextualization, as if I will simply describe the genre of Southwestern Humor, show that Faulkner both draws on and surpasses generic form and content, then leave you comfortable and happy with a fuller, more satisfying understanding of the novel. While that may happen, my intention is quite different: I intend to discuss how *The Hamlet* makes its readers uncomfortable and unhappy by resisting any attempt to confine and control meaning within a standard readerly strategy or critical context. I am fascinated with *The Hamlet*'s indeterminacy, its incongruities, and its grotesquery—and I am therefore unsatisfied with any critical approach that claims to provide a tidy and coherent account of the novel. *The Hamlet* calls for a readerly strategy that illuminates its textual problems, not with the intention of explaining them away but with the goal of better understanding their implications.

I would like to suggest that the source of *The Hamlet*'s complexity lies in Faulkner's representation of the South—or specifically of Frenchman's Bend—as a frontier. We know from the work of several critics that Faulkner drew heavily on the literary context of Southwestern Humor and the cultural context of frontier storytelling for the characters and plots in *The Hamlet*.[1] What I propose to add to this scholarship is a sense of *why* Faulkner looked back to those traditions—an understanding of how these contexts should influence our reading of Faulkner's text. In the pursuit of that goal, I begin with a discussion of frontier that illuminates the grotesquery inherent in the concept, then examine Southwestern Humor as a record of this frontier grotesque. Only when we understand the relationship between frontier grotesque and Southern culture as it is represented in the tales of the Southwestern Humorists will we be in a position to understand Faulkner's extension of these traditions in *The Hamlet*.

We begin, then, with the frontier. The concept of frontier in American studies dates back to Frederick Jackson Turner's classic essay "The Significance of the Frontier in American History."[2] In that essay, Turner describes the frontier as the line on a census map that separates European settlement from wilderness. This model of the frontier does not correspond to a material or historical reality, however; instead, it grows out of the jingoism of the cultures that settled the United States, the ideological desire to divide all space into two categories: the region occupied by culture and the region outside of it.

The cultural inside, or settlement, consists of space that is thoroughly controlled by the institutions of European culture. This cultural hegemony begins with the establishment of definitions and categories that become part of the language and mind of the people: masculine and feminine gender roles; rich and poor; slave and free; citizen and alien; law-abider and criminal; the list continues and branches out beyond these simple, binary oppositions into various shades of distinction. During the colonial period European culture not only located people within categories but also sought to keep them in their physical and cultural places. These categories were enforced by institutions of culture that became associated with civilization in America: the English language, English legal tradition, Christian churches and morality, and a colonialist and capitalist economy. Settlement can therefore be defined as geographical space that has been thoroughly scrutinized and imprinted with ideology, where cultural definitions and categories are visible and enforced, where the highest values of the culture appear in material form in the lives of the citizens.

While the space occupied by culture is known and scrutinized, the space outside of culture remains unseen and unknown. Trained to recognize civilization only in the material forms and institutions of European culture, the colonizer was unable to recognize the wilderness as the settlement of other cultures. The colonizer either regarded native culture as a state of nature or projected the dark underside of European culture onto the Other. Where the stability and order of European culture suggested the categories of mind that Freud would name the ego and superego (conscious identity and the restraint of conscience), the wilderness became associated with the unconscious, forbidden, and repressed desires of the id. In the colonial mind, the natives lived disordered, transgressive, and sinful lives governed by the passions and likely to erupt in unrestrained violence or sexuality. Native cultural institutions— language, religion, the hunting and gathering economy—and all the material forms of native culture were dismissed as barbaric, animalistic, demonic, or nonexistent.

The ideological construct of settlement versus wilderness forms a dyadic structure that clearly supports the cultural hegemony of the European: everything that is inside European culture is good and godly; everything outside—everything associated with the Other—is inferior or evil. The idea of frontier as a line, a clearly recognizable border, maintains the distinction between inside and outside and keeps the cultures from interacting. It is important to note that while the colonial powers wanted their culture to expand, they did not want it to change. The linear conception of frontier operates as a figurative Great Wall of China, keeping the barbarians out and the citizens and their culture safely within. As European settlement expanded, Turner's frontier line moved westward in an orderly progress—almost as if the Great Wall were pushed across the continent, instantly and irrevocably transforming wilderness into settlement and leaving the two spaces forever separate, forever distinct.

When we understand Turner's linear model as a projection of

ideology, it becomes possible to resist the ideology, deconstruct the model, and develop a new conception that more accurately describes the geographical and cultural reality of frontier. Frontier is not a line between settlement and wilderness but is in fact an irregular, illicit, and tenuous European settlement located *within* the wilderness. Frontier space is created when a group of Europeans leaves the settlement and invades the wilderness. Arriving in native territory, they begin to transform the environment into something suitable for Europeans, clearing trees and building fortified stockades for protection against hostile natives and wild animals. These pioneers hunt and gather until their farms produce enough food to sustain the population; they also borrow from native material culture whatever forms—food, shelter, clothing, or weapons—will help them to survive.[3]

This mixing of cultures that takes place on the frontier creates a hybrid that can best be understood as a grotesque. Geoffrey Galt Harpham locates the grotesque in a response to category confusion.[4] We might, for example, recognize the categories of fish and human being as separate and distinct. Presented with the figure of a mermaid, we experience a momentary confusion: is it a fish? or is it a woman? The figure is not unrecognizable, pure phantasm, but all *too* recognizable: it evokes both categories—fish and human—at once, thus calling into question the matrix of definitions that we use to make sense of the world around us. According to Harpham, we react to the grotesque with simultaneous attraction and revulsion, in part because the image breaks through the tidy categories of the conscious mind into the unsettling yet fascinating realm of the unconscious. Harpham argues that the conscious mind cannot rest in this category confusion; it quickly breaks the image down, recognizes each individual part, and names the hybrid, thereby creating a new category: *mermaid*. In this way, the mind moves beyond the grotesque to expand the matrix of definitions that constitute both language and culture. The grotesque does not consist of this process of fracturing and reconstitution, however, but only of that unsettling moment in which the categories are fluid and unstable.

The frontier is just such a grotesque: an illicit space that represents neither wilderness nor settlement, but somehow, illogically, both at once. It comprises a third term in the settlement-wilderness dyad, that closed system of inside versus outside, the logic of which neither requires—nor allows—a middle term. This grotesque quality of the frontier becomes clear when you attempt to view it from either side of the wilderness-settlement dyad. Bring to mind a frontier stockade: place it, for example, in central Tennessee in 1780. Viewed from the perspective of settlement culture—from, say, Boston Common—the stockade is considered wilderness: it resembles nothing so much as an Iroquois fort; it lies outside European-American control; and the people who inhabit the place, while Europeans, have adapted many forms of native culture. From the wilderness or native perspective, however, the frontier stockade represents the leading edge of European encroachment; it lies on land that the natives claim as their own, and in that sense it is no different from Boston Common.

While each culture rejects the idea of frontier, placing it within the realm of the Other, the frontier develops an independent cultural perspective that, borrowing from both wilderness and settlement values, collapses the distinction between insider and outsider. This frontier perspective is best described by reference to a second definition of the grotesque, that articulated by Mikhail Bakhtin in *Rabelais and His World*.[5] Bakhtin locates the grotesque in the European tradition of carnival, a time when popular or folk culture triumphs over the otherwise dominant high culture. According to Bakhtin, carnival involves transgressive behavior of every kind, notably including parody, a comic art involving the reversal of high and low cultural positions: the crowning of a *king of fools*, for example. Other carnivalesque transgressions involve the indulgence of libidinal desire in sex, gluttony, and violence. Bakhtin celebrates carnival as a dynamic period in which otherwise marginal elements in society take center stage, vent their anger against the system, and produce democratic or liberal change. On the other hand, several of Bakhtin's critics object that the parodic laughter and authority reversals of the carnival actually serve institutional high culture as much as they do the people: the sanctioned transgressive moments of carnival allow the people to vent their excessive libidinal energies in nondestructive forms, at times and in places chosen—and thus controlled—by the state.[6]

Because cultural categories were fluid and unstable there, the frontier attracted people who were marginalized or dispossessed within settlement culture: criminals, religious separatists, the landless, the poor, or radical individualists who sought to escape the control of cultural institutions. These marginal groups were further debased in the eyes of high culture by their relocation to the wilderness where they became less civilized, relaxing their mores and adopting "barbaric" and "uncivilized" native ways. The state allowed or sometimes forced these marginal groups to leave the settlement because their unchannelled libidinal energies threatened to erupt in transgressive behaviors that might jeopardize the order of settlement society.[7] The frontier provided a space in which the pioneer was free to expend these dangerous energies in pursuits which were forbidden in settled regions. Settlement mores forbade violence against human beings, for example, yet on the frontier such violence—turned against Native Americans, criminals, or European enemies—was not only permitted but encouraged. For the most part, however, the pioneers vented their libidinal energies in hard work—hunting, clearing land, building homes, and raising families—rather than in criminally transgressive behavior.

Richard Slotkin argues that despite its marginalization and Otherness, frontier culture threatened the hegemony of high settlement culture. The pioneers felt that their lives—lived in more immediate contact with the land, with native culture, with violence and the subconscious powers associated with the wilderness—made their cultural perspective more authentically human, more powerful, and therefore of more value than the settlement perspective. As Turner points out, the frontier was a place of "rapid Americanization," where the European hierarchy of birth was discarded in favor of a hierarchy of individual effort; where rigid systems of institutional law were replaced by a loosely enforced code of behavior; where the rights of individuals took precedence over the requirements of society. Viewed from within this fluid, dynamic, and democratic cultural environment, settlement culture appeared enervated by luxury, hidebound, tyrannical, and corrupt.

The frontier's transgressive challenge to the authority of high culture is balanced by the material support that the frontier provides for the settlement. As the leading edge of colonial economics, frontier provides the settlement with raw materials and a market for finished goods. Frontier also increases the security of settlement by providing a buffer zone against attack by natives and a safe zone in which to pursue inter-European conflict. The frontier also allows European culture to expand—but not in the linear and orderly fashion described by Turner. When a frontier region became relatively secure, the state would authorize the settlement of the area. A different sort of people—not as brave, individualistic, or transgressive as the original frontiersmen—then brought the values and institutions of high culture into the region, thereby completing the process of cultural expansion that transformed the land from wilderness to frontier to settlement.

This moment—when the representatives of high culture are struggling with the frontiersmen for control of the region and its culture—is the period in the cultural history of the South that is recorded in Southwestern Humor.[8] In the years 1835–1861, the heyday of Southwestern Humor, the South experienced an incredibly rapid transformation from wilderness to settlement, leaving Southern society an unstable mixture of many groups: frontier hunters and small farmers, large plantation owners, urban professionals, African slaves, and Native Americans. The tales and sketches of Southwestern Humor record and preserve this grotesque frontier identity which was already being challenged by the high cultural definition of the South that was emerging from the plantation and the city.

The fictional world of Southwestern Humor is a late-stage frontier populated by hunters and hardscrabble farmers, horse-traders, and hell-raising scoundrels, but also by newly arrived city folk including wealthy gentry, ministers, and constables. The humor of this genre arises through the interplay between these groups. Many of these tales employ a cultured, educated narrator who introduces a frontier character who tells his own story in a distinctive, dialect-laden voice. This narrative frame involves the reader in thorny political issues. The cultured narrator presents the frontier subject as a curiosity, with the understanding that the reader will join the narrator in laughing at the subject's rough speech and foolish behavior. But when the frontier subject gains the floor, he often describes an episode in which he outsmarts or humiliates a representative of settlement culture. The narrative frame introduces a question of gaze, "Who is looking—and laughing—at whom?" and also a question of reader-response, "With which of the two storytellers should the reader identify? Should we laugh with the narrator and at the frontiersman, or vice versa?"

The traditional reading of Southwestern Humor suggests that these sketches emerge from a high cultural position. The authors, implied authors, and narrators collapse into one figure: urban, educated, literary, and identified with high settlement values; the implied reader of these tales, which were published in gentleman's sporting magazines and newspapers, would presumably share the politics of the author-narrator. This reading suggests that the sketches are simply meant to poke fun at the disappearing frontier culture. While this reading is true to the rhetoric of the narrative frame, it ignores the contradictory rhetoric of the frontier subject's narration, which pulls the reader in the opposite direction—toward a low cultural perspective. In fact, the transgressive humor and colorful language of the frontier subject leave many readers more interested in—and more satisfied by—his perspective than that of the cultured narrator. This apparent contradiction suggests a third possibility: that the narrative rhetoric of Southwestern Humor pulls the reader into a grotesque frontier perspective from which both positions, that of the cultured narrator and that of the transgressive subject, appear equally clear and equally compelling. Reading Southwestern Humor in the spirit of the frontier allows the reader to reserve judgment, to participate fully and equally in both perspectives, and to laugh with—and at—both narrators. If we allow these contradictory voices to coexist and resist the impulse to impose outside values on the text, we can read Southwestern Humor as a record and a celebration of the grotesque contradictions and carnivalesque spirit of Southern frontier culture.

This understanding of Southwestern Humor leads us back to Faulkner and *The Hamlet*. I began this essay with the observation that I was dissatisfied with most critical interpretations of *The Hamlet* because they fail to account for its grotesquery. In the act of reading, we make use of critical matrices that categorize, define, and order the various elements of a text, leaving us with a coherent accounting of them. This kind of reading cannot account for the grotesque, those incongruous and transgressive elements in a text which challenge tidy theoretical interpretations. While I claim no special dispensation for my own approach—I, too, read the novel selectively, emphasizing features that support my contentions—I do find that restoring the context of Southwestern Humor and frontier grotesque allows a more balanced reading of the novel, one that accounts for the grotesque and carnivalesque features of the text. If this context leads to interpretations which are themselves untidy, contradictory, or transgressive, then we know that we have achieved a frontier perspective.

The famous opening paragraph of *The Hamlet* identifies Frenchman's Bend as a geographical and cultural frontier where the progress of civilization has reversed. The clearly demarcated "gardens and brick terraces and promenades" of the plantation have reverted into "cane and cyprus jungle" here on "the frontier the Yankee made," as W. J. Cash called a South broken down by years of war and Reconstruction.[9] "Definite yet without boundaries, straddling two counties and owning allegiance to neither," Frenchman's Bend is both carnivalesque and grotesque space, recognized by the people who live there but not by the institutions of culture that maintain the record of property lines in the county courthouse.[10] The culture of Frenchman's Bend consists of farming, hunting, horse trading, moonshining, fighting, and storytelling—the same elements of frontier culture found in Southwestern Humor. The residents of the Bend also exhibit the transgressive, individualistic frontier *ethos*—insisting, for example, on their individual freedom even in the face of Will Varner's complete control over their economic lives. The few institutions of culture present in Frenchman's Bend—the church, the school, and the legal system—exert very little influence over individuals in the community.

The various plot lines in *The Hamlet*, each of which tells the story of one individual, draw together into a communal narrative that tells the story of Frenchman's Bend and its discontents. Engaged in the classic frontier struggle to build and maintain civilization, Faulkner's characters negotiate between individual and communal desires as they channel their libidinal energy into labor, sex, and violence. I would like to examine two stories from the novel that illustrate the complexity with which Faulkner treats this theme.

We begin with the love story of Jack Houston and Lucy Pate, an extremely conventional gendering of the frontier experience. Jack's masculinity is represented as unrestrained libidinal energy directed toward individual satisfactions, while Lucy's femininity consists of an attempt to redirect masculine libidinal energy into forms that construct and support community. These opposed gender roles turn their youthful relationship into "a feud, a gage, wordless, uncapitulating, between that unflagging will not for love or passion but for the married state, and that furious and as unbending one for solitariness and freedom" (230). When Jack realizes the threat that Lucy poses—her ability to force him if not into conformity with the system then at least into the appearance of conformity—he defends his independence by running away. In a scene reminiscent of the Biblical parable, Jack borrows money against his inheritance and leaves his father's home—but this prodigal son quickly repays his debt with money earned in a game of craps. Jack then puts his libido to work, building the railroads which were taming the prairie frontier.

Jack's frontier experience is marked by carnivalesque transgression: he challenges the authority of patriarchal culture by renouncing his place within it, but he never quite escapes its influence. Jack enters into a long-term relationship with a former prostitute, but the relationship can hardly be called transgressive because the woman adopts Houston's name and all of the traditional domestic roles of the wife. Jack never marries his lover because, unconsciously at least, he still supports the patriarchal order: "up to this time, with all that he had done and failed to do, he had never once done anything which he could not imagine his father also doing, or at least condoning" (235). When his father dies, Jack reverses the pattern of his life, undoing all of his transgressions and accepting the social position he originally rejected: he abandons his "wife," leaving his savings behind in a gesture that reconfigures the woman as a prostitute; he returns to Frenchman's Bend, builds a home, and furnishes it; he farms his father's land; he marries a socially acceptable woman and—with the help of the moonlight— begins to plan a family.[11]

Jack's story suggests that his transgression was sanctioned by the system as part of young manhood, a prelude to accepting the adult role of husband and father. In order to accept this adult role, however, Jack must relinquish the libidinal individuality that constitutes his masculinity and then redirect his libido into socially constructive channels such as agricultural labor and conjugal sex. In other words, marriage represents a triumph of the feminine in which the masculine is emasculated, civilized, and tamed. The final denouement of Jack and Lucy's relationship confirms the notion that uncivilized masculinity cannot safely exist inside the domestic space or in contact with the feminine. Jack buys a stallion that symbolizes "that polygamous and bitless masculinity which he had relinquished" to his wife. Lucy accepts the symbolic equivalence between the horse and Jack but mistakenly believes the stallion to be as tame as her new husband. The unbridled masculinity in the stallion erupts into violence and Lucy is killed.

The gender scheme presented in this frontier story is utterly conventional. Gender roles are carefully defined and stable: libidinal masculinity is confined within male bodies and domestic femininity within female bodies. This dichotomy represents another configuration of the settlement-wilderness dyad, with the masculine associated with wilderness and the feminine with settlement. However, this clear and stable dichotomy is not upheld throughout the book; in fact, gender bending seems to constitute an essential feature of the Bend's grotesque frontier culture. Eula Varner most richly complicates the simple gender matrix established in Jack and Lucy's story and so it is to her that we now turn.[12]

Even as a child, Eula rejects the traditional feminine role, refusing to make use of the domestic tools that her parents give her as playthings. Where Lucy uses her mind and will to limit masculine libido, as a child Eula seems to lack both mind and will, existing only within a body that incites men's passion without her effort or intention. Eula's effect on Labove illustrates how uncontrolled masculine passion threatens the social order.[13] Labove's erotic passion eventually overwhelms his self-control and leads him to seek a libidinal release that collapses the distinction between sexuality and violence. When Eula resists his advances, he tells her: "That's it. . . . Fight it. Fight it. That's the way it is: a man and a woman fighting each other. The hating. To kill, only to do it in such a way that the other will have to know for ever afterward he or she is dead" (134). Because it does not require—or even consider—the partner's participation in desire, Labove's passion takes the form of attempted rape. After Eula rebuffs him, Labove transfers his passion onto Jody, enthusiastically welcoming the patriarchal violence that he believes will follow his crime: "That would be something, anyway. It would not be penetration, true enough, but it would be the same flesh, the same warm living flesh in which the same blood ran, under impact at least— a paroxysm, an orgasm of sorts, a katharsis, anyway—something" (135). Labove's passion threatens society because in conflating sex with violence and by ignoring the age, sex, and consent of the partner it completely disregards the categories that settlement culture establishes to regulate human sexuality.

Eula does not merely incite this dangerous passion in men, however; she possesses it herself. As a young woman, Eula again finds herself the object of male desire. She attracts a group of suitors who participate in a libidinal dance around her: they direct their energy into work from Monday through Saturday, then spend Sunday afternoon sitting with Eula on the porch; later that evening, they release their pent-up libido by savagely beating each other until they are "for the time being freed even of rage and frustration and desire" (146). When the jealous suitors turn this violence against her favorite, Hoake McCarron, Eula changes from passive object to aggressive subject, savagely beating three attackers with a buggy-whip. Like Labove, Eula connects violence with sexuality because the fight stimulates her passion for McCarron. After vigorously defending her chosen suitor—an extension of the rape scene in which she also defends her right to control her own sexual activity—Eula takes an equally active role in the sex act, supporting McCarron's body from below as he attempts, despite a broken arm, to satisfy her desire.

Eula's story reverses the direction of Jack's. She stimulates masculine libido *within* the community, which disturbs the peace and leads to unsettled, even criminal, behavior. Her own sexuality consists of a grotesque combination of "masculine" libido with an unmistakably female body, thereby undermining the patriarchal dichotomy established in Jack and Lucy's story. Eula's sexual transgression, which also occurs within the community, leads to the literal unsettling of the community as her suitors (both successful and unsuccessful) leave Frenchman's Bend for Texas. We should note, however, that the men's transgression leads to their escape to a new frontier, thus producing a net gain for civilization.

This discussion seems to suggest that Frenchman's Bend is not frontier but rather a settlement culture dominated by patriarchal values. If that were the case, Eula's transgression would end with extreme patriarchal violence—the violence imagined by Jody, who wants to force his sister and her lover to follow patriarchal convention. But in the frontier community of Frenchman's Bend, high cultural systems including the patriarchal gender scheme do not exert absolute control over individuals. Will Varner rejects Jody's strict patriarchalism but, knowing that his position in the community requires that he at least appear to conform to its values, he insists that his pregnant daughter have a husband. In marrying Eula to Flem Snopes, Will acts out of self-interest rather than communal or ethical responsibility: his "solution" does nothing to control Eula's transgressive sexuality (Flem cannot satisfy her desire) or to protect the family name (everyone knows that the wedding is a farce). In the end, Eula threatens patriarchal hegemony not because of her transgression but because her father's reaction to it uncovers the arbitrary, selfish, and destructive nature of man's attempt to control female sexuality.

The stories of Jack and Lucy and of Eula Varner illustrate that the fictional world of *The Hamlet* is a frontier still in the process of negotiating civility: high cultural systems like patriarchy exist in this world, but their authority is weak; communal values like Protestant morality also exist, but individuals manipulate those values in the pursuit of individual will and power. By simultaneously invoking familiar cultural matrices and calling them into question, the novel places its readers in an uncomfortable position: how should we evaluate the novel's grotesques? Do we identify ourselves with high cultural values, with the individualism of the frontier community, or with the interests of one particular individual? Like the work of Southwestern Humor, *The Hamlet* deliberately places its readers into this frontier perspective where multiple perspectives seem equally compelling and where choosing any single perspective embroils the reader in problematic ethical situations.

Consider Ike Snopes's romance with the cow. The very idea of a "stock-diddling" idiot is unsettling, but the rhetorical context in which we encounter the image adds to its grotesque quality. The episode begins in book 3, chapter 1, section 1 when Ratliff, already upset by the marriage of Eula and Flem, hears that there is something mysterious in Mrs. Littlejohn's paddock—something that makes Bookwright uncomfortable. The narrative point of view follows Ratliff as he leaves the store and walks toward the lot, obsessing about Flem. Before Ratliff reaches Mrs. Littlejohn's, section 2 begins with the story of Ike's relationship with the cow; this narrative follows Ike's point of view but employs a rhetoric that "makes use of the conventions of comedy and romance, adorning Ike with honored stylistic formulas."[14] Parodically mingling high culture rhetoric with a low culture subject, this carnivalesque section confuses the reader: are we really supposed to believe that Ike loves this cow? that his relationship is comparable to Romeo's? Should we agree with Donald Kartiganer, who argues that the rhetoric "rescues [Ike] from his pathetic state"? Or should we argue that Faulkner's subject degrades the genres of comedy and romance, that the author is poking fun at worn out cultural forms?

In this moment of confusion, when the reader does not know how to interpret Ike's relationship with the cow, chapter 3 begins with Jack Houston's attempts to confine and control Ike's transgression. Once Houston transfers control of the cow to Mrs. Littlejohn, the narrative returns to Ratliff's point of view as he arrives at the paddock. What he sees there so disturbs him that he immediately intervenes, shutting down the peep show and brokering an end to Ike's bestiality. Ratliff's reaction and the specific solution that he endorses seem to suggest that he feels an understandable revulsion at bestiality, at the community's voyeurism, and at Lump's profiteering. With a few alterations of his own, Ratliff adopts Whitfield's plan to cure Ike of his transgressive desire: the afflicted individual's family must buy the animal, slaughter it, cook it, and force the transgressor to eat it in full knowledge of what he is doing. This formula is carefully constructed to reassert a high cultural matrix of definition and control. Within a context of Protestant morality, family honor, and communal responsibility, this ceremony defines Ike as human, the cow as animal and potential foodstuff, and any sexual desire between them as unthinkable.

Many readers praise Ratliff's actions as supportive of communal values, but in this reading we fall into a rhetorical trap. Because we see Ike and the cow before Ratliff does, we are already experiencing the category confusion introduced by the grotesque combination of rhetoric and subject. When Ratliff reasserts order in the familiar terms of high culture, he settles our confusion and many of us fall gratefully, and too uncritically, into line with his perspective. In fact, Ratliff has no interest in maintaining Snopes family honor, communal responsibility, or Protestant morality.[15] Ratliff convinces I. O. to support the plan not by emphasizing the importance of family honor but by pointing out that his job as schoolteacher depends on his cooperation; he even allows I. O. to dupe Eck into paying an unfair share of the cost of the cow. The idea that Ratliff is a puritanical supporter of sexual codes can be challenged by recalling that he allows Mink's wife to live in his house while she is "working nights" at the boarding house.

If Ratliff is not acting as "a pharisee"—enforcing cultural values for the good of the community—why does he act the way he does? The answer lies in Ratliff's reaction to the spectacle of Ike and the cow. While he does experience a moment of confusion, it is not the same category confusion experienced by the reader: "He did look, leaning his face in between two other heads; and it was as though it were himself inside the stall with the cow, himself looking out of the blasted tongueless face at the row of faces watching him who had been given the wordless passions but not the specious words" (217). As Ratliff's gaze moves from his own perspective, looking at Ike, to Ike's, looking at the crowd, to the crowd's, looking at Ike, he finds himself involved in a sexual situation—participating in Ike's bestial passion as well as the voyeuristic titillation of the crowd. The image of Ike and the cow threatens Ratliff's definition of himself as an asexual observer and challenges his self-control. His cure destroys this threat to his power with immediate and total brutality.

Ratliff's reaction to Ike and the cow also violates the frontier ethic of minding one's own business and letting others mind theirs. The community's reaction to Ike and the cow is no different from its reaction to other "freaks"—everyone turns out to gawk at Flem and his bowtie, Labove's shiny lantern, the spotted horses, and Henry Armstid's insane digging. Ratliff's "solution" to this grotesque is no different from Will Varner's treatment of Eula: both mask the pursuit of selfish, individual goals beneath a facade of support for high cultural values. The reader becomes involved in this ethical situation because whenever we interpret literature, we impose a set of values onto the text; in the case of *The Hamlet*, when we employ the values of high/settlement culture we violate the logic of the frontier context. Like Ratliff and Will Varner, we become guilty of deliberately flattening the transgressive meanings that a genuine frontier perspective would allow to stand.

Consider how much more complicated, transgressive, and interesting the cure of Ike appears when we resist Ratliff's tidy (and selfish) interpretation and restore the grotesque possibility that Ike is genuinely in love with the cow. The cure, which Ratliff would define as a familiar domestic ritual—a meal—now appears as ritual cannibalism, a man eating his lover. The fact that a self-proclaimed pharisee sacrifices the beloved to support the hegemony of a ruling class suggests that we might even consider the cure a bizarre Eucharist-manque.[16] In his last appearance in the novel, Ike is fully contained within the cultural category, drooling idiot, to which Ratliff's cure assigned him. He no longer evokes a grotesque reaction from Ratliff, but we should find this scene disturbing. In the image of the shattered Ike holding the effigy of the cow, Faulkner invokes the familiar image of Benjy Compson holding Caddy's slipper. As readers of *The Sound and the Fury*, we should bring to this scene a store of sympathy for Ike-as-Benjy, and in that context, we appreciate the enormity of what Ratliff has done: how would we react if the Compsons had fed Caddy to her brother?[17]

Nowhere is this tendency to simplify the grotesque more problematic than in the critical response to Flem Snopes. The conventional reading of Flem describes him as a demon, an economic being without genuine humanity, and therefore an excellent representation of the modern, impersonal capitalism that was replacing the traditional, paternalistic economy of the South. Described in this way, Flem appears to be an Andersonian grotesque: in the introductory chapter of *Winesburg, Ohio*, Sherwood Anderson defines a grotesque as a figure with one personality trait that is exaggerated beyond proportion with the rest of the character.[18] I believe, however, that Flem's economic life seems disproportionate only because the rest of his character is flat. The narrative never reveals the interior of Flem's consciousness and Flem has no other interests or passions that might make his economic behavior seem more human—the Old Frenchman, for instance, had his dreams of baronial splendor and Will Varner has his "Rabelaisian" lust. Without any humanizing virtues or vices, Flem's economics seem grasping and ruthless, but in fact his economic strategy merely continues a pattern of frontier economics established by the Old Frenchman and Will Varner.[19]

The history of frontier economics began with the Old Frenchman who, supported by a rhetoric of racial superiority, exploited the labor of African slaves who cleared the land and farmed it for cotton. The planter's land management was as exploitative as his labor practice. He straightened the riverbed to keep his land from flooding, which guaranteed short-term profit but also produced the nutrient-deficient, unproductive soil of the novel's narrative present. Will Varner is a different sort of frontiersman who colonizes the Old Frenchman's Place by purchasing the land as it becomes available through foreclosed mortgages. Once the region is under his control, he replaces the rhetoric of racial superiority with a frontier rhetoric of equality, which masks the fact that he has simply replaced African slaves with white (tenant-farming) wage slaves. Flem Snopes rises to power simply by copying Varner's progress; he does nothing to alter the means of production. The only change made by Flem is his abandonment of the rhetoric of equality; he shamelessly reveals the ruthless greed that has always supported the leader of this economy. Faulkner connects that economy to the colonial-frontier project when he describes the settlement of accounts at the store: "Varner and Snopes resembled the white trader and his native parrot-taught headman in an African outpost. That headman was acquiring the virtues of civilization" (67). The "virtues of civilization" that Flem learns consist of only one thing: the same ruthless, profiteering business that supported his predecessors.

When we read Flem as a demonic representative of a modern, capitalist economy instead of an extension of the traditional system, we are again accepting the interpretation of V. K. Ratliff, who not only compares Flem to the devil but who also—unlike anyone

else in the novel—actively opposes him. Here too, I believe that
Ratliff tries to eliminate a threat to his own power. It is Ratliff,
after all, who is more directly tied to modern, industrial capitalism.
He sells one of only two machines mentioned in the novel, and
carefully masks his almost scientific management of his customer
base—he knows exactly when Eustace Grimm will be able to afford a sewing machine—beneath his role as itinerant storyteller;
and his primary income consists of the profit generated by his
capital investment in the sandwich shop in Jefferson. Faulkner collapses the distinction between Ratliff's industrial-sales business
and the Bend's agricultural business by tying both to the ruthless
profiteering of colonial economics. Arriving in Tennessee on a
business trip, Ratliff "looked around him with something of the
happy surmise of the first white hunter blundering into the idyllic
solitude of a virgin African vale teeming with ivory, his for the
mere shooting and fetching out" (61).

As a fellow pioneer, Ratliff understands that Flem's land- and
power-grab need not stop with his accession to the barrel-throne
of the Old Frenchman's Place, an action that signifies his economic
domination of Frenchman's Bend. After this achievement, which
takes place at the end of the first chapter, it is only a matter of
time before Flem seeks a new frontier, new territory to exploit.
But Flem never goes out on his own; he operates only by copying
his predecessors, and the only character whose business extends
beyond the hamlet is Ratliff. Unlike Ike, whose limited intellect
held him back, Flem resists Ratliff's attempt to confine and control
his transgression. The novel ends with Flem, having loaded his
entire household onto the Texas frontier wagon, removing to Jefferson where he will live in a pioneer tent behind the restaurant
he has swindled from Ratliff.

Flem is not an economic monster but a frontier hero. A number
of voices in the text support a more positive view of Flem, ranging
from Lump's enthusiastic approval of Flem's most ruthless action
(giving Mrs. Armstid a one percent return, in candy, on her five
dollars), to the anonymous voice who respectfully notes that
"couldn't nobody but Flem Snopes have fooled Ratliff," to Tull's

neutral appraisal of Flem's usury: "It aint right. But it aint none of our business" (405, 79). When we interpret Flem from within the frontier context, allowing these contradictory interpretations to remain unresolved, we restore Flem to his grotesque position. Like other grotesque Southwestern Humor characters—George Washington Harris's Sut Lovingood, for example—Flem is frightening, attractive, and ridiculous. We should react to him with fear—he is certainly ruthless and probably evil as well—but we should also respect him for rising from the bottom to the top of his community. Of course, we should also laugh at him.

As with all of the grotesque figures, Flem is the subject of parodic humor. There are three sources of parody in the novel. The first comes from generic intertextuality—the parodic mixture of high culture rhetoric and low subject in Ike, Mink, and Eula's sections. The second comes from Faulknerian intertextuality—the comic repetition of characters from other novels; besides the example of Ike and Benjy Compson, I should also mention I. O.'s wife, who arrives at Varner's store on a wagon, buys sardines and crackers, then chases after her man—an obvious repetition of Lena Grove. The third type of parody is internal to the novel. Flem is described as an ersatz copy of the Varners, not only replicating their economic activities but also adopting their clothes. Flem is further degraded through Jody's mocking comparison of Saint Elmo—the voracious, candy-chewing Snopes—to Flem: "He's worse than a goat. First thing I know, he'll graze on back through that lace leather and them hame-strings and lap-links and ring-bolts and eat you and me and him all three clean out the back door. And then be damned if I wouldn't be afraid to turn my back for fear he would cross the road and start in on the gin and the blacksmith shop" (352). Compared with the appetite of an idiot child, Flem's economic devouring of Frenchman's Bend seems much less threatening, if not positively ridiculous.[20]

The parodic humor in this novel does not produce carnivalesque laughter—defined by Bakhtin as pure joy, free of fear—but instead a grotesque combination of fear and joy. Each of the major figures in the novel—Flem, Eula, Ike, Mink, and Ratliff—produce this grotesque reaction, which combines horror and comedy, attraction and repulsion. The question that faces the reader at the end of the novel is this: How do *you* feel about Ike and that cow? If you can smirk at the barnyard humor, laugh at the overblown rhetoric, and still mourn for the spiritual damage inflicted by Ratliff—or, better, if you can be both grateful and horrified at Ratliff's actions—you have read the scene from a frontier perspective. Reading *The Hamlet* from within the context of frontier grotesque, as an extension of the carnivalesque tradition of Southwestern Humor, allows us to understand the full implications of the grotesquery in the novel and, in the end, to place the novel into the context of Faulkner's career. Faulkner's modernist project—turning to the forms of the past for an understanding of the present—seems to hit a dead end in *Absalom, Absalom!*; Quentin Compson cannot survive the present because he cannot escape the legacy of the plantation and institutional slavery. In *The Hamlet*, Faulkner's historical vision looks beyond the plantation to the frontier myth that produced it—and finds that frontier *ethos* alive and well in Frenchman's Bend. Viewing the South as a frontier allows Faulkner to see a continuity in Southern cultural history: the same cultural myth that produced the plantation and the post-War (Varner) South will soon produce and sustain a modern, capitalist South. While the novel seems to regret the loss of traditional cultural forms and to fear the ones that replace them, overall the novel suggests at least a cautious openness to the future. After all, the South can only stay the same (remain a dynamic frontier) by moving forward and accepting change.[21]

NOTES

1. See, for example, Thomas L. McHaney, "What Faulkner Learned from the Tall Tale" in *Faulkner and Humor: Faulkner and Yoknapatawpha 1984*, ed. Doreen Fowler and Ann J. Abadie (Jackson: University Press of Mississippi, 1986), 110–35 and the third chapter of Daniel Hoffman, *Faulkner's Country Matters: Folklore and Fable in Yoknapatawpha* (Baton Rouge: Louisiana State University Press, 1989), 71–106.

2. *The Frontier in American History* (New York: Henry Holt, 1920).

3. My understanding of frontier draws on the pioneering work of Richard Slotkin in *Regeneration Through Violence: The Mythology of the American Frontier, 1600–1860* (Hanover, N.H.: Wesleyan University Press, 1973).

4. Geoffrey Galt Harpham, *On the Grotesque: Strategies of Contradiction in Art and Literature* (Princeton: Princeton University Press, 1982).

5. Mikhail Bakhtin, *Rabelais and His World*, trans. Helene Iswolsky (Bloomington: Indiana University Press, 1984).

6. First raised by Fredric Jameson, the objection forms the basis of Peter Stallybrass and Allon White's critique in the introduction to *The Politics and Poetics of Transgression* (Ithaca, N.Y.: Cornell University Press, 1986), 1–26.

7. Both here and in the later section on gender roles, I refer to ideas found in Sigmund Freud's *Civilization and Its Discontents*, trans. and ed. James Strachey (New York: Norton, 1961).

8. Because the frontier is both fluid and mobile, and because the word more properly describes a cultural atmosphere than a geographic location, I find it more useful to locate the frontier temporally rather than spatially as Turner does. A place is frontier during that time in which elements of high European culture form a grotesque mixture with elements of low European and native cultures—and when a carnivalesque *ethos* characterizes the society.

9. W. J. Cash, *The Mind of the South* (New York: Knopf, 1941).

10. William Faulkner, *The Hamlet: The Corrected Text* (New York: Vintage International, 1991), 3. Further references are to this edition.

11. Jack's rejection of his "wife" supports Luce Irigaray's contention that prostitutes, while possessing a sexual use value, lose the exchange value that makes virgins suitable for marriage in a patriarchal society; see "Women on the Market" in *This Sex Which Is Not One*, trans. Catherine Porter (Ithaca, N.Y.: Cornell University Press, 1985), 170–91.

12. The novel directly contrasts Houston with Mink Snopes, who marries the passionate, sexually active woman he meets on the frontier. Because of his wife's previous sexual experience and because of the passion she stimulates in him, Mink's marriage never tames his libidinal individuality; this helps to explain why he chooses violent revenge over family responsibility during his dispute with Houston.

13. A fuller discussion of the danger of passion, especially in women, to the fabric of patriarchal society can be found in Tony Tanner's *Desire in the Novel* (Baltimore: Johns Hopkins University Press, 1979).

14. Donald M. Kartiganer, *The Fragile Thread: The Meaning of Form in Faulkner's Novels* (Amherst: University of Massachusetts Press, 1979), 121.

15. The idea of resisting Ratliff's ideology can be inferred in John T. Matthews's analysis of Ratliff's morality in *The Play of Faulkner's Language* (Ithaca, N.Y.: Cornell University Press, 1982). Matthews describes Ratliff's storytelling as nostalgia, supporting values that Ratliff understands to be ungrounded and arbitrary.

16. Faulkner's description of the toy as a "battered wooden effigy of a cow such as children receive on Christmas" seems to support the Eucharistic reading: the figure could be part of a manger scene, intended to recall the birth and subsequent death of Christ. Then, too, when Ratliff sees him, Ike is lying in a manger. This interpretation of the toy radically alters our perception of Eck. His generosity—"I felt sorry for him. I thought maybe anytime he would happen to start thinking, that ere toy one would give him something to think about" (296)—now seems a deliberately cruel reminder of Ike's loss.

17. The intertextuality with *The Sound and The Fury* works both ways, of course: we are reminded that Caddy is also a transgressive female sacrificed to maintain the social position of a family.

18. See "The Book of the Grotesque," in *Winesburg, Ohio* (New York: B. W. Huebsch, 1919).

19. My understanding of the economic history of Frenchman's Bend draws on the work of John T. Matthews, *The Play of Faulkner's Language*, Richard C. Moreland, *Faulkner and Modernism: Rereading and Rewriting* (Madison: University of Wisconsin Press, 1990), and James A. Snead, *Figures of Division: William Faulkner's Major Novels* (New York: Methuen, 1986).

20. Perhaps the most comic of these internal repetitions is the scene in which Eck tries

to stoke the fire at the blacksmith shop. Unlike Ab, who used coal oil to burn DeSpain's barn, this incompetent Snopes uses water.

21. The subject of this conference reminds us that no writing takes place in isolation, that every text is influenced by the context in which it was produced. For that reason, I gratefully acknowledge my debt to the following for the part they played in the production of this essay: the members of Carla Mulford's seminar, Colonialism and Its Discontents (Fall 1992), Don Kartiganer's Faulkner seminar (Fall 1993), Jay Watson's Southern Literature and Literary Theory (Fall 1993), Ann Fisher-Wirth's Gender Theory seminar (Fall 1993), Bob Brinkmeyer's Theories of the Grotesque in Southern Literature (Spring 1994), Wes Berry, John Cox, Thomas Easterling, Joy Harris, and Dan Williams.

Faulkner and the Post-Confederate

NEIL SCHMITZ

Think of Ken Burns's 1990 PBS documentary, *The Civil War*, eleven hours long, nine episodes, shown on five consecutive nights in September 1990, coming at us like the Army of the Potomac, richly funded, beautifully equipped, with its own anthem, Jay Ungar's 1984 composition for three fiddles and two guitars, "Ashokan Farewell." GM, NEH, CPB, the Arthur Vining Davis Foundation, the MacArthur Foundation are up front, announcing their support, as the first and longest episode, "The Cause," begins. At the end, credits almost interminable, long supply trains going on and on, section after section: a stellar cast of readers, Archival Materials, Special Thanks, to many individuals and agencies.

The first word is "We," Oliver Wendell Holmes Jr. speaking. "We have shared," he says, "the incommunicable experience of war." An officer in the Union Army, seriously wounded first at Balls Bluff, then at Antietam, later Chief Justice, of that resonant New England name, Holmes is as Federal blue as one can get. He speaks in the epigraph. First word of text-proper is "American," and it is heavily stressed, repeated. "American homes became headquarters, American churches and schoolhouses sheltered the dying," says the principal narrator (David McCullough), who is never identified or seen. "In two days at Shiloh, on the banks of the Tennessee River, more American men fell than in all previous American wars combined." The repetition insists on closure, on completion, the resolution of the issue. "American," this is the Unionist designation, and it is stamped on everything we see.

Ohio's Geoffrey C. Ward, sometime editor of *American Heritage* magazine, author of *Lincoln's Thought and the Present* (1978) and

A First Class Temperament: The Emergence of Franklin Roosevelt (1989), is the principal writer. Pennsylvania's David McCullough, longtime editor and writer at *Time* magazine, longtime contributing editor at *American Heritage*, then at work on *Truman, A Biography* (1993), is the primary narrator. McCullough's trans-Allegheny/Pittsburghian is the Voice of this History, not Shelby Foote's softly drawling Greenville, Mississippi, voice, though we see a lot of Foote, epic "American" historian of *The Civil War, A Narrative* (1954–1974), in Burns's film, representing the Confederate position, delivering a certain post-Confederate narrative. McCullough's unseen narration is collective, connective, seemingly sideless. Experts, who never converse, argue, or confront each other in the film over the direction of the narrative, singly address its camera eye, report to it. We accept immediately that Foote is the minor historian, that he represents a side, a Southern reading that is incomplete, partial. He won't speak for Frederick Douglass. Barbara J. Fields, the African American historian featured in Burns's documentary, doesn't do battles and leaders, won't represent Bedford Forrest. Everyone is exactly in his or her Civil War place, Northerners, Southerners, whites, blacks.

Talking about battles and leaders, about Lee and Stuart, Lee and Longstreet, in that sad ironically resigned Southern voice, Foote does an elegant post-Confederate, plays his nonthreatening part in this celebratory Unionist text. He does in fact a kind of Faulknerian performance, is a sort of rueful Gavin Stevens, the patriot attorney in William Faulkner's embattled *Intruder in the Dust* (1948), but disciplined, restrained. No danger here of racisms, of embarrassing usages, of inadvertent revelations, of sudden defiances. In 1990, in this major Unionist Civil War documentary, Foote represents the Southern narrative, and he everywhere summons the Southern narrative's great genius, invokes his statement and feeling, often questionably.

In episode 3, "Gettysburg," wanting to essentialize Confederate Southern feeling, Foote cites Faulkner's now classical Gettysburgian speech in *Intruder in the Dust*, "For every Southern boy fourteen years old," a speech strongly established in Gettysburg literature. Foote reads it straight, as perhaps we should, in some sense. "For every Southern boy fourteen years old," that passage reads, tacitly excluding Chick Mallison's African American comrade, Aleck Sander, "not once but whenever he wants it, there is the instant when it's still not yet two oclock on that July afternoon in 1863, the brigades are in position behind the rail fence, the guns are laid and ready in the woods and the furled flags are already loosened to break out and Pickett himself with his long oiled ringlets and his hat in one hand probably and his sword in the other looking up the hill waiting for Longstreet to give the word and it's all in the balance, it hasn't happened yet, it hasn't even begun yet, it not only hasn't begun yet but there is still time for it not to begin."[1] Foote does not read the entire passage. He assumes we know it as we know the final passage in F. Scott Fitzgerald's *The Great Gatsby* (1925), and therefore briefly refers to it. He points to the speech, acknowledges its statement. It memorializes this moment of intense Confederate nationality, all the Southern states there, valiant in the cause. All Anglo-Southern boys, Mississippian, Alabamian, Georgian, know the order of battle, where its divisions stood. This is the Confederate thing they share, the glory of this fatal charge, the fantasy of victory.

Faulkner, of course, ironically records this post-Confederate feeling. In the vault of the hyperbole, a suspension of reality, a delay of historical truth, an echo of John Wilkes Booth, a glimpse of Tom Sawyer. Chick Mallison, the boy, and Gavin Stevens, the man, can both enjoy this exaltation of nationality, this outcome, only by rigorously denying sociopolitical actualities, by excluding the issue of slavery, of all that is at stake for Aleck Sander.

Gettysburg is indeed a difficult subject for the post-Confederate, Southern writing in Unionist discourse, early and late. In Barry Hannah's 1993 story, "Bats Out of Hell Division," the Army of the Potomac, unable to endure any more Confederate Southern reliving of the grand suspended Gettysburgian moment, surrenders. Raggedy Confederate specters invest the Federal works. Hannah's story at once answers Gavin Stevens's Gettysburg address and seeks its own escape from the field, memorial Southern writing centered by the Confederate thing. For post-Civil War Southern writers, the issue of repudiation, of relinquishment, required tough delicate thinking, balancing statement, feats of logical and lexical engineering, of circumlocution and ellipsis. How to enjoy at Gettysburg the greatness of this military Confederate moment, when the post-Confederate had always fundamentally to swear: "We understand that when Lincoln signed the emancipation proclamation, your victory was assured, for he then committed you to the cause of human liberty, against which the arms of man cannot prevail—while those of our statemen who trusted to make slavery the corner-stone of our Confederacy doomed us to defeat as far as they could, committing us to a cause that reason could not defend or the sword maintain in the sight of advancing civilization."[2] Henry Woodfin Grady speaks here, delivering his celebrated 1886 banquet speech, "The New South," at a formal dinner of the New England Society in New York, General Sherman seated among the glittering array of Northern bankers and capitalists, his gaze fixed on Grady. Grady let Sherman have it. "I want to say to General Sherman," he said, "who is considered an able man in our parts, though some people think he is kind of careless about fire, that from the ashes he left us in 1864 we have raised a brave and beautiful city."[3] The New South, he told his Yankee auditors, "had nothing for which to apologize."[4] Post-Confederate Southern statement, even as it finds its place in Unionist discourse, is barbed and bristly.

I want to rethink the post-Confederate narrative Faulkner presents in *Intruder in the Dust*, to observe, as it were, his struggle with it, focusing in particular on the usage "Sambo," this blatant racism, a racism constantly calling Gavin Stevens's version of the post-Confederate into question. It is a usage the younger Chick Mallison scrupulously evades. "Lucas Beauchamp, Sambo," as Stevens so awkwardly and ambiguously has it, recalls Huck Finn's trials with his usage, "Nigger," in referring to Jim. *Intruder in the Dust* everywhere refers to the *Adventures of Huckleberry Finn*. Lucas gives Chick the gaze. "Jim won't ever forget you, Huck; you's de bes' fren' Jim's ever had; en you's de only fren' ole Jim's got now."[5] *Intruder in the Dust* takes up the question Mark Twain engages in *Huckleberry Finn*: how to set Jim free, and it, too, addresses the resources of the language, listens to Pap Finn, listens to Gavin Stevens, is unlikely, screwed into a Tom Sawyer plot. How to set Southern writing free, this, too, was Mark Twain's question.

Post-Confederate, as I see it, exactly names the discursive pact Mark Twain, Joel Chandler Harris, Thomas Nelson Page, George Washington Cable, and other Southern writers, in the 1870s and '80s, differently negotiated and signed with William Dean Howells, Richard Watson Gilder, Robert Underwood Johnson, Thomas Bailey Aldrich, Charles Dudley Warner, with *The Atlantic*, *Harper's*, *The Forum*, *Scribner's/The Century*, *The Critic*, the pact that enabled these young Southern writers to have access to the new bicoastal national literary market, to have national careers, to figure in the new postwar American literature. They produce a remarkable set of texts: Cable's *The Grandissimes* (1880), Harris's *The Songs and Sayings of Uncle Remus* (1881), Mark Twain's *The Adventures of Huckleberry Finn* (1884) and *Life on the Mississippi* (1885), which theorizes the post-Confederate, Page's *In Old Virginia* (1887), parts of which appear in the *Century* as it commences *Battles and Leaders of the Civil War*, the first mounting of Unionist Civil War documentary. Readers of the series could turn from the bitter jangling of Confederate generals, the likes of Joseph E. Johnston and P. G. T. Beauregard, that old South, to the sweetness and light of Harris and Mark Twain, to stories of white lads and black uncles, the New South.

It was understood that this reconstructed Southern writing repudiated the principal articles of Confederate discourse, abjured its Confederate nationality, repudiated the political Confederate Father, though it might still relish the glory of the military Confederate Father. It was understood that this Southern writing accepted the dictate of the new Unionist Republican Federal Constitution, accepted the dictate of the Gettyburg Address: be in, and of, and for, the new nation, that it couldn't advocate racial injustice, that it had to answer, at some point, the Unionist question always there, waiting, the question Grady reached midway through his 1886 speech to the New England Society. "But what of the negro? Have we solved the problem he presents, or progressed in honor and equity toward solution?"[6] It was understood that this Southern writing might present African American experience as its special knowledge, as its cultural capital, report African American narratives, construct scenes of racial amity, produce work that served racial healing.

Post-Confederate, of course, is not a term these Southern writers used. Grady's "New South" was in general usage. Post-Confederate nonetheless better describes the activity of this writing, more accurately positions it, this Southern writing which appears after conquest, during and after occupation, relocated, part of the Unionist discursive work of phrasal consensus, doing the work, along with African American writing, of refiguring plots and characters, yet always in relation to the Confederate moment, the one celebrated by Gavin Stevens in *Intruder in the Dust*, a relation that necessarily excluded Southern African-American writing. In *Life on the Mississippi* Mark Twain puts three writers into it, himself, Cable, and Harris, the Cable of *The Grandissimes*, of the controversial *Century* articles: "The Freedman's Case in Equity," "The Silent South." These few Southern writers are modern, Mark Twain argues, in the world, beyond the dead Confederate thing, Scott [Robert E. Lee], outside its language. The success of the postwar Unionist national narrative, whose mission it was to integrate races and regions, contain their interests, depended on this distinctive Southern articulation, had its first important justification in the transsectional popularity of Harris and Mark Twain. In his wonderfully possessive final tribute, *My Mark Twain* (1910), Howells would call Mark Twain the Lincoln of our literature. Howells's Mark Twain was our Mark Twain.

With the prompt encouragement of Unionist media, post-Confederate writing took up the reconciliatory project of Harriet Beecher Stowe in *Uncle Tom's Cabin* (1851), the first Anglo-American novelist to write biracial fiction, to sentimentalize African American subjectivity. Harris's immensely popular *Uncle Remus: His*

Songs and His Sayings (1880) begins with this *mise-en-scene*: Miss Sally, looking for her seven-year-old boy, "heard the sound of voices in the old man's cabin, and looking through the window, saw the child sitting by Uncle Remus. His head rested against the old man's arm, and he was gazing with an expression of the most intense interest into the rough, weather-beaten face that beamed so kindly upon him."[7] The post-Confederate reading of *Uncle Tom's Cabin* effectively cut out everything between young George Shelby's tearful farewell to sold Uncle Tom, the gift of young George's precious silver dollar as a redemptive token, his promise of rescue, their mutual gaze, and that final gorgeous scene where young George Shelby "appeared among them with a bundle of papers in his hand, containing a certificate of freedom to every one on the place, which he read successively, and presented, amid the sobs and tears and shouts of all present."[8] Harris generously acknowledged his debt: "I owe a great deal to . . . the author of Uncle Tom's Cabin."[9] In its brilliant opening scene, as we shall see, *Intruder in the Dust* recalls the foundational instance in Stowe's novel—the cabin, the gift of money, the gaze—ironically altering the elements, redoing the feeling. "What of the negro?" Responding to this question was a major operation in post-Confederate discourse.

To appear in diverse Unionist publications, this early post-Confederate had therefore to revise its tropes, redo its characters, let go the Pym plots of Edgar Allan Poe, the racist invective of George Washington Harris, yet still define, assert, a recalcitrant sense of nationality, of cultural difference, which was, after all, its principal literary interest. There are tolerances and tensions in the early post-Confederate, partisans left, right, and center. William H. Andrews has recently returned William Wells Brown's *My Southern Home* (1880), a strangely voiced, insidiously subversive African American memoir, to the archive he labels "New South writing." Just as Brown tropes the post-Confederate, his possessive pronoun compact with ironies, Charles Chesnutt's *The Conjure Woman* (1899) is certainly in an ironic play with post-Confederate discourse, with all its fabulous uncles, critically revising Harris's

Uncle Remus (1880). Northern Unionist, Radical Republican, Albion Tourgee, of *A Fool's Errand* (1879), *Bricks Without Straw* (1880), and *The Invisible Empire* (1883), is also contentiously here, though he saw himself as excluded from Southern literature and scorned its racist mythologizing.

Retro, crypto, and neo-Confederate writing surrounds post-Confederate discourse in the Reconstruction and Redemption period, disagrees with it, writes angry letters to it, has its own fiction and poetry. Thomas Dixon, of *The Clansman* (1905) and *The Leopard's Spots* (1906), is definitely retro. Page begins his career publishing sketches in the *Century*, begins with *In Old Virginia* (1887), begins in the post-Confederate, but is soon defining a neo-Confederate. Uncles are his primary narrators, the Uncle Sam of "Marse Chan" and the Uncle Billy of "Meh Lady." They are choric figures. Page could not break from Scott's heroic nationalist romance into a new conception of race relations in his fiction. There are no Jims to free in his fiction, no Lucases to save. His uncles never want freedom. Telling their stories of Marse and Mistis, these uncles bask in the glory of their masters. His uncles set Marse free, save Mistis. When Faulkner begins the Yoknapatawpha chronicle in 1928–29 with *Flags in the Dust*, Page informs his racial writing. There are instances where Faulkner's Uncle Simon nearly repeats the lines Page gives to Uncle Sam in "Marse Chan." Here is Simon: "Yessuh, de olden times comin' back again, sho'. Like in Marse John's time, when de Cunnel wuz de young marster en de niggers f'um de quawtuhs gethered on de front lawn, wishin' Mistis en de little Marster well."[10] Even the militant Caspey, home from the war in France, is comical. "I dont take nothin' f'um no white folks no mo'. War done changed all dat."[11] *Flags in the Dust* has its neo-Confederate turns, as Faulkner ventures into racial writing, yet there are also scenes—Bayard Sartoris seeking refuge in a black sharecropper's barn, sharing a meal with the family, entering their cabin, coming in upon their interiority—that turn the novel toward *Intruder in the Dust*, Mark Twain's racialized territory, the cabin Jim builds on the raft, Lucas's house.

Huckleberry Finn is indeed the telling post-Confederate text, a demonstration of the options, an irony of the fictional means, a painstaking setting forth of the available narratives, the possible resolutions. Mark Twain begins with a Unionist decree nailed to a Southern Courthouse door, asserts his mastery of Southern speech, then promptly denounces *Tom Sawyer*, Tom Sawyer's St. Petersburg. What are the lies Mr. Mark Twain tells in *Tom Sawyer*? No matter which way Huck turns in his text, and there are diversions, the race question is before him. How to set Jim free? There is Huck's way, which is to fold, reluctantly, but decently, into the major narrative, Jim's, the slave narrative, or Tom's, which is to write Jim's liberation script, deciding the time, determining the conditions, of said liberation. Ultimately, of course, in the post-Confederate, there is only Tom's white supremacist way, but his version is exposed, his narration discredited, the raft will not move at his command, and we turn back to Huck's failure, to his interrupted text, to the issue of his tortured identification with Jim, his recognition of the integrity of Jim's narrative.

In the gaze that beholds this horrific tableau of relapse, Tom's triumph, Jim's debased gratitude, we get to see an outside, the end of this particular cultural adventure. Huck won't go back. Beyond this, another kind of Southern writing, but what it is, in that new territory, who can suppose it? The ending of *Intruder in the Dust* also declares such an impasse, the enmeshment of Gavin and Lucas in racist routines, their ongoing contestation, Chick witnessing, the narrator giving Lucas the last word, receipt, letting us ponder the true extent of debt and payment in American race matters.

Edmund Wilson's 1948 *New Yorker* review of *Intruder in the Dust*, at once beautifully High Unionist and High Modernist, memorably grieved over Faulkner's prose style, its arrest, its atrophy. It was, finally, Wilson argued, too rhetorically Southern, too provincial, to sustain a serious High Modernist attention. Wilson worked in close on Faulkner's syntax and grammar, parsing sentences, checking off Faulkner's "mismanagement of relatives," his improper punctuation, his confusion of pronouns, his incorrect usages. Wilson acknowledged the novel's humanities, its "reconditioned Southern chivalry," the greatness of Faulkner's previous fiction, and then abruptly interrogated the politics of *Intruder in the Dust*, took it up as a tract, as a public message, Faulkner doing a Confederate Gettysburg Address, reasserting a contraposed Anglo Southern nationality, the old familiar one, even as the novel exactly performed the post-Confederate's major operation, set Lucas free. It was an antilynching novel, Wilson argued, that was also "a counterblast to the anti-lynching bill and to the civil rights plank in the Democratic platform."[12] He underlined "Sambo," exposed the novel's intrinsic racism, rejected its answer to the Unionist question, *what of the negro*, rejected it in this contemptuous high Unionist phrasing, sounding very much like Charles Sumner in the 1850s. "So the Southerners must be allowed, on their own initiative, in their own way, with no intervention by others, to grant the Negro his citizenship. Otherwise— / Otherwise, what?"[13]

Wilson's dismissive reading remains, to a very large extent, the definitive reading. Walter Taylor, James A. Snead, Eric Sundquist, and others, have incisively extended and elaborated Wilson's *New Yorker* critique. Faulkner's contrived plotting in *Intruder in the Dust*, Taylor writes, only works to "justify Gavin's polemics." These "manipulations bordered on the ridiculous, and they were there for all to see."[14] Sundquist similarly regards *Intruder in the Dust* as a "ludicrous novel and a depressing social document." He especially derides Faulkner's application of *Huckleberry Finn*. Mark Twain's "painfully convoluted" ending is "tragically exacting," profoundly ironic. "In Faulkner's new vision there is almost no irony at all, and the burden of shame that is lifted from Charles's shoulders therefore leaves too little of the resonant ambiguity and fully realized moral complicity of Huck's struggle with his conscience."[15]

This is, I think, an exhausted reading, not necessarily a wrong reading, just a concluded reading, and I want to look elsewhere in the text, to retrieve Cleanth Brooks's insistence that Faulkner is not Gavin Stevens. *Intruder in the Dust* certainly marks a crisis in the post-Confederate, marks it succinctly in the foregrounded usage, "Sambo," interactively moves within the complex of the post-Confederate, reworking its practices, always addressing, especially through the usage, "Sambo," Unionist media, Unionist discourse, the editors at Random House, Malcolm Cowley of the 1946 Viking *Portable William Faulkner*, Edmund Wilson in the *New Yorker*. It humorously defends its position, that it does not participate in the subjection of Uncle Tom, and its prerogatives, that it speaks for Jim, that it frees Lucas. It recalls the discursive pact that reconstructed Southern writing signed with the *Atlantic* and the *Century* in the 1870s and '80s, refurbishes its terms, reviews its project, what it repudiates (racism), what it won't relinquish (nationality), delicately distinguishing an older post-Confederate from a younger. A lot of heavy work is done in this text, and all it has for transport is Chick's horse, Highboy, and Miss Habersham's old truck.

The biggest load is the racism, Sambo, constantly before us, either in actual or virtual parenthesis, always glaring in its wrongness. It is a softening euphemism, a pseudoaffectionate idiomatic usage, that Gavin Stevens tries to manage in his post-Confederate speeches, mixing into it a certain irony. He wants at once to recapture Lucas's transgressive character with it and to distance himself from the worse usages of the retro-Confederate, the racist invective one might find in the political speeches of James K. Vardaman and Theodore Bilbo. Finally his Sambo transforms into Booker T. Washington, the honorific Gavin Stevens humorously gives to Lucas at the end of the novel. The text itself gives Stevens no warrant for its usage, shows him immediately as obtuse [his first utterance is racist, names Aleck Sander as Chick's "boy"], so the usage isn't tied down, isn't managed, is loose in the text, always a sore point, a stoppage. Stevens's own distance from it is too shaky. He seems at times to be drawn into it, stuck to it. It is a kind of tarbaby term, Sambo, and of course Stevens doesn't shake it loose with Booker T. Washington.

Should anyone who can't control the racism, Sambo, be trusted to articulate Lucas's case? *Intruder in the Dust* raises the question of entitlement, the question Martin Delany promptly framed in his 1852 reading of *Uncle Tom's Cabin*: can Anglo-American writers do faithful justice to African American experience? What is Faulkner's answer to James Baldwin's 1956 *Partisan Review* article, "Faulkner and Desegregation," to Baldwin's charge that Faulkner's fictional Negroes are always "tied up in his mind with his grandfather's slaves?"[16] He can't speak. He's in the prison-house of male Anglo-Southern race writing, Uncle Tom's cabin. In the fifties, Faulkner would consistently avoid public discussion with African American writers, who, for their part, continually addressed him. In 1956 W. E. B. Du Bois wanted to stage a public debate. Faulkner promptly mailed Du Bois a concession speech, playing Cass to Du Bois's Ike. "We both agree in advance that the position you will take is right morally legally ethically. If it is not evident to you that the position I take in asking for moderation and patience is right practically then we will both waste our breath in debate."[17] In 1966, for Random House (Faulkner's publisher), can William Styron, in the first person, *The Confessions of Nat Turner*, present a lubricious Nat lusting after the white Southern belle, Margaret Whitehead?

Faulkner's "Sambo" in *Intruder in the Dust* marks an evacuation, declares an end to a certain kind of post-Confederate writing, reinscribed here, responding to the present crisis, Unionist invasion, Confederate secession. History crunches in on the novel. In 1946 the CIO was intrusively organizing in Mississippi. In 1947 a prestigious federal commission called for an end to segregation. In 1948 President Harry S. Truman sent an ambitious civil rights package to Congress. In 1948 Mississippi Democrats left the national party to form the Dixiecrat party, giving us Strom Thurmond as its first presidential candidate. Says a wiseacre citizen in *Intruder in the Dust*: "Aint you heard about that new lynch law the Yankees passed? the folks that lynches the nigger is supposed to dig the grave?"[18] Here it is, that reconciliatory post-Confederate discourse, Gavin Stevens's version, stuck to Sambo, besmirched, invalidated, as it strives to inform Charles Mallison's understanding, to establish a position for him.

If Faulkner's public statement on civil rights is conflicted in the fifties, his discourse in interviews, letters to the editor, at conferences, leaking racisms, his grip on racist usage in the besieged 1948 *Intruder in the Dust* seems fairly secure. The narrator, virtually some older Charles Mallison, though never identified as such, presents himself as someone who appreciates and affirms the older Chick's raised consciousness. In his supportive critical language, we observe Chick's thinking through the grips and seizures of elemental racisms seemingly visceral in their truth, racisms of the senses, racisms of odor, racisms of taste. *Intruder in the Dust* begins with this exchange, Roth Edmonds and Gavin Stevens, linking the history told in *Go Down, Moses* (1942), and all its rich ironies, to *Intruder in the Dust*. Bachelor Roth Edmonds, whose big house in *Intruder* is womanless, had once a woman in *Go Down, Moses*, has in fact, elsewhere, unrecognized, a son who is just the sort of boy he names in this exchange. Gavin Stevens is right there in Roth's oblivious language, peer patrician.

"'Come out home with me tomorrow and go rabbit hunting:' and then to his mother: 'I'll send him back in tomorrow afternoon. I'll send a boy along with him while he's out with his gun:' and then to him again: 'He's got a good dog.'

"'He's got a boy,' his uncle said and Edmonds said:

'Does his boy run rabbits too?' and his uncle said:

'We'll promise he wont interfere with yours.'[19]

These boys, in a category with dogs, are "one of Edmonds' tenant's sons," thereafter referred to, with a certain remote irony, as "Edmonds' boy," whom Lucas calls "Joe," and Aleck Sander, Chick's best friend. "Edmonds' boy" is older; both "boys" are larger than Chick, skilled hunters who can nail a fleeting rabbit with a tapstick, who would not tumble from a log bridge. Every racism in this first chapter is carefully marked and promptly disvalued, even the most personal racism, given up to a reductio: "he could smell that smell which he had accepted without question all his life as being the smell always of the places where people with any trace of Negro blood live as he had that all people named Mallison are Methodists."[20]

In this first order of racisms cluttering everyday discourse, damaging conversational discourse, Faulkner is still astute in his hearing and seeing, immediately showing us Joe and Aleck, older, larger, competent black youths, constrained in the racism, "boy," immediately presenting the majesty of Lucas's stature, Lucas's patriarchal authority unquestionably sounding in his commands: "Get the pole out of his way," "Come on to my house," "Tote his gun," "Strip off," Lucas as the absolute transcendent negation of "boy." Here he is, not only not, but actually an ireful castrating (axe on the shoulder) Grandfather Patriarch, who has you naked, at his mercy, who stands over you, looming. Chick must nonetheless fit him into a racism, regain the security of that designation, give this ominous figure coins, a tip, and this is the dark humor of the first section, his act a futility, the coins (racisms) spurned, spilled to the floor.

A reconstructed confident narrator drives the engine of this antiracist surveillance. When Gavin Stevens, in full rhetorical stride, says: "Lucas Beauchamp, Sambo," there it is, a glaring exposure, a stupidity, a racism pressed too far as an ironic euphemism, a stupidity, and ridiculous, too. The narrator's attentive bracketing of all such instances asks that we acknowledge what he repudiates, a benighted racist language, indeed asks that we respect his privileged sensitivity, his privileged knowledge. Lucas Beauchamp, after all, especially the Lucas Beauchamp in *Go Down, Moses*, might very well be Faulkner's response to the challenge that he lacked the "necessities" to do "black" experience. *"You say (with sneer),"* says Gavin Stevens, anticipating Edmund Wilson's supercilious reading, *"You must know Sambo well to arrogate to yourself such calm assumption of his passivity and I reply I dont know him at all and in my opinion no white man does,"*[21] speaking only for himself, not for the narrator, not for the novel, and certainly not for Faulkner.

It is at the next order of racism, the literary racism of plots and narratives, of situations and characters, of fantasies and resolutions, that the text is problematic. At the level of utterance, of everyday speech, a scrupulous discovery of racisms, constantly operating, always reassuring us. At the level of story, the curious return of racisms, of antiracisms as racism, of counterracisms, Lucas's own racism, racism reentering as constitutive, racism the construction of this world: "the house and the ten acres of land it sat in—an oblong of earth set forever in the middle of the two-thousand acre plantation like a postage stamp in the center of an envelope,"[22] racism the already-there of the *mise-en-scene*, the turn in the road. Here we recognize that Lucas has only two sites in the novel, Uncle Tom's cabin and Jim's shed, that Faulkner's exemplary deconstruction of everyday racist discourse circulates within the paradigms and plots of the post-Confederate, takes place within its limitation.

After *Light in August* (1932), after *Absalom, Absalom!* (1936), after *Go Down, Moses* (1942), the abject failures of Gail Hightower and Gavin Stevens to save Joe Christmas from lynching, the challenges of Charles Bon (*"I'm the nigger that's going to sleep with your sister."*),[23] the racist relapse of old Isaac McCaslin in "Delta Autumn," what is Faulkner's relation to the post-Confederate, to its project, its primordial scenes, its appropriate figures, and what, in 1948, does he seek to gain with this recourse to its narrative strategies, its specific language games? He means certainly to engage Harriet Beecher Stowe and Mark Twain, to engage their fundamental moves, restage their classic presentations, as answer to Malcolm Cowley and Edmund Wilson, as response to a new intrusively judging Unionist discourse, Truman's civil rights legislation. Here is Lucas, axe-bearing Grandfather, as anti-Tom; Lucas with his antique wallet, his dollars and cents, as non-Jim, the Jim who gladly takes his forty dollars from Tom Sawyer at the end of *Huckleberry Finn*, and here, too, is a restoration of Sir Walter Scott in the Gowrie tragedy, the Gowries as Highlanders along with the Ingrums and the Workitts and the Frasers, Beat Four the center of their Southern nationality, their sovereignty. The pleasures of Scott factored through these distinctive Southern things—family, place, Protestant church in piney woods—Gavin Stevens gets high on this nationalism as he drives up into the hills toward Caledonia Church, talking excitedly, sailing off into his convoluted paradoxes, and we see absolutely the misery of its blindspots, its double binds, the constraints of Stevens's post-Confederate. His New

South upholds "the postulate that Sambo is a human being living in a free country and hence must be free," declares itself in Unionist discourse, "what the outland calls (and we too) progress and enlightenment," even as it asserts, evoking Confederate discourse: "we must resist the North," defend "our homogeneity from a federal government to which in simple desperation the rest of this country has had to surrender voluntarily more and more of its personal and private liberty in order to continue to afford the United States."[24]

Up, up, into these formulas, and what holds the two priorities together (Sambo must be free, Anglo-American Southerners must be free) in a single coherent emancipatory narrative, is a dependence on, the need for, an Uncle Tom. Just as we reach Caledonia Church, epitome of Confederate nationality, "intractable and independent, asking nothing of any, making compromise with none,"[25] Gavin Stevens reaches this final point in his post-Confederate discourse, describing the necessary Sambo as the one who "loved the old few simple things . . . a little of music (his own), a hearth, not his child but any child, a God a heaven which a man may avail himself a little of at any time without having to wait to die, a little earth for his own sweat to fall on among his own green shoots and plants,"[26] a Sambo prized from the person of Lucas Beauchamp, the figure who sets this final passage into motion. Chick's thought is close to his uncle's as they make their ascent to Caledonia Church, especially at those verges where the prospect discloses Yoknapatawpha spread mapwise below, county as country, his "whole native land." Confederate feeling, state nationality, *Maryland! My Maryland!*, these are the surges, but Chick's anthem differs, swirls around the intractable figure of Lucas Beauchamp. Chick is still smarting from his first traumatic encounter with Lucas, this "damned highnosed impudent Negro,"[27] he calls him, in the midst of his anthem, so there are rifts and rents in his discourse. He doesn't have the ready usage of his uncle's Sambo, can't postulate him.

Uncle Tom, Uncle Remus, Uncle Lucas. Christina Zwarg has already admirably catalogued and described the decor of Uncle

Tom's cabin, read the symbolic import of all its objects, the "brilliant scriptural prints" over the fireplace, the portrait of a colored George Washington, shown us how Stowe uncles this space, makes us rethink the foundational father. It is all there, the flowers, the bedstead, the carpet, table and table cloth, cups and saucers, these objects on the mantel. Zwarg's Stowe is supersophisticated in her discursive racializing. Working through Uncle Tom and his political alter-ego on the Shelby plantation, Sam, doing their different discourses, Zwarg's Stowe invents new subject-positions for patriarchal men, "uncles," creates a space and a speech that escapes the traditional binaries of race and gender. Zwarg's Stowe playfully gets into the dialectical play of Sam's lecturing, Sam's philosophizing, is doing minstrel Emerson in blackface, ironically using blackface in a wily feminist way.

This is not the cabin Faulkner reads in *Intruder in the Dust*, though the objects he sees are the same: furniture, a print over the mantel and by the bed a portrait on an easel. The print, a calendar lithograph "in which Pocahontas in the quilled fringed buckskins of a Sioux or Chippewa chief stood against a balustrade of Italian marble above a garden of formal cypresses," specifically indicates the racism of Stowe's idealization of Uncle Tom as it exposes generally the appropriative racism of all Anglo-American racial representation. Everything is wrong here, costume and setting. Opposite it, Faulkner's portrait, the wedding portrait of Lucas Beauchamp and Molly Worsham, singularities, actual persons. Here, too, something is wrong. A racism mars this wedding portrait. When Chick finally scrutinizes it, he sees, with a shock, the same "calm intolerant face" he confronts in the present pressing Lucas.[28] Everything in Uncle Tom's cabin operates to dispel the uncanny racist horrors of sameness/difference, to calm racist anxieties. Everything in Lucas's cabin works oppositely, to upset the conceit of the sentimental, to heighten racist anxieties. No boyish George Shelby is comfortably at home in this cabin. Showing the grassless way to Lucas's cabin, Faulkner defoliates Stowe's embowering flowers, the garden greenery, and what is for dinner, what wonderful thing from Aunt Molly's oven?

It is a crisis, Chick's innocent racism, his failure to recognize the young hair-styled Molly Worsham in the wedding portrait. He only knows her as wearing a headrag. His apparent confusion at the easel stirs up in the observing Molly ancient race-caused griefs in her marriage, causes her to speak, to distance herself from the falsified person in the portrait, and brings Lucas necessarily into the logic of this discussion. We are already in Lucas's doings, she says, as she explains the portrait. " 'That's some more of Lucas's doings.' "[29] She exposes Lucas in this very racism, the present tense situation, the forced intrusion of Chick, the awkwardness of his being there, Lucas's inappropriate, possibly mean, transgression of racial codes, Chick just a boy and obviously disconcerted, shaken. More of his doings, this grand hospitality that catches Molly unprepared, without enough food in the house to feed the guests. It is Lucas's worst moment in the section, this expression of his internalized racism, his intolerance, his sexist disdain of Molly. He has to justify the act, and first fibs, displaces responsibility, says the photographer made Molly take her headrag off. He must say it finally, admit his own racism, his own derogation of Molly: " 'I told him to . . . I didn't want no field nigger picture in the house.' "[30]

Aunt Chloe and Uncle Tom, here redone. It is also a warning, Lucas's disclosure, a complex admonition: *and there ain't no field nigger in this house,* direction as to how Chick is to treat Lucas, and therefore weak. Molly has forced Lucas from the chain of his imperatives. Clutching his coins, already himself defeated, unable to deal directly with Lucas, Chick turns toward Molly, establishing social ties, to give her Lucas's payment, and she would charitably take the payment, receive it inside the racism, which neither Chick nor Molly herein hurtfully designates. It is a sort of refuge in racism, this racism as a brief haven, this racism as an anti-Lucas measure. Lucas's defiance of white racism, always prompt, is itself racist, therefore vulnerable, open to irony. Still, for all its peremptory treatment of Molly, Lucas's rough usage is a shock therapy, a disabling of white racist descriptives, *boy, uncle, Sambo,* and the like. There is indeed no field nigger in this house. Lucas's challenge ultimately sets Chick relatively free of such racisms, allows the instance of a nonverbal communicative gaze, gives us the anti-racist wit and wisdom of our narrator, a skillful operator in advanced post-Confederate.

In *Huckleberry Finn*, after Cairo is missed, Jim's experience has only two representational sites: Huck's ongoing escape narrative, which has only a limited space for him, as accomplice, as caregiver and storyteller, as social dependent, a life somewhere between the Je suis of Aunt Chloe and the Ich bin of Uncle Tom, and Tom's surreal prison-break scripts, Jim in whiteface writing: "Here's a captive heart busted."[31] The king and the duke paint Jim blue, put him in "King Leer's outfit," placard him: "Sick Arab." Tom's scripts take from Alexander Dumas, prefigure Ralph Ellison, weirdly evoke scenes and situations from classic slave narratives: chains sawn off, secret notes exchanged, disguises, messages of betrayal, work like Hollywood movies in the thirties and forties, dehistoricizing the manacle, emptying the secret note of its socio-political meaning. Subject-categories in advanced post-Confederate, these two suspect Jims. Huck's discourse is privileged because it can partially admit Jim's narrative, see him, hear him, outside the clutter of racisms, and it can regard Tom's plotting, report, and sometimes protest, its demands, its dangers. In Huck's narrative there is a thin outside, a documentary gaze, which lets us see, enacted, the complicity of the versions, the limitation of the one, the brutality of the other.

Some such gaze is surely operating at the end of *Intruder in the Dust*, positioning the three persons, giving the final word to Lucas Beauchamp, "receipt," Lucas's racism. White folks lie, cheat, break their promises. Get it in writing. Get a receipt. "If you aint stealing the lumber," Lucas says to Crawford Gowrie, "get me Uncle Sudley Workitt's receipt." What do you want, Stevens asks, seeing that the dismissed Lucas is not going, but standing there, looking at them. "My receipt," says Lucas, out-patronizing Stevens, out-ironizing him, the last move his. Isn't this final scene necessarily a valedictory, Faulkner's effective withdrawal from the field of African American representation? Lucas pushes that pile of pennies across Gavin Stevens's desk, thanks for "representing my case," two dollars worth of help for the due process and the habeas corpus. What, after all, is Stevens's reputation in doing such legal work? Joe Christmas, Nancy Mannigoe. Receipt is closure. Surely this ending reflects Faulkner's tacit understanding of what is about to happen, African American writing evicting Anglo-American writing, post-Confederate and High Unionist alike (Joel Chandler Harris, Mark Twain, Gertrude Stein, Carl Van Vechten, Faulkner, Styron) from the field of African American representation. The beginning of *Intruder in the Dust* an exorcism in the post-Confederate, confronting Uncle Tom in his cabin, the ending a post-Confederate valedictory. There is, of course, a reprise in *The Reivers* (1962). Uncles return, Ned and Parsham, one wily, the other noble, acting out their post-Confederate parts, but with a certain signal attached: ". . . Ned said; he wasn't being Uncle Remus or smart or cute or anything now."[32]

Lucas enters the final scene addressing Stevens and Chick Mallison with a forbidden usage, one declaring Lucas's parity, Lucas's true social position. "Gentle-men," he says, and it brings immediately into play Jim's great line in *Huckleberry Finn*: "Dah you goes, de ole true Huck; de on'y white genlman dat ever kep' his promise to ole Jim." Between Lucas's "Gentlemen," and Lucas's "My receipt," a dumb-show from the post-Confederate. Like Tom Sawyer, Stevens insists on the formality of Lucas Beauchamp taking flowers and gratitude to Miss Habersham. Like Huck, Chick worries that Stevens might have put Lucas in harm's way, out there on the street, where lynch-minded white racists are still moving about, some maybe angry at Miss Habersham for coming to the assistance of a "damned highnosed impudent Negro," lurking in her bushes. Like Tom, Stevens airily brushes these considerations aside. Lucas does not do the grateful Sambo that Jim does at the end of *Huckleberry Finn*, but he is archaic in his McCaslin clothes, that "old-time white waistcoat," his cocked beaver hat, a comic figure.

Faulkner's advanced post-Confederate in *Intruder in the Dust* achieves this surveillance. By insisting on a bill, "within reason," on payment and receipt, on the routine of this exchange, Lucas sets up the situation where racism must routinely occur, be fore-grounded, and immediately takes charge of it, captures it, enters its routines, its language game. He has come to pay the defense lawyer who presumed him guilty. This is, as it were, more of Lu-cas's doings, his kind of signifying, the McCaslin outfit, counting out the pennies. There is no other language for Lucas, or for Gavin Stevens, just this one, routine, prescriptive, limited, and for all that, complex, hurtful, heavy. Though truces may be struck, and escapes engineered, it goes on.

What happens to Chick's advanced post-Confederate discourse in the fifties and sixties? Hard discursive demands are put on Chick, as hard as those put on Huck out there on the water dealing with the slave-catchers, to say whose side he is on, whose story he must privilege. What kind of beautifully racialized antiracist Southern writing exists outside the conditions and protocols of the post-Confederate, intermediate and advanced? Faulkner doesn't get there. Historical time in Faulkner's fiction stops in 1947. *Intruder in the Dust* everywhere marks boundaries, the Beats, the county, the highlands and bottomlands, marks the distinctive place of Southern writing in American literature, just as, in some other sense, in its action, its patriotic speeches, the novel anticipates, prefigures, in the distant dust of travelled roads, intruders, trans-gressions, boundaries crossed, the end of Southern writing, as the novel knew it.

NOTES

1. William Faulkner, *Intruder in the Dust* (New York: Vintage International Edition, 1991), 190–91.

2. Henry Woodfin Grady, "The New South," in the New York *Daily Tribune*, 23 December 1886.

3. Ibid., 312.

4. Ibid., 320.

5. Mark Twain, *Adventures of Huckleberry Finn*, ed. Walter Blair and Victor Fischer (Berkeley: University of California Press, 1985), 125.

6. Grady, "The New South."

7. Joel Chandler Harris, *Uncle Remus: His Songs and His Sayings* (New York: Schocken Books, 1974), 3–4.

8. Harriet Beecher Stowe, *Uncle Tom's Cabin*, ed. Elizabeth Ammons (New York: W. W. Norton & Company), 379.

9. Quoted in Jay Hubbell, *The South in American Literature, 1607–1900* (Durham: Duke University Press, 1954), 786.

10. William Faulkner, *Flags in the Dust* (New York: Random House, 1973), 359.

11. Ibid., 53.

12. Edmund Wilson, *Cannibals and Christians* (New York: Farrar Straus and Company, 1958), 465.

13. Ibid., 476–78.

14. Walter Taylor, *Faulkner's Search for a South* (Urbana: University of Illinois Press, 1983), 163.

15. Eric J. Sundquist, *Faulkner, The House Divided* (Baltimore: Johns Hopkins University Press, 1983), 149.

16. James Baldwin, *Nobody Knows My Name* (New York: Dell Publishing Company, 1961), 108.

17. *Selected Letters of William Faulkner*, ed. Joseph Blotner (New York: Random House, 1977), 262.

18. *Intruder in the Dust*, 137.

19. Ibid., 4.

20. Ibid., 9–10.

21. Ibid., 210.

22. Ibid., 8.

23. William Faulkner, *Absalom, Absalom! The Corrected Text* (New York: Vintage Books, 1987), 446.

24. *Intruder in the Dust*, 150–51.

25. Ibid., 154.

26. Ibid., 153.

27. Ibid., 148.

28. Ibid., 10, 14.

29. Ibid., 14.

30. Ibid., 15.

31. *Huckleberry Finn*, 322.

32. William Faulkner, *The Reivers* (New York: Random House, 1962), 261.

Race Fantasies: The Filming of
Intruder in the Dust

CHARLES HANNON

I first visited Oxford, Mississippi, in June of 1991, to examine Oxford's city and county courtrooms, and to consider how the formal construction of the law in Faulkner's hometown might inform the writer's career-long interest in that most official of cultural discourses. While there, I learned to distinguish between the law as a prediscursive body of rules and regulations, and the law as one of several "delivery systems" that mediate the individual subject's imaginary relation to the Symbolic Order of culture. The manner in which apparatuses such as law, literature, newspapers, and film produce a particular reality for their audiences became especially clear after I finished reading Faulkner's murder mystery *Intruder in the Dust*, viewed Clarence Brown's film adaptation (thanks to the Center for the Study of Southern Culture), and attempted to learn more about the context of Faulkner's story about lynching narrowly averted by researching what the local paper, the *Oxford Eagle*, had reported of two events: the actual 1908 lynching of Nelse Patton for the alleged murder of a white woman named McMillin, and MGM's filming of Faulkner's story "on location" in the spring of 1949. I found very little on Nelse Patton in the *Oxford Eagle*: approximately two column-inches, six sentences in all, with the headline "Negro Lynched by Mob," and a short narrative in which Mr. McMillin, serving a jail sentence, sends Patton to deliver a message to his wife.[1] According to the story, Patton had "remained about the place," prompting Mrs. McMillin to attempt to frighten him away with a revolver. This allegedly led to Patton

disarming Mrs. McMillin and then slitting her throat. I was struck
by the absence of detail in this front-page story: for what crime
had Mr. McMillin been jailed? What message did he send his
wife? Why did he choose Patton to deliver the message? What
witnesses were there to tell that Patton "remained about the
place"? Why would he do this? How do we know Mrs. McMillin
pulled a gun on Patton, or what her motives were? Why would
Patton kill Mrs. McMillin? How was Patton captured? Who was
in the lynch mob that took him from the jail? How did they overcome the jailers, or did they even have to? Finally, although this
hardly exhausts the number of questions a motivated journalist
might have pursued regarding the event, what had happened to
Patton's body?[2]

Although I was puzzled at the time, the absence of these details
made more sense after I understood the story's ideological function as a rehearsal of the dialectic of racial subject-formation, in
which white Southern men are offered a position of superiority,
what the narrator of *Intruder in the Dust* calls the "white man's
high estate," over the black Other.[3] The Nelse Patton of the *Oxford
Eagle* story was no longer an actual person, but the ideological
figure of the Negro used throughout Southern history to "stitch
up" inconsistencies within the fantasy-construction of white superiority.[4] As an ideological apparatus, the newspaper story had
transformed the actual Nelse Patton into an object of erasure, delivering for its readers a particular version of reality in which clear
racial divisions exist between blacks and whites. Yet the necessity
of Patton's rhetorical transformation attests to a fundamental irrationality in the ideological system supported by the newspaper. To
apply Slavoj Žižek's phrasing, the newspaper served as a support
for the ideology of white supremacy, producing "an illusion which
structures the effective, real social relations" of the segregated
South, yet also masking some "insupportable, real, impossible kernel" which is inconsistent with the illusion.[5] Žižek's formulation of
the process by which the Symbolic is mapped onto the unconscious is thus open to a concept of social antagonism, unlike the
Althusserian instance of interpellation, which for Žižek "never

fully succeeds": "there is always a residue, a leftover, a stain of traumatic irrationality and senselessness sticking to it."[6] As several readers of Faulkner have shown, his fiction is most critical of Southern racial ideology when it represents its irrationalities and internal inconsistencies, especially as these inflect individual subjectivity.[7] Quite often, this irrationality emerges in the form of a dialectic of dependence and disavowal: the white subject requires the presence of some black Other to supplement the fantasy of uncorrupted racial boundaries, yet hates this dependence and enters into any number of delusions in order to disavow it. The figure of the Negro in the *Oxford Eagle* story on Nelse Patton represents this kind of half-willed, half-unconscious delusion: it "stitches up" the inconsistencies in segregation ideology by rehearsing the sublation of white dependence upon the black Other that defines both lynching, as an extreme act of racial division and disavowal, and the everyday experiences of whites in a segregated society.

I will occasionally refer to the Nelse Patton story as I explore events surrounding the filming of *Intruder in the Dust* in the spring of 1949, which also strikes me as an episode of subject-formation, but one uniquely determined by alterations in the discourses of culture available to Southerners after World War II. My primary focus will be the elaboration of film as a vehicle for the fantasies of the South's dominant classes, where this function had previously been performed in the discourse of American historiography and in the legal rhetoric of manifest destiny.[8] Marxist analyses have long recognized film's capacity to create the illusion of mastery in the subjects it produces through the apparatus of the camera lens. This illusion reifies the relation between capital and labor, encouraging the spectator "to desire and possess a consumable space from his or her own perspective, a space in fact requiring the presence of 'an individual' for its lines (perspectival) to be justified."[9] While film's perpetuation of capitalist paradigms is an important consideration for any discussion of film and American culture, we need to recognize that in the segregated South, the same technology would reinforce regional assumptions about racial difference, which legitimated, for white Southerners, the practice of subordinating black experience to white. Although theorists generally understand the illusion of mastery as it is created for audiences viewing a finished film, I will discuss it as a deferred object of desire analogous to the endlessly deferred moment of racial purity, which is the impossible object of desire in the segregationist fantasy. Following Žižek, I will seek the kernels of irrationality that always threaten to erupt within the field of ideology produced by such apparatuses as the novel, the camera, and the newpaper.

American historiography of the Civil War and Reconstruction is fraught with the dialectic of dependency and disavowal. In one example found throughout the literature, the Union's dependence upon black labor and black soldiers is disavowed through the perpetuation of proslavery stereotypes of the benevolent planter, the loyal slave, the evil carpetbagger, and the freedman quickly learning to miss the old days under slavery. Although revisionist historiographers such as W. E. B. Du Bois had corrected many of these misrepresentations by the late 1930s, by then they had become staples of American cinema, and remained so until at least the 1950s.[10] Not only did the first American films rewrite *Uncle Tom's Cabin* in the same proslavery vocabulary as the historiographers were then using to write American history, but America's first great film director, D. W. Griffith, who pioneered techniques of feature filmmaking still in use today, directed and produced the viciously racist *The Birth of a Nation* (1915), and this, along with its virtual remake *Gone with the Wind* (1939), cemented proslavery ideology in white America's cultural imaginary.[11] Recognizing how profitable these films had been, MGM marketed *Intruder in the Dust* as the third installment of a Southern trilogy beginning with *The Birth of a Nation* and *Gone with the Wind*.[12] Although Faulkner's narrative takes place in the late 1940s and not in the Reconstruction past, both it and Oxford's collaboration with MGM deploy the same dialectic of dependency and disavowal that these earlier films—and the discourse of New South historiography— had made available to white subjectivity.

For example, just as the Southern plantocracy and its avatars historically have disavowed their dependence upon black labor, whites in *Intruder in the Dust* ritually scorn their economic reliance upon blacks. The novel registers this dependence in several places—not least in Lucas's annual payment of his property taxes—yet Faulkner's narrator describes "the whole white part of the county" driving into Jefferson to witness Lucas's lynching, travelling the new roads to the town's jail and courthouse, all of which, in their minds, "existed only by their sufferance and support" (143).[13] Moreover, each time Chick half-remembers something, he is recalling and then disavowing a similar example of dependence, as with the memory that Miss Habersham and Molly, Lucas's wife, had been "born in the same week and both suckled at Molly's mother's breast and grown up together almost inextricably like sisters, like twins" (86). When he first recalls this biography, we see that Chick has already learned to disavow its details: "here again something nagged at his mind his attention but already in the same second gone, not even dismissed: just gone" (76). This disavowal in the face of dependency predicates most of the violence performed or contemplated in the novel, and its essential role in the production of white subjectivity is always on the verge of exposure. Indeed, most of Chick's education in this *Bildungsroman* is tied to his exposure of the dialectic he temporarily has refused to activate with regard to Lucas's lynching. "[I]t seemed to him now," the narrator observes at one point, "that he was responsible for having brought into the light and glare of day something shocking and shameful out of the whole white foundation of the county" (135).

Chick's critical examination of the cultural and psychological processes that produce him as a Southern white male contrasts with anything Southern film audiences might have expected from Brown when he proposed to film Faulkner's novel in Oxford. As was the case with the earlier films by Griffith and Selznick, audiences would have expected Brown's film to reproduce these processes as essentially "real" and natural. They could rely upon film as an ideological apparatus, in other words, to reproduce and thereby support the effective relations of existence under segregation. The claim that Brown's film would represent "the real" Oxford was made repeatedly in the *Oxford Eagle* during Brown's filming. Of particular interest was the number of local buildings that would appear in the film, and the percentage of finished product that would be filmed on location. Speaking of the "substantial resemblance" between Faulkner's "word picture" and the environs of Oxford, one writer for the paper continued: "That 'substantiality' and the 'character' that is real in these real scenes is what Mr. Brown says he hopes to capture in this film, a reality which he could not simulate in Hollywood."[14] Some articles even spoke of the "Oxford Method" of filmmaking, claiming that the more a movie is filmed where the story "takes place," the more accurate it will be.

Our awareness of the strategies of exclusion that ideologically determined discourses such as newspapers, literature, and film rely upon to represent the "real" induces us to recognize, however, that the Oxford in Brown's film is a reflection of the white fantasy—in this case, the fantasy of a South whose black population is either erased, or subject to erasure at any moment. Chick ruminates throughout Faulkner's novel upon the "simple and uncomplex" vocabulary available to the people of Jefferson and Beat Four for "the deliberate violent blotting out obliteration of a human life" (88). Brown's film begins in the aftermath of this blotting out: "Where they all at?" the man looking for a shoe-shine boy asks in the film's earliest lines; "Seems to me I ain't seen one darkey in the road since yesterday." Jefferson's blacks are hiding: as Chick, Miss Habersham, and Aleck Sander travel that night to Caledonia Chapel, we see three scenes that Brown has inserted to emphasize black fear of white retributive violence. In one, a black woman covers her children with a bed cover; in another, three adults drink coffee in the dark; and in the third, a single man watches fearfully as the car and horse go by. The succession of these images amounts to an obsession in Brown's film with the power of whites to remove the town's black presence. Chick's father, similarly obsessed, uses a metaphor of sanitation as he cautions Chick to "stay home until this thing is cleaned up—over, finished, and done with." Finally, Brown's film represents the racially "cleansed" town in a celebratory atmosphere: while the townspeople wait for the Gowries to lynch Lucas, they game, flirt with one another, and generally enjoy the festive music broadcast over their heads.

Intruder's obsession with the power of whites to remove the black presence from a protected town square speaks volumes about the development of film as a discursive domain producing its audiences as racial subjects in the late 1940s. The sudden acceptance of Faulkner's story among his otherwise antagonistic neighbors suggests they are in need of some new apparatus to support the dialectic of white superiority which had sustained their vision of an Anglo-Saxon South since the days of Andrew Jackson. Cheryl Lester's thesis about black migration suggests one cause of this anxiety: migrating in droves since World War I, African Americans had been protesting the region's oppressive racial climate and asserting an agency denied them in white representations of the South and Southern history.[15] In this context, the man whose desperate search for some black Other opens Brown's film represents the white South's anxiety over black migration, which threatened the dialectical foundation of its racial identity. But Brown's film also creates the reassuring fiction that blacks would always be available, once empowered whites created the conditions for their reemergence. In this, it follows Faulkner's text rather closely: "they were still there," Faulkner's narrator repeatedly suggests, "they had not fled, you just didn't see them" (95). In the context of black migration, then, the filming of *Intruder* evoked a mass nostalgia over a South that no longer existed by 1949. As several film theorists have noted, film has this delusional capacity to "fix" a particular view *as* historical reality.[16] For the residents of Oxford, film could project a segregationist fantasy that excluded blacks from a protected white center, but maintained their availability as binary references in both the social and psychological construction of white racial identity.

As it came to represent the effective relations of whites and blacks under segregation, the filming of Faulkner's novel supported the everyday fantasies of white privilege. In fact, filming became a metonym for these relations, an "associated idea substituted" for segregation.[17] Implicitly, every moment of filming referred to a future moment of viewing the film in segregated movie houses across the South. But MGM's presence in Oxford represented segregation most fully when it exposed the daily inconveniences and irrationalities of a racially divided society. Juano Hernandez, like the character Lucas Beauchamp he portrayed, forced Brown and others to confront many of these irrationalities. Hernandez obviously required lodging while in Oxford, but law and custom prevented his housing with other white actors. The dilemma was resolved when prominent members of Oxford's African American community volunteered to house Hernandez and other black members of the MGM crew, but this solution only raised another difficulty, when Faulkner found he could not invite Hernandez to the cast party he hosted at Rowan Oak. As Joseph Blotner reports, "He was a fine actor and a cultivated man, but if they invited him they would have to include the Bankhead family [his hosts] as well, and they felt that they could not do that."[18] In addition to these high-profile instances, one can imagine the number of daily aggravations segregation created for Brown's film—a film Brown himself had championed as "the most eloquent statement of the true Southern viewpoint of racial relations and racial problems ever sent out over the nation."[19] The Chamber of Commerce, for instance, encountered difficulties casting local African Americans for the film's jail scene, because, as the *Oxford Eagle* reported, "The colored people don't appear to fancy being in the jail even in make believe."[20] Like the system of segregation itself, producing *Intruder in the Dust* as a support for segregation ideology gave Brown and the residents of Oxford daily opportunities to deny and disavow their dependence upon blacks.

One might think that the daily irrationalities of an ideological fantasy would eventually discredit it in the eyes of those experiencing them, but according to Žižek, they actually ensure its "unconditional authority" by simultaneously deferring and making real the object of desire.[21] Instead of discrediting the segregationist fantasy, each example of white dependence upon blacks makes the desired future moment of racial division and disavowal more real—the moment of viewing Brown's film in a segregated cinema house, for instance; or the moment of lynching, in the case of both Faulkner's characters and the mob that acted against Nelse Patton forty years earlier. Each time the promised moment of racial separation approaches, however, it immediately withdraws again as the impossible object of desire. *Plessy v. Fergusson*'s one-drop rule is an excellent example of this phenomenon, since it posited an impossible standard as the proof of racial purity and thus necessitated a truly absurd taxonomy of legal distinctions in order to support it. *Plessy* was by no means the first legal decision to promise and then endlessly defer the South's desired object of racial homogeneity. The Indian Removal Act of 1830 generated an array of similar legal technicalities as the basis of deciding who would count as an Indian for the purposes of removal and, later in the century, land allotment in the West. Since the early nineteenth century, Southern discourses of racial differentiation have tended to conflate Native Americans and African Americans as a single, threatening Other, because they have been motivated by a similar desire to remove racial Others from an imaginary white space. In the 1940s federal cooperation with the fictions of law and custom that segregated whites from other races in the South began to weaken, however. The unconstitutionality of Jim Crow laws received increased federal scrutiny in the 1940s, just as, according to Felix Cohen, there had run in federal Indian legislation since the 1930s "the motive of righting past wrongs inflicted upon a nearly helpless minority."[22] Again Oxford's taking up of Faulkner's story in the spring of 1949 can be seen in relation to anxieties caused by these contextual historical events, because both Faulkner's text and Brown's film offer the discourse of Native American removal as a way of cancelling Lucas's claim to a white ancestry and fixing him firmly in the position of the Other.

When we first see Lucas in *Go Down, Moses* (1942), he is hiding his still in an Indian burial mound so he can then tell the landowner, Carothers Edmonds, that George Wilkins, Lucas's aspiring

son-in-law, is manufacturing on his property. Lucas's digging un-
settles the mound and it collapses, covering him in dirt and pot-
tery, and depositing in his hand a single gold coin. This coin
symbolically connects Lucas with the South's racial Other of a
hundred years earlier—the Cherokee of Georgia, and the Chock-
taw and Chickasaw of northern Mississippi—and with the desire
for gold that motivated whites to dispossess Indians of their lands.
In a crucial scene from *Intruder in the Dust,* the discourse of Indian removal again separates Lucas from the white South and
marks him as essentially different. As Chick enters the sitting room
of Lucas's home to dry off from his mishap at the creek, readers
are presented with alternate frameworks for interpreting Lucas's
racial identity. In one of these, Lucas is represented in a painting
reminiscent of Grant Wood's *American Gothic:*

> there looked back at him again the calm intolerant face beneath the
> swaggering rake of the hat, a tieless starched collar clipped to a white
> starched shirt with a collarbutton shaped like a snake's head and al-
> most as large . . . and beside him the tiny doll-like woman in another
> painted straw hat and a shawl. (14)

Nearby this portrait hangs a second framed image, a "lithograph
of a three-year-old calendar in which Pocahontas in the quilled
fringed buckskins of a Sioux or Chippewa chief stood against a
balustrade of Italian marble" (10). In the revised American Gothic,
Lucas's claim to both a white and a black identity is undercut by
the permanence of the frame surrounding his relationship with his
all-black wife, Molly. The threat posed by Lucas's dual heritage is
thus contained within this frame. At the same time, the historical
figure of Pocahontas and her actual role as a uniter of races are
repudiated in the insistence upon essential difference which domi-
nates the legend of Pocahontas, and its representation in the lithograph of Pocahontas wearing "quilled fringed buckskins." While
the framing of the Italian balustrade does suggest her voyage
across the Atlantic, it marks her as essentially different in the same
way that the portrait frame marks Lucas. Moreover, the lithograph
of Pocahontas erases both her life with colonist John Rolfe and

her symbolic crossing of racial and cultural boundaries among the British. Significantly, Chick's contemplation of these images precedes his own attempt to instate an essential racial barrier between himself and Lucas, when he paternalistically offers Molly coins in return for what Lucas had intended as common decency.

In Brown's film, the lithograph presenting Pocahontas as a symbol of essential difference is replaced by a painting that represents Euro-American expansion in the nineteenth century. Although our view of the painting is obstructed by actors Claude Jarman Jr. and Juano Hernandez, we can just glimpse a team of horses pulling a covered wagon, and a scout on horseback with his back turned in a gesture that indicates his responsibility to protect the white pioneers from Indian attackers. Like the gold coin that drops into Lucas's hand in the Indian burial mound in *Go Down, Moses,* this painting subordinates Lucas's claim as a Southerner to the discourse of expansion and Euro-American domination of the continent. Moreover, just as each of these images placed in Lucas's home rehearses a particular fiction about America's European discovery and Euro-Americans' subsequent "manifest destiny," the scene acted out before them, Chick's demand that Lucas pick up the coins Chick has dropped on the floor, rehearses the ideology of white superiority, even in Lucas's own home.

In different but similarly motivated ways, then, Faulkner's novel and Brown's film modify nineteenth-century discourses of racial removal as they participate in the dialectic of dependency and disavowal that has sustained white identity in the South for nearly two hundred years. This dialectic relies upon a rhetoric of purity at the center and threat at the margins, and possibly Gavin Stevens's espousal of this rhetoric—his theory of a homogeneous South— will further explain Oxford's uncharacteristic sympathy with him in the spring of 1949. For Gavin, purity is evident in the ubiquity of Anglo-Saxon surnames, names like Workitt "that used to be Urquhart only the one that brought it to America and then Mississippi couldn't spell it" (146). This use of common names to prove the dominant culture's "pure" genealogy is echoed by a columnist in the *Oxford Eagle*, who, backing up Lafayette County's "historic contention that it is the most Anglo Saxon spot in the entire United States," notes that "among the hundreds of Oxford citizens who appear in 'Intruder in the Dust,' scarcely six non-Anglo-Saxon names could be found!"[23] The Southerner's interest in supporting the ideal of pure origins is indicated by the final line of this writer's story: "the Anglo-Saxon blood has been kept intact down the years." For both Gavin and this nameless columnist, proper names signify racial purity, a quality invoked in any justification of white hegemony. As James Snead has observed, this is why Lucas's name is so disturbing to whites in *Intruder in the Dust*.[24] Already a sign of miscegenation whose physical presence repudiates the dominant culture's basic racial philosophy, Lucas is also very careful that people know the proper genealogical referent of his name: "'I aint a Edmonds,'" Lucas corrects the sawmill lout who harasses him at the crossroads store, "'I belongs to the old lot. I'm a McCaslin'" (19). Lucas's presence thus denies Gavin and his community the right to tell themselves stories about the county's pure, Anglo-Saxon origins. In response, this community seeks to rewrite Lucas's white ancestry in Native American terms, and thus exclude him from their vision of an homogeneous Anglo-Saxon South.

This desire to remove Lucas from the protected center of the white South, evident in Faulkner's novel and Brown's film, suggests Southerners' anxieties in the late 1940s over their losses in the national debate over segregation, following Truman's desegregation of the military during World War II, and his party's reelection in 1948 despite, possibly because of, the civil rights plank in its campaign platform. If one could isolate a single event that launched this debate into the 1948 campaign it would be the skirmish that erupted at the Democratic nominating convention over the language of the civil rights plank.[25] The drafting committee at the convention had cooperated with Truman's campaign team in crafting a moderate civil rights statement, asserting the following: "We again call upon the Congress to exert its full authority to the limit of its constitutional powers to assure and protect these rights."[26] This ambiguous language was a concession to Southern Democrats, who could read it as a recognition of the limits of federal jurisdiction, and of the validity of the doctrine of states' rights. When minority drafts were put to a floor vote, however, this language was replaced by the following statement:

> We call upon Congress to support our President in guaranteeing these basic and fundamental rights: (1) the right of full and equal political participation, (2) the right to equal opportunity of employment, (3) the right of security of person, and (4) the right of equal treatment in the service and defense of our nation.[27]

Obviously, this language repudiated the doctrine of states' rights. As a consequence of its adoption, delegates from Southern states including Mississippi and Alabama walked out of the Convention, and on 17 July, dissatisfied Southern Democrats met in Birmingham, Alabama, to nominate Governor Strom Thurmond of South Carolina, and Governor Fielding L. Wright of Mississippi, for President and Vice-President on a States' Rights ticket. In several Southern states, including Mississippi, this ticket was listed on the official ballot as the nomination of the Democratic Party.

One reason the story of Lucas's near-lynching in *Intruder in the Dust* should be read in relation to the Democratic split in 1948 is that this split was a culmination of Southern opposition to federal antilynching legislation throughout the first half of this century.[28] Although Strom Thurmond was himself considered a "liberal-minded" governor because he was known to pursue the perpetrators of lynching in his state, "he always opposed a federal anti-lynching law as an unconstitutional invasion of states' rights."[29] Southerners like Thurmond and Wright had always resisted this legislation because of the precedent it would set for federal intervention in the South, especially in matters relating to segregation. While desegregation was thus the paramount consideration of the States' Rights party, it had been articulated before World War II primarily through opposition to federal antilynching legislation, which amounted, for the Dixiecrats, to the unconstitutional extension of federal powers into state law enforcement. As Anne Goodwyn Jones notes in her contribution to this collection, much of the lobbying on behalf of antilynching legislation was done by members of the Association of Southern Women for the Prevention of Lynching.[30] How is the political activism of Southern women against the criminal actions of white men represented in Faulkner's novel? Like the transformation of African Americans into a rhetorical figure which is then always available as an object of erasure, the politically active woman is transformed by novel and film into the stereotype of the passive "kinless spinster" (75), always on the verge of political irrelevancy. "Good evening, sir," Chick says to Miss Habersham as he interrupts her conference with his uncle (74). She is in his blind spot, but even when he acknowledges her presence he simultaneously can forget her: "He had dismissed her; he had said 'Excuse me' and so evanished her not only from the room but the moment too" (77). Although Miss Habersham's role in freeing Lucas is crucial, the ludicrous scene at the jail in which she passively resists Crawford Gowrie's attack shows that Faulkner's text too is blind to the active role of women in the battle against lynching. The spinster stereotype allows both the novel and the film to "stitch over" the ideologically inconsistent fact of "radical" Southern women with the socially acceptable image of a respectful white male (Crawford Gowrie!) bowing to the wishes of a venerable lady.

The South's opposition to the intrusion of outsiders into "regional" affairs is familiar to anyone who has studied civil rights history. It also formed initial responses to the idea of filming Faulkner's story on location, as Faulkner himself had related in a conversation quoted by Blotner: "people were saying, 'We don't want no one comin' into our town to make no movie about no lynchin'.'"[31] And in an article for the *Oxford Eagle* that looked back to early concerns about the "public relations problem" of bringing non-Southern black actors into Oxford, Phil Mullen writes, "just at the time, racial tension throughout the country had been inflamed by the politicians. That certain type of red-tinged racial extremist could have created incidents which would have done great harm."[32] Although the elections thus contributed to an atmosphere in Mississippi and in Oxford that was hostile to outsider commentary about racial relations, this atmosphere dissipated when Brown and MGM pitched the idea to local merchants. Soon after Brown arrived in February 1949 to scout the area for filming in the spring, the local Chamber of Commerce met and voted to support Brown: the film would be "of great economic, cultural, and advertising value to Oxford," Chamber of Commerce President C. S. Haney claimed, as he pledged Oxford's full support.[33] Oxford's merchants overcame their initial reluctance because it made good business sense, but their decision combined economics with a concern for the region's national image, apparently convinced by Brown that the film could be "a great credit to Oxford and to the South."[34]

We could say that Oxford's merchants saw an opportunity for profit in Brown's proposal, and leave it at that. But I want finally to show how these merchants and professional men and women were also concerned that only a lower-class, bigoted view of race relations was reaching the North, and saw the presence of Hollywood's cameras as an opportunity to define the "real" South as primarily mercantile and middle-class. "Class" thus describes an additional category of removal outlined by the discursive arrangements of Faulkner's story in Oxford in 1949. It is distinguished from the nineteenth-century removal of Indians to the Western territories, and from the twentieth-century removal of both black-white interdependence and the political protests of Southern women from the "real" South, primarily in the degree to which the removal of lower-class whites necessitated the simultaneous refashioning of white Southernness. To be sure, the doctrine of a pure, Anglo-Saxon South is itself evidence of the dominant culture's self-constructions in relation to its underrepresented populations. But the process by which the white South was redefined as primarily middle class, merchant, and professional is unlike these earlier episodes of subject-formation because it involves the sacrifice of one whole class of whites in order to continue the illusion of a pure center threatened by hostile margins.

Unlike the Agrarians' touting of the poor yeomanry in the 1930s, or *Gone with the Wind*'s portrayal of aristocratic landowners, the people behind the filming of *Intruder in the Dust* celebrated a middle-class, professional identity for themselves and their region. In the premiere edition of the *Oxford Eagle,* the editors call attention to Oxford notes written by MGM publicist Barrett Kiesling and scattered throughout the nation's media. Most of these celebrate the realism of the film by noting, for example, its use of Oxford's own St. Peter's Episcopal Church, rather than a Hollywood set, in the opening scene. But the notes also stress the mercantile and professional image of Oxford that Brown's film would publicize across the country. "St. Peter's was built in 1851," one note reads; "It now joins the Lafayette County Jail, a college professor's home, a cotton farm, a dress shop, a drug store and a lawyer's office in the list of authentic settings which Brown used."[35] Moreover, an anecdote printed under these notes suggests how class image was a pervasive issue during Brown's filming. Brown, looking for a local resident to portray the proprietor of Fraser's Store, found George Galloway at his own general store and cast him on the spot:

> It disturbed him that director Brown had thrust him before the camera just as he was, and somewhat mussed from moving merchandise. So at noon he went home, washed, shaved and changed his clothes. The shave could be obliterated with make-up . . . but it was necessary for store-owner Galloway to return home and don the togs in which he had been registered by the cameras during the morning!

Just as local blacks had not wanted to cooperate with Brown by willingly jailing themselves, so this local merchant, George Galloway, wanted to avoid being filmed in the trappings of the lower class, because of the separation of this class from the empowered classes that was occurring at the time.

Faulkner's novel is replete with middle-class success stories of the sort that would have appealed to Oxford's Chamber of Commerce. Most of these involve transplanted farmers who now own property in town, sometimes their own homes, and are prospering as office workers or in some profession. This is true of individual characters like Sheriff Hampton (105) and Jefferson's town marshall (133); but the phenomenon is also evinced in Faulkner's descriptions of neighborhoods, "where the prosperous young married couples lived with two children each and (as soon as they could afford it) an automobile each and the memberships in the country club/and the bridge clubs" (118). Following Faulkner's interest in Jefferson's changing class structure, the story of Brown's filming, as it is told in the pages of the *Oxford Eagle,* offers the city's mayor as a symbol of the "arrived" middle class in the South. R. X. Williams figures prominently, as a promoter of the city, as the owner of the local theater where the "world premiere" took place, and, as one *Eagle* photo caption reads, "practically the 'location manager' for the M-G-M film company."[36] He is also one of the city's residents chosen to play a character in the film, the role of Mr. Lillie, "a countryman," Faulkner's text reads, "who had moved to town a year ago and now owned a small shabby side street grocery" (46). The text dwells upon Lillie's house as a harbinger of middle-class suburbia: "a small neat shoebox of a house built last year between two other houses already close enough together to hear one another's toilets flush." And in the film Mayor Williams's suit, seemingly out of place for someone watering his grass, suggests the story of a transplanted yeoman pursuing a nobler class identity for himself. Williams—by extension, all the merchants and business owners who participated in the filming—thus performed roles both in Brown's film, and in the story of the New South that grew out of Hollywood's presence in Oxford.

In the process of producing Oxford as a white, middle-class success story, Brown's filming followed Faulkner's text in sacrificing lower-class whites in order to demonstrate equal racial treatment under segregation. Like the removal of black subjectivity that describes Reconstruction historiography, we should recognize that the removal of poor whites from the image of the New South fashioned in both Faulkner's text and Brown's film is predicated upon a certain revision of the middle and upper classes' role in the South's racial past. After all, it was a former U.S. Senator from Mississippi, W. V. Sullivan, who asserted with pride to a reporter for the Jackson *Daily Clarion-Ledger* that he had led the mob against Nelse Patton.[37] And as late as 1950, Faulkner had identified

a prominent banker as the author of a hate letter in response to
Faulkner's advocacy of integrated public schools.[38] Thus the dialectic of class identity-formation relies upon a process of dependency and disavowal similar to that with regard to race: the middle
and upper classes depended upon their rural, agrarian past to
demonstrate their own economic progress, but disavowed this dependency by explaining the South's remaining prejudices as a
problem of the lower, unreconstructed classes.

As with any process founded upon artificial binary oppositions,
Oxford's fashioning of a white, middle-class identity for itself is
fraught with contradiction and irrationality. Perhaps the fantasy of
a unified, white middle class is exposed most when it is confronted
by the double-impossibility, according to its logic, of a black middle class. As the cotton farm included in the list of "authentic" film
scenes suggests, the ownership of property—as Lucas owns the
ten acres at the center of the antebellum McCaslin plantation—
qualifies one for middle-class status in Jefferson as in Oxford. Lucas's final appearance in Faulkner's fiction, demanding a written
record of the financial transaction he had conducted with the most
visible white professional in Jefferson, thus confirms his own "arrival" in the face of efforts by the white community in general, and
by Gavin Stevens in particular, to exclude him. As I have already
suggested, Hernandez's Hollywood celebrity presented the people
of Oxford an analogous refutation of the system of exclusions upon
which their segregated society was based.

I would not want to reduce these various instances of subject-
formation to a *single* formula of dependency and disavowal, however. Doing so would be to participate in the same longing for
order and cohesion this dialectic served to support. Doing so
would allow one to rationalize the white South's history of racial
exclusion, for instance, as fundamentally the same as the wealthy
white South's economic and political scapegoating of poor whites.
Middle-class whites have depended upon blacks, poor whites, and
politically active women, and have disavowed this dependence in
similar ways. But the consequences of the dialectic are different
in each case. When Chick says the people of Jefferson will "make

a nigger" (31) out of Lucas, his phrase refers to the same process by which Nelse Patton became the figure of the Negro in the 1908 *Oxford Eagle*. The actual Lucas with a home, a family, and a history would be transformed into an ideological object of ridicule and mutilation, which could be used in subsequent retellings of his lynching to reinforce the white fantasy of uncorrupted racial boundaries. When Crawford Gowrie emerges as the real murderer, the nearest thing to an ideological figure for the people of Jefferson and Beat Four to transform him into is a fratricide, understood in terms of the Old Testament. But in the postwar context of Faulkner's story, this rhetorical transformation anticipates no communal violence against Crawford, as it does in the case of Lucas. Instead, Crawford conveniently is allowed to take his own life with comparative honor. A final, perhaps obvious difference between these cases is the speed with which the two objects of disavowal are inserted into the dominant class's dialectic of self-ratification. Lucas is immediately accepted as a suitable object of scorn and ritual erasure, whereas Crawford, still a visible reminder of the white middle class's own recent experiences, is only disavowed when the facts of Vinson's murder become irrepressible.

Previous schools of literary criticism tended to reduce narratives of social injustice to a single plot, without considering the differential spaces between them. One important goal of cultural criticism should therefore be to retrieve the details of cultural events that seem most impossible, most irreducible to a single narrative of symbolization. A final example from what happened to Faulkner's novel during Brown's filming will illustrate this point. Literally, we know the body of Jake Montgomery gets lost somewhere between Faulkner's novel and Clarence Brown's film. Like the details of the Nelse Patton affair which would have confused the formula of "white womanhood protected" for the readers of the *Oxford Eagle* in 1908, Jake Montgomery's connection to the Gowries, and the second corpse this subplot introduces to Faulkner's narrative, would have complicated Ben Maddow's screenplay beyond the coherence of a Hollywood film. But cultural events like the filming of *Intruder in the Dust* are best understood if we retrieve the incoherent details that others have determined to forget, and seek all the technologies of removal that have collaborated to disavow them.

NOTES

1. "Negro Lynched by Mob," *Oxford Eagle*, 17 September, 1908, 1. The story gives "Lawson" as Patton's proper name. The spelling of the female victim's surname differs in the various discussions of this case, further evidence, to me, that the particulars were of less importance than the formula these events reproduced.

2. For answers to some, but not all, of these questions, see John B. Cullen, *Old Times in the Faulkner Country* (Chapel Hill: University of North Carolina Press, 1961), 89–98.

3. William Faulkner, *Intruder in the Dust* (1948; New York: Random House, Vintage Books, 1991), 134; subsequent page references are to this edition.

4. This is a reformulation of Slavoj Žižek's discussion of the ideological figure of the Jew in *The Sublime Object of Ideology* (New York: Verso, 1989), 48.

5. Ibid., 45.

6. Ibid., 43.

7. See Philip Weinstein, *Faulkner's Subject: A Cosmos No One Owns* (New York: Cambridge University Press, 1992); and Cheryl Lester, "Racial Awareness and Arrested Development: *The Sound and the Fury* and the Great Migration (1915–1928)," *The Cambridge Companion to William Faulkner,* ed. Philip Weinstein (New York: Cambridge University Press, 1994), 123–45.

8. For an analysis of film as fantasy-construction, see Timothy Murray, *Like A Film: Ideological Fantasy on Screen, Camera, and Canvas* (New York: Routledge, 1993). Žižek provides numerous readings of film, desire, and ideology in *Looking Awry: An Introduction to Jacques Lacan through Popular Culture* (Cambridge: Massachusetts, MIT Press, 1991).

9. Dudley Andrew, *Concepts in Film Theory* (New York: Oxford University Press, 1984), 23.

10. On the representation of slavery in American historiography, see John David Smith, *An Old Creed for the New South: Proslavery Ideology and Historiography, 1865–1918* (Westport: Greenwood Press, 1985). For Du Bois's revisionist historiography, see *Black Reconstruction in America, 1860–1880* (1935; New York: Atheneum, 1992).

11. The relation between minstrel stereotypes of the nineteenth century and the development of the American film industry is the subject of Donald Bogle, *Toms, Coons, Mulattoes, Mammies, and Bucks: An Interpretive History of Blacks in American Films* (1973; New York: Continuum, 1989); and Edward Campbell, *The Celluloid South: Hollywood and the Southern Myth* (Knoxville: University of Tennessee Press, 1981).

12. A Brandt's Mayfair advertisement in the *New York Times*, for example, proclaims the following: "*The Birth of a Nation* created a sensation in 1915; *Gone with the Wind* did the same in 1939; *Intruder in the Dust* gives the dramatic answer in 1949." *New York Times*, 21 November 1949, 29.

13. Other examples of taxable black labor in the novel occur on pages 94, 119, and 145.

14. "These Lafayette Scenes To Become Movie Sets," *Oxford Eagle*, 17 February 1949, 1.

15. See Cheryl Lester's essay in this collection. Emigration from Mississippi slowed during the 1930s, but by the 1940s it had regained its pre-Depression pace. The 1950 census recorded a black population in Mississippi of 986,494, down 8.2 percent compared to 1940, according to Donald B. Dodd, *Historical Statistics of the States of the United States: Two Centuries of the Census, 1790–1990* (Westport: Greenwood Press, 1993), 50.

16. Marc Ferro, for instance, writes that "Unlike a work of history, which necessarily

changes with distance and analytical developments, a work of art becomes permanent, unchanging." *Cinema and History,* trans. Naomi Greene (Detroit: Wayne State University Press, 1988), 159.

17. This definition comes from Trevor Whittock, *Metaphor and Film* (New York: Cambridge University Press, 1990), 59.

18. Joseph Blotner, *Faulkner: A Biography,* 2 vols. (New York: Random House, 1974), 1284.

19. Quoted in Blotner, 1277.

20. "MGM Seeking More Local Actors As Movie Progresses," *Oxford Eagle,* 17 March 1949.

21. Žižek, *Sublime Object,* 43.

22. Felix S. Cohen, *Handbook of Federal Indian Law* (1941; Washington: U.S. Government Printing Office, 1945), 83.

23. "In Most Any Newspaper in the Country, May Appear Something About Oxford," *Oxford Eagle,* 6 October 1949, 10.

24. See James Snead, *Figures of Division: William Faulkner's Major Novels* (New York: Methuen, 1986), 197.

25. Much of this history of the 1948 Democratic Convention comes from Irwin Ross, *The Loneliest Campaign: The Truman Victory of 1948* (New York: New American Library, 1968).

26. Ibid., 121.

27. Ibid., 122.

28. Indeed, one reason Walter White of the NAACP worked the Democratic Convention as thoroughly as he did was the pressure Southern members of Congress exerted upon Senate and House committees earlier that spring to write weak antilynching legislation. See Robert L. Zangrando, *The NAACP Crusade Against Lynching, 1909–1950* (Philadelphia: Temple University Press, 1980), 192–94.

29. Ross, 132.

30. For the history of this and other antilynching organizations, see Jacquelyn Dowd Hall, *Revolt Against Chivalry: Jesse Daniel Ames and the Women's Campaign Against Lynching* (New York: Columbia University Press, 1993).

31. Blotner, 1277.

32. "Negro Star Was Well Liked, Well Respected in Town," *Oxford Eagle,* 6 October 1949, 19.

33. "Movie Folk Enthused Over Oxford: Expect Film Start Early in March," *Oxford Eagle,* 10 February 1949, 1.

34. Ibid.

35. "In Most Any Newspaper in the Country, May Appear Something about Oxford," *Oxford Eagle,* 6 October 1949, 9.

36. "A New Star Is Born!" *Oxford Eagle,* 21 April 1949, 6.

37. See Cullen, 97.

38. See the "Weeping Willie" letters in James B. Meriwether, ed., *Essays, Speeches, and Public Letters by William Faulkner* (New York: Random House, 1965), 93–94.

Culture in a Faulknerian Context

SACVAN BERCOVITCH

By "Faulknerian Context" I mean to suggest a reversal of tradition. As a rule, interdisciplinary study places literature in the context of another discipline: once mainly theology; now mainly the disciplines associated with cultural studies: anthropology, psychology, sociology, and so forth. And now as then, the result has been disciplinary colonization: literature anthropologized, psychologized, sociologized—literature as an exemplum for something else. The reason for this is not far to seek. Disciplines are systems of knowledge. They provide solutions, however tentative, and solutions are the stuff that professional careers are made of: monographs, essays, public lectures. And there's no ready alternative. Disciplines are artificial, but necessary. They're the product of the distribution of intellectual labor in our fallen world. We'd like to know everything there is to know, but we can't, and disciplinarity—dividing up the job of knowledge—is the best compromise we've found.

Artificial, but necessary; and also vice-versa: necessary, but artificial. Take *Light in August*. Faulkner's novel is not just literature. Or rather, as literature, it's also psychology, sociology, anthropology. Disciplinarity is an enabling form of compromise that Faulkner's work invites us to *resist*. The problem is that resistance itself then takes the form of disciplinarity. Formalist approaches to works of art, like other disciplinary approaches, have tended to close out connections—to separate the aesthetic from the cognitive, and, within aesthetics, to separate high from low culture, literary from ordinary language. Disciplinarity thus denies a truth that's central to *Light in August* and other literary classics across time and place. For although some works persist by institutional fiat or because of esoteric appeal (cult objects, *romans-à-clef*), by and large their persistance attests to commonality. What's distinctive about those texts is the extent of their connectedness; what's extraordinary about them is the depth of their embeddedness in the ordinary. Is there a method of study, a disciplined way of understanding, commensurate with that achievement? That's what I mean to affirm by "Faulknerian Context." I will call the method this entails counterdisciplinary (for lack of a better term)—counterdisciplinary as distinct from antidisciplinary, for what I have in mind is more or less specialized. A method is a context appropriate to the materials being analyzed. Thus a literary context is appropriate to a novel by Faulkner, whereas a philosophical context is appropriate to a treatise by Ludwig Wittgenstein. What's the difference? Take a quick look at the two passages I've xeroxed.[1] A *quick* look, noting the parts underlined, for just a minute. I'll return to these passages later.

You'll have noticed that both writers make use of a chess analogy, but for very different ends. Faulkner invokes it only to move, unexpectedly, rather illogically, to a religious image. At the start, a man is compared to a pawn; the analogy is timeless, absolute (capital-P Player and pawn). But it leads to a vividly detailed scene of a lynching, and at the end we're left wondering, like the townspeople, what to make of it all. The victim's blood rushes out and he seems "to soar into their memories forever and ever"— apparently an allusion to the crucifixion. Chess and the cross, then, serve as pretexts for a certain fictional event. These pretexts are (to repeat) timeless, absolute, applicable to situations across time and place. But their applicability *here*, in this passage, seems puzzling. Is Faulkner suggesting some relation between the crucifixion and a fixed chess match? The answer requires us to see those ahistorical images (chess, the cross) in the framework of the event in question, a specific action in a specific place, Jefferson, Mississippi. The absolutes called Fate and Christ are contextualized by that local fiction. Each term means something in its own right, of course—philosophically, theologically—but here those abstract meanings become flexible, volatile, because they have been localized. Their significance, in connection with chess, depends upon what we make of *this* scene in *this* novel.

Wittgenstein's passage works in the opposite way. Here the analogies function (as he says) like an "x" in logic; they are local instances designed to prove an ahistorical abstraction. And both instances, you'll notice, are highly imaginative. In the first case, someone decides: "Now I will make myself a queen with very frightening eyes, she will drive everyone off the board." Bizarre, but it's surrounded by a series of abstractions which erase time and place. The point is: chess equals syntax, equals the way that language functions. We've got to play by the rules. That "we" includes anybody, anywhere. To emphasize the point, Wittgenstein concludes with another analogy, this time to a hypothetical chess-planet, Mars, where theory and practice merge, so that you can win a war by proving that the king will be captured in three moves. Again: bizarre, but it makes perfect sense. Those made-up specifics (a man inventing a chess queen, a world governed by the laws of chess) are contextualized by an ahistorical concept. The point is that this is the way language, any language, works. Wittgenstein's analogy is a thought-experiment that makes the imagination a vehicle of logic. Faulkner's analogy is an image-experiment that makes conceptual absolutes a vehicle of specificity.

It's a difference of means and ends. Philosophy transcends, by which I mean it moves from particulars to abstract totalities—in this case, the totality of language (Wittgenstein even includes the language of mathematics). By contrast, the literary text moves *through* transcendence to convey a local event. We could interpret the event philosophically—life is a game of chess—but that would be an inversion of aesthetic means and ends. The literary counter-move would then be to interpret Wittgenstein's analogy in specific local terms. That man who decided to reinvent the queen: was he black or white? The problem with this sort of confrontation is that each interpreter has a different purpose in view. They're contestants playing by opposite means to opposite ends, whereas a contest requires a common context, a mutually binding set of rules, as in a chess game. Under what common rules, then—since Faulkner's passage is also philosophy and Wittgenstein's passage is also literature—can Faulkner's pawn be played alongside Wittgenstein's queen?

The advantage of literature for this purpose lies in its peculiar mixture of rationality and artifice. On one hand, literary study is the aesthetic field that's most closely connected with fields of rational understanding, such as philosophy. Language is their common denominator. As I said, Wittgenstein is also a writer, and Faulkner also a philosopher. But philosophy deals in logical necessity, whereas literary texts are worlds of make-believe. We can say, then, on the other hand, that as a discipline—a method whose proper subject is imaginary—literary study is more transparently *constructed* than any other body of knowledge. Perhaps I should put the emphasis elsewhere—it's more *transparently* constructed—since my point is not uniqueness but commonality. Literary study highlights the constructedness of all disciplines. Professionally, it's barely a century old; grounded in the vagaries of genteel appreciation (taste, tact, and sensibility); and in its brief career, it has gone through several startling metamorphoses, from philology to poststructuralism. *Is* there a *literary* body of knowledge? Does it constitute *an* area of specialization? A discipline, after all, is a *system* of understanding. In this sense, I take Wittgenstein's chess analogy to stand not only for philosophy, but for disciplinarity in general. A discipline demands a certain rigor, certain modes of persuasion, certain standards of validation and invalidation. It is responsible to the language of logical coherence.

Literary study tries to be coherent, too, of course, but it's responsible to the language of the literary text (as we've come to define it)—the language of the imaginary world of *Light in August*, rather than the real world under investigation by Wittgenstein, or the real world to which Jesus brought redemption (according to the Gospels). That literary world, the "aesthetic realm" to which Wittgenstein himself denied philosophy access, has a different kind of logic, with its own professionally different rules of cognition. We've been told that we learn about the "deep meaning" of

Joe Christmas by seeing that he's like Christ. But that's reversing
ends and means. The character's significance here depends on a
branch of theology, whereas understanding the novel requires us
to see theology through the lens of Joe Christmas. Suppose that
we adjust the analytic context accordingly. What if we seek the
meaning of Jesus in Joe Christmas or that of Fate in Percy Grimm?
Whatever we learn in these cases, it involves a logic which calls
disciplinary knowledge into question. What's known beforehand
as representing something that claims to be objectively true
(Christ, Fate), is being recontextualized in terms of fictions, which
by definition are made up by specific persons at specific times.
And that specificity, let me add, applies even when authors claim
omniscience, even when they tell us it's not *them* speaking, but
History or God. Disciplinarily, Gibbon's *Decline and Fall* describes what happened in Roman history, even though the author
vividly specifies himself at the start. Literarily, the scripture of "J"
is specific, local, and (more or less) subject to the sorts of questions
raised by dramatic irony, even though, disciplinarily, as theology,
it's the timeless voice of Jahweh.

   This reversal of means and ends is epitomized by what I called
the "question of context" on your handout. "Whereof one cannot
speak, thereof one must be silent."[2] Disciplines tell us what we
can articulate knowingly—what works; what makes sense; what
we can verify or predict. In this view, literature is the realm of
cognitive silence. That's what philosophers from Plato through
Kant have been telling us. Wittgenstein's remark about Kafka is
typical: "This man gives himself a lot of trouble not writing about
his trouble."[3] That rigorous disciplinary judgment applies to
Faulkner as well. Wittgenstein's image of trouble is a fly trapped
in a bottle. The philosopher shows the fly the way out. So does
the sociologist, the economist, and the psychologist. Faulkner, like
Kafka, tells us what it's like to *be* the trapped fly. Like all literature,
his fiction works on a counterdisciplinary principle: it keeps recalling us from abstractions to our bottled-in condition.

   This is not because writers abhor abstractions. Quite the contrary: literature is a grand procession of abstractions that writers

have endorsed, from the anonymous medieval Everyman to Bunyan's Christ-like Pilgrim and Goethe's Eternal Feminine to what Faulkner called his tales of the Human Heart. But for the writer, the abstraction is the vehicle for constructing specifics. Bunyan's Christian turns out to be a seventeenth-century Baptist Englishman. The medieval Everyman, Goethe's Marguerite, and Joe Christmas all have human hearts, but that's the least interesting thing you can say about them, even from a medical point of view. From a literary point of view, not even that banality counts, since these examples of the human heart are life*like* people, realistic as distinct from real. Cognitively, therefore, they open a gap between the truth—what a disciplined thinker would call evidence, a database—and the truths they claim to represent. Is Goethe's Marguerite truly Feminine? Is *that* why we find her credible two centuries later? And if so, does credibility mean things as they are, or as they have been, or as they *have* to be, absolutely? Or is aesthetic "truth," as moralists have long warned us, simply whatever *this* fiction persuades you is true?

What I'm calling a literary approach is the cognitive field established by the interaction between these three questions. Literary truth is: (1) status quo, the norms (e.g., femininity) of *this* culture; (2) transcendence, the putative capital-T Truth; and (3) this fiction or artifact, a special world of make believe. The result is a volatile state of meaning that redefines cognition itself. In strictly aesthetic terms, that redefinition is confined to the interpretive possibilities of the text. But if we extend the analysis to the world as we know it disciplinarily—that is, if we extend the rules of the made-up text to the made-up rules of cultural analyses—if, in short we see culture in a Faulknerian context—then I believe we have the grounds for an interdisciplinary project. To that end, I have referred to the literary approach as counterdisciplinary rather than antidisciplinary. I mean by this both resistance and reciprocity. I want to distinguish literary analysis from standard methods of cultural study *and* to indicate its relatedness to these methods.

So understood, the relation between Faulkner and culture requires a context by negation. The term I used earlier, cognitive silence, is a fair description if we take the term cognitive seriously, as a particular mode and understanding of how culture works. We learn something which we know, like gender, from the standpoint of what we don't know, like a science fiction planet. The assumption of disciplinarity is that we can extend our rational methods of understanding (propositional logic, empirical research) to all times and places. The counterdisciplinary assumption is that we can recognize the limits of our rational and experimental methods by understanding a specific area that never existed, like Yoknapatawpha County. What sort of knowledge does that yield? Consider the Wittgenstein dictum again. "Whereof one cannot speak, thereof one must be silent." Abstractly understood, this reads like a tautology—"cannot speak" is just another way of saying "be silent"—and as such it applies to anyone, anywhere. It sounds like *the* truth, a logical imperative. Whoever you are, don't talk knowingly about what you don't know. That's the tautological, self-consistent structure of all disciplines. But there's another possible reading of Wittgenstein's aphorism. Contextually, the aphorism comes at the end of a modern treatise in symbolic logic called the *Tractatus Logico-Philosophicus*. Perhaps, then, Wittgenstein had a modern specialist in mind. His "one" may stand not for everyone, but for philosophers only. He would then be reminding his colleagues that they don't know everything; that there are matters of which philosophers should not speak—religion, for example, or literature.

"Whereof one cannot speak, thereof one must be silent": who *does* the "one" represent? Once we ask that question—once we contextualize the abstraction by trying to specify the "one"—we are on literary grounds. After all, that "one" (German: "man") is a fiction, much like the "man" who reinvented the queen. And that fiction, moreover, ends up in a question: "one" *what*? One composite human being? one specialist? one madman? Suppose we pursue that last line of inquiry. What if we read the aphorism ironically, as the author's *mocking* commentary on the entire enterprise of philosophy. For let me point out another detail about this specific context: the *Tractatus* is a work that claims to solve all the problems of philosophy: all of them, once and for all. What if the author *really* meant to ridicule all such claims? "Whereof one cannot speak, thereof one must be silent": are we expected to read into this a condemnation of the entire philosophic *pretence* to knowledge? Is "Ludwig Wittgenstein," the ostensible author, really a figure of satire, a Don Quixote of disciplinary truth, driven mad by academic learning, and speaking on and on about that whereof anyone, especially a philosopher, ought to be silent?

This is not perversity on my part. It's a standard literary device. One term for it is narrative irony, and it becomes a dominant technique in modern literature, with its emphasis on subjectivity and point of view—think of the multiple narrators in *Light in August*— but actually it's endemic to all literary works. That is to say, it's potential in the text—intrinsic to what we've come to identify as literary context—whether or not the author meant it to be so. William Blake said famously of *Paradise Lost* that its author was of the Devil's Party without knowing it. Blake was wrong about Milton the theologian, but not about the epic itself. To specify the abstraction Evil as a lifelike rebel named Satan is to narrow the focus from a timeless absolute to a time-bound fiction. And here, as in Joe Christmas's case, or as in the case of Wittgenstein's "one," to narrow down in that literary sense is to open up in terms of cultural context: from everyone (an absolute) to a group of people (religious, racial, academic) to a certain person. I've termed this a reversal of ends and means because it marks a direct turnabout in the use of evidence and the work of language. The philosophic approach specifies in order to abstract. The literary approach, on the contrary, enlarges by specifying. I would go so far as to say that it *universalizes* by specifying. By his specificity, Milton's Satan, like Joe Christmas, represents, first, a spiritual absolute; then, more directly, a cultural norm, an example of a particular set of Christian beliefs; and then, more concretely still, and more universally, a certain man whose fictionality grounds him in time and place, and opens his significance to interpretation, as in a question whose answer is still to be ascertained.

We might compare that question to the primal doubleness of the word "prove" in the popular expression "the exception proves the rule." This concrete instance, the exception, challenges, tests, and perhaps confirms certain cultural rules and spiritual absolutes. By analogy: this invented person, Joe Christmas, is universal insofar as he *proves* the truth-value of Christ, or the archetype Everyman, or the modern stereotype Marginal Man. That is to say, he's universal because he incorporates several layers of identity, the deepest of which is the concrete fictional character in *Light in August* whose credibility at once entails and challenges—calls into question *as opposed* to dismissing—the certainty of both absolutes and relativist truths.

That volatile reciprocity is literary context, and by its cognitive silence it elicits crucial aspects of who we are, universally. To begin with, it teaches us that a main characteristic of our bottled-in condition is the dream of beyondness, the urge to transcend. So understood, disciplinarity is the fly that *thinks* its way out of the bottle—thinks, that is, that it's on the way out, almost *there*; or more grandly, thinks that it has already been there, and returned for our benefit, to show us the way out. Literature often serves to illustrate routes to transcendence, but in doing so it also reminds us, by virtue of its specificity—in the very process of *literary* illustration—that those directions are inside narratives, susceptible to narrative irony. Thus the literary does not invalidate disciplinarity; rather, it draws disciplinarity into a dialogue between local, cultural, and transcendent issues. Can you willfully reinvent a chess piece? The disciplinary answer is No; absolutely not. The literary text opens the No to qualifications or even reversal: that specific person saying No may be wrong, or only half-right. Precisely because he or she is credible—life*like*, like *a* person historically located and circumscribed by *a* language, *a* set of principles, *a* form of morality—therefore we don't know, or can't be sure. This is not because literary texts are inherently mysterious, or endlessly ambiguous, or absolutely irreconcilable. It's because the literary tends to challenge the disciplinary bond between the abstraction we "know" and its textual representation. That's the counterdisciplinary form of knowledge to which literary study is committed by the nature of its evidence, just as a chess player is committed to a certain set of rules and regulations.

My analogy is not accidental. Chess is well-suited as a model for both literary and cultural studies. It has been a favorite analogy of writers across time and place, from Abelard to Stephan Zweig; and in English literature alone, from Chaucer through Shakespeare to George and T. S. Eliot, and in our time from Nabokov to Pynchon and Morrison. It's also a commonplace in the social sciences for the laws of history, institutional structures, and the rules of cultural continuity and change. For the sociologist Georg Simmel, it's a paradigm of the way people think and behave. For Ferdinand de Saussure, it's the single best image of the science of linguistics. Most directly for my purpose, chess has served, philosophically, as *the* model of disciplinary cognition. Wittgenstein tells us that it represents the nature of all propositions, the basic relation between words and the world. A disciplined thinker argues, according to Wittgenstein, "as we would talk about the rules of chess."[4]

Let's suppose, then, that we could resolve the relation between Faulkner and culture by recourse to those rules. What sort of game would we be playing? Wittgenstein gives us the disciplinary answer: a game is a contract to abide by fixed regulations within a self-consistent system. For the literary answer, I return to Faulkner's analogy. It comes in a climactic scene in *Light in August*. The protagonist, Joe Christmas, who embodies the Southern race problem (is he black or white?), has murdered his benefactor, Joanna Burden, and set fire to her house. The hunt for the killer is a major plot-frame of the novel. Faulkner underlines its significance by allusions to *Paradise Lost* and *Oedipus Rex*. The lynch mob is led by Percy Grimm, a patriot-fanatic who's driven (we're told) by "a belief that the white race is superior to any and all other races and that the American is superior to all other white races and that the uniform is superior to all men."[5] As the chase draws to a close the townspeople gather in a kind of outraged festivity, almost a holiday mood:

> [Grimm] was moving again almost before he had stopped, with that lean, swift, blind obedience to whatever Player moved him on the

Board. . . . He seemed indefatigable, not flesh and blood, as if the
Player who moved him for pawn likewise found him breath. . . .

But the Player was not done yet. When the others reached the
kitchen they saw . . . Grimm stooping over the body . . . and when
they saw what Grimm was doing one of the men gave a choked cry
and stumbled back into the wall and began to vomit. Then Grimm too
sprang back. . . . "Now you'll let white women alone, even in hell," he
said. But the man on the floor had not moved. He just lay there, with
his eyes empty of everything save consciousness . . . [looking] up at
them with peaceful and unfathomable and unbearable eyes. Then his
face, body, all, seemed to collapse . . . and from the slashed garments
about his hips and loins the pent black blood seemed to rush like a
released breath. It seemed to rush out of his pale body like the rush
of sparks from a rising rocket; upon that black blast the man seemed
to rise soaring into their memories forever and ever. (437, 439–50)

Imagine this passage as the final move in a chess game. An abstract player, like a god in a Greek tragedy—like the destiny that
drives Oedipus to Thebes—moves a white piece in position to
capture what appears to be its black counterpart. The capture itself, however, turns into a surprising reversal. Metaphorically, it's
the black pawn that wins, or seems to, and it does so by starting
an entirely new game. It captures our imagination by emerging
as the crucified Jesus, a triumphant black king, in a scene that's
memorable for its details (the "choked cry," the vomit, the
"slashed garments," the "unbearable eyes"). But can *this* man, an
arsonist and killer, represent Christ? Can it be that *these* racist
fundamentalists have seen Christ in Christmas? It is those local
problems, and not the Christian interpretation of the cross, which
provide the context of meaning. The Christian interpretation is
part of a larger frame of explanation which works by interpreting
the very pre-texts it builds upon. The question is: once we set out
the problem in this way, are we trying to find a solution or to begin
anew? Is it the end of a game or the beginning of another?

That question is a model of what I mean by literary approach.
Light in August is my example for the entire range of what we've
come in this century to call literature—the sort of texts we expect
to find under "literature" in a college catalogue—in its relation to

what we understand as the disciplinary study of culture. Let me therefore elaborate the model by analogy to two types of chess problems: (1) the endgame puzzle, a problem in endings, and (2) the gambit, a problem in openings. The endgame is a familiar puzzle. You've all seen it in the newspaper. White to win in three moves. You're asked to complete a game that's already resolved, like an acrostic or a murder mystery. The answer is already there, somewhere, challenging your ingenuity. Let this endgame puzzle stand for the disciplines that we associate with cultural studies. Literature, by contrast, resembles the gambit. This is less familiar, but just as simple. Here the challenge is not to win, but something like the opposite. You're asked to detect the trap in what seems to be a clear-cut advantage. Your opponent offers (as it were out of the blue) to give up his pawn. It seems to be a blunder, but if you accept, you'll soon find yourself in a difficult position. In puzzle language: you're presented with an apparent gift, and your task is to see why it's a trap.

Endgame versus gambit: we can generalize this contrast into the language of game theory. Chess is traditionally known as *the* game of rules and regulations. That's why the endgame is such a good image of chess. It stands for systemic order. You and I are just starting to play this particular chess match, but we can play only if we already know the rules. Our free agency hinges on that stern recognition of necessity. I have in mind Faulkner's impersonal Player, but you might think also of Ingmar Bergman's image of the chessmaster, Death, in *The Seventh Seal*, or of Samuel Beckett's familiar emblem of things-as-usual in his play *Endgame* and his endgame novel, *Watt*: "[White:] All life long the same questions, the same answers." "[Black:] I can't go on." "[White:] That's what you think."[6]

An endgame is a closed system, no matter how many moves you're allowed, three or thirty. The gambit, on the contrary, is an epitome of possibility. It specializes in indirections and circumventions. By declining to capture your opponent's pawn, you're neither giving up the game nor declaring checkmate. You're simply recognizing that the way to win, whatever it is, is not *this* way.

You're demanding that the game continue with all pieces in play and all options open. That's the strategy behind Faulkner's shift in images. He doesn't refute the endgame analogy (pawn takes pawn, checkmate). He simply declines to play it out, or he plays it out in a way that opens other possible lines of play, suggested by analogy to the Gospels, and thence connecting, through earlier analogies, to *Oedipus Rex* and *Paradise Lost*.

These connections have often been noted. Suffice it, therefore, to say that they are central to Faulkner's meaning, and that as such they're not just intertextual, but intercontextual. They constitute a cultural framework of interpretation, and thereby provide the ground of what I called solutions, meaning the rules by which we play at overcoming our limitations. In this case, they're the absolutes called Fate and the Cross. In general, they're the absolutes, large and small, shallow and profound, through which certain groups (united by common secular or religious interests) make sense of the world, all too often, though not necessarily, at the expense of other groups. These absolutes shape the different games we play, in academia and elsewhere: our standards of excellence, our bases of selection, our norms of good and bad, right and wrong. A culture coheres through such rules, which are abstracted from a multiplicity of particulars, and thus *made* coherent, *called* rules, in much the same way that on July 4, 1776, the thirteen Anglo-American colonies declared themselves free, independent, and united: because they were *not*. Independence was advanced as an ahistorical ideal, the edict of Nature's God, in order to solve, once and for all, a particular set of problems. The ideal may or may not be absolutely true. The problems themselves pointed then and still point to dependencies: the sorts of limitations that apply anywhere, in one way or another, to the human quest for community.

Hence the contrast I outlined between frameworks of explanation. The literary frame is the fictional "one" that opens several layers of meaning. This literary move, from an abstract pretext, *the* crucifixion, to a textual specific, *this* lynching, I associate with the gambit. It's an instance of the transcultural *limitations* I just referred to, the specific problems that call for solutions, and so lead to the kinds of generalizations we live by. The disciplinary frame of explanation is the generalization itself. I associate this with the endgame puzzle. The literary explanation raises a question; the disciplinary explanation answers it; or more accurately, it represents an answer that's accepted by a particular culture. The theory of the Fall abstracts *the* meaning of evil in such a way as to explain why a certain interpretation of a death, that of Jesus, encapsulates the reason for Death (capital D). That explanation tells us why we not only must but *should* die, either for our own good or for the greater glory of God. It's an absolute attended by *a* set of rules, concerning Justice and Mercy. The proper disciplinary terms of interpretation require the reader to fit all experience into that particular set of propositions. The lynching in question thus becomes what social scientists call a case history and theologians an exemplum. In the case of the Faulkner passage: certain dilemmas then (Adam's choice, Christ's passion) and certain very different dilemmas now (a house on fire, a double murder) are *made* to correspond through *an* abstraction that accounts totally, absolutely, as in an endgame, for all facts of violence and death.

That's the theological endgame solution (Joe Christmas, Jesus Christ), and its parallels in the endgames of the human sciences should be obvious (the Foucauldian endgame, the Lacanian endgame, etc.). The literary explanation, the gambit, does not necessarily undermine that sort of solution. It may actually confirm it, but also it may not, or it may bear it out partially, in a specific, perhaps surprising way as when Faulkner tells us that Fate is an American legionnaire, Percy Grimm, engaged in an act of violence marked by "black blood" and lit up by a festive "rush of sparks."

That was Blake's mistake in reading *Paradise Lost*. Milton was not a secret Satanist, nor is his poetry deeper than theology. It has a different kind of depth: the multilayered experience of living by a particular set of absolutes, within *a* cultural framework or set of beliefs. Disciplines speak from the vantage of cognition. They tell us how far we've come; they report on how things cohere to the best of our knowledge. They tend toward closure, therefore, even when closure is a paradise still to be regained; even, for that matter, when *the* answer is atheism or agnosticism. The literary text speaks from the other side of the divide between knowing and not-knowing. It tends towards open-endedness, even when its premise is the doctrine of predestination, as in Fate or Adam's Fall. In either case, the specifics it builds on constitute layers, not levels of meaning.

Layers, not levels. Levels imply an objective and totalizing answer—a depth of meaning which is always the same, more or less, since it's *the* answer: sexuality for Freud; class for Marx; Christ for Christians. By contrast, the layers I speak of are reversible, interchangeable, because the relation between the general theory and its specific literary manifestation point towards the *limitations* of human knowledge. This is culture in a Faulknerian context. The context highlights the fictional quality—the inventedness—of the traditions (symbols, stories, belief-systems) through which we make, unmake, and remake meaning. Fiction in this sense is not a lie. On the contrary: it's an index to the truths we live by—but a volatile index, one that requires us to judge the universality of those truths in terms of specifics that reveal, among other things, the depth of our ignorance—problematic specifics that recontextualize endgames as gambits.

Faulkner's work is exemplary in this respect because of its *deliberate* volatility. I have argued that volatility itself inheres in the "literary." We could probably extend literary context in this sense to those moments in any text where language creates a gap between cultural explanation and textual specific, between the truth as we know it and an incident that implies the limitations of what we know. In Faulkner, this method is explicit. Fate and Christ—and (as the text makes clear) also sexuality and class—are the overlapping "deep meanings" of a figure whose significance hinges on the specifics of a life, a time, a place, a set of circumstances. We can infer a variety of explanations from those meanings. I think this would hold true of any "literary" description of a lynching—not only novelistic, but historical, ethnographical, psychological. But for Faulkner the process of inference on our part signals an aesthetic strategy on his. Fate and Christ function together in this passage as obstacles to a comprehensive meaning. One analogy doesn't quite fit the other, unless we stretch it (as Huck Finn might say), and the stretching process requires us by definition to confront what we don't know. Contextually Fate/Christ works *against* the interpreter's impulse to totalize. So does the trinitarian context of race, class, and sexuality. One example: Faulkner consistently revised the description of Joe Christmas through the novel—elaborated and detailed the person, place, and time—in such a way as to problematize the fateful issue of race. In other words, Joe Christmas emerges as a racial type through questions of context. Those questions don't necessarily undermine the abstractions that make up the type. As you recall, the "black blood" in that scene has been interpreted, by Gavin Stevens for one, as a confirmation of race. But the confirmation itself comes by way of questions that specify the abstractions. Gavin Stevens said so. Thus in Faulkner's final version we simply cannot know whether Joe is black, white, or both, or neither (he *may* be Mexican). The blackness of the blood that rushes out at the end is in the *mind's* eye of the beholder. I emphasize *mind* as the vehicle of disciplinary logic: it's an abstraction that has been recontextualized by the text as a particular assumption. It seemed so to an astonished group of townspeople. In that *seeming* crucifixion, as throughout the passage, the depths of meaning direct us away from an answer towards possibilities of various kinds. Whatever our gameplan of interpretation is, it has to include an incomplete correspondence (or dissonance) between layers of representation.

You'll have noticed by now that I'm using a number of terms—*deep, universal,* and *absolute*—in a peculiar sense. Please bear with this for an hour. By *deep,* I mean common questions, rather than revelatory answers. By *universals* I mean abiding limitations—our universal human limitations of will, reason, imagination, and endurance; the limitations of history, agency, and chance. And by *absolutes* I mean the solutions we devise to overcome those limitations, or at least to make do with them. Since these definitions are counterconventional, perhaps counterintuitive, let me explain myself briefly one more time. Solutions differ from one society to another, one century to the next: *a* theory of justice, *a* standard of beauty, *a* justification for death. These are culture bound: the products of certain minds, nurtured in history. Literary specifics lead down to the problems which are always there, humanly, across time and place. *These* are universal. According to a famous dictum in statistical science—a founding principle of the insurance industry—"nothing is more uncertain than the life span of a man; nothing is more certain than the life span of a thousand men."[7] The second claim, regarding the certainty of the thousand, is a cultural abstraction; it describes a certain society at a certain time. The first claim, regarding that characteristically uncertain one man—characteristic because *a* life span is uncertain, contingent—is universal. What it tells us is applicable alike to ancient Athens, to first-century Judea, and to the modern South.

The literary approach is a mediation between the one and the one thousand, between the specific act and the rule. For Aristotle, that kind of mediation issues in what he called the probable, by which he meant a certain instance abstracted to the dimensions of the norm. The one is probable because it represents the one thousand. Faulkner's art suggests a model that works in the opposite direction. Here, mediation is a movement downward, from the (temporarily) secure abstraction to the volatile historical common. Christians think that they know more than others about God because of the Incarnation. Psychiatrists are certain that premodern theories of the dream are as outmoded as the Ptolemaic system. Wittgensteinians think they can reason more clearly than Platonists. But no Faulknerian will claim that *Light in August* teaches us more about religion, psychology, or philosophy, than *Oedipus Rex* does, or *Paradise Lost*, and certainly not more about literature.

These texts are universal because they do *not* transcend. This does not mean that they deny transcendence. They almost always allow for it; sometimes beckon towards it; often invoke it; but ultimately they return (like Melville's *Moby-Dick*) from a pursuit of *the* answer, there and then, to predicaments that extend, circuitously, from wherever *there* was to whatever *now* is. Such specifics connect *Light in August* to *Oedipus Rex* and *Paradise Lost*.

The universality of Faulkner's passage lies in the peculiar quotidian problems that Joe Christmas represents beyond his resemblance to Jesus—problems of a consciousness, a modern ritual, a form of religion, and a concept of manhood (black male sexuality), in an unforgettably specified region of a country. The Christian archetype works aesthetically because Faulkner has contextualized it as the fugitive Joe Christmas, circa 1932. In other words, it works aesthetically by opening up the various possibilities available to us, culturally and disciplinarily, under the rules. *Under*, as in subject to the rules, but also within them, at once undergirding the rules and undermining them; *under*, as in underlie, involving possibilities that in some sense *these* absolutes really do speak the truth—possibilities, too, of an unsettling kind, prospects that have been declared out of bounds, or that have not yet been explored—variations, transformations, or innovations that may effect the rules themselves, and so alter the nature of the game.

Literary depth is an invitation to recommence. Disciplinary depth is a directive towards ending the game. Plato's *Republic* and Marx's *Capital* explain the world by projecting its essences and ends. They aspire to become (in Beckett's words) our "same old answers." *Oedipus Rex* and *Paradise Lost* contextualize essences and ends in terms of problems we continue to live with. Literature is not a criticism of life. It is life's criticism of absolutes, language's skepticism about totalizing answers. In this game, endings are a sacrifice to be declined. And *sacrifice* is the right word, even for the player who declines the gambit. For the truth is, disciplinarity is an offer that's hard to refuse. You've received a certain body of knowledge as a gift of education, a cultural heritage. You're trained to believe in it, and when you test it against experience it often works; or what's more important, you believe it works. Then, in this instance, for this literary occasion, you're asked to suspend belief, to put your training aside, and from this perspective, a perspective of ignorance to renegotiate apparent solutions.

What you can learn from this is the inverse of Foucault's equation of knowledge and power. It's the importance of acknowledging boundaries. Closed systems are systemically imperial. They triumph by incorporating new, hitherto unresolved problem areas. Ideally, a certain endgame strategy enlarges to the point where it becomes *the* endgame, a master key to the great code, even if the key is constructivism, relativism, or solipsism. The gambit carries the opposite set of assumptions. It requires you to give up the ready answer, however compelling, in order to grasp the nature of *this* specific problem. The reward is a recognition of the traps of transcendence and thereby, perhaps, a recognition of the limitations that connect our particular worldview to those of others. Along with this, if we're lucky, we gain a certain access to difference and otherness; a sense of the cognitive *dis*advantages of illegitimate appropriation; and, particularly in the area of cultural study, a salutary wariness about the totalitarian impulse inherent in disciplinarity itself, even in its programmatically tolerant forms.

This is by no means to disavow professionalism. I seek neither to privilege literature not to mystify ignorance. I believe absolutely in the move towards closure. We *should* want to find the answers (*the* truth, the *best* way to organize society, the *highest* moral principles). The language games we play would become less human, less than human, if we gave up on absolutes. It would be scandalous to revise the past without believing in some sense in historical truth, or to institute social change without believing in some sense in progress. It's the job of cognitive disciplines to try to get us closer to answers, however distant *the* answer remains. It's the job of literature, and by extension of literary study, to keep the game going by demonstrating that we don't know enough to claim answers.

Literary study is a discipline in non-progressivism. It builds upon the recognition that literature moves forward—say, from Sophocles to Faulkner—by refuting theories of closure. What aestheticians have termed progress—perspective, the novel, free verse—is not a ground of consensus but a locus for debate, and in any case it indicates development only in the photographic sense: as an enlargement, innovation, or variation in methods of representing specifics. Progressivism is a disciplinary frame of explanations which the literary text challenges. That's not because authors are essentially rebels (the archetype of the Subversive Artist is a Romantic invention, one more time-bound absolute) but because the language games they're playing are grounded in a commitment to recommence the games of culture.

That act of recommencement is no less moral and political in its way than the commitment to absolutes. It teaches by negation—by our refusing to sacrifice specificity—that we are always already more than the endgames we play. We are always more, that is, than our culture tells us we are, just as a language is more than a discipline, just as a human being is more than the statistics he or she fits into, and just as a literary text is more than the sum of the ideologies it accumulates as it travels across time and space. What's "more" in all these instances is precisely what we *can't* speak of disciplinarily, and its *cognitive* value extends to all disciplines. Scientifically, God may be dead; historically, we may be advancing towards some end-time utopia. But it requires enormous ignorance or arrogance on our part to draw those conclusions from what science or history have taught us. The truth is, we don't know.

What the evidence does show, from a literary point of view, is that absolutes are never universal and universals are never absolute. I should probably repeat that. *Absolutes are never universal*: they're cultural Particulars, made up by time-bound human beings. *And universals are never absolute*: they're the specific limitations that are always with us. That's the nontranscendent Faulknerian approach to culture. Let me now draw out its positive implications by contrasting it with the standard disciplinary approach. And the first thing to note here is that there's something wrong with the chess analogy I've used. I refer not just to Faulkner's shifty pawn, but to what I should now confess has been my own sleight-of-hand. For in any rigorous sense, the gambit cannot stand as a model of the game at large. It's one move in a game, and it's prompted, like any other move, by the drive to win by the rules. As Wittgenstein points out:

> every syntax . . . [is] a system of rules. . . . Chess does not consist in my pushing wooden figures around a board. If I say "Now I will make

myself a queen with very frightening eyes, she will drive everyone off
the board" you will laugh . . . [because] the totality of the game determines the [piece's] logical place. A pawn is . . . like the "x" in logic.
. . . [And so, too, by extension, is any particular strategy or ruse. Theoretically, a gambit is] a scientific question, [similar to the question of]
whether the king could be mated . . . in three moves.

What's striking about this dictum is its absolutist tone. It's meant
to be a guide to practice, but it issues as a warning against the
illusions of freewill. The gambit is an "x" in the logic of the game.
In this view, the literary represents one line of play in the game of
cultural studies. But suppose that we persist instead with Faulkner's literary logic and try to expand the gambit into a model of
chess at large. In order to do so, we would have to reconceive the
game. Just think of it: a game of endless traps, ruses, circumventions, and recommencements! What would it look like? Answer
One: it would look like a Faulkner novel. Answer Two: it would
look like a lot of literary texts. Answer Three: it would look a lot
like the world we inhabit. Answer Four: it would look exactly like
the game of chess. Specialists discuss chess as the story of a hundred great games; but in fact it's the story of continual transition,
the zigzag histories of cultures, a shifting configuration of the most
unlikely reciprocities between rules governing different areas of
life, the ancient, multilingual transnational "game of games."

The specific origins of chess remain problematic; but we know
that in Malaya the rules of chess changed with successive religious
influences (Hindu, Shintoist, Islamic); that in India, China, and
the Middle East chess moves were directly linked to large-scale
war games; and that the original Near Eastern and Arabic names
for chess ("chatrang," "shantranj") reflect variations in political hierarchy, as do early Korean forms of the game. We know further
that, during the Renaissance, chess was played at tournaments
with human "pieces" on enormous fields; that the meanings of
chess pieces have fluctuated with the fate of empires; and that
fluctuation has brought with it constant crisscrossings of institutional, conceptual, and even technological structures—in our day,
for instance, the radical changes introduced by the Fischer time

clock. A contemporary match could be contextualized through the overlappings of feudal Spanish knight and caste-bound Indian pawn with our space age timer at a courtly Renaissance tournament.

Think of what it would mean to describe a chess match in this context! It would be like explaining the castration of Joe Christmas through Sophocles, Milton, local histories, and theories of race. We would have to account for the most unlikely transhistorical correspondences. The point of analysis would be to explain why the game did *not* end. Why did the wisdom of the ancient Greeks fail to solve our moral problems? Why, as *Light in August* testifies, did the triumph of Christianity turn into a world of the same old questions, sometimes the same old answers? And conversely: why, as *Light in August* also testifies, did Christianity and the wisdom of the Greeks prevail in spite of those de facto failures? Why, in spite of all we've learned, do we still invoke Fate? How did chess, with its antique, mixed-up hierarchy, persist in our democratic world? And how can we account, except by negation, for the Alice-in-Wonderland-like metamorphoses that constitute the mix—as for example in medieval Rome, when the Persian vizier or counselor was replaced by the queen; or again, several centuries later, when the queen assumed what we now consider to be her lawful place on the board.

That last moment is significant enough to stand as a paradigm for chess in general. It inaugurated the rules of modern chess, the game as we now play it. Evidently, half a millennium ago, in the last quarter of the fifteenth century, somewhere in Spain, Portugal, or Italy, the game of chess changed qualitatively. The significant developments centered on speed of contact and scope of personal initiative. The main innovation lay in the expanded powers of the queen, which, from being the weakest player—weaker than the pawn—suddenly became the strongest single unit on the board. By 1492, chess had begun anew. According to experts, the game had developed "a coherent new system" with a complete "theory of its own," sometimes known as the theory of the mad queen, "eschés de la dame enragée," "ala rabiosa."[8] Chess historians have made the predictable Renaissance correspondences: expanded mobility, the new individualism, the invention of the printing press, and the great queens of empire, from Isabella of Spain to Elizabeth of England. And indeed Isabella herself is directly implicated: the first published treatise on the New Chess was dedicated to her in 1496 by its author, the courtier-poet Luis de Lucena, who had it bound together with a group of Petrarchan sonnets, and entitled it all *The Game of Love*.

Lucena's Mad Queen is an emblem of literary context. She's a fit opponent for the queen with frightening eyes, emblem of the disciplinary taboo: thou shalt not violate the rules of the game. "Totality," declares Wittgenstein, "the game determines": the picture at which we are asked to laugh—a player suddenly, willfully, reconceiving the function of the queen—implies the impotence of radical innovation, the absurdity of "my pushing" against the object's "logical place," my impudence in talking about that "of which we cannot speak." It abstracts what's given, the chessboard as we find it, into a fixed, prescriptive meaning, as though its eight-square shape were not a relatively late development, derived from another game, "ashtapada," but a symbol of Fate.

That move toward totalization inheres in philosophy itself. When Descartes says, "I think, therefore I am," he requires me to erase the multitude of particulars that literature builds upon—for example, all the particulars that differentiate me from Descartes. To understand Heraclitus's theory of flux ("We never step into the same river twice") requires me to banish the specific questions that literature starts and ends with: "Which river?" "At what time of year?" "Who is 'we'?" Ahistoricism, we might say, is a disciplinary requirement, expressing an abiding human limitation: the urge to say it all, which by definition includes things whereof we do not know and therefore should not speak. Philosophy is typical of disciplinarity in that it represents the specific as an absolute, even if that absolute is anti-absolutism, as in William James, John Rawls, or Richard Rorty. Faulkner's chess analogy is the counter-disciplinary contrast: it begins in a know-it-all absolute (the capital-P Player) and it ends in an allusion to God, but the analogy itself resists totalization. Wittgenstein's logical pawn is an emblem of the limitations of reason: it pictures the arbitrary itself as necessity. Faulkner's mutable pawn is an emblem of the limitations of literature: it transforms Fate itself into a knot of hard facts. Philosophy says: "I think, therefore I am." Literature says: "That's what *you* think."

I realize that my own argument here is both historically conditioned in its definitions (what our culture has come to call literature) and prescriptive in its method (the "literary" requires a disciplined suspension of systemic truth and cultural belief). Let me emphasize, therefore, what I hope has been implicit all along, that my concept of counterdisciplinarity is offered as practice, not theory. It's a strategy for resisting the pressures of totalization inherent in the methodologies derived from the human sciences (much as the literary has served in the past to resist the totalizing pressures of theology). So understood, the value of literary context in our time is that it calls into question the sort of impasse I've just outlined. The opposition between the literary and the cognitive is one more culture-bound absolute—in this case, the absolute of disciplinarity. For what I called at the start Faulkner's unaccountable linguistic shift is really a kind of multidisciplinary spectacle. The lynching of J. C. is a specific, limited, concrete, and hence universalized enactment of the confluence of religion, history, politics, and philosophy. What makes for that volatility is the fact that Faulkner's gambit does not contradict the endgames it builds upon. Its premise, that really we *don't* know, appeals to the truths both of daily experience and of conceptual abstraction, even as it builds upon the disparities between those kinds of different truths. Faulkner's analogy invokes absolutes *as endgames*—it may even be said to celebrate them as endgames (to underscore the force of Fate and the passion of Christ)—and at the same time it represents their acts of closure (the self-blinding of Oedipus, the resurrection) as traps of transcendence.

The literary differs from the disciplinary in that it frees us, momentarily, from the necessity of endgames, in precisely the area, language, which bears most responsibility for the way we understand the world. This does not lift us beyond the rules of the game; but it does allow us to test limits, to transgress disciplinary boundaries between what one can and cannot speak of, and (in imitation of Faulkner's art) to turn endgames into a standing invitation to resist appropriation. Literary criticism is cognitive insofar as it teaches us through literary texts—or any other kinds of texts considered as literature—that all rules are subject to variation, even transformation; so that any one of them may in time become an opening gambit, a specific point of departure, as when the thousand-year-old doctrine of the king's divine right became a key player in the language-game of American individualism—Jefferson's "kingly commons," Whitman's "divine average," Faulkner's pawn-become-king, the black and/or white king with unbearable eyes.

I take that last, surprising, willful, overdetermined, and arbitrary figure to represent culture in a Faulknerian context. It's a language game that requires us to play for keeps (win, lose, or draw) in an intercontextual match which we expect will leave us, wherever we end, at some point of recommencement—which is to say, in the midst of things, as in fact we now are, professionally and humanly.

APPENDIX: A QUESTION OF CONTEXT

"Whereof one cannot speak, thereof one must be silent."
"Wovon man nicht sprechen kann, darüber müß man schweigen."
　　—LUDWIG WITTGENSTEIN, *Tractatus Logico-Philosophicus*

1. The Disciplinary Approach

Every syntax can be regarded as a system of rules for a game. Chess does not consist in my pushing wooden figures around a board. *If I say, "Now I will make myself a queen with very frightening eyes, she will drive everyone off the board," you will laugh. It does not matter what a pawn looks like. What is rather the case is that the totality of rules of the game determines the logical place of a pawn. A pawn is a variable, like the "x" in logic.* The difference between chess and the syntax of a language [is] solely in their application. *If there were men on Mars who made war like the chess pieces*, then the generals would use the rules of chess for prediction. It would then be a scientific question whether *the king could be mated by a certain deployment of pieces in three moves*. (Wittgenstein, in conversation; italics added, ellipses deleted)

2. The Literary Approach

[Grimm] was moving again almost before he had stopped, with that lean, swift, blind obedience to whatever Player moved him on the board. He seemed indefatigable, not flesh and blood, as if the Player who moved him for pawn likewise found him breath.

But the Player was not done yet. When the others reached the kitchen they saw Grimm stooping over the body *and when they saw what Grimm was doing one of the men gave a choked cry and stumbled back into the wall and began to vomit.* Then Grimm too sprang back. "Now you'll let white women alone, even in hell," he said. But the man on the floor had not moved. He just lay there, with his eyes empty of everything save consciousness, [looking] up at them with peaceful and unfathomable and unbearable eyes. Then his face, body, all, seemed to collapse, and *from the slashed garments about his hips and loins the pent black blood seemed to rush* like a released breath. It seemed to rush out of his pale body like the rush of sparks from a rising rocket; upon that black blast *the man seemed to rise soaring into their memories forever and ever.* (Faulkner, *Light in August*; italics added, ellipses deleted)

NOTES

1. See Appendix. The references are to William Faulkner, *Light in August* (New York: Random House, 1932), 139–41, and Ludwig Wittgenstein, quoted in *Wittgenstein and the Vienna Circle: Conversations Recorded by Friedrich Waismann*, ed. Brian McGuinness, trans. Joachim Schulte and Brian McGuinness (Oxford: Oxford University Press, 1979), 103–4. I would like to thank Donald Kartiganer for his warm hospitality at this conference. A different version of this argument appears in *"Culture" and the Problem of the Disciplines*, ed. John Carlos Rowe, forthcoming from Columbia University Press.

2. See Appendix. The reference is to Ludwig Wittgenstein, *Tractatus Logico-Philosophicus*, trans. C. K. Ogden (London: Routledge, 1989), 189.

3. Quoted in Ray Monk, *Ludwig Wittgenstein: The Duty of Genius* (New York: Viking Penguin, 1990), 498.

4. Wittgenstein, *Philosophical Investigations*, 46e–47e (no. 108). See Ferdinand de Saussure, *Course in General Linguistics*, trans. Roy Harris, ed. Charles Bally and Albert Sechehaye (New York: Philosophical Library, 1959), 88–89, and Georg Simmel, diary excerpt from *Fragmente und Aufsätze*, quoted in Kurt Wolff, introduction to *The Philosophy of Georg Simmel*, trans. and ed. Kurt Wolff (New York: Free Press, 1950), xx–xxi.

5. Faulkner, *Light in August*, 425–26.

6. Samuel Beckett, *EndGame: A Play in One Act* (New York: Grove Press, 1958), 5, and *Watt* (New York, Grove Press, 1958), 5. See also the chess game annotated in *Murphy* (New York: Grove Press, 1938), where the point is to *lose* the game, so that the opening move, P-K4, is "the primary cause of all White's subsequent difficulties" (244).

7. Elizur White, 1856, quoted in Susan L. Mizruchi's forthcoming *The Science of Sacrifice: American Literature and Modern Social Theory*. Elizur White, a founder of the insurance industry, was President of the Prudential Insurance Company.

8. Richard Eales, *Chess: The History of the Game* (New York: Oxford University Press, 1985), 18–38. The references to chess history are drawn from a variety of sources, the best of which remains H. J. R. Murray, *A History of Chess* (Oxford: Oxford University Press, 1913).

Contributors

Sacvan Bercovitch is the Charles H. Carswell Professor of English and American Literature at Harvard University. He is the author (among other works) of *The Puritan Origins of the American Self, The American Jeremiad, The Office of "The Scarlet Letter,"* and *The Rites of Assent: Transformations in the Symbolic Construction of America.* Currently he is General Editor of the multi-volume *Cambridge History of American Literature.*

Don H. Doyle is professor of history at Vanderbilt University and is the author of *New Men, New Cities, New South: Atlanta, Nashville, Charleston, Mobile, 1860–1910,* as well as other studies of Southern history. He is currently working on a history of Lafayette County, with special attention to the ways in which Faulkner's historical fiction can illuminate our understanding of Southern history.

Peter Alan Froehlich is a doctoral candidate in English at the University of Mississippi, with an M.A. from Pennsylvania State University and a B.A. from Georgetown University. He is currently working on a dissertation that investigates the presence of frontier grotesques in various cultural contexts and their impact on regional and national identities. An assistant curator at Rowan Oak, he is also a founding director of the annual Southern Writers, Southern Writing Graduate Conference at the University of Mississippi.

Charles Hannon received his Ph.D. from West Virginia University in 1994 and is currently a Lecturer in the Department of American Thought and Language at Michigan State University. He has published on Faulkner, Carson McCullers, and Richard Wright. He is currently working on a book, "Faulkner and the Discourses of Culture."

Anne Goodwyn Jones received the Jules F. Landry Award for *Tomorrow Is Another Day: The Woman Writer in the South, 1859–1938*, a book that combines biography, social history, feminist criticism, and textual analysis. Associate professor of English at the University of Florida, she is the author of *Theory and the Good Old Boys: White Masculinity in the South*. She also coedited *Haunted Bodies: Gender and Southern Texts* with Susan Donaldson.

Cheryl Lester is associate professor of English and American Studies at the University of Kansas. With support from a 1995 NEH Fellowship, Lester recently completed *Faulkner, Black Migration, and the Commerce of Culture* (forthcoming, Cambridge University Press). In the summer of 1996, she codirected an NEH Summer Seminar for College Teachers devoted to the topic of African American migration and American culture. Currently, she is studying oral history and narratives of migration to and from Kansas, Mississippi, Tennessee, Michigan, and Senegal.

Gena McKinley is a doctoral candidate in English at the University of Virginia. Having received two M.A. degrees, in philosophy and in English, at the University of North Carolina and the University of Virginia, she has also studied at the Sorbonne in Paris. Her doctoral dissertation is entitled "Southern Literature Revisited: The Construction of Race and Region."

John T. Matthews, professor of English at Boston University, is the author of *The Play of Faulkner's Language* and *"The Sound and the Fury": Faulkner and the Lost Cause*, as well as numerous essays on Faulkner in leading journals and collections. He has recently received a fellowship from the National Endowment for the Humanities for a book titled *Raising the South: Literary Modernism and the Imagination of History*.

Kevin Railey is associate professor of English at Buffalo State College. He has published and presented a number of essays on Faulkner, as well as on ethnic American Literature and the relationship between pedagogy and politics. He has recently completed a booklength study, *Natural Aristocracy: William Faulkner in Ideology and History*.

Neil Schmitz, professor of English at the State University of New York at Buffalo, is the author of *Of Huck and Alice: Humorous Writing in American Literature* and essays on a wide range of subjects, from Abraham Lincoln to Donald Barthelme, and including such figures and topics as William Lloyd Garrison, Civil War photography, regional humor, Native American texts, Mark Twain, Gertrude Stein, Robert Coover, and Ishmael Reed. He received a Guggenheim Fellowship in 1984–85 for a study of the Civil War.

Dawn Trouard is professor of English and chair of the Department of English at the University of Central Florida. Currently managing editor of the *Faulkner Journal*, she is editor of *Eudora Welty: Eye of the Storyteller* and coauthor of *Reading Faulkner's "Sanctuary."* She has been a Fulbright Lecturer in American Literature at the University of Catania, Italy.

Warwick Wadlington is the Joan Negley Kelleher Centennial Professor at the University of Texas at Austin. He is the author of *The Confidence Game in American Literature, Reading Faulknerian Tragedy*, and *"As I Lay Dying": Stories Out of Stories*, as well as essays on such writers as Melville, Nathanael West, Theodore Dreiser, and Wallace Stevens.

Index

Absalom, Absalom!, 68, 128, 170–72, 178–79, 182–87
"Ad Astra," 142
Adorno, Theodor, 41
Althusser, Louis, 96
As I Lay Dying, 188
Autobiography of an Ex-Colored Man (Johnson), 148–49, 152–53, 155–57, 159–63

Babouk (Endore), 179–82
Bakhtin, Michail, 222
Baldwin, James, 214–15, 252
"Barn Burning," 28–29, 172–74
Barrett, Michele, 49, 51
"Bear, The," 56
Beauchamp, Lucas, 254–55, 257–61, 271–77, 280–81
Benbow, Cassius Q., 23
Benbow, Horace, 68–69, 75–89, 128, 142
Benbow, Narcissa, 90–91

Christmas, Joe, 60, 68–69, 130–31, 139, 151–64, 288, 291–92, 299, 307
Coldfield, Goodhue, 16, 36
Companionate Marriage (Lindsey), 61–66, 70–71
Compson, Quentin, 47–48, 60, 68, 76, 95, 178–79, 183
Cook, Sylvia Jenkins, 169–70
Cooper, Minnie, 44–45, 58

"Delta Autumn," 160
Derrida, Jacques, 188–89
Dilsey, 6
Drake, Judge, 77, 83
Drake, Temple, 46–49, 65–67, 70–72, 83, 92–96, 101–03, 112–13, 115–19
"Dry September," 44–45, 53, 56, 161–62
Du Bois, W. E. B., 252

Edmonds, McCaslin, 140–41
Ellison, Ralph, 195, 197, 203

Fable, A, 137, 144
Flags in the Dust, 128, 142–43, 248

Flaubert, Gustave, 107–12
Foucault, Michel, 50–51

Go Down, Moses, 134–35, 144, 254
Gold, Mike, 168–69
Gramsci, Antonio, 49–53
Grimm, Percy, 135, 137–38, 293–94
Gwin, Minrose, 45

Hamlet, The, 30–31, 38, 174–75, 218–40
Hannah, Barry, 243–44
Harpham, Geoffrey Galt, 221
Hightower, Gail, 130, 139
Houston, Jack, 227–32

If I Forget Thee, Jerusalem, 62–63, 66–67, 69, 187, 191–215
Intruder in the Dust, 168, 242–61, 263–82
Irigaray, Luce, 117–18

"Jail (Nor Even quite Yet Relinquish), The," 35

Kartiganer, Donald, 151–53
Killers of the Dream (Smith), 56, 61
Knight's Gambit, 143

Light in August, 26, 60, 68–69, 125–46, 148–64, 284–85
"Lo!," 135–36

McCaslin, Ike, 64, 140–41
Madame Bovary (Flaubert), 107–12, 119
Mallison, Chick, 255–58, 267–69
Mansion, The, 187
Medici, Marie de, 113–15, 119
Mohataha, 9
Morrison, Toni, 194

Newman, Francis, 60–61

"Odor of Verbena," 68
"Old Man," 201–03
Olsen, Tillie, 187–88

Pate, Lucy, 227–29
Popeye, 85–89
Porter, Katherine Anne, 61
Pylon, 143

Ransom, John Crowe, 59
Ratliff, V. K., 231–38
Ringo, 20–21, 26
Rittenmeyer, Charlotte, 197–200
Roberts, Diane, 45–46
"Rose for Emily, A," 67

Sanctuary, 46–49, 61, 65–67, 70–72, 75–
    98, 100–19
Sartoris, Bayard, 67–69
Sartoris, Colonel John, 20–21, 24, 139–40
"Shall not Perish," 143–44
"Skirmish at Sartoris," 26–27, 53
Slotkin, Richard, 223
Snopes, Ab, 26, 28
Snopes, Ike, 231–34
Snopes, Flem, 30–33, 234–37
Sound and the Fury, The, 47–48, 95, 118,
    234
Souls of Black Folk, The (Du Bois), 198
Stevens, Gavin, 242, 244, 251–56, 260
Sutpen, Judith, 15

Sutpen, Thomas, 11, 28, 182–87

Theweleit, Klaus, 78–81, 83, 90
Turner, Frederick Jackson, 219–21,
    223–24
Twain, Mark, 244–46, 248–49, 259

Uncle Tom's Cabin (Stowe), 246–47,
    256–58
Unvanquished, The, 17–18, 20–21, 25, 26,
    52, 67–68

Varner, Eula, 229–31
Varner, Will, 28, 227, 230–31, 235
Velde, Van de, 58–59, 70–71

Warren, Robert Penn, 5
"Wash," 170–72
Washington, Booker T., 204–05
Wilbourne, Harry, 199–200, 215
Wild Palms, The. See *If I Forget Thee, Je-
    rusalem*
"Wild Palms," 62–63, 66–67, 69,
    197–200
Wilson, Edmund, 249–50
Wittgenstein, Ludwig, 285–93, 303–04,
    307
Woodward, C. Vann, 3–4